INTERNATIONAL TRADE:
ESSAYS IN THEORY

STUDIES IN INTERNATIONAL ECONOMICS

Volume 4

NORTH-HOLLAND PUBLISHING COMPANY
AMSTERDAM · NEW YORK · OXFORD

INTERNATIONAL TRADE: ESSAYS IN THEORY

RONALD W. JONES

1979

NORTH-HOLLAND PUBLISHING COMPANY
AMSTERDAM · NEW YORK · OXFORD

Publishers

NORTH-HOLLAND PUBLISHING COMPANY
AMSTERDAM · NEW YORK · OXFORD

Sole distributors for the U.S.A. and Canada
ELSEVIER NORTH-HOLLAND, INC.
52 VANDERBILT AVENUE
NEW YORK, N.Y. 10017

Library of Congress Cataloging in Publication Data

Jones, Ronald Winthrop, 1931-
International trade.

(Studies in international economics ; v. 6)
Includes index.
1. Commerce--Addresses, essays, lectures.
2. International economic relations--Addresses, essays, lectures. I. Title.
HF1411.J63 382 79-10705
ISBN 0-444-85226-3

PRINTED IN THE NETHERLANDS

INTRODUCTION TO THE SERIES

This series is intended to embrace all aspects of international economic analysis: theoretical, empirical and econometric. It will equally encompass contributions to pure and monetary theory.

The series will include the publication of collected essays, conference proceedings of exceptional professional quality and interest, and edited volumes addressed to specific phenomena of importance in the analysis of international economics. It will particularly encourage, however, the publication of hitherto unpublished studies which represent fresh and valuable contributions to the analysis of international economic problems.

The Journal of International Economics now provides an excellent outlet for original scientific work in international economics in article length form. For pamphlet length contributions, the different series published by the *International Finance Section* at Princeton have long been of exceptional value, even though they have not generally extended beyond international monetary issues. It is the hope of the editors that the launching of this series, *Studies in International Economics*, will now fill the lacuna in the systematic publication of monograph and volume length research output of international economists, and succeed in doing so consistently with the high quality that the promotion of scientific study of international economic issues requires.

THE EDITORS

To the Five-by-fives:

Deane
Laura
Dylan
Brenn
and
Polly

PREFACE

This collection of essays brings together works of widely ranging vintage, from my first published work in 1956 (Chapter 1) to several previously unpublished papers. The focus is upon the pure theory of international trade instead of the monetary or balance of payments aspects of the field.

For some years I had thought of preparing a volume of essays centered upon my 1965 *Journal of Political Economy* article, 'The Structure of Simple General Equilibrium Models' (appearing here as Chapter 4), since I have over the years published a series of papers which make direct applications of this model. Further thought convinced me that since the field of trade theory encompasses many topics not directly related to the simple general equilibrium model of production, this volume might more usefully gather together work on the transfer problem, international factor mobility, technology and trade and Ricardian models as well as the standard Heckscher–Ohlin approach.

Although each essay stands on its own, I have tried to arrange this collection so that the volume comes close to being a graduate level 'text'. Thus, the subject matter of these papers covers at least three-quarters of the material I traditionally present in my graduate seminar in trade theory at the University of Rochester. I have arranged the chapters under six groupings and added introductory remarks to each section. These serve to place the essays in somewhat wider perspective and, on occasion, to correct statements made in the original publication (see, for example, my remarks in the Introduction to Part I on the possibility of ranking commodities by factor intensity in a Heckscher–Ohlin setting). The final section of the book reproduces my 1976 Graham lecture at Princeton which, while discussing the issue of 'dimensionality' in trade theory, serves to bring together many of the substantive issues discussed in other essays.

Many of the essays which have been previously published are left intact save for minor typographical corrections. Others have been revised or abridged, such as Chapters 8, 12, 13, and 16, and the Appendix to Chapter 14. Chapters 7 and 17, as well as the new Appendix to Chapter 10, have not previously been published.

For this new work (as well as many of the previously published pieces) I am indebted to the National Science Foundation for research support.

Since this volume contains work spanning my academic career, there are many people whose influence and suggestions warrant mention. My interest in trade theory was kindled as an undergraduate at Swarthmore in the excellent seminars conducted by the late Joe Conard, and received further nourishment at M.I.T. from Charles Kindleberger, Paul Samuelson, and Bob Solow. Many of the others who should be acknowledged hopefully are in each chapter. I should especially single out for thanks several co-authors: José Scheinkman (whose piece with me in the *Journal of Political Economy*, 1977, has been shortened and revised as Chapter 8), Roy Ruffin (Chapter 13), and Eitan Berglas (Chapter 16). All have kindly given permission for our joint products to appear here. Typing preparation for the manuscript was excellently provided by Marge Adams.

R.W. Jones

CONTENTS

III THE TRANSFER PROBLEM

IV INTERNATIONAL FACTOR MOBILITY

V TECHNOLOGY AND TRADE

PART I

THE PURE THEORY OF TRADE

INTRODUCTION TO PART I

Two basic models of trade and production, those associated with David Ricardo on the one hand and Eli Heckscher and Bertil Ohlin on the other, provide the pillars upon which most of the pure theory of international trade rests. The first two chapters in Part I explore and extend the Heckscher–Ohlin theory, while Chapter 3 is devoted to the Ricardian model in its many-country, many-commodity version analyzed by Frank Graham and Lionel McKenzie.

Fundamental developments of the two-country, two-commodity, two-factor version of Heckscher–Ohlin theory had been made prior to 1953, especially by Stolper and Samuelson (on the effect of tariffs on income distribution) and Lerner and Samuelson (on the tendency of free trade to equalize factor prices). However, it was Leontief's application of input – output analysis to the structure of trade in the American economy in his now classic 1953 paper that shocked trade theorists, practitioners, and half a generation of graduate students into re-examining the connection between factor endowments and the pattern of trade. Chapter 1, my first published work in economics, focuses upon the role of demand differences between countries and of factor-intensity reversals in technology in challenging the Heckscher–Ohlin theorem that relatively capital-abundant countries export capital-intensive commodities. This early work goes further in attempting to describe relationships in a multi-commodity Heckscher–Ohlin setting. As Jagdish Bhagwati [1] and others have observed, I overextended myself (in section 6 of Chapter 1) in suggesting that if two countries share a common technology for producing a variety of commodities, these commodities can be ordered from the most capital-intensive to the least and demand conditions would provide a dividing line between those more-capital-intensive commodities that would be exported by the capital-abundant country and the commodities at the labor-intensive end of the chain exported by the labor-abundant country.

The problem with an assertion of this type is that a model with more commodities than productive factors has a ruled transformation surface. That is, the pattern of production becomes indeterminate as the price plane is tangent to a 'rule' or 'flat' of the transformation surface. If factor prices have been equalized with free trade, costs of production for all commodities are equated between countries and the location of production of any single item becomes indeterminate. My remarks in section 6 must presuppose that factor prices are not driven to equality by trade (as they need not be, even if transport costs are absent), in which case relative costs of production are strictly ordered by the factor-intensity ranking.

Chapter 2 pursues the analysis of a two-factor, many-commodity Heckscher–Ohlin model by taking advantage of the 'small country' assumption. This allows commodity prices to be given from the outside, thus making easier the task of analyzing how a country's production pattern and factor prices depend upon its underlying factor endowment base. Trade patterns typically involve a country importing a variety of commodities, some of which are more capital-intensive than its exports, while some are more labor-intensive. Furthermore, if a non-traded commodity is produced, local demand patterns always can influence factor prices even with given world commodity prices (for traded goods) and a given factor endowment.

Chapter 3 illustrates how the simplification provided by the Ricardian assumption that only one productive factor (labor) requires renumeration allows an analysis of production patterns in a world of many commodities *and* many countries. Building upon earlier work of Graham and McKenzie, this chapter discusses the generalization of the concept of comparative advantage and how it is related to the familiar bilateral cost ratios of Ricardian theory.

Reference

[1] Bhagwati, J., 'The Heckscher–Ohlin Theorem in the Multi-Commodity Case', *Journal of Political Economy*, 80 (September/October 1972) 1052–1055.

Chapter 1

FACTOR PROPORTIONS AND THE HECKSCHER–OHLIN THEOREM*

1.

Recent contributions to the pure theory of international trade have relied heavily on the variable-proportions account of trade developed by Heckscher [2] and Ohlin [9], who linked export–import patterns to factor endowments and methods of production. Their hypothesis is expressed in summary form in the *Heckscher–Ohlin theorem*: a country exports those commodities produced with relatively large quantities of the country's relatively abundant factor. Perhaps the most controversial application of this theorem to appear recently is that based on Leontief's input–output studies of the American economy. According to Leontief [5], America is not capital-rich compared with the rest of the world, as popularly supposed. His data suggest that American exports require a higher proportion of labor to capital than do American imports (or rather, American import-competing commodities). Leontief's conclusions then follow from his unqualified support of the Heckscher–Ohlin dictum.

However, there are significant exceptions to the Heckscher–Ohlin theorem.[1] The theorem rests both upon a concept of factor abundance related to pre-trade factor-price ratios and special shapes for the production functions. Should these strict conditions be modified, the Heckscher–Ohlin theorem in some cases no longer holds, in others becomes meaningless. The purpose of this chapter is to clarify the meaning of the Heckscher–Ohlin theorem and to demonstrate that there is no *a priori* basis for accepting the Leontief conclusions; his

**Review of Economic Studies* (October 1956) 1–10. In preparing this article I have benefited greatly by conversations with Professor Robert Solow and my colleagues, Louis Lefeber and Michael Moss.

[1] The tendency towards factor-price equalization, a corollary of the Heckscher–Ohlin theorem, has been challenged by James and Pearce [3]. For a statement and discussion of the factor-price equalization theorem see Samuelson [11, 12], and McKenzie [7].

data are not inconsistent with the commonly-held notion of American factor endowments.

2.

The two-country, two-factor, two-commodity framework customary in the variable proportions account of trade is retained in what follows unless explicitly altered. That is, each commodity in the two countries is sold in a purely competitive market and produced under constant returns to scale. No transfer costs of any kind exist, so that the prices of internationally traded commodities are equalized in the two countries. Fixed endowment quantities of two homogeneous factors of production, capital and labor, are fully employed in each country. The quality (but not quantity) of each factor in the two countries is identical, as are the production functions. This assumption is made so that differences in trading patterns and pretrade price ratios are ascribable to differences in factor endowments on the supply side and/or to differences in demand conditions, rather than to differences in technology.

Within the framework set out by these assumptions the concepts of relative factor abundance and factor intensity each admit of more than one interpretation. The concept of relative factor *abundance* is examined first; this part of the discussion is based on the strong Samuelson notion of factor *intensity*: for *any* set of factor-price ratios optimal resource allocation in each country entails that one commodity (X) is always produced with a greater amount of capital per unit of labor (ρ_x) than the capital/labor ratio (ρ_y) employed in the other commodity (Y) (Samuelson [11, p. 165 n] and [12, p. 182]).

In addition, initially it is assumed that trade does not lead to complete specialization in either country.

3.

Ohlin's definition of relative abundance rests on the pretrade ratio of factor prices in the two countries. Denoting the countries by the subscripts 1 and 2, capital and labor by K and L, and the wage rate and rental on capital by w, r, respectively, country 1 is relatively capital abundant in the Ohlin sense if before trade is initiated:

$$\left(\frac{w}{r}\right)_1 > \left(\frac{w}{r}\right)_2. \tag{1}$$

By definition capital is relatively cheaper in the capital-rich country before trade. As suggested by Samuelson in his factor-price equalization articles, if the strong factor-intensity property holds, the assumptions underlying the Ohlin theory imply a unique relationship between factor price ratios and commodity price ratios. This relationship is identical for the two countries. Equality of commodity prices with trade must involve an equalization of the returns to the same factor in each country. Furthermore, any given factor-price ratio is associated uniquely with a ratio of commodity prices, as illustrated in fig. 1.1. The fact that capital is relatively cheaper in country 1 before trade implies that the capital-intensive commodity (X) is relatively less expensive in that country. Thus, with trade the capital-rich country must export the capital-intensive commodity. With Ohlin's definition of factor abundance and the strong assumptions of section 2 the Heckscher–Ohlin theorem, although true, is trivial. The converse of the theorem also holds: if a country exports the capital-intensive commodity, capital must have been the relatively cheap factor of production in that country before trade.

However, this seems not to be the notion of factor abundance employed by Leontief and most others who discuss this question. Applications of the Ohlin dictum hint at a relationship between physical factor endowments and patterns of trade, rather than the latter and the pretrade constellation of factor prices.

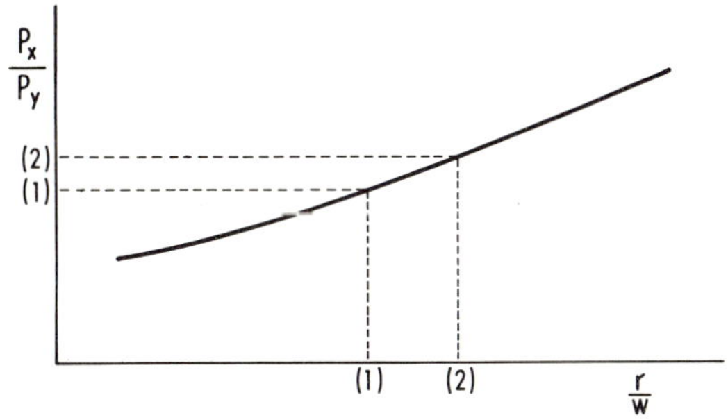

Figure 1.1

Indeed, Ohlin himself makes this point succintly: '... the real problem is to demonstrate what lies behind such inequality in prices, or, more precisely, to show in what way *differences in equipment* come to be expressed in differences in money *costs and prices*' [9, p. 13, my italics].

4.

An alternative definition of relative factor abundance goes back to physical factor endowments. According to this definition a country is relatively capital abundant if and only if it is endowed with a higher proportion of capital to labor than the other country. Thus, country 1 is relatively capital-rich if:

$$\frac{\overline{K}_1}{\overline{L}_1} > \frac{\overline{K}_2}{\overline{L}_2}, \tag{2}$$

where the bars denote the fixed factor quantities available in each country. This definition and the Ohlin (1) definition are certainly not equivalent. Pretrade factor-price ratios are determined both by conditions of supply and demand and are uniquely related to pretrade commodity price ratios, whereas factor endowment proportions may be outweighed by dissimilarities in demand in influencing price ratios.[2] Differences in relative endowments impart a *bias* on the supply side, but not sufficient to insure validity of the Heckscher–Ohlin theorem if this new definition (2) of factor abundance is used.

The nature of the bias introduced by differences in factor endowments is most clearly seen in the relationship between the transformation schedules of the two countries. If both countries were endowed with the same factor proportions, the constant-returns-to-scale assumption would be sufficient to insure that the transformation schedules of the two countries, if not identical, would be radial blowups of each other. Differences in relative factor endowments are reflected by transformation schedules differing in shape. Suppose that country 1 is relatively capital abundant by the non-Ohlin definition (2). The transformation schedule of the capital-rich country must be flatter than that of the other country along any ray from the origin, as illustrated in fig. 1.2. That is, *if the output of the two commodities is in the same proportion in both countries, the relatively capital abundant country will be able to expand its production of the capital intensive commodity at a lower opportunity cost than the other country.* In this sense the relatively

[2] For example, cf. James and Pearce [3, p. 113].

capital abundant country has a production bias in favor of the capital intensive commodity.[3]

That this production bias may not be sufficient to insure that before trade capital and the capital intensive commodity are relatively cheaper in country 1 than in country 2 is seen in fig. 1.2.[4] The pretrade price ratio, P_x/P_y, is greater in country 1 at *b* than in country 2 at *a*, despite the production bias. Thus, with trade the capital-rich country concentrates on the production of the labor-intensive commodity in order to export *ei* of this commodity (Y) in exchange for imports (*ig*) of the capital-intensive commodity. In this case differences in tastes outweigh differences in factor endowments and the Heckscher–Ohlin theorem (using definition (2) of factor abundance) does not hold. Conversely, without specifying demand conditions it is invalid to infer factor endowment proportions from the pattern of trade.[5]

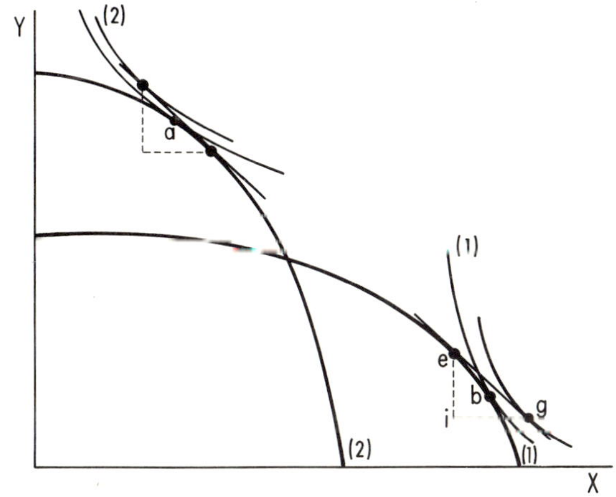

Figure 1.2

[3] In an original version of this article I made use of the production box diagrams of each country to prove this relationship between the slopes of the two transformation schedules. Since then, Rybczynski [10] has demonstrated the equivalent proposition that should the supply of one factor (capital) in a country be augmented, the transformation schedule becomes flatter.

[4] Two sets of community indifference curves are drawn in fig. 1.2. Essentially this amounts to assuming that each country behaves like a single rational consumer in a competitive market. For a demonstration of the graphical procedure, cf. Leontief [4].

[5] Even the assumption of identical taste patterns in the two countries is not sufficient to assure validity of the Heckscher–Ohlin theorem, as there is no necessary relationship among the slopes of different indifference curves along any ray. It is easy to demonstrate, however, that if both countries' taste patterns are identical and homothetic (implying unitary income elasticities), the Heckscher–Ohlin theorem must hold with either definition of factor abundance.

5.

The previous comments may be used to examine the meaning of the term 'comparative advantage'. In a Ricardian, one-factor, constant-returns world, technology alone determines which commodity is exported from each country. Furthermore, each country is said to possess a comparative advantage in producing that commodity. Thus, the concept of comparative advantage satisfied the following two criteria: (i) comparative advantage is determined by production conditions alone, and (ii) each country exports that commodity in which it enjoys a comparative advantage.

However, in a two-factor, variable proportions model of trade, the concept of comparative advantage does not always satisfy these criteria, so some sacrifice in the meaning of the term must be made. Under the assumptions of section 2, and employing the Ohlin definition of factor abundance in terms of pretrade factor prices, it is possible to define the capital-rich country to have a comparative advantage in producing the capital-intensive commodity. It is then true, but trivial, to state that each country exports that commodity in the production of which it enjoys a comparative advantage. However, the first criterion is not satisfied, for a knowledge of factor endowment proportions alone is not sufficient, with Ohlin's definition, to determine the 'comparative advantage' commodity, so defined. Demand conditions must be considered as well.

An alternative approach consists in selecting the 'comparative advantage' commodity for each country merely from a knowledge of factor endowments. Thus, using the definition of factor abundance related to endowment proportions rather than to factor prices, state that the capital abundant country has a comparative advantage in producing the capital-intensive commodity. Unlike the Ohlin definition, the alternative definition satisfies the first criterion, although demand conditions may invalidate the second.

The meaning of comparative advantage in production is reflected in the production bias arising from differences in factor endowments. Whatever the conditions of demand and patterns of consumption, with free trade there is a unique relationship between the ratios of commodities *produced* in each country. In the country possessing a greater relative supply of capital, the ratio of the quantity of the capital-intensive commodity produced to the production of the labor-intensive commodity must always be larger than in the other country. Retaining the assumptions in section 4, the ratio X/Y in country 1 must, in free trade, always be larger than the X/Y ratio of production in country 2. In this sense it is meaningful to state that the capital-rich country has a comparative advantage in producing the capital-intensive commodity.

6.

As suggested in the previous sections, the relationship between factor-price and commodity-price ratios is unique granted constant returns to scale and the strong definition of factor intensity. This is clearly demonstrated if the analysis is extended to include more than two commodities produced in each country. Suppose each country produces three commodities, X, Y, Z, each subject to constant returns to scale. Furthermore, suppose that for any given factor-price ratios commodity X always employs a higher capital/labor ratio than Y, which employs a higher capital/labor ratio than Z. That is, let

$$\rho_x > \rho_y > \rho_z. \tag{3}$$

Regardless of demand conditions in the two countries, if commodity X is cheaper relative to Y in country 1 than in country 2, so also must Y be cheaper relative to Z in country 1.

This binding relationship among commodity price ratios may be proved in straight-forward fashion. Since each commodity is produced subject to constant returns:

$$\begin{aligned} X &= L_x f(\rho_x), \\ Y &= L_y g(\rho_y), \\ Z &= L_z h(\rho_z). \end{aligned} \tag{4}$$

Optimal resources allocation requires the ratio of factor prices to be equal to the ratio of the marginal physical products of labor to capital in each commodity:

$$\frac{w}{r} = \frac{f(\rho_x) - \rho_x f'(\rho_x)}{f'(\rho_x)} = \frac{g(\rho_y) - \rho_y g'(\rho_y)}{g'(\rho_y)} = \frac{h(\rho_z) - \rho_z h'(\rho_z)}{h'(\rho_z)}. \tag{5}$$

Pick any two commodities, e.g. Y and Z. The ratio of the prices of Y and Z in equilibrium is given by the ratio of the marginal physical products of either factor in Z and Y:

$$\frac{P_Y}{P_Z} = \frac{h'(\rho_z)}{g'(\rho_y)}. \tag{6}$$

This price ratio varies inversely with the capital/labor ratio employed in any commodity. For

$$\frac{\mathrm{d}(P_Y/P_Z)}{\mathrm{d}\rho_y} = \frac{g'h''\,\mathrm{d}\rho_z/\mathrm{d}\rho_y - h'g''}{(g')^2}. \tag{7}$$

Differentiating eq. (5), solving for $d\rho_z/d\rho_y$ and substituting into (7) yields

$$\frac{d\left(\dfrac{P_Y}{P_Z}\right)}{d\,\rho_y} = \frac{\dfrac{g''\,(h')^2 g}{h\,g'} - h'\,g''}{(g')^2}. \tag{8}$$

But eq. (5) may be solved for g/g':

$$\frac{g}{g'} = \frac{h}{h'} + \rho_y - \rho_z. \tag{9}$$

Substituting (9) into (8) yields

$$\frac{d(P_Y/P_Z)}{d\,\rho_y} = \frac{g''(h')^2}{h(g')^2}(\rho_y - \rho_z). \tag{10}$$

Since g'' is negative (reflecting a falling marginal physical product of capital) and since commodity Y has been assumed more capital-intensive than Z for *any* common factor price ratio, $d(P_Y/P_Z)/d\rho_y$ must be negative.[6]

Commodities Y and Z were picked arbitrarily. With any number of commodities, $(1, \ldots, n)$,

$$\frac{d(P_i/P_j)}{d\rho_i} < 0, \quad \text{if } \rho_i > \rho_j. \tag{11}$$

Therefore an X to Y commodity price ratio in country 1 lower than in country 2 must reflect a capital to labor ratio employed in any commodity in country 1 that is higher than that found in the production of the corresponding commodity in country 2. This latter relationship, and eq. (11), implies a lower Y to Z commodity price ratio in country 1 as well, regardless of demand conditions.[7]

This strong relationship among commodity price ratios has implications for the concept of comparative advantage as well. Ordering the commodities with respect to the capital/labor ratios employed in production is to rank them in order of comparative advantage. Demand conditions merely determine the dividing line between exports and imports; it is not possible to break the chain of comparative

[6] I wish to thank Professor Harry Johnson for recommending a more simple form of the original proof. The relationship between factor intensities and commodity price ratios proved here has also been demonstrated in slightly different fashion by James Meade [8].

[7] Although demand conditions are important in determining the relationship between ρ_i in one country and ρ_i in the other, note that the relationships proved here apply as well in the two-commodity case and serve as verification of the previous remarks.

advantage by exporting, say, the third and fifth commodities and importing the fourth when they are ranked by factor intensity.[8]

7.

The preceeding analysis seems unduly restricted by the strong factor-intensity criterion suggested by Samuelson. That is, previously technology has assumed X to require a higher proportion of capital than Y for *any* set of factor prices common to both commodities. By using an alternative concept of factor intensity it is possible to include cases heretofore ruled out; these cases not only qualify the meaning of the Heckscher – Ohlin theorem but may also invalidate the Leontief procedure.

The alternative notion of factor intensity has meaning only when factor endowments are specified. Given the initial level of resources, it is possible to define X as capital-intensive if $\rho_x > \rho_y$ for any equilibrium combination of outputs.[9] Alternatively, X is capital-intensive if ρ_x is greater than the endowment ratio, $\overline{K}/\overline{L}$. Stated in terms of common factor-price ratios, commodity X is capital-intensive if $\rho_x > \rho_y$ for all common *possible* equilibrium factor-price ratios once a set of endowments is specified.

The relationship between this definition of factor intensity and the Samuelson definition is clear: to be labeled capital-intensive *à la* Samuelson, commodity X must require a higher capital/labor ratio than Y for *any* common factor-price ratio, whether or not this ratio can exist in equilibrium once factor endowments are specified. This requirement is not satisfied by all pairs of constant-returns production functions. On the other hand, any pair of linear homogeneous production functions may be subjected to the suggested alternative criterion.[10]

The significance of this different interpretation is clearly seen if two production functions that do not satisfy the strong Samuelson condition are examined. By continuity, if $\rho_x > \rho_y$ for some set of common factor price ratios and $\rho_x < \rho_y$ for some other set, the capital to labor ratios employed in the production of the two commodities must be equal for some factor price ratio.[11] In fig. 1.3 a member of

[8] This is similar to the relationships that hold in the one-factor case. Cf. Haberler [1].

[9] Constant returns to scale in each commodity insure that a greater ρ_x than ρ_y at one point along the contract curve is sufficient for $\rho_x > \rho_y$ everywhere on the contract curve.

[10] Except in the singular case in which the contract curve and the diagonal of the production box are identical.

[11] Assume for simplicity the existence of only one such critical factor-price ratio. This excludes the

each isoquant family is depicted.[12] If the endowment ratio is country 1, $\bar{K}_1/\bar{L}_1$ is greater than the λ-ratio, while the endowment ratio in country 2, $\bar{K}_2/\bar{L}_2$, is less than the λ-ratio, X must be the labor-intensive commodity in country 1 and the capital-intensive commodity in country 2.[13]

Should the endowment proportions in both countries lie on the same side of the λ-ratio, all the previous conclusions of this paper hold, despite the fact that the

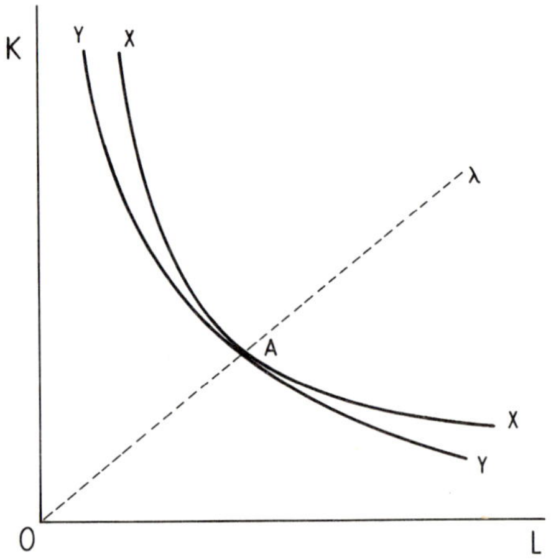

Figure 1.3

Footnote 11 continued
main case considered by James and Pearce [3]. In their excellent demonstration of the fact that capital may be relatively cheaper in the labor-abundant country before trade and that factor prices may diverge rather than be equalized once trade is initiated, they concentrate on the case in which two critical factor-price ratios exist (although their terminology and graphical demonstration differ substantially from that employed in this paper). Both ratios lie between the endowment proportions of the two countries; thus, the same commodity is capital-intensive in both countries. However, our primary concern here is not the effect of trade on factor prices but rather the relationship between pretrade factor-price ratios in the two countries and the pattern of trade. Suffice it to say that in the James and Pearce case, as well as in our one-critical-price-ratio case, it is possible for the capital-abundant country to export the labor-intensive commodity.

[12] The pioneering examination of these cases is that of Lerner [6].

[13] A heuristic proof, which can be made quite rigorous, is sketched here. As in fig. 1.3, assume the X-isoquant to be more concave than the Y-isoquant, reflecting the fact that there is less possibility for factor substitution in X-production than in Y-production. That is, for any factor-price ratio common to both industries (excluding the price ratio at A), the critical λ-capital/labor ratio must more closely correspond to ρ_x than to ρ_y. In country 1 the λ-ratio is 'labor-intensive' relative to factor endowments. Therefore ρ_x must be less than ρ_y at any point on the contract curve. In country 2, $\rho_x > \rho_y$ at all points.

Samuelson criterion is not satisfied (except in the special case of complete specialization, to be discussed in section 9).[14]

8.

If the factor endowment ratios in each country lie on opposite sides of the λ-ratio, as suggested above, $\rho_x < \rho_y$ in country 1, and $\rho_x > \rho_y$ in country 2. But the literal meaning of the Heckscher – Ohlin theorem is, in this case, open to question, as is Leontief's procedure of comparing capital/labor ratios in exports and import-competing industries.

The contract curves in the two countries are shown in fig. 1.4. Since $\rho_x < \rho_y$ in country 1, P_X/P_Y is an increasing function of ρ_x (cf. section 6). In country 2,

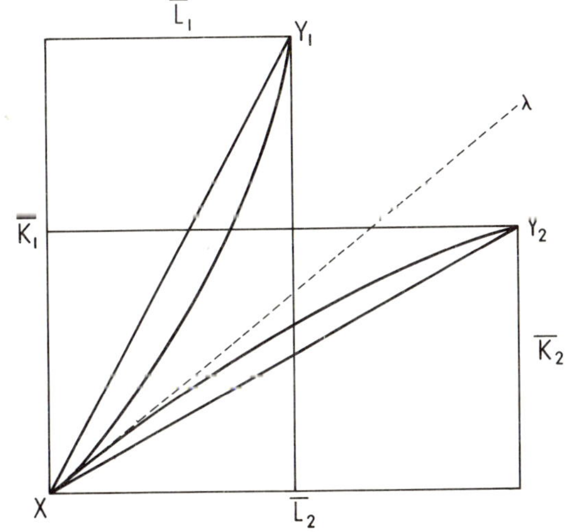

Figure 1.4

[14] In the general case of more than one λ-ratio the previous conclusions of this paper hold if factor endowments for both countries lie between the same two consecutive critical factor ratios, λ_r and λ_{r+1}. As has been pointed out to me by Professor Pearce, the above conditions, although sufficient, are not necessary for the previous conclusions. For if factor endowments in the two countries are separated by an *even* number of λ-ratios the same commodity is capital intensive in both countries and the capital abundant country may export the capital intensive commodity (although not in all cases, cf. n.11 above). The case cited in the text is the special case in which only one λ-ratio exists; if both sets of factor endowments lie on the same side of this λ-ratio, its existence creates no new problems and all previous conclusions hold.

P_X/P_Y is a decreasing function of ρ_x. But, as is seen in fig. 1.4, ρ_x and ρ_y in country 1 are both greater than either ρ_x or ρ_y in country 2; these sets of ratios are separated by the critical λ-ratio. The relationship between commodity and factor price ratios and ρ_x in each country is shown in fig. 1.5.

Country 1 is relatively capital-abundant; not only is $\bar{K}_1/\bar{L}_1$ greater than $\bar{K}_2/\bar{L}_2$ but, as fig. 1.4 demonstrates, ρ_x in country 1 must always be higher than in country 2, which implies (cf. fig. 1.5) that capital must be relatively cheaper in country 1, regardless of demand conditions. As shown by points A and B in fig. 1.5,[15] it may be the case that the relatively capital-abundant country exports its labor-intensive commodity. *America may be capital-rich, either by the Ohlin definition or in terms of factor endowment proportions, and export commodities employing relatively less capital than in its import-competing industries.*

Closer inspection reveals that, in a formal sense, the Heckscher–Ohlin theorem as applied to both countries in this case cannot possibly hold. For the exports of each country are either both capital-intensive (relative to the other commodity produced in the country) or labor-intensive. It is impossible for both countries to

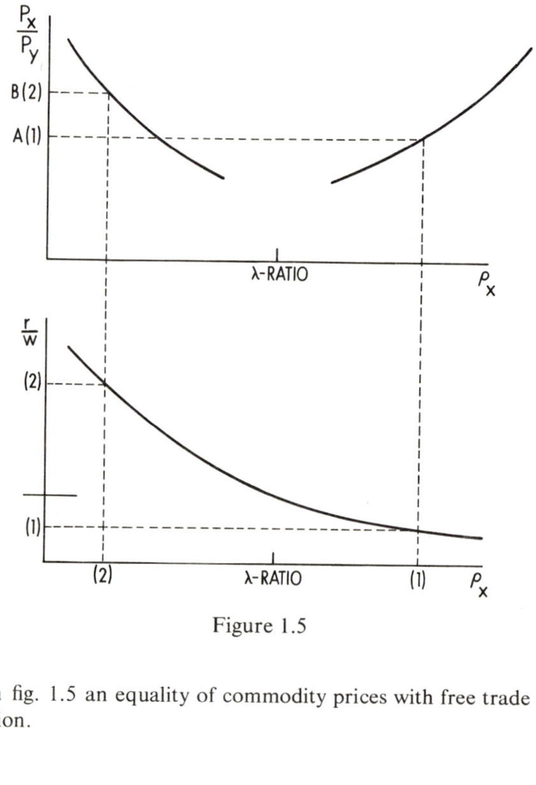

Figure 1.5

[15] Note also that in fig. 1.5 an equality of commodity prices with free trade could never result in factor-price equalization.

export that commodity requiring a relatively high quantity of the factor in which the country is relatively well endowed.

This is only a formal objection to the Heckscher–Ohlin theorem, however. For no matter which commodity is exported from the capital-rich country, it must embody a higher proportion of capital than either commodity produced in the other country. Although validated in this sense, the Heckscher–Ohlin theorem cannot be put into reverse in the Leontief manner. In concluding that America must be labor-abundant, Leontief compared the capital/labor ratios in American exports and American import-competing industries; no comparison was made with factor proportions abroad. If both American exports and import-competing products are produced with more capital-intensive methods than abroad, Leontief's paradoxical conclusion is no longer valid. In this case, and there is no *a priori* reason to believe this case is more unlikely than any other, Leontief's method tells us nothing about American factor endowments relative to the rest of the world.

9.

The case of complete specialization offers the best support to the Heckscher–Ohlin theorem and Ohlin's factor-price equalization views. Suppose commodity X is produced by capital-intensive methods in both countries,[16] country 1 is relatively capital-abundant by the definition that compares endowment proportions, and its transformation schedule is *everywhere* flatter than country 2's transformation schedule. In this case before trade (and after trade) capital must be relatively cheaper in country 1 than in country 2, and one country must specialize completely in its export commodity. The Heckscher–Ohlin theorem must hold and Ohlin is justified in his supposition that trade brings about a tendency, *necessarily incomplete*, towards factor-price equalization.[17]

10.

Thus, in the two-commodity model, with identical constant-returns-to-scale technology in the two countries, the Heckscher–Ohlin theorem may not hold in

[16] Assume the existence of no more than one critical λ-ratio.

[17] As pointed out by Professor Pearce, an incomplete tendency towards factor-price equalization also follows if factor endowments are separated by one or more λ-ratios, even if specialization is incomplete.

all cases. If production functions are of the strict Samuelson type, the Heckscher–Ohlin theorem must hold if relative factor abundance is tied to pretrade factor prices. However, it may not be valid to use the Heckscher–Ohlin theorem to infer relative endowment proportions from existing trading patterns if demand conditions in the two countries are quite dissimilar.

If the Samuelson restriction is lifted, strict application of the Heckscher–Ohlin theorem may not be valid if factor endowments differ considerably. And the Leontief procedure of comparing factor intensities in only one country may be invalid.

As suggested in section 6, similar binding relationships exist in a three-or-more commodity world. However, lifting the two-factor assumption poses problems for analysis; unless two or more factors are completely substitutable, the concept of factor intensity, upon which, in part, the Heckscher–Ohlin theorem rests, loses some of its meaning.[18] Finally, taking into account differences in technology or quality of the factors of production as well as endowment proportions makes for sterile analysis, as trading patterns could then be explained by differences in factor endowments, or in the quality of the factors, or in technology, or in conditions of demand.

References

[1] Haberler, G., *The Theory of International Trade* (Hodge & Co. Ltd., London, 1936) p. 137.

[2] Heckscher, E., 'The Effect of Foreign Trade on the Distribution of Income', *Ekonomisk Tidskift*, 21 (1919) 497–512; reprinted as chapter 13 in *Readings in the Theory of International Trade* (Blakiston, Philadelphia, 1949) pp. 272–300.

[3] James, S.F. and I.F. Pearce, 'The Factor-Price Equalization Myth', *Review of Economic Studies*, 19 (2) (1951–1952).

[4] Leontief, W., 'The Use of Indifference Curves in the Analysis of Foreign Trade', *Quarterly Journal of Economics*, 47 (May 1933) 493–503; reprinted as chapter 10 in *Readings in the Theory of International Trade* (Blakiston, Philadelphia, 1949).

[5] Leontief, W., 'Domestic Production and Foreign Trade: The American Capital Position Re-examined', *Proceedings of the American Philosophical Society*, 97 (4) (September 1953); reprinted in *Economica Internazionale*, 7 (February 1954) 9–38.

[6] Lerner, A., 'Factor Prices and International Trade', *Economica* (N.S.), 19 (73) (February 1952) 1–15.

[7] McKenzie, L., 'Equality of Factor Prices in World Trade', *Econometrica* (July 1955) 239–257.

[8] Meade, J., *Trade and Welfare* (Oxford University Press, 1955) pp. 600–601.

[18] The case in which there are more factors than commodities, and vice versa, and implications for factor-price equalization have been handled by James and Pearce [3] and by Samuelson [13].

[9] Ohlin, B., *Interregional and International Trade* (Harvard University Press, Cambridge, Mass., 1933).

[10] Rybczynski, T., 'Factor Endowment and Relative Commodity Prices', *Economica* (N.S.), 22 (88) (November 1955) 336–341.

[11] Samuelson, P.A., 'International Trade and the Equalization of Factor Prices', *Economic Journal* (June 1948).

[12] Samuelson, P.A., 'International Factor-Price Equalization Once Again', *Economic Journal* (June 1949).

[13] Samuelson, P.A., 'Prices of Factors and Goods in General Equilibrium', *Review of Economic Studies*, 21 (1) (54) (1953–1954).

Chapter 2

THE SMALL COUNTRY IN A MANY-COMMODITY WORLD*

1. Introduction

A distinction increasingly made in the theory of international trade focuses on the influence which producers and consumers in a particular country can exert on prices of commodities that are freely traded on world markets. On the one hand, there exists that body of theory that envisages trade between two countries (or one country and the rest of the world) of roughly similar size, wherein any change in tastes, technology, or resources in either country disturbs the equilibrium terms of trade and, through this change, affects real incomes in both countries. The possibility of immiserizing growth, based on the adverse impact on a country's terms of trade of growth heavily biased towards the export sector, and the theory of the optimal tariff, illustrated by one country's choosing a tariff rate that puts it on the most preferred point of the other country's offer curve, are two illustrations in the theory of trade based upon the assumption that each country is sufficiently large to influence world prices. On the other hand, a 'small country' is assumed to be incapable of affecting world prices of internationally traded commodities. Its optimal tariff is zero and, assuming its prices are world prices, growth must increase real incomes.

With a few exceptions the analysis of the 'large country' case has been restricted to two commodities.[1] The problems posed by different degrees of substitutability

* *Australian Economic Papers* (December 1974) 225–236. I am indebted to the National Science Foundation for support of this research.

[1] Obvious exceptions are customs-union theory, multi-commodity Ricardian models, and the highly technical discussion of the Stolper–Samuelson theorem and factor-price equalization theorem in an n-commodity, n-factor setting.

or complementarity when price ratios among several commodities are endogenous has served to inhibit analysis of many markets in the large country case. This need not be a problem for the small country case, as Salter's use of the Hicksian composite commodity theorem some years ago demonstrated [3]. If world prices of traded goods are given, they may be lumped together and treated as one commodity. This is a real convenience for illustrating the distinction between traded goods and nontraded goods, for even in a small country local changes in tastes, technology, or policy can alter the price of nontraded goods in terms of traded goods. See for example, Salter [3] or Caves and Jones [1, suppl. to ch. 19].

The purpose of this chapter is to analyze the patterns of production, specialization, and trade in a small country with a given technology. I assume the existence of two mobile factors, labor and capital, capable of producing any of a number of commodities with constant returns to scale. Subsequently the case in which a nontraded commodity is also produced is analyzed, and a comparison made with the model in which all commodities are traded at given world prices.

2. The composite traded commodity

With capital and labour the only factors of production, all commodities can be ranked by factor intensities. Fig. 2.1 illustrates the case in which factor intensities are never reversed for the set of five commodities shown. At any given wage/rent

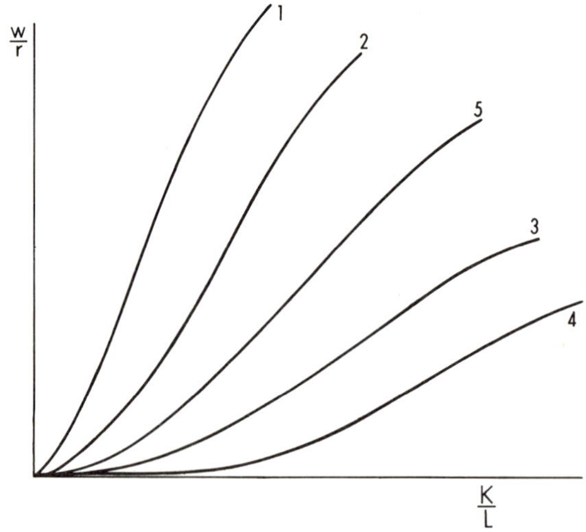

Figure 2.1

ratio (w/r), the ranking of capital/labor ratios ($K_i/L_i = \rho_i$) is: $\rho_4 > \rho_3 > \rho_5 > \rho_2 > \rho_1$. The diagram captures one essential feature of the small country's given technology: the factor proportions that would be used if each commodity were produced.

The technology available in the small country is not assumed to be identical to that in the rest of the world. This is reflected in the assumption that at the prevailing factor prices in the small country and at the given world prices for the five commodities, not all commodities could be produced in the small country. Fig. 2.2 illustrates a set of unit-*value* isoquants for these five commodities, determined both by technology at home and by the given world prices. Technology dictates the shape of the unit-physical isoquants. Given world prices determine for each good which isoquant has unit value. In fig. 2.2 it is clear that commodity 5 cannot be produced at the assumed world prices. No competitive equilibrium would allow positive production of commodity 5 in the small country at zero profit without some other productive activities yielding positive profits. Alternatively phrased, commodity 5 is an example of a commodity too-low priced on world markets relative to the home country's technology ever to be produced at home.

The dashed chords *BA*, *DC*, and *FE* are tangent to the appropriate isoquants and they form part of the unit-value isoquant for the composite commodity. They delineate the pattern of production and factor prices that correspond to each capital/labor endowment ratio. For capital/labor ratios even lower than shown by a ray from the origin through point A, only commodity I would be produced,

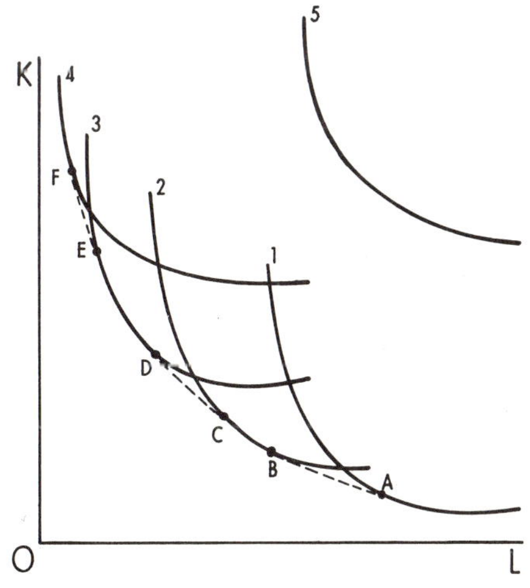

Figure 2.2

and the wage/rent ratio would be indicated by the slope of the x_1 isoquant at that point. If the K/L ratio lies within the cone formed by the rays OA and OB, the wage/rent ratio is given by the slope of chord BA and both commodities 1 and 2 are produced. For slightly higher values of the K/L ratio, in the cone formed by the OB and OC rays, the small country would again be completely specialized, but in commodity 2. The unit-value isoquant for the composite commodity is the convex-hull of all the individual unit-value isoquants for traded goods.

Clearly the home-country's factor-price ratio is, in general, determined both by world prices of traded goods and its own factor endowment proportions (given its own technology). Fig. 2.3 based on fig. 2.1 (with the absence of the factor proportions curve for commodity 5 since at these world prices commodity 5 is never produced at home), highlights the strict association of the factor-price ratio and the production pattern with the factor endowment K/L ratio once world prices for traded commodities are given. The heavy curve shows the unique wage/rent ratio that would correspond to each endowment ratio. Along the upward sloping sections the small country is completely specialized in producing the commodity indicated by the numbered curve. Along the horizontal stretches the country produces both the commodities shown by the supporting curves. For example, for any K/L ratio in the range CD the country produces both commodities 2 and 3, whereas in the range DE it is specialized only to commodity 3. The lettering in fig. 2.3 corresponds with that in fig. 2.2.

Fig. 2.3 reveals the general monotonic relationship between factor returns and factor endowments when commodity prices are given. Complete specialization implies strict monotonicity: any increase in the capital/labor ratio must drive up labour's relative return. Incomplete specialization ties factor prices

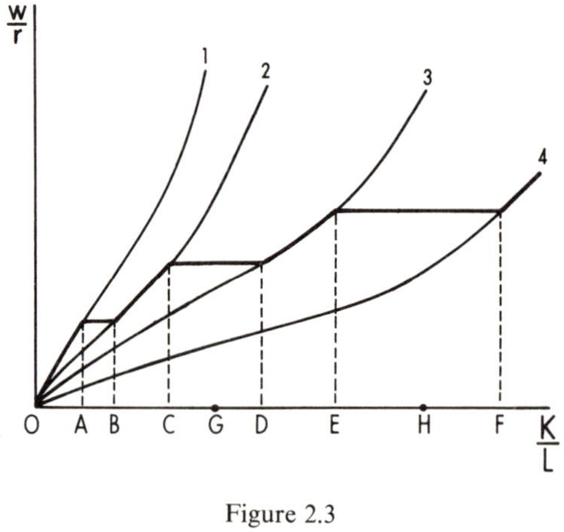

Figure 2.3

rigidly to given world commodity prices. Factor endowments may change, but if the country still produces the same two commodities, factor prices remain unaltered. However, if the growth of the capital/labor endowment ratio is sufficient to change the pattern of production, relative wages must rise. For example, if the K/L ratio rises from OG to OH in fig. 2.3, w/r rises, despite the fact that for small changes of the K/L ratio near OG on the one hand or OH on the other the wage/rent ratio is uniquely determined by the given world commodity prices.

For an alternative interpretation suppose that there are several small countries with identical technologies and facing the same set of world prices. Differences in factor endowments (e.g. one country with an OG capital/labor ratio and another with an OH ratio) can lead to incomplete specialization in each country without factor-price equalization.

To compare this case with the standard two-commodity model, note that it is not merely 'extreme' factor endowment proportions that lead to complete specialization. Instead, as K/L rises from very low values, the pattern of production alternately changes from complete to incomplete specialization.

3. A change in world prices

Although a small country cannot, by definition, alter world commodity prices by its own actions, these prices may change as a consequence of disturbances in the rest of the world. And such a change can alter factor returns and the pattern of production in the small country.

Consider the unit-value isoquants depicted in fig. 2.2 and assume that the price of commodity 3 changes, all other commodity prices remaining constant. A price rise shifts the unit-value isoquant uniformly towards the origin, as lower input levels are now required to achieve the same unit value of output. Such an inward shift would cause the tangent chord FE in fig. 2.2 to become steeper, and the chord DC to become flatter. A price fall, on the other hand, would shift the unit-value insoquant radially outwards and have the opposite result. Indeed, a sufficient price fall would exclude the possibility of producing commodity 3; its unit-value isoquant would lie above the convex hull of the remaining isoquants much as that for commodity 5 illustrated in fig. 2.2.

The effects of price changes are illustrated in fig. 2.4. Assume the price of commodity 3 rises. This lowers the position of the horizontal segment to the left of OD and raises the height of the horizontal segment to the right of OE. This corresponds to the aforementioned steepening of chord FE and flattening of DC in fig. 2.2. Complete specialization in commodity 3 now obtains for a wider range of K/L ratios $(I-J)$ than previously $(D-E)$ in fig. 2.4. The effect of this

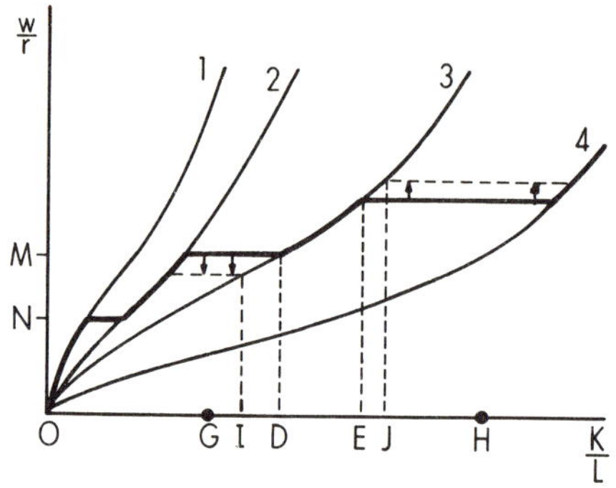

Figure 2.4

price change on factor prices depends on the pattern of production. If the country is specialized completely in commodity 3, or if the country produces no commodity 3, the wage/rent ratio is unaffected. But if the country produces commodity 3 and some other commodity (2 or 4), the price change does alter the factor-price ratio. Suppose the K/L endowment ratio is shown by OG, implying that the country produces both commodities 2 and 3. Compared with commodity 2, commodity 3 is capital intensive, and an increase in p_3 must lower the wage/rent ratio. However, as fig. 2.4 illustrates, if the endowment ratio is given by OH, an increase in p_3 must raise the wage/rent ratio. With the small country producing 3 and 4, commodity 3 is relatively labor-intensive and an increase in its relative price must raise relative wages.

A sufficiently large rise in p_3 would make it impossible to compete in the production of commodity 2, regardless of factor endowments. In fig. 2.2 this would occur if the inward shift in the unit-value isoquant for commodity 3 moved point C south-eastwards past point B. In such a case the tangent chord between the new unit-value isoquant for commodity 3 and that for commodity 1 would lie strictly below the unit-value isoquant for commodity 2. In fig. 2.4 this would be shown by a drop in the horizontal stretch (to the left of curve 3) from OM to some point below ON.

4. Nontraded goods and the transformation schedule

If all commodities are freely traded at given world prices, factor endowments determine a unique value for factor prices. This strong result requires modification if the small country produces a commodity consumed locally but incapable of being imported or exported because of high transport costs. That is, suppose the small country produces a nontraded commodity, *N*, in addition to one or more traded commodities.

With given world prices for all traded commodities, the heavy curve in fig. 2.3 can be thought of as the curve showing factor proportions for any given factor prices for the composite traded commodity (T). This is reproduced in fig. 2.5 together with the curve *N* depicting technology in producing the nontraded commodity. It is assumed that some traded commodities (4) are more capital-intensive than is *N*, while others (1, 2, and 3) are less capital-intensive. Therefore *N* and *T* exhibit the factor-intensity reversal phenomenon. However, for any given factor-endowment ratio, say α in fig. 2.5, the nontraded commodity is capital-intensive relative to any traded commodities which, at the given world prices, could be produced. With an exception to be discussed later, this is a general result: if the small country faces given prices for all traded goods and has a given endowment base, the nontraded commodity must either be more or less capital-intensive than any of the traded commodities it may produce.

Given K/L equal to α in fig. 2.5 factor prices are not uniquely determined. The wage/rent ratio can lie anywhere in the range $\beta_N\beta_T$. At the lower extreme, if w/r equals β_N the country produces only the non-traded good; *N* uses factors in exactly the proportions available in the α-endowment bundle. At the other extreme, if w/r equals β_T, only tradeables are produced. Indeed, only commodity 3 would be produced. Any factor-price ratio outside this range could not be maintained, as

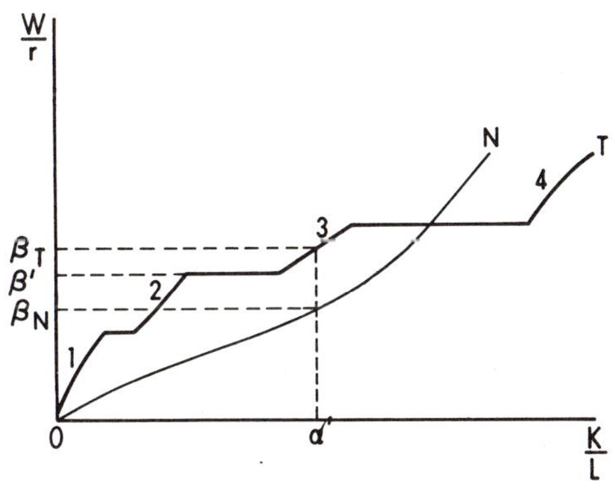

Figure 2.5

it would involve traded and nontraded goods both using a capital/labour ratio higher than (or lower than) the α-endowment ratio.[2]

To trace out the production possibilities for this small country, suppose initially only the nontraded commodity is produced, so that the wage/rent ratio is given by β_N. If any resources are released for traded goods production, at first only commodity 2 can be produced. Such a shift of resources must raise the wage/rent ratio above β_N. With given world prices for all tradeables, and with tradeables labour-intensive (in this range) compared with N, the price of nontradeables must fall. If the wage/rental ratio reaches β', the small country can be incompletely specialized in both commodity 2 and commodity 3 (as well as in N). When sufficient resources are pulled out of the nontradeable commodity, the wage/rent ratio can rise above β', all production of commodity 2 ceases, and only commodity 3 (and N) are produced.

These patterns of production are illustrated in fig. 2.6, showing alternative output patterns for the nontraded good, N, and the composite traded good, T. The transformation schedule has an interior 'flat', the stretch AB. Along this flat both traded goods 2 and 3 are produced. At point B just commodities 2 and N are produced. A reduction in the output of nontradeables from point B releases resources to the traded goods sector, but the ratio of capital to labor released exceeds the requirements of either commodity 2 or commodity 3. Of these two traded goods, commodity 3 is the more capital-intensive, and its output must rise and that of commodity 2 fall to absorb the resources being released by N.

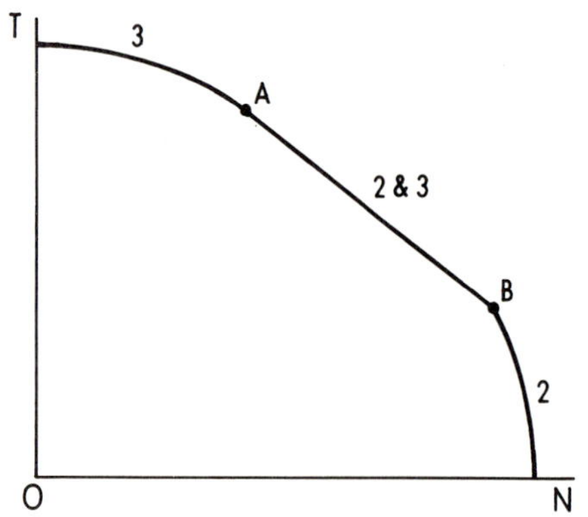

Figure 2.6

[2] For a simple explanation of this kind of diagram in the two-commodity case, see Caves and Jones [1, ch. 9].

These are the output changes predicted by the Heckscher-Ohlin theory at constant factor prices – and the wage/rent ratio (as well as all commodity prices) is constant (w/r equals β') along the linear AB stretch in fig. 2.6. At point A only commodities 3 and N are produced. Any further release of resources from nontradeables cannot be absorbed just by commodity 3 (which is labor-intensive compared with N) without a rise in the wage/rent ratio. This factor-price change makes each industry use capital more intensively and serves to drive down the relative price of capital-intensive N.

The shape of the transformation schedule shown in fig. 2.6 is rather special in that it shows the existence of one, internal, flat. It is easy to show that: (i) there may be no flats, indicating that besides the nontraded commodity there is only one traded commodity that could be produced at the given prices of tradeables and the given factor endowments. This is illustrated by fig. 2.7. With K/L equal to α, the wage/rent ratio must lie between β_N and β_T, only commodity 3 can be produced amongst all the tradeables, and the transformation schedule between T and N would be strictly bowed out. (ii) A flat on the transformation schedule may hit an axis instead of being interior. (iii) The transformation schedule may possess more than one flat.

Both points (ii) and (iii) are illustrated in fig. 2.8. Suppose the wage/rent ratio is at its maximal value, β_T, given that K/L equals α. The factor proportions required by 3, 4, and N at this wage/rent ratio are shown by the three rays in fig. 2.9. E is the factor-endowment point. If all resources are devoted to tradeables, quantity OA of good 4 and OB of good 3 are produced. (AE is parallel to the ρ_3-ray and EB is

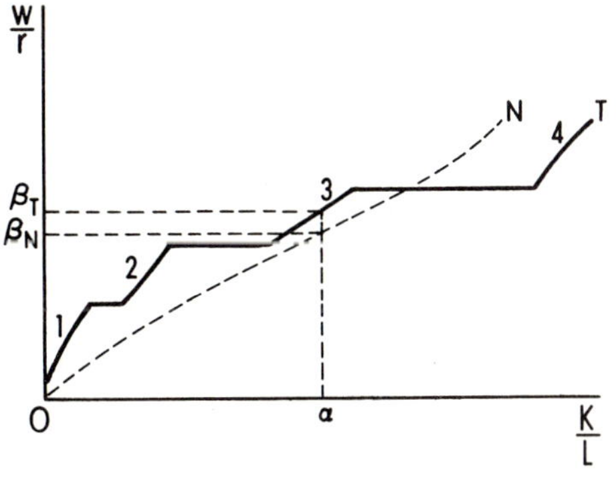

Figure 2.7

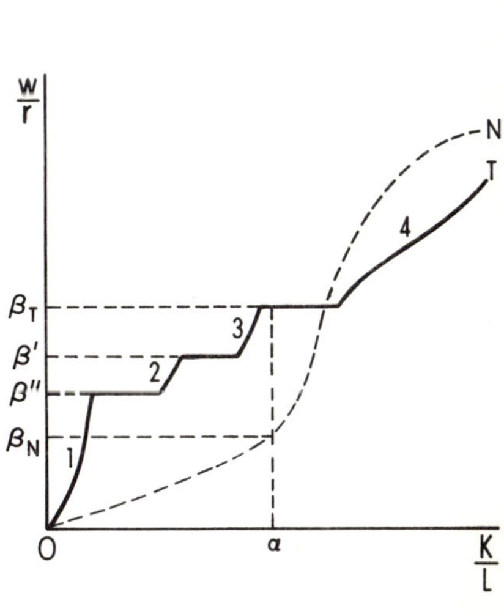

Figure 2.8

parallel to the ρ_4-ray.) As resources are pulled into nontradeables, the bundle of factors available for goods 3 and 4 is reduced from E to, say, F in fig. 2.9. FE is parallel to the ρ_N-ray and indicates the quantity of N now produced. Output of commodity 4 is reduced from OA to OC and of commodity 3 is reduced from OB to OD. This process can continue, at the same w/r given by β_T and therefore at fixed prices for all commodites, until EG of nontradeables is produced, at which point production of commodity 4 goes to zero and of commodity 3 is reduced to OG. This illustrates point (ii) above; there is a flat on the transformation schedule emanating from the T-axis (along which 3, 4 and N are produced). Furthermore, it illustrates the exception mentioned earlier to the proposition that the capital/labor ratio in the nontraded good must exceed (or fall short of) that for all traded goods that can be produced given the endowment base. In particular, commodity 4 is more capital intensive than is the nontraded good. The spirit of the proposition is retained by noting that the capital/labor ratio required by the nontraded good exceeds the endowment ratio and, therefore, the appropriately weighted average of the ratios in goods 3 and 4.

As the wage/rental ratio drops below β_T in fig. 2.8, only commodities 3 and N are produced until β' is reached. At this point the transformation schedule has another flat, along which N, 2, and 3 are produced. The story continues in a fashion shown explicity by fig. 2.10, which illustrates the possibility of many flats on the transformation schedule. Indeed, for the small country with K/L equal to α in fig. 2.8 there exists some price of nontraded goods (relative to the given prices of traded goods) at which each of the four traded goods can be produced.

There is a difference, however, in output patterns for traded goods along an interior flat, on the one hand, and along a flat which hits an axis, on the other. Suppose the economy initially produces at point A in fig. 2.10 – most resources

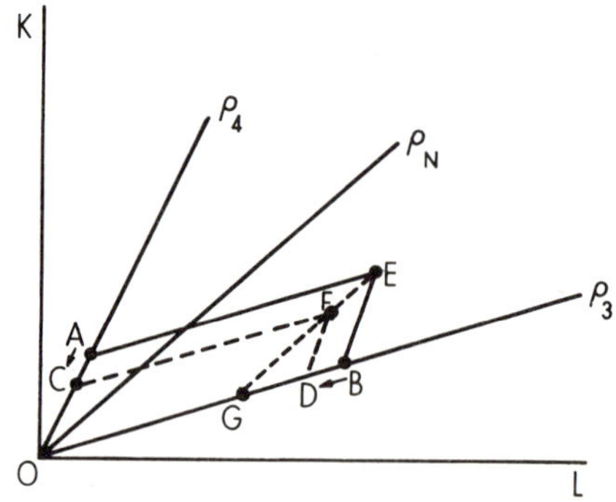

Figure 2.9

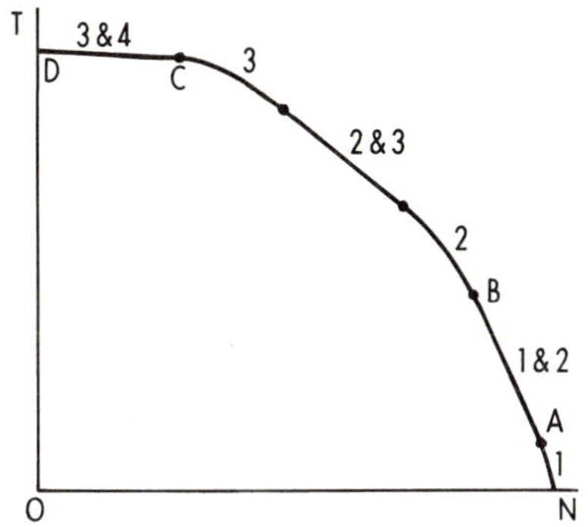

Figure 2.10

are devoted to nontradeables but some quantity of commodity 1 is produced. As outputs change along the flat moving from *A* to *B*, resources are shifted out of nontradeables into tradeables. But the composition of the output changes for tradeables is highly asymmetric: the output of commodity 2 steadily rises and of commodity 1 steadily falls in moving from *A* to *B*. (This is precisely the kind of behaviour already described along the flat in 2.6.) The reason lies in the fact that resources released by the *N*-sector are more capital-intensive than in either traded sector. By contrast, consider the economy at point *C* in fig. 2.10, producing the nontradeable and commodity 3. As further resources are released from nontradeables, the output of commodity 4 commences, but that of commodity 3 also rises. As fig. 2.9 illustrates, the factor proportions released by the *N*-sector now lie between those required by these two traded commodities, allowing a rise in both of them.

5. The trade pattern for a small country[3]

This chapter has concentrated on the details of the production and specialization pattern for a small country embedded in a many-commodity world. Specialization tends to be narrow (one or two traded commodites) in this model for two reasons. (i) The technology of the small country was assumed not to be identical with all other countries. This implies that relative world prices of traded goods need bear no resemblance to relative costs of production in the small country. Put more geometrically, this implies that the convex hull of the unit-value isoquant for the

[3] I am indebted to Dermot McAleese of Trinity College, Dublin, for suggestions as to the pattern of trade.

composite traded commodity (such as illustrated in fig. 2.2) may have flats, but it would be accidental for *more* than two traded commodities to have unit-value isoquants tangent to the same line. (ii) There are assumed to be only two, mobile, factors of production. To appreciate the impact of such an assumption suppose each sector also made use of some factor of production incapable of moving into productive employment in other sectors. Then a number of traded commodities could be produced simultaneously, with those sectors relatively efficient at given world prices yielding high rents on factors specific to those sectors, while relatively inefficient sectors still produce because rentals are low on their specific factors.[4]

The trade pattern reflects not only the production pattern but also demands. A rather neutral assumption is made concerning demand: the small country has a positive demand for most traded commodities at given world prices. If the country produces only one traded good, it must export that commodity and import all others for which its demand is positive. If it produces two traded commodities, it could conceivably import one of them in addition to those commodities which it does not produce. But the pattern is clear: the country will tend to import a wide range of commodites compared to a fairly narrow export base. More importantly, its exports need not be the most labor-intensive commodities – or the most capital-intensive. Instead, its exports will typically display factor proportions that are 'intermediate' in the array of its imports. As an example, consider fig. 2.6. Depending upon taste patterns at home for tradeables and nontradeables, the small home country produces either commodity 2 or 3 or both. If it consumes all commodities it must be importing commodity 1 (the most labor-intensive), commodity 4 (the most capital-intensive), as well as those commodities (commodity 5) which, regardless of their required factor proportions, are too cheaply produced abroad compared with home technology. This is a different view of the typical trade pattern than that provided by the standard two-commodity analysis where both countries share the same technological knowledge.

References

[1] Caves R.E. and R.W. Jones, *World Trade and Payments* (Little, Brown, Boston, 1973).

[2] Jones, R.W. 'Income Distribution and Effective Protection in a Multi-Commodity Trade Model', *Journal of Economic Theory* (August, 1975) 1–15.

[3] Salter, W.E.G., 'Internal and External Balance. The Role of Price and Expenditure Effects', *The Economic Record*, 35 (1959).

[4] For a general model with specific factors see Jones [2].

Chapter 3

COMPARATIVE ADVANTAGE AND THE THEORY OF TARIFFS: A MULTI-COUNTRY, MULTI-COMMODITY MODEL*

1.

The classical discussion of comparative advantage within the framework of a two-country, two-commodity model provides the basis for Graham's attack on classical theory. The method of numerical example used by Graham [2] in setting out a multilateral theory of international specialization was greatly improved upon in two articles by McKenzie [6, 7]. The application of activity analysis enabled McKenzie systematically to explore the many-country, many-commodity examples of world production introduced by Graham. The equivalence between a competitive solution in a trade model and an efficient solution was proved in these articles by McKenzie and used by him in applying the competitive profit conditions of pure competition to solve for efficient specializations.

In this chapter I make use of both the competitive profit conditions and the concept of efficiency in world production in order to extend McKenzie's contributtions to develop necessary and sufficient conditions for efficient multilateral specialization. Emphasis is placed on relating the results to the bilateral comparative cost ratios found in the classical treatment. In addition, the case in which intermediate products are freely traded is explored. The 'rest-of-the-world' concept often used in trade models to reduce a many-country to a two-country framework is discussed in relation to the criterion for efficiency proved early in the paper. Graham-type demand functions are then introduced in developing a 'no-trade' production locus. This locus is employed in the concluding section of the

**Review of Economic Studies* (June 1961) 161–175. I am indebted to the Ford Foundation for support of this research project in the summers of 1958, 1959 and to Lionel McKenzie for helpful suggestions and encouragement.

paper in which an introduction is given to a multilateral theory of the effects on production and trade of tariffs and subsidies.

Throughout the article I employ the two assumptions basic to Ricardian and Graham trade models: (i) the existence of only one primary factor of production (labor), immobile between countries and fixed in supply (and fully employed) within countries and (ii) constant-cost (linear homogeneous) technology.

2.

Table 3.1 shows the constant labor costs of producing a unit of corn and linen in America (A) and Britain (B). If intermediate products are used, they are assumed not to enter into trade, so that the activities are integrated in linking units of output to the labor costs of table 3.1. Since 5/10 is less than 7/10, America has a bilateral comparative advantage in linen compared with Britain (and relative to corn). Once the total labor supplies are specified, a world efficiency frontier can be drawn (fig. 3.1).

The world efficiency frontier shows the maximal combinations of world outputs subject to the labor constraints in each country. It is composed of the two solid line segments joined at ②, the world output of corn and linen when America specializes completely in linen and Britain completely in corn. Any point on the frontier is a linear combination of points ① and ② or ② and ③. That is, it is sufficient, in drawing the world efficiency frontier, to compute all the efficient *complete* specializations – in which each country is devoting its entire labor supply to the production of one commodity. In fig. 3.1, ①, ②, ③, and ④ are the complete specializations. However, ④ is inefficient since it lies inside the locus. If Britain specialized completely in linen and America in corn (shown by ④, it would be possible to produce more of at least one commodity with no less of any other by reallocating labor in each market (moving along the arrow).[1]

Although America has a comparative advantage in linen, demand conditions may allow Britain to produce linen as well. For example, ⑤, a pattern of special-

Table 3.1

	America	Britain
Corn	10	10
Linen	5	7

[1] Note that ② does *not* lie northeast of ④, because of the larger size of America. Nonetheless, ② is definitely the efficient pattern of specialization in which one country is completely in corn and the other completely in linen.

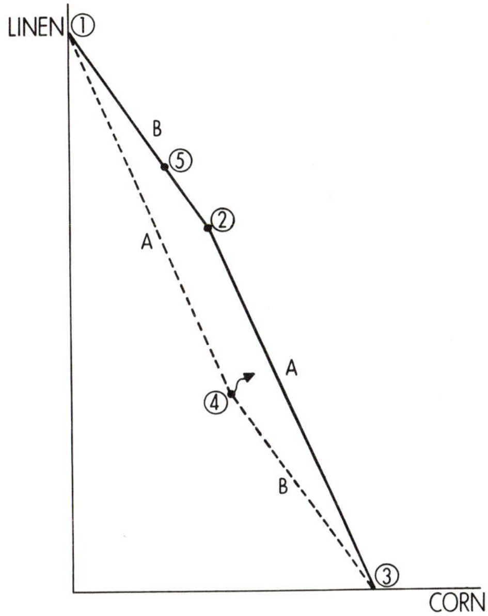

Figure 3.1

ization with Britain producing both corn and linen and America only linen, is a linear combination of complete specializations ① and ②, and is efficient. In fact, America might not produce linen at all (point ③) if the demand for linen is especially weak. Thus, without knowledge of demand conditions the actual production pattern is unknown. But the efficient production *possibilities* in fig. 3.1 are completely specified once the efficient complete specializations are determined.

Both Haberler [3] and Viner [8] in their treatises discuss the extensions made by the classical writers to a two-country, many-commodity or a many-country, two-commodity model. In each case a ranking is made, either of countries or of commodities, with demand conditions providing the dividing line (between comparative cost ratios) determining the actual production pattern. But what of the simple 3 × 3 case, shown in table 3.2? One country, Continental Europe (C), and one commodity, cloth, have been added to the labor cost figures from table

Table 3.2

	America	Britain	Continental Europe
Corn	10	⑩	10
Linen	⑤	7	3
Cloth	4	3	②

3.1. Note that if Continental Europe specializes completely in cloth production, with America in linen and Britain in corn as before, each country has a bilateral comparative advantage in the commodity it produces compared with any other country and the commodity that country is assigned. For example, 2/3 is less than 4/5, so that Continental Europe has a bilateral comparative advantage in cloth compared to America (and relative to linen). However, as the next section demonstrates, this pattern of specialization, shown by the circles in table 3.2 is *inefficient*.[2]

3.

As the preceding section illustrates for the 2×2 case, the task of determining the world efficiency frontier involves selecting the efficient *complete* specializations. Any point on the efficiency locus must be a convex linear combination of efficient complete specializations.[3]

Accordingly, I define an *assignment* as a pattern of complete specializations – each country's labor resources are devoted exclusively to the production of one commodity. Two (or more) assignments belong to the same *class* if and only if every commodity has the same number of countries assigned to it in one assignment as in the other. Thus, in the previous 2×2 case, it is possible to distinguish four assignments and three classes; two assignments each specified one of the countries in linen and the other in corn.

Excluding the possibility of ties (e.g. two countries having the same relative set of costs), there is a unique *optimal* assignment in each class – the assignment lying on the world efficiency locus. If an assignment is optimal (or efficient) in its class, it is impossible to increase world output of any commodity without reducing the output of at least one other commodity by diverting labor from this assignment towards any other assignment in its class.[4]

[2] That is, it is *not* sufficient (for efficiency) for these bilateral comparisons to hold. Lionel McKenzie, in correspondence with P.A. Samuelson, was the first to give an explicit example of this. The example McKenzie cited is the specialization shown in fig. 1 of his first *Review of Economic Studies* article (McKenzie [6]), in which *A* produces corn, *B* linen, *C* cloth, and *D* corn. This specialization satisfies the bilateral ratio comparisons. But when Richard Rosett pointed out to McKenzie that this part of the diagram was in error (*A* in corn, *B* in cloth, *C* in corn, and *D* in linen representing the efficient specialization), McKenzie realized that he had an example of an inefficient specialization that satisfied the bilateral comparisons.

[3] But the converse does not hold. For example, a linear combination of ① and ③ in fig. 3.1 does not yield an efficient specialization. In higher dimensional cases, it may not be *easy* to map out the world efficiency frontier from a knowledge of the efficient complete specializations, but in principle it can be done.

[4] As mentioned in a previous footnote, the optimal assignment may not dominate other assignments in its class. But by shifting *some* labor out of the pattern given by these other assignments it is possible to increase the output of some commodities without reducing the output of any.

The set of optimal assignments determines the world efficiency frontier, which is made up of zero-dimensional facets (the outputs corresponding to the optimal assignments) and higher dimensional facets up to $n - 1$ dimensional hyperplane segments (where n is the number of commodities).[5] Actual production, of course, need not correspond to any particular optimal assignment. Demand conditions need to be stated in determining where on the world efficiency locus actual production takes place.

In what follows I am concerned solely with the problem of determining the assignment that is optimal in its class. The special assumption of this section is the absence of traded intermediate products (to be lifted in the next section) so that the activities are integrated with respect to the one primary resource in each country, labor. For purposes of exposition, I consider the symmetrical case of n countries and n commodities and the *class* of assignments for which each country is assigned a different commodity (and therefore all commodities are produced). Other assignment classes and asymmetrical cases are treated in the next section.

Suppose countries and commodities are numbered such that the optimal assignment (for the class in which each country specializes in a different commodity) places country i in commodity i (referred to hereafter as the $i - i$ assignment). Compare this with one of the inefficient assignments, e.g. where country i produces commodity $j = i + 1$ for $i = 1, \ldots, n - 1$ and $j = 1$ for $i = n$ (the $i - j$ assignment). Suppose world production takes place according to the inefficient $i - j$ assignment, and consider the result of operating a set of *switching* activities whereby each country diverts some labor from the commodity it produces in the inefficient assignment into the commodity it produces in the optimal assignment.

In country i, this switching activity is the vector $A_i^i - (a_{oi}^i/a_{oj}^i)\, A_j^i$, where A_i^i is a column vector with a plus one in the ith row and zeros elsewhere. Similarly, A_j^i has the unit element in the jth row and zeros elsewhere, and a_{oi}^i and a_{oj}^i are the labor costs in country i of producing one unit of i and j, respectively.[6] If production of commodity j is reduced by a_{oi}^i/a_{oj}^i units, a_{oi}^i units of labor are released which, if put into commodity i, yield an output of 1 unit of i. Let s_i denote the level of this switching activity.

The switch from the inefficient assignment $i - j$ results in a change in world output of the n commodities given by the ΔY vector in eq. (1), where s is the column vector of

$$\Delta Y = Bs \tag{1}$$

[5] Cf. McKenzie [6] for a geometrical exposition in the three-country case. Also note the correction to this graph discussed above in footnote 2.

[6] The zero in the subscript refers to labor.

switching activities and B is the matrix defined in (2); B is a matrix with a unit diagonal

$$B = \begin{bmatrix} 1 & 0 & 0\ldots & 0 & \dfrac{-a_{0n}^{n}}{a_{01}^{n}} \\ \dfrac{-a_{01}^{1}}{a_{02}^{1}} & 1 & 0\ldots & 0 & 0 \\ 0 & \dfrac{-a_{02}^{2}}{a_{03}^{2}} & 1\ldots & 0 & 0 \\ \cdot & \cdot & \cdot & \cdot & \cdot \\ \cdot & \cdot & \cdot & \cdot & \cdot \\ \cdot & \cdot & \cdot & \cdot & \cdot \\ 0 & 0 & 0\ldots & \dfrac{-a_{0,n-1}^{n-1}}{a_{0n}^{n-1}} & 1 \end{bmatrix}, \tag{2}$$

and nonpositive off-diagonal elements. Clearly if the $i-i$ assignment is optimal, there exists an $s > 0$ such that $\Delta Y > 0$. But by the familiar Hawkins-Simon results of Leontief input-output theory [4], this requires the principal minors of the B matrix all to be positive. Clearly all principal minors of dimensions less than n have the value unity, and $|B|$ itself has value $1 - \Pi_i(a_{0i}^{i}/a_{0j}^{i})$, where $j = i + 1$ for $i = 1, \ldots,$ $n-1$ and $j = 1$ for $i = n$. Thus $\Pi_i(a_{0i}^{i}/a_{0j}^{i})$ is smaller than unity if the $i-i$ assignment is optimal. The converse also holds: comparing just these two assignments, if $\Pi_i(a_{0i}^{i}/a_{0j}^{i}) < 1$, $i-j$ cannot be the optimal assignment.[7]

The switching activity matrix shown in (2) involved all countries changing production patterns. To obtain the classical bilateral results compare the $i-i$ assignment with $i-j^*$, where $j^* = 2$ for $i = 1$, $j^* = 1$ for $i = 2$, and $j^* = i$ for $i > 2$. The new B matrix (B^*) is shown in (3), and $s_i = 0$ for $i > 2$. Clearly ΔY_1 and ΔY_2 can be made positive

$$B^* = \begin{bmatrix} 1 & \dfrac{-a_{02}^{2}}{a_{01}^{2}} & 0\ldots & 0 \\ \dfrac{-a_{01}^{1}}{a_{02}^{1}} & 1 & 0\ldots & 0 \\ 0 & 0 & 0\ldots & 0 \\ \cdot & \cdot & & \\ \cdot & \cdot & & \\ 0 & 0 & 0\ldots & 0 \end{bmatrix}, \tag{3}$$

[7] Compare this result with the essentially similar statement of eq. (6) in McKenzie [6].

for positive s_1, s_2 if and only if country 1 has a (bilateral) comparative advantage in commodity 1 compared with country 2 (and relative to commodtity 2).

The generalization is clear. Of all the assignments in the class, $i - i$ is optimal (efficient) if and only if $\Pi_i a^i_{0i}$ is less than $\Pi a^i_{0j(i)}$ where $j(i)$ is any other assignment in this class. Thus, the criterion for the optimal assignment involves *minimizing* the product of labor coefficients involved in the assignment.[8]

According to this criterion, the assignment in table 3.2 where America is in linen, Britain in corn, and Europe in Cloth, is inefficient. The product of labor coefficients for that assignment is 100, whereas the assignment America in corn, Britain in cloth and Europe in linen has a product of labor coefficients of 90 and is the optimal assignment in which each country specializes in a different commodity. Thus, a comparison of bilateral ratios is not enough. The economic significance of this is discussed in more detail in section 5.

4.

A fundamental result in activity analysis states that efficient outputs are outputs that satisfy the profit conditions of competitive equilibrium. The equivalence between an efficient solution and a solution sustainable in pure competition (if demand conditions are appropriate) in the Graham-type model of this paper is exploited in this section to develop the criterion for optimal assignments by the

[8] It is interesting to note that the 'optimal-assignment' problem in linear programming refers to a problem of minimizing (or maximizing) the (weighted) *sum* of rating coefficients rather than their product. Cf. Gale [1] for a discussion of and references to the assignment problem. For an earlier exposition of an assignment problem cf. Markowitz [5]. The minimum *product* criterion of this chapter could be turned into a minimum *sum* problem by taking logarithms. Thus the mathematical techniques for solving the literature's 'optimal-assignment' problem could be transferred to the international trade problem. The fact that sums appear in the literature is indicative of the value terms in which 'ratings' are listed. In my treatment the use of price-weighted values is avoided.

Whitin [9] analyzed the trade problem by maximizing the value product of world output. This leads to a linear programming problem if prices are taken as given (instead of depending upon demand factors as Whitin supposed). But the advantage of the approach used in this chapter lies in the dependence of the optimality criterion solely upon labor costs. It is also interesting to recall the classical attempts to use logarithms in extending the 2×2 case to cases of many countries *or* of many commodities (cf. Viner [8]).

In comparing the treatment in this chapter with the mathematical literature, consider the following problem: select the assignment in a class that maximizes the value of world output when prices are given for each commodity. The assignment that is optimal on this criterion may not be efficient (in the sense defined in this chapter)! For example, if the relative price of corn is sufficiently high, specialization ④ in fig. 3.1 yields a higher value output than does ②. But ③ would have a still higher value, as would some linear combinations of ② and ③.

profit conditions of competitive equilibrium. In addition, the model is expanded to allow free trade in intermediate products, although the intermediate product structures are assumed the same in all countries.[9]

Start by examining the symmetrical $n \times n$ case and the class of assignments in which all commodities are produced. Let a_{kj} represent the input requirement of commodity k in producing one unit of commodity j in all countries (net of own use, i.e. let $a_{jj} = 0$ for all j), p_j the world price of commodity j and w^i the wage rate in country i.

Suppose the assignment $i - i$ is optimal. Then there exists a set of positive prices and wage rates such that the competitive profit conditions of (4) are satisfied:

$$\begin{aligned} p_i &= \sum_{k \neq i} p_k a_{ki} + w^i a^i_{0i}, \quad \text{for all } i, \\ p_j &\leqq \sum_{k \neq j} p_k a_{kj} + w^i a^i_{0j} \quad \text{for all } i, j \neq i. \end{aligned} \tag{4}$$

To simplify, let $h_i = \Sigma_{k \neq i} p_k a_{ki} > 0$. Substitute into (4) and solve for w^i to obtain (5):

$$\begin{aligned} w^i &= \frac{p_i - h_i}{a^i_{0i}}, \quad \text{for all } i, \\ w^i &\geqq \frac{p_j - h_j}{a^i_{0j}}, \quad \text{for all } i, j \neq i. \end{aligned} \tag{5}$$

Assuming w^i positive for all countries, $p_i - h_i > 0$ for all i. This leads to the inequalities

$$\frac{p_i - h_i}{p_j - h_j} \geqq \frac{a^i_{0i}}{a^i_{0j}}, \quad \text{for all } i, j \neq i, \tag{6}$$

shown in (6). Assume no ties, so that the strict inequality holds. It is by multiplying these inequalities together that the same product criterion developed in the preceding section is obtained, as the left hand side reduces to unity and the right hand side to $\Pi_i(a^i_{0i}/a^i_{0j(i)})$, where $j(i)$ is any other assignment in the class.

Although the criterion yields the optimal assignments, they are not all feasible. That is, the world efficiency frontier consists only of the intersection of the effi-

[9]Partial justification for this assumption may seem to be obtained from the fact that the prices of intermediate (and final) commodities are the same in all countries with free trade and zero transport costs. But labor coefficients differ, so there is no necessity, in a world of variable production coefficients, for intermediate product structures actually used to be similar from country to country.

ciency locus with the non-negative orthant. Since i is an intermediate product, not enough i may be produced to satisfy world production demands if country i is small. This is most clearly seen by examining the class of assignments for which only one commodity (i) is produced. There is only one assignment that accomplishes this, but unless no other commodity, $j \neq i$, is an input into i, such an output is clearly not feasible (it does not lie in the non-negative orthant). The same objection would obtain even if all intermediate requirements were zero if minimum consumption requirements for all commodities had to be satisfied.

In this treatment all commodities serve both as intermediate products and final (consumption) products. Suppose, instead, that no product could be traded if it were to be used as an intermediate product in some other country. In such a case, activities within each country could be treated as integrated activities with congealed labor inputs, A^i_{0i}. Even if intermediate product structures were the same, however, the ratios of the A^i_{0j} would bear no resemblance to the ratios of the direct labor coefficients, a^i_{0j}. The indicated pattern of optimal specialization would be entirely different in the two cases. As McKenzie [6, p. 179] states, '. . . Lancashire would be unlikely to produce cotton cloth if the cotton had to be grown in England'.[10] Thus, if the labor cost figures of table 3.2 reflected direct and indirect labor costs, under the assumption that corn, linen, and cloth could not be traded if they were to be used as intermediate products, the specialization cited as efficient (A in corn, B in cloth, and C in linen) might not remain so if these products could be freely traded as intermediate goods. In the latter case the criterion changes to the minimum product function of the *direct* labor costs.

The asymmetric case, as well as the case where the number of commodities differs from the number of countries, is handled in precisely the same fashion. For example, consider the case of four countries and three commodities and the class of assignments, for which two countries are assigned to commodity 1, one country to commodity 2, and one to commodity 3. If the assignment: country 1 in 1, 2 in 2, 3 in 3, and 4 in 1 is optimal, the product $a^1_{01}a^2_{02}a^3_{03}a^4_{01}$ must be less than any other product $\Pi_i a^i_{oj(i)}$ in the same assignment class. If assignments from the class are selected, $\Pi\left[(p_i - h_i)/(p_j - h_j)\right]$ reduces to unity as every element in the numerator is matched by a corresponding element in the denominator.

The problem becomes much more complicated if intermediate product structures differ between countries and free trade in intermediate commodities is allowed. The profit conditions of competitive equilibrium still apply, but prices do not cancel out of the product of elements in (6). Alternatively, if the problem is

[10]The same pattern of specialization would hold in the 2×2 case, but not others.

set up in terms of switching activities, as in the previous section, the B matrix of (2) contains both positive and negative off-diagonal elements and the problem is of the general activities analysis type with no readily established criterion involving a^i_{oj} and a^i_{kj} in a simple fashion. Trade patterns are then influenced both by differences in labor costs and differences in intermediate product technology.

5.

The minimum product criterion for optimal assignments suggests that the bilateral ratios of comparative costs significant in the two-country or two-commodity case are also relevant in the general model. But as the discussion of table 3.2 illustrates, it is not sufficient for optimality that each country have a bilateral comparative advantage in the commodity it produces compared with any other country (and the commodity that country produces in the assignment class). The assignment: A in linen, B in corn, and C in cloth in table 3.2 satisfies the bilateral criteria, but is not efficient, since the product of the labor coefficients is not minimal. In this section I shall point out the economic interpretation of these added criteria.

For simplicity, I consider again the $n \times n$ case and the class of assignments for which each country is assigned a different commodity. If the optimal assignment is country i in commodity i, the inequality in (7) must hold for all other assignments $[j(i)]$ in this

$$\prod_i \frac{a^i_{oi}}{a^i_{oj(i)}} < 1 \tag{7}$$

class. Consider, first, the alternative assignments in which two countries, j and k, switch their products while all other countries $i \neq j, k$, remain specialized in commodity i. The

$$\frac{a^j_{0j}}{a^j_{0k}} < \frac{a^k_{0j}}{a^k_{0k}} \tag{8}$$

criterion, (7), reduces to (8) for these assignments, as the cost ratios for $i \neq j, k$ cancel out. That is, country j must have a bilateral comparative advantage in commodity j compared with country k and commodity k.

Consider now the assignments (in the same class) for which country m switches as well. One of these assignments leads to the inequality shown in (9). The left-hand side

$$\frac{a_{0j}^{j}}{a_{0k}^{j}} < \frac{a_{0j}^{m}}{a_{0m}^{m}} \frac{a_{0m}^{k}}{a_{0k}^{k}} \tag{9}$$

is the opportunity cost of producing j in country j, expressed in k units. This is smaller than the similar cost ratio in country k, as shown by (8). Furthermore, it is smaller than this relative cost for countries k and m together; this is the meaning of (9). For the right-hand side of (9) shows the amount of commodity k that must be sacrificed to produce a unit of commodity j when country k reduces k production and transfers its labor into commodity m allowing country m to reduce its production of commodity m to produce commodity j. And (8) and (9) show that this (comparative, or opportunity) cost of producing j is lower in country j than in k, and lower in j than in countries k and m together.

Continuing in this fashion, inequalities such as (9) result with a larger number of countries shown on the right side of (9). If all other countries are considered, inequality (10) results. The right-hand side shows the comparative cost (expressed in units of k) of

$$\frac{a_{0j}^{j}}{a_{0k}^{j}} < \frac{a_{0j}^{s}}{a_{0s}^{s}} \cdots \frac{a_{0m}^{r}}{a_{0r}^{r}} \frac{a_{0r}^{k}}{a_{0k}^{k}} \tag{10}$$

producing a unit of j in the 'rest of the world' (all countries except j) when this is accomplished indirectly by country k reducing k production and going into some commodity $r \neq j, k$, allowing country r to release some of its labor from r into m production, etc. until some country, s, releases labor to produce j.

The pattern is now clear. In this multilateral setting, with reference to this class of assignments, country j has a (multilateral) comparative advantage in producing commodity j relative to commodity k compared with the 'rest of the world' if and only if the sacrifice of one unit of commodity k in country j yields a greater increase in the production of commodity j than (with reference to the optimal assignment) would a sacrifice of one unit of commodity k in the rest of the world. The transfer of resources in the rest of the world can take place *directly* by having country k (the producer of commodity k in the efficient specialization) reduced k output and switch its labor into commodity j. Or it can take place *indirectly* by having country k reduce its output of commodity k and apply the released labor to *any other* commodity and have the other countries in the rest of the world so adjust that the output of j increases while the outputs of commodities $i \neq k, j$ remain constant. It is these *indirect* routings that are neglected in the simple bilateral comparative cost ratios; but the result of complicated reallocations in production patterns can be expressed by the *product* of the simple bilateral terms.[11]

6.

The world efficiency frontier discussed in the preceding sections is also the locus of world outputs that are compatible with free trade and pure competition. It could be termed the free-trade frontier. As a preliminary to the next section's discussion of tariffs, a locus of the no-trade production possibilities is developed in this section. Let n = number of countries and m = the number of commodities.

In the complete absence of trade, and assuming every country is producing somewhere on its own efficiency frontier (transformation surface), world output is contained in an m-dimensional convex set bounded by the world efficiency frontier and a surface representing the *least* efficient world outputs. In fig. 3.2, with $n = 3$, $m = 2$, the set of possible world outputs with *no* trade is represented by the shaded area.

It would be misleading to suppose the shaded area represents the gains (in terms of world output) to be obtained by moving from the no-trade to the free trade position. For demand conditions may be such as to allow *any* point in the shaded area, including the boundaries, to be the no-trade world output. In the face of this difficulty it is tempting somehow to normalize demand conditions to obtain a locus of points in the shaded area that represents the no-trade production possibilities. This is accomplished by positing the Graham demand assumptions.

Graham assumed (i) demand functions were the same in each country and (ii) in any country the demand for any commodity was of unitary price and income elasticity. The purpose of this section is to prove that with these Graham demand assumptions the world no-trade locus reduces to a section of an $m - 1$ dimensional hyperplane representing the convex linear combinations of maximal world outputs of each commodity. In fig. 3.2, it is the line segment joining Y_1^* and Y_2^*, the outputs of 1 and 2 if all the world's labor were put into 1 and 2, respectively.

The proof consists of two stages. First, I prove that if each country puts the

[11] Note that country j need not have a bilateral comparative advantage in producing j relative to k compared with *every other* country individually. It would be unusual if this happened. For example, in table 3.2 the efficient specialization when all commodities are produced assigns Britain to cloth. Although Britain has a comparative advantage in cloth compared with America and relative to corn, it does *not* have a similar bilateral comparative advantage with Europe in cloth over corn. But this is inessential, as Europe is not assigned to corn – the relevant comparison for Britain (in comparing cloth and corn) is either with America directly or indirectly with Europe *and* America.

same fraction, λ_j, of its labor supply into commodity j, the world output must lie on this $m - 1$ dimensional hyperplane segment.

The allocation of labor in each country, i, into commodity j is given by $\lambda_j L^i$, where $\lambda_j \geqq 0$ and $\Sigma \lambda_j = 1$. Note that by assumption λ_j is the same for all countries. Since one unit of labor in country i yields $1/a^i_{0j}$ units of commodity j, $\lambda_j L^i$ units of labor yield $(\lambda_j/a^i_{0j})\, L^i$ units of j. The vector of country i's outputs is given by y^i in (11):

$$y^i = \begin{bmatrix} \lambda_1 \dfrac{L^i}{a^i_{01}} \\ \vdots \\ \lambda_m \dfrac{L^i}{a^i_{0m}} \end{bmatrix} \tag{11}$$

and the total world output in this no-trade situation is given by Y in (12):

$$Y \equiv \Sigma\, y^i = \begin{bmatrix} \lambda_1 \Sigma \dfrac{L^i}{a^i_{01}} \\ \vdots \\ \lambda_m \Sigma \dfrac{L^i}{a^i_{0m}} \end{bmatrix} = \sum_j \lambda_j\, Y_j^* \tag{12}$$

Y_j^* is a vector with zeros everywhere except in the jth row, whose entry is $\Sigma_i\, (L^i/a^i_{0j})$. But this is the maximal world output of commodity j – obtained by having each country put all its labor into commodity j. Therefore if each country devotes the fraction λ_j of its labor to commodity j, world output, Y, is contained in the $m - 1$ dimensional convex hull of the maximal world output vectors, Y_j^*.

It only remains to be demonstrated that the Graham demand functions require this allocation of labor resources in each country if there is no trade. If y^i_j represents the consumption (and production) of commodity j in country i, r^i the income of country i, and p^i_j the price of commodity j in country i, the Graham demand function is given in (13):

$$y^i_j = b_j \frac{r^i}{p^i_j}, \tag{13}$$

where b_j is the constant fraction of income spent on commodity j in all countries. Now $r_i = w^i L^i$, where w^i is the wage rate in country i. Furthermore, by the competitive profit conditions, $w^i = p^i_j/a^i_{0j}$. Substitution yields (14) as the Graham demand function:

$$y_j^i = b_j \frac{L^i}{a_{0j}^i}. \tag{14}$$

If b_j is interpreted as λ_j, it is clear that if trade between countries is excluded, the Graham demand assumption requires each country to devote the same fraction, b_j, of its labor to commodity j as every other country. And, as I set out to prove, total world output lies in the convex hull spanned by the maximal vectors, Y_j^*.

It is interesting to note that the normalization of demand functions that requires each country to produce outputs in the same proportion as every other country leads to a locus of possible world outputs clearly inferior to this convex hull. The reason for this is seen most clearly in the two-commodity, two-country case. If country 1 has a comparative advantage in commodity 1, and produces according to the Graham demand functions in the no-trade case, it will produce relatively more of commodity 1 than will country 2. This follows because commodity 1 is relatively cheaper in country 1. Requiring both countries to produce outputs in the same proportion leads to a more inefficient allocation of labor.

Still other normalizations could be devised. But the Graham demand assumption has the advantage of being simple to state, widely used, and in addition of leading to the most simple locus of world outputs. And the purpose of the normalization is to allow some control over demand behavior so that problems in which 'it all depends on demand' can be handled more fruitfully.

7.

Free trade and pure competition ensure that the allocation of world resources is such that production is efficient: world output is on the world efficiency frontier. The introduction of tariffs still allows for competitive behavior, but nonetheless may result in inefficient resource allocation. In this final section I explore the implications of tariffs for world patterns of specialization in production and trade in the Graham multi-country, multi-commodity constant labor cost model. In particular I shall develop a criterion to determine what *inefficient* assignments become possible in a world of tariffs.

For simplicity I restrict my discussion to the three-country, three-commodity case, and the class of complete specializations in which all commodities are produced. Suppose country i in commodity i is the efficient assignment. That is, Πa_{0i}^i is less than $\Pi a_{0j(i)}^i$, where $j(i)$ is any other assignment in this class. Then with free trade none of these inefficient assignments can be supported. But suppose country i levies a nondiscriminatory tariff, t_j^i on commodity j. What inefficient patterns of production may then be allowed?

Suppose, as a result of the tariffs, the assignment that puts country 1 into commodity 2, country 2 into 3, and 3 into 1 is allowed. If π_j^i represents the domestic price in i of commodity j, and w^i the wage in i, the competitive profit conditions ensure the system of equalities and inequalities shown in (15):

$$\begin{aligned}&\pi_2^1 = w^1 a_{02}^1; \qquad \pi_3^2 = w^2 a_{03}^2; \qquad \pi_1^3 = w^3 a_{01}^3,\\ &\pi_1^1 \leqq w^1 a_{01}^1; \qquad \pi_2^2 \leqq w^2 a_{02}^2; \qquad \pi_3^3 \leqq w^3 a_{03}^3.\end{aligned} \tag{15}$$

The wage rate can be eliminated in each column pair of inequalities to yield the set (16):

$$\frac{\pi_2^1}{\pi_1^1} \geq \frac{a_{02}^1}{a_{01}^1}; \qquad \frac{\pi_3^2}{\pi_2^2} \geq \frac{a_{03}^2}{a_{02}^2}; \qquad \frac{\pi_1^3}{\pi_3^3} \geq \frac{a_{01}^3}{a_{03}^3}. \tag{16}$$

Multiplying these together yields inequality (17):

$$\frac{\pi_2^1}{\pi_1^1}\frac{\pi_3^2}{\pi_2^2}\frac{\pi_1^3}{\pi_3^3} \geq \frac{a_{02}^1}{a_{01}^1}\frac{a_{03}^2}{a_{02}^2}\frac{a_{01}^3}{a_{03}^3}. \tag{17}$$

Although the price of j in each country need not be the same, prices cannot be more widely spread than the tariff rates allow. In particular, π_1^3, π_2^1, and π_3^2 must be bounded as in (18):

$$\begin{aligned}&\pi_1^3 \leqq (1 + t_1^3)\,\pi_1^1\\ &\pi_2^1 \leqq (1 + t_2^1)\,\pi_2^2.\\ &\pi_3^2 \leqq (1 + t_3^2)\,\pi_3^3\end{aligned} \tag{18}$$

Multiplying these inequalities together and substituting into (17) yields (19)

$$a_{01}^1 a_{02}^2 a_{03}^3 \geqq \frac{a_{02}^1 a_{03}^2 a_{01}^3}{(1 + t_2^1)(1 + t_3^2)(1 + t_1^3)} \tag{19}$$

as the inequality that must be satisfied if the system of tariffs is to permit country 1 to produce commodity 2, 2 to produce 3, and 3 to produce 1. Since the $i - i$ assignment was optimal, $a_{01}^1 a_{02}^2 a_{03}^3$ is less than the product $a_{02}^1 a_{03}^2 a_{01}^3$. In order for the latter specialization to be possible, tariff rates must be sufficiently great to reduce the right-hand side of (19) at least to the optimal product, $a_{01}^1 a_{02}^2 a_{03}^3$.

The pattern is clear. Consider the general case, for any particular class of assignments, α. If $k(i)$ and $j(i) \in \alpha$, and $k(i)$ is the efficient assignment of commodities (k) to countries (i), $\Pi_i a^i_{0k(i)}$. But a system of tariffs will allow country i to produce commodity j, for all i, only if (20) is satisfied:

$$\prod_i \frac{a^i_{0j(i)}}{1 + t^i_{j(i)}} \leqq \prod_i a^i_{0k(i)}. \tag{20}$$

The analysis of inefficient *trade* flows leads to somewhat different results. To return to the assignments discussed above, can i be an exporter of j, where $j = i + 1$ for $i = 1, 2$, and $j = 1$ for $i = 3$? First consider the possibility of the inefficient producers exporting to the efficient sources of supply. Country i will import commodity i from country j only if the import price of i is lower than the internal cost of producing i in country i. This requires the inequalities shown in (21):

$$\pi^3_1 (1 + t^1_1) \leqq w^1 a^1_{01}; \qquad \pi^1_2 (1 + t^2_2) \leqq w^2 a^2_{02}; \qquad \pi^2_3 (1 + t^3_3) \leqq w^3 a^3_{03}. \tag{21}$$

The wage rates, w^i, are given in (15) and, upon substitution, the inequalities in (22) are required for this trade to take place:

$$\frac{\pi^1_2}{\pi^3_1} \geqq \frac{a^1_{02}}{a^1_{01}} (1 + t^1_1); \qquad \frac{\pi^2_3}{\pi^1_2} \geqq \frac{a^2_{03}}{a^2_{02}} (1 + t^2_2); \qquad \frac{\pi^3_1}{\pi^2_3} \geqq \frac{a^3_{01}}{a^3_{03}} (1 + t^3_3). \tag{22}$$

Multiplying these together, the π_i's cancel to yield (23):

$$a^1_{01}\, a^2_{02}\, a^3_{03} \geqq a^1_{02}\, a^2_{03}\, a^3_{01}\, (1 + t^1_1)\, (1 + t^2_2)\, (1 + t^3_3). \tag{23}$$

Since i in i is the efficient assignment, this condition clearly can not be satisfied if the t^i_i's are positive.

But a different multilateral trading pattern must also be considered, namely the one in which country i exports commodity j to country $k \neq i, j$. If this trade pattern is to emerge, it must not be the case that country j could make a profit by producing commodity j and supplanting country i as an exporter to country k. For example, the price in country 3 of commodity 2 exported by country 1 is $w^1 a^1_{02}(1 + t^3_2)$. Country 2 could supply consumers in country 3 with commodity 2 at a tariff-ridden price of $w^2 a^2_{02}(1 + t^3_2)$. The inefficient pattern of trade can be sustained in a competitive equilibrium only if the inequalities in equation (24) hold. Multiplying these inequalities together yields $\Pi_i a^i_{0i} \geqq \Pi_i a^i_{0j}$, which was ruled out by assumption.

$$w^2 a^2_{02}(1 + t^3_2) \geqq w^1 a^1_{02}(1 + t^3_2); \qquad w^3 a^3_{03}(1 + t^1_3) \geqq w^2 a^2_{03}(1 + t^1_3),$$
$$w^1 a^1_{01}(1 + t^2_1) \geqq w^3 a^3_{01}(1 + t^2_1). \tag{24}$$

By protecting inefficient industries, a system of tariffs allows inefficient patterns of *production*. Nondiscriminatory tariffs[12] serve to choke off trade, but never to allow inefficient producers also to *export*.

This conclusion rests on having $t_i^i \geqq 0$. But suppose subsidies are employed. Although subsidies are often thought preferable to tariffs, they may allow inefficient patterns of trade to emerge. Suppose the t_i^i are all zero. Instead, country i contributes a subsidy, s_j^i, to commodity j assigned it in the inefficient specialization (1 in 2, 2 in 3, 3 in 1). Then if (25) is satisfied,

$$a_{02}^1 a_{03}^2 a_{01}^3 \leqq \frac{a_{01}^1 a_{02}^2 a_{03}^3}{(1 - s_2^1)(1 - s_3^2)(1 - s_1^3)}, \tag{25}$$

inefficient *trade* may develop.

Return to the previous section's discussion of the no-trade locus. If Graham demand conditions are specified, a system of tariffs allows world production in the shaded region north-east of the $Y_1^* Y_2^*$ line segment of fig. 3.2. At worst, if all tariffs were prohibitive, production would take place somewhere along line $Y_1^* Y_1^*$. But a system of subsidies could permit production below this line as well. By allowing inefficient producers to export to the efficient region, a system of

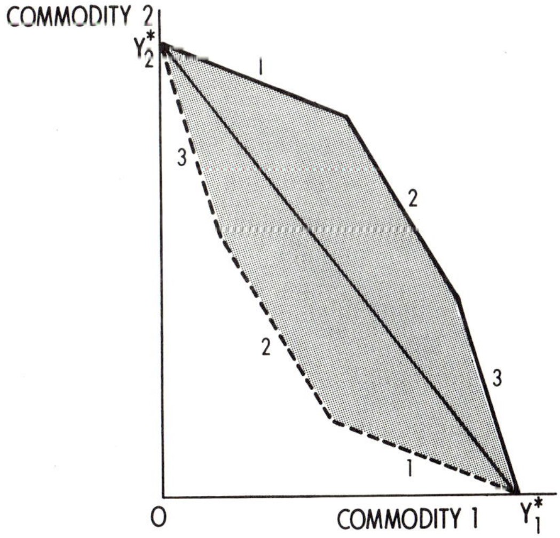

Figure 3.2

[12]The tariff terms cancel in each inequality of (24) only if each country has a uniform duty regardless of sources of supply.

subsidies may depress world output further than any system of tariffs would permit. Some trade is better than no trade – if the impediments to trade are in the form of tariffs.

References

[1] Gale, D., *The Theory of Linear Economic Models* (McGraw-Hill, New York, 1960).
[2] Graham, F. D., *The Theory of International Values* (Princeton Unviersity Press, 1948).
[3] Harberler, G., *The Theory of International Trade* (Hodge & Co. Ltd., London, 1936) pp. 136–140.
[4] Hawkins, D. and H. Simon, 'Note: Some Conditions of Macroeconomic Stability', *Econometrica* (July–October) 1949).
[5] Markowitz, H., 'Concepts and Computing Procedures for Certain X_{ij} Programming Problems', in: *Proceedings of the Second Symposium on Linear Programming*, vol. II (1955) pp. 509–565.
[6] McKenzie, L., 'Specialization and Efficiency in World Production', *Review of Economic Studies*, 21 (3) (June 1954).
[7] McKenzie, L., 'Specialization in Production', *Review of Economic Studies*, 23 (1) (1956).
[8] Viner, J., *Studies in the Theory of International Trade* (Allen & Unwin, London, 1955) pp. 453–467.
[9] Whitin, T., 'Classical Theory, Graham's Theory, and Linear Programming in International Trade', *Quarterly Journal of Economics* (November 1953).

PART II

STRUCTURE IN TRADE MODELS

INTRODUCTION TO PART II

The search for simple general equilibrium models of trade and production that would capture both the importance of factor endowment differences in explaining trade patterns and the impact of trade on the internal distribution of income led to formal developments of the Heckscher–Ohlin two-factor, two-commodity model described in Chapter 1. A simple version of this model, the 'small open economy' case, treats commodity prices as parameters and thus avoids the problem of analyzing the determination of prices in world markets. Further typical simplification had each country's factor endowment base autonomously given, cut off from dependence on factor or commodity prices. But even these simplifications leave a model with eight unknowns for each country; the two output levels, the two factor prices, and the quantities of each factor allocated to each sector.

Chapters 4 and 5 represent my attempt to recast the description of the Heckscher–Ohlin 2×2 model to highlight the dual relationship between such standard trade results as the Stolper–Samuelson theorem linking factor and commodity prices and the Rybczynski theorem dealing with factor endowment – commodity output relationships at constant prices. Techniques borrowed from activity analysis and present in neoclassical form in Walras's classic treatise helped simplify matters by focusing on factor requirements per unit output instead of total factor allocations. If factor endowments and/or commodity prices change, solutions for relative changes in the eight unknowns of the model can be obtained without ever having to handle more than a pair of equations at a time.

Chapter 6 attempts to harness the structure of the 2×2 model to a model with three productive factors. The rigid link between commodity and factor prices is broken if the number of factors exceeds the number of commodities. In this chapter the connection between the 3×2 model and the Heckscher – Ohlin 2×2 model is easier to visualize since I assume each sector uses only two factors. It is precisely this assumption that allows the 3×2 model to emerge as the most simple case in which the distinction between mobile factors and specific factors can be made. In a subsequent article [11], I show that the structural properties of this specific-factors version of the 3 × 2 model are maintained intact in the general $(n + 1) \times n$ version – each sector using a factor specific to it plus one common mobile factor.

In the 2 × 2 Heckscher–Ohlin model the key distinction between factors is that they are required in different proportions in the two sectors. In the 3 × 2 specific factors version of Chapter 6, the key distinction between factors resides in the assumed degree of intersectoral mobility. Chapter 7 picks up this contrast in asking how responsive, in each model, is the composition of output along the transformation schedule to a change in the terms of trade.

Chapter 8, based on joint work with José Scheinkman, seeks to generalize the structural properties of the 2 × 2 and 3 × 2 models. An important precursor is Samuelson's 1953 piece [17] on the relationship between commodity and factor prices in multi-sector, multi-factor models. Chapter 8 avoids the path taken by Chipman, [2], Uekawa, [20], Kemp and Wegge, [14], Inada, [5], and others who ask what restrictive assumptions on technology are required to yield unique one-to-one assignments of factors to commodities so that each commodity price rise leads to an increase in the real return to the factor uniquely assigned it (decrease, in Inada's case) and a decrease in all others (increase, in Inada's case). Instead, it follows Ethier's suggestion [4] that one should investigate what general properties emerge without such restrictions on the technology. The material in Chapter 8 overlaps with several other recent pieces of independent research, namely Kemp and Wan [13], Diewert and Woodland [3], and Chang [1].

The Stolper–Samuelson and the Rybczynski results point to the asymmetrical effect of commodity price changes on factor prices, on the one hand, and of endowment changes on outputs at constant commodity prices, on the other. As Chapter 4 notes, and Chapter 8 stresses, the asymmetry stems in large part from a basic asymmetry typically assumed about the technology: that joint production is absent. That is, each separate process requires more than one factor to produce each good. Suppose, by contrast, the existence of n productive activities, each requiring as inputs all (say n) factors and each yielding as outputs all n commodities. In such a case a rise in the price of commodity no. 35, holding other commodity prices constant, might raise every input price by the same relative amount as every other; completely absent would be the Stolper–Samuelson effect whereby at least one factor's real return would rise relative to p_{35} and at least one other factor return would absolutely fall.

If joint production is a rare phenomenon, the Stolper–Samuelson and Rybczynski types of results are useful special cases of what Chapter 4 terms the 'magnification effect'. But should these results be scrapped if joint production is prevalent? I would argue that even with joint production a basic asymmetry exists that can be used to derive results analogous to Stolper–Samuelson and Rybezynski. Many factors are combined in each (single) productive *process* (or activity), even if each process spews out a number of commodities. Trade theory can then focus on the international dispersion of these processes and how changes in commodity prices affect the factoral distribution of income through their effects upon the *net* output value of each process.

Applications of the 2×2 and 3×2 models are briefly discussed in Chapters 4 and 6. Some of my work on technology, appearing below in Part V, is based upon the demonstration in Chapter 4 that arbitrary (small) alterations in technology affect outputs and prices much as would a set of subsidies and factor endowment changes. But space limitations have precluded other work which is based on these models. In [6] I extended the 2×2 case to analyze production and pricing relationships when constant returns to scale no longer prevail. In such cases it becomes important to recognize that the commodity which requires overall a higher proportion of capital to labor may nonetheless, for small output variations, require smaller increments of capital to labor. The analogy for such behaviour is found in the literature on the transfer problem, where differences between countries' *marginal* propensities to consume a commodity determine how transfer affects relative commodity prices. Indeed, this kind of analogy motivated a later piece [9] in which I reinterpreted the 2×2 model in Chapter 4 to handle a case in which 'technology' represents utility functions, with inputs of commodities being used nonjointly to produce outputs of real income for each of two consumer groups. 'Demand' in such a model could be provided by a Bergsonian welfare function, in which case the model illustrates the relationship between the community indifference curves of Scitovsky [19] and the social indifference curves of Samuelson [18]. Alternatively, if individuals possess bundles of commodities as endowments, the model can be adapted to show how and why there may be a presumption that net income effects act in a stable manner.

When relative changes replace absolute changes as the basic variables under consideration, Chapter 4 shows how two transforms of the technology matrix of input–output coefficients become significant. The first of these is the matrix of factor allocation coefficients, λ_{ij} (the fraction of the total supply of the ith factor used in the jth industry). These fractions bind output changes to endowment changes at constant factor prices. The second matrix displays distributive factor shares in each industry, θ_{ij}. The relative change in the price of commodity j is the distributive-share weighted average of factor price changes. As Chapter 4 demonstrates, factor intensity rankings are equivalently displayed either by the determinant of λ-coefficients or of θ-coefficients. But if the same factor earns different returns in the two sectors, because of factor market distortions or differential taxes, a ranking of industries by *physical* factor proportions (as given by the λ-determinant) might differ as compared with *value* factor proportions (reflected in the θ-determinant). As I discuss in [8], the focus on the λ and θ matrices described in Chapter 4 usefully reveals the sources of paradoxical behaviour (e.g. an increase in price leads to a reduction in output) in models characterized by factor market distortions.

In [7] and [10] I found this structure helpful in handling cases in which imported intermediate commodities are subject to duty. In this setting, changes in tariff rates imply different alterations in rates of effective protection. Both in [7] and [11] I have argued that effective protection is a more reliable indicator of changes in income distribution than in outputs. Indeed, in extremely simple cases it is still possible that the industry that receives effective protection may nonetheless contract. An example of this phenomenon, provided by Ramaswami and Srinivasan [15] is dissected and analyzed in [7].

Some applications in trade theory involve a comparison between the 2×2 and 3×2 models. For example, in [16] Roy Ruffin and I discuss the presumption concerning protection and real wages in these and other models. Finally, an incursion into the balance of payments literature in a joint article with Max Corden [12] suggests how a currency devaluation when the government is involved in incomes policy that introduces factor price rigidity may have profoundly different real repercussions depending upon the degree of intersectoral factor mobility. In all these applications I found it useful to develop the model along the lines set out in the material in Part II.

References

[1] Chang, W., 'Some Theorems of Trade and General Equilibrium with Many Goods and Factors', unpublished.

[2] Chipman, J., 'Factor Price Equalization and the Stolper–Samuelson Theorem', *International Economic Review*, 10 (October 1969) 399–406.

[3] Diewert, W.E. and A.D. Woodland, 'Frank Knight's Theorem in Linear Programming Revisited', *Econometrica* (March 1977) 375–398.

[4] Ethier, W., 'Some of the Theorems of International Trade with Many Goods and Factors', *Journal of International Economics*, 4 (May 1974) 199–206.

[5] Inada, K., 'The Production Coefficient Matrix and the Stolper-Samuelson Condition', *Econometrica*, 39 (March 1971) 219–240.

[6] Jones, R.W., 'Variable Returns to Scale in General Equilibrium Theory', *International Economic Review* (October 1968) 261–272.

[7] Jones, R.W., 'Effective Protection and Substitution', *Journal of International Economics* (February 1971) 59–81.

[8] Jones, R.W., 'Distortions in Factor Markets and the General Equilibrium Model of Production,' *Journal of Political Economy* (May/June 1971) 437–459.

[9] Jones, R.W., 'Activity Analysis and Real Incomes: Analogies with Production Models', *Journal of International Economics* (August 1972) 277–302.

[10] Jones, R.W., 'The Metzler Tariff Paradox: Extensions to Nontraded and Intermediate Commodities', in: Horwich and Samuelson, eds., *Trade, Stability, and Macroeconomics* (Essays in Honor of Lloyd Metzler) (Academic Press, 1974) pp. 3–18.

[11] Jones, R. W., 'Income Distribution and Effective Protection in a Multi-Commodity Trade Model', *Journal of Economic Theory* (August 1975) 1–15.

[12] Jones, R.W., and W. Max Corden, 'Devaluation, Non-Flexible Prices, and the Trade Balance for a Small Country', *The Canadian Journal of Economics* (February 1976) 150–161.

[13] Kemp, M.C. and Henry Wan, 'Relatively Simple Generalizations of the Stolper-Samuelson and Samuelson-Rybczynski Theorem', in: M.C. Kemp, *Three Topics in the Theory of International Trade* (North-Holland, Amsterdam, 1976) pp. 49–59.

[14] Kemp, M.C. and L. Wegge, 'On the Relation Between Commodity Prices and Factor Rewards', *International Economic Review*, 10 (October 1969) 407–413.

[15] Ramaswami, V.K. and T.N. Srinivasan, 'Tariff Structure and Resource Allocation in the Presence of Factor Substitution', in: Bhagwati, Jones, Mundell and Vanek, eds., *Trade, Balance of Payments, and Growth* (North-Holland, Amsterdam, 1971) 291–299.

[16] Ruffin, R. and R.W. Jones, 'Protection and Real Wages: The Neo-Classical Ambiguity', *Journal of Economic Theory* (April 1977) 337–348.

[17] Samuelson, P.A., 'Prices of Factors and Goods in General Equilibrium', *Review of Economic Studies*, 21 (1953) 1–20.

[18] Samuelson, P.A., 'Social Indifference Curves', *Quarterly Journal of Economics* (February 1956) pp. 1–22.

[19] Scitovsky, T., 'A Reconsideration of the Theory of Tariffs', *Review of Economic Studies* (1942) 89–110.

[20] Uekawa, Y., 'Generalization of the Stolper-Samuelson Theorem', *Econometrica*, 39 (March 1971) 197–213.

Chapter 4

THE STRUCTURE OF SIMPLE GENERAL EQUILIBRIUM MODELS*

1. Introduction

It is difficult to find any major branch of applied economics that has not made some use of the simple general equilibrium model of production. For years this model has served as the work-horse for most of the developments in the pure theory of international trade. It has been used to study the effects of taxation on the distribution of income and the impact of technological change on the composition of outputs and the structure of prices. Perhaps the most prominent of its recent uses is to be found in the neoclassical theory of economic growth.

Such intensive use of the simple two-sector model of production suggests that a few properties are being retranslated in such diverse areas as public finance, international trade, and economic growth. The unity provided by a common theoretical structure is further emphasized by the dual relationship that exists between sets of variables in the model itself. Traditional formulations of the model tend to obscure this feature. My purpose in this chapter is to analyze the structure of the simple competitive model of production in a manner designed to highlight both the dual relationship and the similarity that exists among a number of traditional problems in comparative statics and economic growth.

The model is described in sections 2 and 3. In section 4 I discuss the dual nature of two theorems in the theory of international trade associated with the names of Stolper and Samuelson on the one hand and Rybczynski on the other. A simple

* *Journal of Political Economy*, 73 (December 1965) pp. 557–572. I am indebted to the National Science Foundation for support of this research in 1962–1964. I have benefited from discussions with Hugh Rose, Robert Fogel, Rudolph Penner, and Emmanuel Drandakis. My greatest debt is to Akihiro Amano [1], whose dissertation was a stimulus to my own work.

demand relationship is added in section 5, and a problem in public finance is analyzed – the effect of excise subsidies or taxes on relative commodity and factor prices. The static model of production is then reinterpreted as a neo-classical model of economic growth by letting one of the outputs serve as the capital good. The dual of the 'incidence' problem in public finance in the static model is shown to have direct relevance to the problem of the stability of the balanced growth path in the neoclassical growth model. In the concluding section of the chapter I show how these results can be applied to the analysis of technological progress. Any improvement in technology or in the quality of factors of production can be simply viewed as a composite of two effects, which I shall term the 'differential industry' effect and the 'differential factor' effect. Each effect has its counterpart in the dual problems discussed in the earlier part of the paper.

2. The model

Assume a perfectly competitive economy in which firms (indefinite in number) maximize profits, which are driven to the zero level in equilibrium. Consistent with this, technology in each of two sectors exhibits constant returns to scale. Two primary factors, labor (L) and land (T), are used in producing two distinct commodities, manufactured goods (M) and food (F). Wages (w) and rents (r) denote the returns earned by the factors for use of services, whereas p_M and p_F denote the competitive market prices of the two commodities.

If technology is given and factor endowments and commodity prices are treated as parameters, the model serves to determine eight unknowns: the level of commodity outputs (two), the factor allocations to each industry (four), and factor prices (two). The equations of the model could be given by the production functions (two), the requirement that each factor receive the value of its marginal product (four), and that each factor be fully employed (two). This is the format most frequently used in the theory of international trade and the neoclassical theory of growth.[1] I consider, instead, the formulation of the model suggested by activity analysis.

The technology is described by the columns of the A matrix,

$$A = \begin{pmatrix} a_{LM} & a_{LF} \\ a_{TM} & a_{TF} \end{pmatrix},$$

where a_{ij} denotes the quantity of factor i required to produce a unit of commodity

[1] As an example in each field see Kemp [14] and Meade [15].

j. With constant returns to scale total factor demands are given by the product of the *a*'s and the levels of output. The requirement that both factors be fully employed is thus given by eqs. (1) and (2). Similarly, unit costs of production in each industry are given by the columns of *A* multiplied by the factor prices. In a competitive equilibrium with both goods being produced, these unit costs must reflect market prices, as in eqs. (3) and (4).[2]

$$a_{LM}M + a_{LF}F = L, \quad (1)$$

$$a_{TM}M + a_{TF}F = T, \quad (2)$$

$$a_{LM}w + a_{TM}r = p_M, \quad (3)$$

$$a_{LF}w + a_{TF}r = p_F. \quad (4)$$

This formulation serves to emphasize the dual relationship between factor endowments and commodity outputs on the one hand (eqs. (1) and (2) and commodity prices and factor prices on the other (eqs. (3) and (4)).

In the general case of variable coefficients the relationships shown in eqs. (1)–(4) must be supplemented by four additional relationships determining the input coefficients. These are provided by the requirement that in a competitive equilibrium each a_{ij} depends solely upon the ratio of factor prices.

3. The equations of change

The comparative statics properties of the model described in section 2 are developed by considering the effect of a change in the parameters on the unknowns of the problem. With unchanged technology the parameters are the factor endowments (*L* and *T*) and the commodity prices (p_M and p_F), the right-hand side of eqs. (1)–(4).

Let a hat (ˆ) indicate the relative change in a variable or parameter. Thus, $\hat{p}_F$ denotes dp_F/p_F and $\hat{L}$ denotes dL/L.[3] The four equations in the rates of change

[2] These basic relationships are usually presented as inequalities to allow for the existence of resource(s) in excess supply even at a zero price or for the possibility that losses would be incurred in certain industries if production were positive. I assume throughout that resources are fully employed, and production at zero profits with positive factor and commodity prices is possible. For a discussion of the inequalities see, for example, Dorfman *et al.* [5] or Hicks [9].

[3] This is the procedure used by Meade [15]. The λ and θ notation has been used by Amano [1]. Expressing small changes in relative or percentage terms is a natural procedure when technology exhibits constant returns to scale.

are shown in (1a)–(4a):

$$\lambda_{LM}\hat{M} + \lambda_{LF}\hat{F} = \hat{L} - [\lambda_{LM}\hat{a}_{LM} + \lambda_{LF}\hat{a}_{LF}], \tag{1a}$$

$$\lambda_{TM}\hat{M} + \lambda_{TF}\hat{F} = \hat{T} - [\lambda_{TM}\hat{a}_{TM} + \lambda_{TF}\hat{a}_{TF}], \tag{2a}$$

$$\theta_{LM}\hat{w} + \theta_{TM}\hat{r} = \hat{p}_M - [\theta_{LM}\hat{a}_{LM} + \theta_{TM}\hat{a}_{TM}], \tag{3a}$$

$$\theta_{LF}\hat{w} + \theta_{TF}\hat{r} = \hat{p}_F - [\theta_{LF}\hat{a}_{LF} + \theta_{TF}\hat{a}_{TF}]. \tag{4a}$$

The λ's and θ's are the transforms of the a's that appear when relative changes are shown. A fraction of the labor force is used in manufacturing (λ_{LM}), and this plus the fraction of the labor force used in food production (λ_{LF}) must add to unity by the full-employment assumption (shown by eq. (1)). Similarly for λ_{TM} and λ_{TF}. The θ's, by contrast, refer to the factor shares in each industry. Thus, θ_{LM}, labor's share in manufacturing, is given by $a_{LM}w/p_M$. By the zero profit conditions, θ_{Lj} and θ_{Tj} must add to unity.

In this section I assume that manufacturing is labor-intensive. It follows that labor's share in manufacturing must be greater than labor's share in food, and that the percentage of the labor force used in manufacturing must exceed the percentage of total land that is used in manufacturing. Let λ and θ be the notations for the matrices of coefficients shown in ((1a), (2a)) and ((3a), (4a)).

$$\lambda = \begin{pmatrix} \lambda_{LM} & \lambda_{LF} \\ \lambda_{TM} & \lambda_{TF} \end{pmatrix}; \quad \theta = \begin{pmatrix} \theta_{LM} & \theta_{TM} \\ \theta_{LF} & \theta_{TF} \end{pmatrix}.$$

Since each row sum in λ and θ is unity, the determinants $|\lambda|$ and $|\theta|$ are given by

$$|\lambda| = \lambda_{LM} - \lambda_{TM} \quad \textit{and} \quad |\theta| = \theta_{LM} - \theta_{LF}\text{'}$$

and both $|\lambda|$ and $|\theta|$ are positive by the factor-intensity assumption.[4]

If coefficients of production are fixed, eqs. (1a)–(4a) are greatly simplified as every a_{ij} and, therefore, the λ and θ weighted sums of the $\hat{a}_{ij}$'s reduce to zero. In the case of variable coefficients, sufficient extra conditions to determine the $\hat{a}$'s are easily derived. Consider, first, the maximizing role of the typical com-

[4] Let P and W represent the diagonal matrices,

$$\begin{pmatrix} p_M & 0 \\ 0 & p_F \end{pmatrix} \text{and} \begin{pmatrix} w & 0 \\ 0 & r \end{pmatrix},$$

respectively, and E and X represent the diagonal matrices of factor endowments and commodity outputs. Then $\lambda = E^{-1}AX$ and $\theta = P^{-1}A'W$. Since $|A| > 0$ and the determinants of the four diagonal matrices are all positive, $|\lambda|$ and $|\theta|$ must be positive. This relation among the signs of $|\lambda|$, $|\theta|$, and $|A|$ is proved by Amano [1] and Takayama [22].

petitive entrepreneur. For any given level of output he attempts to minimize costs; that is, he minimizes unit costs. In the manufacturing industry these are given by $(a_{LM}w + a_{TM}r)$. The entrepreneur treats factor prices as fixed, and varies the a's so as to set the derivative of costs equal to zero. Dividing by p_M and expressing changes in relative terms leads to eq. (6). Eq. (7) shows the corresponding relationship for the food industry:

$$\theta_{LM}\hat{a}_{LM} + \theta_{TM}\hat{a}_{TM} = 0, \tag{6}$$

$$\theta_{LF}\hat{a}_{LF} + \theta_{TF}\hat{a}_{TF} = 0. \tag{7}$$

With no technological change, alterations in factor proportions must balance out such that the θ-weighted average of the changes in input coefficients in each industry is zero.

This implies directly that the relationship between changes in factor prices and changes in commodity prices is *identical* in the variable and fixed coefficients cases, an example of the Wong–Viner envelope theorem. With costs per unit of output being minimized, the change in costs resulting from a small change in factor prices is the same whether or not factor proportions are altered. The saving in cost from such alterations is a second-order small.[5]

A similar kind of argument definitely does *not* apply to the λ-weighted average of the $\hat{a}$'s for each factor that appears in the factor market-clearing relationships. For example $(\lambda_{LM}\hat{a}_{LM} + \lambda_{LF}\hat{a}_{LF})$ shows the percentage change in the total quantity of labor required by the economy as a result of changing factor proportions in each industry at unchanged outputs. The crucial feature here is that if factor prices change, factor proportions alter in the same direction in both industries. The extent of this change obviously depends upon the elasticities of substitution between factors in each industry. In a competitive equilibrium (and with the internal tangencies implicit in earlier assumptions), the slope of the isoquant in each industry is equal to the ratio of factor prices. Therefore the elasticities of substitution can be defined as in (8) and (9):

$$\sigma_M = \frac{\hat{a}_{TM} - \hat{a}_{LM}}{\hat{w} - \hat{r}}, \tag{8}$$

$$\sigma_F = \frac{\hat{a}_{TF} - \hat{a}_{LF}}{\hat{w} - \hat{r}} \tag{9}$$

Together with (6) and (7) a subset of four equations relating the $\hat{a}$'s to the change in the relative factor prices is obtained. They can be solved in pairs; for example (6)

[5] For another example of the Wong–Viner theorem, for changes in real income along a transformation schedule, see Jones [13].

and (8) yield solutions for the $\hat{a}$'s of the M industry. In general,

$$\hat{a}_{Lj} = -\theta_{Tj}\sigma_j(\hat{w} - \hat{r}); \quad j = M, F,$$

$$\hat{a}_{Tj} = \theta_{Lj}\sigma_j(\hat{w} - \hat{r}); \quad j = M, F.$$

These solutions for the $\hat{a}$'s can then be substituted into eqs. (1a)–(4a) to obtain:

$$\lambda_{LM}\hat{M} + \lambda_{LF}\hat{F} = \hat{L} + \delta_L(\hat{w} - \hat{r}), \tag{1b}$$

$$\lambda_{TM}\hat{M} + \lambda_{TF}\hat{F} = \hat{T} - \delta_T(\hat{w} - \hat{r}), \tag{2b}$$

$$\theta_{LM}\hat{w} + \theta_{TM}\hat{r} = \hat{p}_M, \tag{3b}$$

$$\theta_{LF}\hat{w} + \theta_{TF}\hat{r} = \hat{p}_F, \tag{4b}$$

where

$$\delta_L = \lambda_{LM}\theta_{TM}\sigma_M + \lambda_{LF}\theta_{TF}\sigma_F,$$

$$\delta_T = \lambda_{TM}\theta_{LM}\sigma_M + \lambda_{TF}\theta_{LF}\sigma_F.$$

In the fixed-coefficients case, δ_L and δ_T are zero. In general, δ_L is the aggregate percentage saving in labor inputs at unchanged outputs associated with a 1% rise in the relative wage rate, the saving resulting from the adjustment to less labor-intensive techniques in both industries as relative wages rise.

The structure of the production model with variable coefficients is exhibited in eqs. (1b)–(4b). The latter pair states that factor prices are dependent only upon commodity prices, which is the factor-price equalization theorem.[6] If commodity prices are unchanged, factor prices are constant and eqs. (1b) and (2b) state that changes in commodity outputs are linked to changes in factor endowments via the λ matrix in precisely the same way as θ links factor price changes. This is the basic duality feature of the production model.[7]

4. The magnification effect

The nature of the link provided by λ or θ is revealed by examining the solution for $\hat{M}$ and $\hat{F}$ at constant commodity prices in (1b) and (2b) and for $\hat{w}$ and $\hat{r}$ in eqs (3b)

[6] Factor endowments come into their own in influencing factor prices if complete specialization is allowed (or if the number of factors exceeds the number of commodities). See Samuelson [18] for a detailed discussion of this issue.

[7] The reciprocal relationship between the effect of a rise in the price of commodity i on the return to factor j and the effect of an increase in the endowment of factor j on the output of commodity i is discussed briefly by Samuelson [18].

and (4b).[8] If both endowments expand at the same rate, both commodity outputs expand at identical rates. But if factor endowments expand at different rates, the commodity intensive in the use of the fastest growing factor expands at a greater rate than either factor, and the other commodity grows (if at all) at a slower rate than either factor. For example, suppose labor expands more rapidly than land. With M labor-intensive,

$$\hat{M} > \hat{L} > \hat{T} > \hat{F}.$$

This *magnification effect* of factor endowments on commodity outputs at unchanged commodity prices is also a feature of the dual link between commodity and factor prices. In the absence of technological change or excise taxes or subsidies, if the price of M grows more rapidly than the price of F,

$$\hat{w} > \hat{p}_M > \hat{p}_F > \hat{r}.$$

Turned the other way around, the source of magnification effect is easy to detect. For example, since the relative change in the price of either commodity is a positive weighted average of factor-price changes, it must be bounded by these changes. Similarly, if input coefficients are fixed (as a consequence of assuming constant factor and commodity prices), any disparity in the growth of outputs is reduced when considering the consequent changes in the economy's demand for factors. The reason, of course, is that each good requires both factors of production.

Two special cases have been especially significant in the theory of international trade. Suppose the endowment of only one factor (say labor) rises. With $\hat{L}$ positive and $\hat{T}$ zero, $\hat{M}$ exceeds $\hat{L}$ and $\hat{F}$ is negative. This is the Rybczynzki theorem in the theory of international trade: at unchanged commodity prices an expansion in one factor results in an absolute decline in the commodity intensive in the use of the other factor. (See Rybczynski [17] and also Chapter 1.) Its dual underlies the Stolper–Samuelson [21] tariff theorem.[9] Suppose $\hat{p}_F$ is zero (for example, F could be taken as numeraire). Then an increase in the price of M (brought about, say, by a tariff on imports of M) raises the return to the factor used intensively in M by an even greater relative amount (and lowers the return to the other factor). In the case illustrated, the *real* return to labor has unambiguously risen.

For some purposes it is convenient to consider a slight variation of the Stolper–

[8] The solutions, of course, are given by the elements of λ^{-1} and θ^{-1}. If M is labor-intensive, the diagonal elements of λ^{-1} and θ^{-1} are positive and exceed unity, while off-diagonal elements are negative.

[9] A graphical analysis of the dual relationship between the Rybczynski theorem and the Stolper–Samuelson theorem is presented in Chapter 5.

Samuelson theorem. Let p_j stand for the *market* price of j as before, but introduce a set of domestic excise taxes or subsidies so that $s_j p_j$ represents the price received by producers in industry j; s_j is one plus the *ad valorem* rate of subsidy to the industry.[10] The effect on factor prices of an imposition of subsidies on commodities is derived from eqs. (3c) and (4c):

$$\theta_{LM}\hat{w} + \theta_{TM}\hat{r} = \hat{p}_M + \hat{s}_M, \tag{3c}$$

$$\theta_{LF}\hat{w} + \theta_{TF}\hat{r} = \hat{p}_F + \hat{s}_F. \tag{4c}$$

At fixed commodity prices, what impact does a set of subsidies have on factor prices? The answer is that all the subsidies are 'shifted backward' to affect returns to factors in a *magnified* fashion. Thus, if M is labor-intensive and if the M industry should be especially favored by the subsidy,

$$\hat{w} > \hat{s}_M > \hat{s}_F > \hat{r}.$$

The *magnification* effect in this problem and its dual reflects the basic structure of the model with fixed commodity prices. However, if a demand relationship is introduced, prices are determined within the model and can be expected to adjust to a change in factor endowments or, in the dual problem, to a change in excise subsidies (or taxes). In the next section I discuss the feedback effect of these induced price changes on the composition of output and relative factor prices. The crucial question to be considered concerns the extent to which commodity price changes can dampen the initial magnification effects that are produced at constant prices.

5. The extended model: demand endogenous

To close the production model I assume that community taste patterns are homothetic and ignore any differences between the taste patterns of laborers and landlords. Thus, the ratio of the quantities consumed of M and F depends only upon the relative commodity price ratio, as in eq. (5):

$$\frac{M}{F} = f\left(\frac{p_M}{p_F}\right). \tag{5}$$

[10] I restrict the discussion to the case of excise subsidies because of the resemblance it bears to some aspects of technological change, which I discuss later. In the case of taxes, $s_i = 1/(1 + t_i)$, where t_i represents the *ad valorem* rate of excise tax.

In terms of the rates of change, (5a) serves to define the elasticity of substitution between the two commodities on the demand side, σ_D:

$$(\hat{M} - \hat{F}) = -\sigma_D(\hat{p}_M - \hat{p}_F). \tag{5a}$$

The effect of a change in factor endowments at constant commodity prices was considered in the previous section. With the model closed by the demand relationship, commodity prices adjust so as to clear the commodity markets. Eq. (5a) shows directly the change in the ratio of outputs consumed. Subtracting (2b) from (1b) yields the change in the ratio of outputs produced:

$$(\hat{M} - \hat{F}) = \frac{1}{|\lambda|}(\hat{L} - \hat{T}) + \frac{\delta_L + \delta_T}{|\lambda|}(\hat{w} - \hat{r}).$$

The change in the factor-price ratio (with no subsidies or taxes) is given by

$$(\hat{w} - \hat{r}) = \frac{1}{|\theta|}(\hat{p}_M - \hat{p}_F),$$

so that, by substitution,

$$(\hat{M} - \hat{F}) = \frac{1}{|\lambda|}(\hat{L} - \hat{T}) + \sigma_S(\hat{p}_M - \hat{p}_F),$$

where

$$\sigma_S \equiv \frac{1}{|\lambda||\theta|}(\delta_L + \delta_T).$$

σ_S represents the elasticity of substitution between commodities on the *supply* side (along the transformation schedule).[11] The change in the commodity-price ratio is then given by the mutual interaction of demand and supply:

$$(\hat{p}_M - \hat{p}_F) = -\frac{1}{|\lambda|\ (\sigma_S + \sigma_D)}(\hat{L} - \hat{T}). \tag{10}$$

[11] I have bypassed the solution for $\hat{M}$ and $\hat{F}$ separately given from (1b) and (2b). After substituting for the factor-price ratio in terms of the commodity-price ratio the expression for $\hat{M}$ could be written as

$$\hat{M} = \frac{1}{|\lambda|}[\lambda_{TF}\hat{L} - \lambda_{LF}\hat{T}] + e_M(\hat{p}_M - \hat{p}_F),$$

where, e_M, the shorthand expression for $\{1/|\lambda||\theta|\}\ (\lambda_{TF}\delta_L + \lambda_{LF}\delta_T)$, shows the percentage change in M that would be associated with a 1% rise in M's relative price along a given transformation schedule. It is a 'general equilibrium' elasticity of supply, as discussed in Jones [13]. It is readily seen that $\sigma_S = e_M + e_F$. Furthermore, $\theta_M e_M = \theta_F e_F$, where θ_M and θ_F denote the share of each good in the national income.

Therefore the resulting change in the ratio of commodities produced is

$$(\hat{M} - \hat{F}) = \frac{1}{|\lambda|} \frac{\sigma_D}{\sigma_S + \sigma_D} (\hat{L} - \hat{T}). \tag{11}$$

With commodity prices adjusting to the initial output changes brought about by the change in factor endowments, the composition of outputs may, in the end, not change by as much, relatively, as the factor endowments. This clearly depends upon whether the 'elasticity' expression, $\sigma_D/(\sigma_S + \sigma_D)$, is smaller than the 'factor-intensity' expression, $|\lambda|$. Although it is *large* values of σ_S (and the underlying elasticities of factor substitution in each industry, σ_M and σ_F) that serve to dampen the spread of outputs, it is *small* values of σ_D that accomplish the same end. This comparison between elasticities on the demand and supply side is familiar to students of public finance concerned with questions of tax (or subsidy) incidence and shifting. I turn now to this problem.

The relationship between the change in factor prices and subsidies is given by (3c) and (4c). Solving for the change in the ratio of factor prices,

$$(\hat{w} - \hat{r}) = \frac{1}{|\theta|} \{(\hat{p}_M - \hat{p}_F) + (\hat{s}_M - \hat{s}_F)\}. \tag{12}$$

Consider factor endowments to be fixed, Any change in factor prices will nonetheless induce a readjustment of commodity outputs. On the supply side,

$$(\hat{M} - \hat{F}) = \sigma_S\{(\hat{p}_M + \hat{p}_F) + (\hat{s}_M - \hat{s}_F)\}.$$

The relative commodity price change that equates supply and demand is

$$(\hat{p}_M - \hat{p}_F) = -\frac{\sigma_S}{\sigma_S + \sigma_D} (\hat{s}_M - \hat{s}_F). \tag{13}$$

Substituting back into the expression for the change in the factor-price ratio yields

$$(\hat{w} - \hat{r}) = \frac{1}{|\theta|} \frac{\sigma_D}{\sigma_S + \sigma_D} (\hat{s}_M - \hat{s}_F). \tag{14}$$

This is a familiar result. Suppose *M* is subsidized more heavily than *F*. Part of the subsidy is shifted backward, affecting relatively favorably the factor used intensively in the *M*-industry (labor). Whether labor's relative return expands by a greater proportion than the spread in subsidies depends upon how much of the subsidy has been passed forward to consumers in the form of a relatively lower price for *M*. And this, of course, depends upon the relative sizes of σ_S and σ_D.

Notice the similarity between expressions (11) and (14). Factors produce commodities, and a change in endowments must result in an altered composition of production, by a magnified amount at unchanged prices. By analogy, subsidies 'produce' returns to factors, and a change in the pattern of subsidies alters the distribution of income. In each case, of course, the extent of readjustment required is eased if commodity prices change, by a factor depending upon the relative sizes of demand and supply elasticities of substitution.

6. The aggregate elasticity of substitution

The analysis of a change in factor endowments leading up to eq. (11) has a direct bearing on a recent issue in the neoclassical theory of economic growth. Before describing this issue it is useful to introduce yet another elasticity concept – that of an economy-wide elasticity of substitution between factors.[12] With no subsidies, the relationship between the change in the factor price ratio and the change in endowments can be derived from (10). Thus,

$$(\hat{w} - \hat{r}) = -\frac{1}{|\lambda||\theta|(\sigma_S + \sigma_D)}(\hat{L} - \hat{T}). \tag{15}$$

By analogy with the elasticity of substitution in a particular sector, define σ as the percentage rise in the land/labor endowment ratio required to raise the wage/rent ratio by 1%. Directly from (15),

$$\sigma = |\lambda||\theta|(\sigma_S + \sigma_D).$$

But recall that σ_S is itself a composite of the two elasticities of substitution in each industry, σ_M and σ_F. Thus, σ can be expressed in terms of the three *primary* elasticities of substitution in this model:

$$\sigma = Q_M\sigma_M + Q_F\sigma_F + Q_D\sigma_D,$$

where

$$Q_M = \theta_{LM}\lambda_{TM} + \theta_{TM}\lambda_{LM},$$

$$Q_F = \theta_{LF}\lambda_{TF} + \theta_{TF}\lambda_{LF},$$

$$Q_D = |\lambda|\cdot|\theta|.$$

Note that σ is not just a linear expression in σ_M, σ_F, and σ_D–it is a weighted average

[12] For previous uses see Amano [2] and Drandakis [6].

of these three elasticities as $\Sigma Q_i = 1$. Note also that σ can be positive even if the elasticity of substitution in each industry is zero, for it incorporates the effect of intercommodity substitution by consumers as well as direct intracommodity substitution between factors.

Finally, introduce the concept, σ, into expression (11) for output changes:

$$(\hat{M} - \hat{F}) = \frac{|\theta|\sigma_D}{\sigma}(\hat{L} - \hat{T}), \tag{11a}$$

and into expression (14) for the change in factor prices in the subsidy case:

$$(\hat{w} - \hat{r}) = \frac{|\lambda|\sigma_D}{\sigma}(\hat{s}_M - \hat{s}_F). \tag{14a}$$

One consequence is immediately apparent: if the elasticity of substitution between commodities on the part of consumers is no greater than the overall elasticity of substitution between factors, the *magnification* effects discussed in section 4 are more than compensated for by the dampening effect of price changes.

7. Convergence to balanced growth

The two-sector model of production described in sections 1–6 can be used to analyze the process of economic growth. Already I have spoken of increases in factor endowments and the consequent 'growth' of outputs. But a more satisfactory growth model would allow for the growth of at least one factor of production to be determined by the system rather than given parametrically. Let the factor 'capital' replace 'land' as the second factor in the two-sector model (replace T by K). And let M stand for machines rather than manufacturing goods. To simplify, I assume capital does not depreciate. The new feedback element in the system is that the rate of increase of the capital stock, $\hat{K}$, depends on the current output of machines, M. Thus $\hat{K} = M/K$. The 'demand' for M now represents savings.

Suppose the rate of growth of the labor force, $\hat{L}$, is constant. At any moment of time the rate of capital accumulation, $\hat{K}$, either exceeds, equals, or falls short of $\hat{L}$. Of special interest in the neoclassical theory of growth (with no technological progress) is the case of balanced growth where $\hat{L} = \hat{K}$. Balance in the growth of factors will, as we have seen, result in balanced growth as between the two commodities (at the same rate). But if $\hat{L}$ and $\hat{K}$ are not equal, it becomes necessary to inquire whether they tend toward equality (balanced growth) asymptotically or tend to diverge even further.

If machines are produced by labor-intensive techniques, the rate of growth of machines exceeds that of capital if labor is growing faster than capital, or falls short of capital if capital is growing faster than labor. (This is the result in section 4, which is dampened, but not reversed, by the price changes discussed in section 5.) Thus, the rate of capital accumulation, if different from the rate of growth of the labor supply, falls or rises toward it. The economy tends toward the balanced-growth path.

The difficulty arises if machines are capital intensive. If there is no price change, the change in the composition of outputs must be a magnified reflection of the spread in the growth rates of factors. Thus, if capital is growing more rapidly than labor, machine output will expand at a greater rate than either factor, and this only serves to widen the spread between the rates of growth of capital and labor even further.[13] Once account is taken of price changes, however, the change in the composition of outputs may be sufficiently dampened to allow convergence to balanced growth despite the fact that machines are capital intensive.

Re-examine eq. (11a), replacing $\hat{T}$ by $\hat{K}$ and recognizing that $|\theta|$ is negative if machines are capital intensive. If σ exceeds $-|\theta|\sigma_D$, on balance a dampening of the ratio of outputs as compared to factor endowments takes place. This suggests the critical condition that must be satisfied by σ, as compared with σ_D and $|\theta|$, in order to insure stability. But this is not precisely the condition required. Rather, stability hinges upon the *sign* of $(\hat{M} - \hat{K})$ being opposite to that of $(\hat{K} - \hat{L})$. There is a presumption that when $(\hat{M} - \hat{F})$ is smaller than $(\hat{K} - \hat{L})$ (assuming both are positive) the output of the machine sector is growing less rapidly than is the capital stock. But the corresponding is not exact.

To derive the relationship between $(\hat{M} - \hat{K})$ and $(\hat{M} - \hat{F})$ consider the two ways of expressing changes in the national income (Y). It can be viewed as the sum of returns to factors or the sum of the values of output in the two sectors. Let θ_i refer to the share of factor i or commodity i in the national income. In terms of rates of change,

$$\hat{Y} = \theta_L(\hat{w} + \hat{L}) + \theta_K(\hat{r} + \hat{K}) = \theta_M(\hat{p}_M + \hat{M}) + \theta_F(\hat{p}_F + \hat{F}).$$

But the share of a factor in the national income must be an average of its share in each sector, with the weights given by the share of that sector in the national

[13] See Shinkai [19] for a discussion of the fixed-coefficients case. At constant commodity prices the impact of endowment changes on the composition of output is the same regardless of elasticities of substitution in production. Thus, a necessary and sufficient condition in Shinkai's case is the factor-intensity condition. For the variable coefficients case the factor-intensity condition was first discussed by Uzawa [24].

income. This, and eqs. (3b) and (4b), guarantee that

$$\theta_L \hat{w} + \theta_K \hat{r} = \theta_M \hat{p}_M + \theta_F \hat{p}_F.$$

That is, the rates of change of the financial components in the two expressions for $\hat{Y}$ balance, leaving an equality between the physical terms:

$$\theta_L \hat{L} + \theta_K \hat{K} = \theta_M \hat{M} + \theta_F \hat{F}.$$

The desired relationship is obtained by observing that θ_K equals $(1 - \theta_L)$ and θ_M is $(1 - \theta_F)$. Thus,

$$(\hat{M} - \hat{K}) = \theta_F(\hat{M} - \hat{F}) - \theta_L(\hat{K} - \hat{L}).$$

With this in hand it is easy to see that (from [11a]) $(\hat{M} - \hat{K})$ is given by

$$(\hat{M} - \hat{K}) = \frac{\theta_L}{\sigma}\left\{-\frac{\theta_F|\theta|}{\theta_L}\sigma_D - \sigma\right\}(\hat{K} - \hat{L}). \tag{16}$$

It is not enough for σ to exceed $-|\theta|\sigma_D$, it must exceed $-(\theta_F/\theta_L)|\theta|\sigma_D$ for convergence to balanced growth.[14] It nonetheless remains the case that σ greater than σ_D is sufficient to insure that the expression in brackets in (16) is negative. For (16) can be rewritten as (16a):

$$(\hat{M} - \hat{K}) = -\frac{\theta_L}{\sigma}\left\{\sigma - \left[1 - \frac{\theta_{LM}}{\theta_L}\right]\sigma_D\right\}(\hat{K} - \hat{L}). \tag{16a}$$

Thus, it is overly strong to require that σ exceed σ_D.[15]

8. Savings behavior

A popular assumption about savings behavior in the literature on growth theory is that aggregate savings form a constant percentage of the national income. (See, for example, Solow [20].) This, of course, implies that σ_D is unity. In this case it becomes legitimate to inquire as to the values of σ or σ_M and σ_F as compared with unity. For example, if each sector's production function is Cobb–Douglas (σ_M and σ_F each unity), stability is guaranteed. But the value 'unity' that has a crucial

[14] The two requirements are equivalent if $\theta_F = \theta_L$, i.e. if total consumption $(p_F F)$ is matched exactly by the total wages (wL). This equality is made a basic assumption as to savings behavior in some models where laborers consume all and capitalists save all. For example, see Uzawa [24].

[15] A condition similar to (16a), with the assumption that $\sigma_D = 1$, is presented by Amano [3].

role in this comparison only serves as a proxy for σ_D. With high σ_D even greater values for σ_M and σ_F (and σ) would be required.

If σ_D is unity when the savings ratio is constant, is its value higher or lower than unity when the savings ratio depends positively on the rate of profit? It turns out that this depends upon the technology in such a way as to encourage convergence to balanced growth precisely in those cases where factor intensities are such as to leave it in doubt.

The capital goods, machines, are demanded not for the utility they yield directly, but for the stream of additional future consumption they allow. This is represented by the rate of return (or profit), which is linked by the technology to the relative price of machines according to the magnification effects implicit in the Stolper–Samuelson theorem. The assumption that the savings ratio (the fraction of income devoted to new machines) rises as the rate of profit rises implies that the savings ratio rises as the relative price of machines rises (and thus that σ_D is less than unity) if and only if machines are capital intensive. Of course the savings assumption also implies that σ_D exceeds unity (that is, that the savings ratio falls as the relative price of machines rises) if machines are labor intensive, but convergence to balanced growth is already assured in this case.[16]

9. The analysis of technological change

The preceding sections have dealt with the structure of the two-sector model of production with a given technology. They nonetheless contain the ingredients necessary for an analysis of the effects of technological progress. In this concluding section I examine this problem and simplify by assuming that factor endowments remain unchanged and subsidies are zero. I concentrate on the impact of a change in production conditions on relative prices. The effect on outputs is considered implicitly in deriving the price changes.

Consider a typical input coefficient, a_{ij}, as depending both upon relative factor prices and the state of technology:

$$a_{ij} = a_{ij}(w/r, t).$$

In terms of the relative rates of change, $\hat{a}_{ij}$ may be decomposed as

$$\hat{a}_{ij} = \hat{c}_{ij} - \hat{b}_{ij}.$$

[16] For a more complete discussion of savings behavior as related to the rate of profit, see Uzawa [25] and Inada [10].

$\hat{c}_{ij}$ denotes the relative change in the input–output coefficient that is called forth by a change in factor prices as of a given technology. The $\hat{b}_{ij}$ is a measure of technological change that shows the alteration in a_{ij} that would take place at constant factor prices. Since technological progress usually involves a *reduction* in the input requirements, I define $\hat{b}_{ij}$ as $-(1/a_{ij})\,\partial a_{ij}/\partial t$.

The $\hat{b}_{ij}$ are the basic expressions of technological change. After the discussion in section 3 it is not surprising that it is the λ and θ weighted averages of the $\hat{b}_{ij}$ that turn out to be important. These are defined by the following set of π's:

$$\pi_j = \theta_{Lj}\hat{b}_{Lj} + \theta_{Tj}\hat{b}_{Tj} \qquad (j = M,\ F),$$

$$\pi_i = \lambda_{iM}\hat{b}_{iM} + \lambda_{iF}\hat{b}_{iF} \qquad (i = L,\ T).$$

If a $\hat{B}$ matrix is defined in a manner similar to the original A matrix, π_M and π_F are the sums of the elements in each column weighted by the relative factor shares, and π_L and π_T are sums of the elements in each row of $\hat{B}$ weighted by the fractions of the total factor supplies used in each industry. Thus, π_M, assumed non-negative, is a measure of the rate of technological advance in the M-industry and π_L, also assumed non-negative, reflects the overall labor-saving feature of technological change.

Turn now to the equations of change. The $\hat{c}_{ij}$ are precisely the $\hat{a}_{ij}$ used in eqs. (6)–(9) of the model without technological change. This subset can be solved, just as before, for the response of input coefficients to factor price changes. After substitution, the first four equations of change (eqs (1a)–(4a)) become

$$\lambda_{LM}\hat{M} + \lambda_{LF}\hat{F} = \pi_L + \delta_L(\hat{w} - \hat{r}), \tag{1d}$$

$$\lambda_{TM}\hat{M} + \lambda_{TF}\hat{F} = \pi_T - \delta_T(\hat{w} - \hat{r}), \tag{2d}$$

$$\theta_{LM}\hat{w} + \theta_{TM}\hat{r} = \hat{p}_M + \pi_M, \tag{3d}$$

$$\theta_{LF}\hat{w} + \theta_{TF}\hat{r} = \hat{p}_F + \pi_F. \tag{4d}$$

The parameters of technological change appear only in the first four relationships and enter there in a particularly simple form. In the first two equations it is readily seen that, in part, technological change, through its impact in reducing input coefficients, has precisely the same effects on the system as would a change in factor endowments. π_L and π_T replace $\hat{L}$ and $\hat{T}$, respectively. In the second pair of equations the improvements in industry outputs attributable to technological progress enter the model precisely as do industry subsidies in eqs. (3c) and (4c) of section 4. Any general change in technology or in the quality of factors (that gets translated into a change in input coefficiencies) has an impact on prices and outputs that can be decomposed into the two kinds of parametric changes analyzed in the preceding sections.

Consider the effect of progress upon relative commodity and factor prices. The relationship between the changes in the two sets of prices is the same as in the subsidy case (see eq. (12)):

$$(\hat{w} - \hat{r}) = \frac{1}{|\theta|}\{(\hat{p}_M - \hat{p}_F) + (\pi_M - \pi_F)\}. \tag{17}$$

Solving separately for each relative price change,

$$(\hat{p}_M - \hat{p}_F) = -\frac{|\theta|}{\sigma}\{(\pi_L - \pi_T) + |\lambda|\sigma_S(\pi_M - \pi_F)\}, \tag{18}$$

$$(\hat{w} - \hat{r}) = -\frac{1}{\sigma}\{(\pi_L - \pi_T) - |\lambda|\sigma_D(\pi_M - \pi_F)\}. \tag{19}$$

For convenience I refer to $(\pi_L - \pi_T)$ as the 'differential factor effect' and $(\pi_M - \pi_F)$ as the 'differential industry effect'.[17]

Define a change in technology as 'regular' if the differential factor and industry effects have the same sign.[18] For example, a change in technology that is relatively 'labor-saving' for the economy as a whole ($[\pi_L - \pi_T]$ positive) is considered 'regular' if it also reflects a relatively greater improvement in productivity in the labor-intensive industry. Suppose this to be the case. Both effects tend to depress the relative price of commodity M: the 'labor-saving feature of the change works exactly as would a relative increase in the labor endowment to reduce the relative price of the labor-intensive commodity (M). And part of the differential industry effect, like a relative subsidy to M, is shifted forward in a lower price for M.

Whereas the two components of 'regular' technological change reinforce each other in their effect on the commodity price ratio, they pull the factor price ratio in opposite directions. The differential factor effect in the above case serves to depress the wage/rent ratio. But part of the relatively greater improvement in

[17]The suggestion that a change in technology in a particular industry has both 'factor-saving' and 'cost-reducing' aspects has been made before. See, for example, Bhagwati and Johnson [4] and Meier [16]. Contrary to what is usually implied, I point out that a Hicksian 'neutral' technology change in one or more industries has, nonetheless, a 'factor-saving' or 'differential factor' effect. The problem of technological change has been analyzed in numerous articles; perhaps those by Johnson [11] and Findlay and Grubert [7] should especially be mentioned.

[18]Strictly speaking, I want to allow for the possibility that one or both effects are zero. Thus, technological change is 'regular' if and only if $(\pi_L - \pi_T)(\pi_M - \pi_F) \geqq 0$.

the labor-intensive M industry is shifted backward to increase, relatively, the return to labor. This 'backward' shift is more pronounced the greater is the elasticity of substitution on the demand side. There will be some 'critical' value of σ_D, above which relative wages will rise despite the downward pull of the differential factor effect:

$$(\hat{w} - \hat{r}) > 0 \text{ if and only if } \sigma_D > \frac{(\pi_L - \pi_T)}{|\lambda|(\pi_M - \pi_F)}.$$

If technological progress is not 'regular' these conclusions are reversed. Suppose $(\pi_L - \pi_T) > 0$, but nonetheless $(\pi_M - \pi_F) < 0$. This might be the result, say, of technological change where the primary impact is to reduce labor requirements in food production. Labor is now affected relatively adversely on both counts, the differential factor effect serving to depress wages as before, and the differential industry effect working to the relative advantage of the factor used intensively in food production – land. On the other hand, the change in relative commodity prices is now less predictable. The differential factor effect, in tending to reduce M's relative price, is working counter to the differential industry effect, whereby the F industry is experiencing more rapid technological advance. The differential industry effect will, in this case, dominate if the elasticity of substitution between goods on the supply side is high enough:

$$(\hat{p}_M - \hat{p}_F) > 0 \text{ if and only if } \sigma_S > -\frac{\pi_L - \pi_T}{|\lambda|(\pi_M - \pi_F)}.$$

The differential factor and industry effects are not independent of each other. Some insight into the nature of the relationship between the two can be obtained by considering two special cases of 'neutrality'.

Suppose, first, that technological change is 'Hicksian neutral' in each industry, implying that, at unchanged factor prices, factor proportions used in that industry do not change (see Hicks [8]). In terms of the $\hat{B}$ matrix, the rows are identical $(\hat{b}_{Lj} = \hat{b}_{Tj})$. As can easily be verified from the definition of the π's, in this case

$$(\pi_L - \pi_T) = |\lambda|(\pi_M - \pi_F),$$

and technological change must be 'regular'. If, overall, technological change is 'labor-saving' (and note that this can happen even if it is Hicksian neutral in each industry), the price of the relatively labor-intensive commodity must fall. Relative wages will, nonetheless, rise if σ_D exceeds the critical value shown earlier, which in this case reduces to unity.

The symmetrical nature of this approach to technological change suggests an alternative definition of neutrality, in which the columns of the $\hat{B}$ matrix are equal. This type of neutrality indicates that input requirements for any factor, i, have been reduced by the same relative amount in every industry. The relationship between the differential factor and industry effects is given by

$$(\pi_M - \pi_F) = |\theta|\,(\pi_L - \pi_T).$$

Again, technological change must be 'regular'. If the reduction in labor coefficients in each industry exceeds the reduction in land coefficients, this must filter through (in dampened form unless each industry uses just one factor) to affect relatively favorably the labor-intensive industry. The remarks made in the case of Hicksian neutrality carry over to this case, except for the fact that the critical value which σ_D must exceed in order for the differential industry effect to outweigh the factor effect on relative wages now becomes higher. Specifically, σ_D must exceed $1/|\lambda|\,|\theta|$, which may be considerably greater than unity. This reflects the fact that in the case of Hicksian neutrality $(\pi_L - \pi_T)$ is smaller than $(\pi_M - \pi_F)$, whereas the reverse is true in the present case.

With Hicksian neutrality the paramount feature is the difference between rates of technological advance in each industry. This spills over into a differential factor effect only because the industries require the two factors in differing proportions. With the other kind of neutrality the basic change is that the input requirements of one factor are cut more than for the other factor. As we have just seen, this is transformed into a differential industry effect only in dampened form.

These cases of neutrality are special cases of 'regular' technological progress. The general relationship between the differential factor and industry effects can be derived from the definitions to yield

$$(\pi_L - \pi_T) = Q_M\beta_M + Q_F\beta_F + |\lambda|\,(\pi_M - \pi_F) \tag{20}$$

and

$$(\pi_M - \pi_F) = Q_L\beta_L + Q_T\beta_T + |\theta|\,(\pi_L - \pi_T). \tag{21}$$

In the first equation the differential factor effect is broken down into three components; the labor-saving bias of technical change in each industry (β_j is defined as $\hat{b}_{Lj} - \hat{b}_{Tj}$) and the differential industry effect.[19] In the second expression the differential industry effect is shown as a combination of the relatively greater saving in each factor in the M industry (β_L, for example, is $\hat{b}_{LM} - \hat{b}_{LF}$) and the

[19] Note that Q_M and Q_F are the same weights as those defined in section 6. The analogy between the composition of σ and that of $(\pi_L - \pi_T)$ becomes more apparent if $|\lambda|(\pi_M - \pi_F)$ is rewritten as $Q_D\{(\pi_M - \pi_F)/|\theta|\}$. The differential factor effect is weighted average of the Hicksian factor biases in each industry and a magnified $(1/|\theta|)$ differential industry effect.

differential factor effect.[20] With these relationships at hand it is easy to see how it is the possible asymmetry between the row elements and/or the column elements of the $\hat{B}$ matrix that could disrupt the 'regularity' feature of technical progress.[21]

For some purposes it is useful to make the substitution from either (20) or (21) into the expressions for the changes in relative factor and commodity prices shown by (17–(19). For example, if technological change is 'neutral' in the sense described earlier, where the reduction in the input coefficient is the same in each industry (although different for each factor), β_L and β_T are zero in (21) and the relationship in (17) can be rewritten as

$$(\hat{w} - \hat{r}) = \frac{1}{|\theta|}(\hat{p}_M - \hat{p}_F) + (\pi_L - \pi_T).$$

To make things simple, suppose π_T is zero. The uniform reduction in labor input coefficients across industries might reflect, say, an improvement in labor quality attributable to education. Aside from the effect of any change in commodity prices on factor prices (of the Stolper–Samuelson variety), relative wages are directly increased by the improvement in labor quality.

Alternatively, consider substituting (20) into (19), to yield (19a):

$$(\hat{w} - \hat{r}) = -\frac{1}{\sigma}\left\{Q_M\beta_M + Q_F\beta_F + Q_D(1 - \sigma_D)\frac{\pi_M - \pi_F}{|\theta|}\right\}. \tag{19a}$$

Will technological change that is Hicks neutral in every industry leave the factor-price ratio unaltered at a given ratio of factor endowments? Eq. (19a) suggests a negative answer to this query unless progress is at the same rate in the two industries ($\pi_M = \pi_F$) or unless σ_D is unity.[22]

There exists an extensive literature in the theory of international trade concerned with (a) the effects of differences in production functions on pre-trade factor and commodity price ratios (and thus on positions of comparative advantage), and (b) the impact of growth (in factor supplies) or changes in techno-

[20] Q_L equals $(\lambda_{LF}\theta_{LM} + \lambda_{LM}\theta_{LF}$, and Q_T is $(\lambda_{TF}\theta_{TM} + \lambda_{TM}\theta_{TF})$. Note that $Q_L + Q_T$ equals $Q_M + Q_F$.

[21] These relationships involve the *difference* between π_L and π_T, on the one hand, and π_M and π_F on the other. Another relationship involving *sums* of these terms is suggested by the national income relationship, as discussed in section 7. With technical progress, $\theta_M\pi_M + \theta_F\pi_F$ equals $\theta_L\pi_L + \theta_T\pi_T$.

[22] Recalling n. 19, consider the following question: If the elasticity of substitution between factors is unity in every sector, will a change in the ratio of factor endowments result in an equal percentage change in the factor price ratio? From section 6 it is seen that this result can be expected only if σ_D is unity.

logical knowledge in one or more countries on the world terms of trade.[23] The analysis of this paper is well suited to the discussion of these problems. The connection between (a) and expressions (17)–(19) is obvious. For (b) it is helpful to observe that the impact of any of these changes on world terms of trade depends upon the effect in each country separately of these changes on production and consumption at constant commodity prices. The production effects can be derived from the four equations of change for the production sector (eqs. (1a)–(4a) or later versions) and the consumption changes from equation (5a).[24] The purpose of this paper is not to reproduce the results in detail but rather to expose those features of the model which bear upon all of these questions.

References

[1] Amano, A., *Neo-Classical Models of International Trade and Economic Growth* (University of Rochester, New York, 1963).

[2] Amano, A., 'Determinants of Comparative Costs: A Theoretic Approach', *Oxford Economic Papers* (November 1964).

[3] Amano, A., 'A Two-Sector Model of Economic Growth Involving Technical Progress' (unpublished).

[4] Bhagwati, J. and H. Johnson, 'Notes on Some Controversies in the Theory of International Trade', *Economic Journal* (March 1960).

[5] Dorfman, R., P.A. Samuelson and R.M. Solow, *Linear Programming and Economic Analysis* (McGraw-Hill, New York, 1958).

[6] Drandakis, E., 'Factor Substitution in the Two-Sector Growth Model', *Review of Economic Studies* (October 1963).

[7] Findlay, R. and H. Grubert, 'Factor Intensities, Technological Progress and the Terms of Trade', *Oxford Economic Papers* (February 1959).

[8] Hicks, J.R., *The Theory of Wages* (Macmillan, New York, 1932).

[9] Hicks, J.R., 'Linear Theory', *Economic Journal* (December 1960).

[10] Inada, Ken-ichi, 'On Neoclassical Models of Economic Growth', *Review of Economic Studies* (April 1965).

[11] Johnson, H., 'Economic Expansion and International Trade', *Manchester School of Economic and Social Studies* (May 1955).

[12] Johnson, H., 'Economic Development and International Trade', in: *Money, Trade, and Economic Growth* (George Allen & Unwin, London, 1962) ch. 4.

[13] Jones, R.W., 'Stability Conditions in International Trade: A General Equilibrium Analysis', *International Economic Review* (May 1961).

[23] See Johnson [12] and the extensive bibliography there listed. The most complete treatment of the effects of various differences in production conditions on positions of comparative advantage is given by Amano [2] who also discusses special cases of Harrod neutrality. For a recent analysis of the impact of endowment and technology changes on the terms of trade see Takayama [23].

[24] Account must be taken, however, of the fact that with trade the quantities of M and F produced differ from the amounts consumed by the quantity of exports and imports.

[14] Kemp, C.M., *The Pure Theory of International Trade* (Prentice-Hall, Englewood Cliffs, 1964) pp. 10–11.
[15] Meade, J.E., *A Neo-Classical Theory of Economic Growth* (Allen & Unwin, London, 1961) pp. 84–86.
[16] Meier, G.M., *International Trade and Development* (Harper & Row, New York, 1963) ch. 1.
[17] Rybczynski, T.M., 'Factor Endowments and Relative Commodity Prices', *Economica* (November 1955).
[18] Samuelson, P.A., 'Prices of Factors and Goods in General Equilibrium', *Review of Economic Studies*, 21 (1) (1953–1954).
[19] Shinkai, Y., 'On Equilibrium Growth of Capital and Labor', *International Economic Review* (May 1960).
[20] Solow, R., 'A Contribution to the Theory of Economic Growth', *Quarterly Journal of Economics* (February 1956).
[21] Stolper, W.F., and P.A. Samuelson, 'Protection and Real Wages', *Review of Economic Studies* (November 1941).
[22] Takayama, A., 'On a Two-Sector Model of Economic Growth: A Comparative Statics Analysis', *Review of Economis Studies* (June 1963).
[23] Takayama, A., 'Economic Growth and International Trade', *Review of Economic Studies* (June 1964).
[24] Uzawa, H., 'On a Two-Sector Model of Economic Growth', *Review of Economic Studies* (October 1961).
[25] Uzawa, H., 'On a Two-Sector Model of Economic Growth – II', *Review of Economic Studies* (June 1963).

Chapter 5

DUALITY IN INTERNATIONAL TRADE: A GEOMETRICAL NOTE*

Two basic relationships in the pure theory of international trade have become associated with the names of Stolper and Samuelson on the one hand and Rybczynski on the other. The former proposition deals with the effect of a change in the terms of trade on the returns to factors of production. In particular, Stolper and Samuelson [6] point out that an increase in the relative price of the labor-intensive commodity (in a two-commodity, two-factor country) results in an increase in the real wage rate. In the past dozen years much has been written about the relationships between changes in factor endowments and the composition of commodity outputs. One of the earlier contributors, Rybczynski [3], established the proposition that an increase in the labor force with constant aggregate endowment of the other productive factor (in a two-commodity, two-factor country) results in a greater than proportionate increase in the output of the labor-intensive commodity and an actual decline in the total output of the other good if the terms of trade are held constant. Although both propositions are well established, it seems that the *dual* nature of the relationship between them has never been stressed.[1] The purpose of this chapter is to illustrate this duality feature of the basic model of trade by simple geometric means.

Assume purely competitive market conditions in a country producing positive quantities of two commodities, say manufactured goods M and food F, with full employment of two factors of production, say labour L and land T. Departing

* *Canadian Journal of Economics and Political Science*, 31 (3) (August 1965) 390–393. I am indebted to the National Science Foundation for support for this research.

[1] However, more than a decade ago Paul Samuelson presented a brief discussion of 'reciprocity relations' in the general equilibrium model. Thus, if X_i and p_i refer to the quantity and price of commodity i, and V_j and w_j to the quantity (endowment) and return (rental or wage) to factor j, $(\partial X_i/\partial V_j) = (\partial w_j/\partial p_i)$. See Samuelson [5].

from traditional procedure, I examine the fixed-coefficients case first. At the conclusion of the note I show what modifications need to be made to allow for the possibility that changes in factor prices may alter factor proportions.

Fig. 5.1 illustrates the relationship between factor endowments and commodity outputs. The labour/land ratios used in producing the two commodities are shown by the slopes of the *M*- and *F*-rays. I have assumed that *M* is labour-intensive. Constant returns to scale ensure that the quantities of *M* and *F* produced can be measured along the respective rays from the origin. Thus if a_{ij} represents the quantity of factor *i* required per unit output of commodity *j*, *OA* represents one unit of *M*, and *OB* represents (*OB*/*OA*) units of *M*. If point *E* is the initial endowment position, commodity outputs are shown by drawing lines through *E* parallel to the *M*- and *F*-rays. The resource bundle shown by vector *OB* is used in *M*, and this plus the resource bundle used in *F* (*OD*) exhausts the endowments.

A number of propositions readily follow. (i) If factor endowments should expand along a ray from the origin through *E*, outputs of both goods expand in the same proportion (the balanced growth case). (ii) If one factor endowment expands relative to another, the commodity intensive in the use of that factor expands relative to the other commodity.[2] (iii) In order for the production of both commodities to increase it is *not* sufficient for both factor endowments to expand. Rather, a necessary condition is expansion within cone *C* in fig. 5.1 determined by the factor proportions in the two industries. (iv) As a special case, if the endowment of land should expand with a constant labour force (e.g. the movement from *E* to *E'* in fig. 5.1), the output of the land-intensive good rises by a greater proportion, and production of the labor-intensive commodity falls. This, of course, is the Rybczynski theorem.

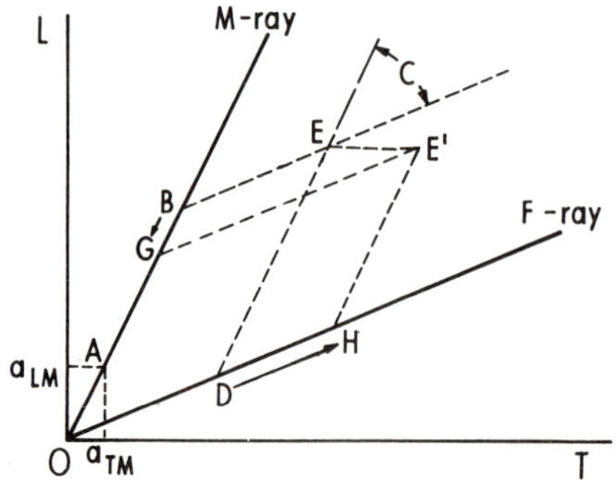

Figure 5.1

[2] For the significance of this remark in the theory of trade, see Chapter 1.

Clearly the argument of fig. 5.1 is virtually the same as that using the Edgeworth Bowley production box.[3] However, the latter device is slightly more cumbersome and, more importantly, its use disguises the fact that the structure of the relationships among physical quantities shown in fig. 5.1 carries over to the (dual) relationships among prices. The assumption that both factors are fully employed is stated algebraically in eq. (1) and geometrically in fig. 5.1. By the zero profit conditions for a competitive equilibrium the sum of wage costs plus land rentals must equal market prices, as in eq. (2):

$$\begin{pmatrix} a_{LM} \\ a_{TM} \end{pmatrix} M + \begin{pmatrix} a_{LF} \\ a_{TF} \end{pmatrix} F = \begin{pmatrix} L \\ T \end{pmatrix}, \tag{1}$$

$$\begin{pmatrix} a_{LM} \\ a_{LF} \end{pmatrix} w + \begin{pmatrix} a_{TM} \\ a_{TF} \end{pmatrix} r = \begin{pmatrix} p_M \\ p_F \end{pmatrix}. \tag{2}$$

Thus, the relationship between factor prices and commodity prices is similar to that between commodity outputs and factor endowments, and can be illustrated by the same geometrical construction, as in fig. 5.2.

The wage component in prices is given by the vector OK, where (OK/OJ) yields the wage rate. This, added to the rental component (ON), gives the costs of production. Alternatively, if P represents the market prices, factor prices are determined by the lines through P parallel to the w-ray and r-ray.

Conclusions (i)–(iv) above can be rephrased to apply to the relationships between commodity price changes and factor price changes. Typically one of the commodities is treated as numeraire. If this should be F, the effect of an increase in the price of M can be shown by an upward movement of P. Analogous to (iv) above, the return to land falls, and the wage rate rises, even relative to the price of the labor-intensive commodity. This is the Stolper–Samuelson theorem.

All that remains is to re-examine the argument in the general case of variable coefficients. In the two-commodity, two-factor model of incomplete specialization, factor prices remain invariant if commodity prices are fixed. Therefore the M- and F-rays in fig. 5.1 remain unaltered if the terms of trade are constant and the factor endowment point changes. The Rybczynski theorem applies to the special case of constant terms of trade,[4] and the argument is thus identical to that used in the fixed coefficients case.[5]

[3] The box is formed by joining E with perpendiculars to the axes. Proofs and extensions of the Rybczynski Theorem have used the box diagram. For example, see Guha [2] and Amano [1].

[4] For any given factor endowments the composition of outputs can vary all along the transformation curve, given an appropriate change in the terms of trade.

[5] Suppose, instead, that the movement from E to E' in fig. 5.1 is associated with an increase in the

At first glance the consequences of allowing input coefficients to adjust to changes in factor prices for the pricing relationships of fig. 5.2 seem more serious. A change in commodity prices from P explicitly changes factor prices – this is what the diagram shows. But this change in factor prices in general causes the slopes of the w-ray and r-ray to change. For example, an increase in p_m (with F the numeraire) would result in an increase in wages and a fall in rents at unchanged input coefficients. As a consequence, labor will be used less intensively in each industry. Thus, it is not clear which way the w-ray and the r-ray swing.[6] But the important point is that for small price changes *it does not matter*. This is a consequence of the Wong–Viner envelope theorem (see Samuelson [4]): if costs are being minimized for any given level of output (as must be the case in a competitive economy), the saving in costs from rearranging factor proportions in response to a small change in factor prices is a second-order small. That is, the relationship between small changes in commodity prices and the consequent changes in factor prices is identical in the fixed and variable coefficients cases.

To see this, differentiate eq. (2) to obtain (3):

$$\begin{pmatrix} a_{LM} \\ a_{LF} \end{pmatrix} \mathrm{d}w + \begin{pmatrix} a_{TM} \\ a_{TF} \end{pmatrix} \mathrm{d}r = \begin{pmatrix} \mathrm{d}p_M \\ \mathrm{d}p_F \end{pmatrix} - \left\{ w \begin{pmatrix} \mathrm{d}a_{LM} \\ \mathrm{d}a_{LF} \end{pmatrix} + r \begin{pmatrix} \mathrm{d}a_{TM} \\ \mathrm{d}a_{TF} \end{pmatrix} \right\} \tag{3}$$

The last bracketed expression is zero. For example, in the M-industry the equality

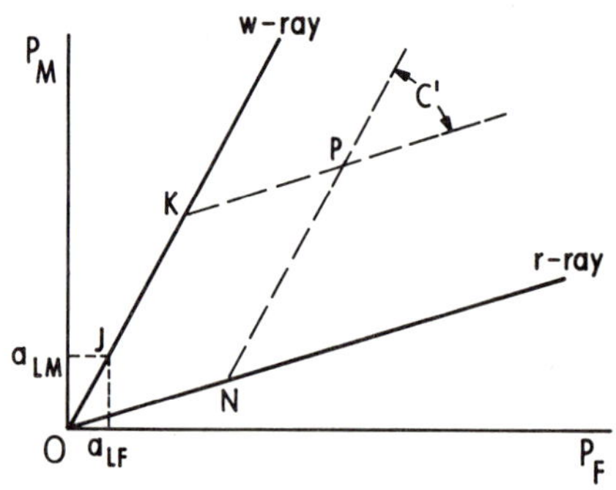

Figure 5.2

Footnote 5 continued
wage/rent ratio. This would serve to reduce labor inputs and increase land inputs per unit of output in both goods. The M-ray and F-ray both become flatter. That is, the cone formed by these rays 'swings' in the direction of the factor endowment point, and the required change in outputs is dampened by the price changes. The increase in T is absorbed, in part, by more intensive land use in each industry.

[6] This depends, *inter alia*, on the relative values of elasticities of substitution in each industry.

of the slopes of an M-isoquant and the iso-cost line yields $w\mathrm{d}a_{LM} + r\mathrm{d}a_{TM}$ equals zero.[7] This serves to re-establish the diagrammatic technique of figs. 5.1 and 5.2 even in the general case of variable coefficients as a device to illustrate the dual relationship between these basic propositions in the theory of international trade.

References

[1] Amano, A., 'Factor Endowment and Relative Prices. A Generalization of Rybczynski's Theorem', *Economica* (November 1963).

[2] Guha, A., 'Factor and Commodity Prices in an Expanding Economy', *Quarterly Journal of Economics* (February 1963).

[3] Rybczynski, T., 'Factor Endowments and Relative Commodity Prices', *Economica* (November 1955).

[4] Samuelson, P.A., *Foundations of Economic Analysis* (Cambridge, Mass., 1947) pp. 34–35.

[5] Samuelson, P.A., 'Prices of Factors and Goods in General Equilibrium', *Review of Economic Studies, XXI (1) 54 (1953–1954) 10.*

[6] Stolper, W.F. and P.A. Samuelson, 'Protection and Real Wages', *Review of Economic Studies* (November 1941).

[7] A more complete algebraic treatment of this and other duality features of the two-sector model is contained in Chapter 4.

Chapter 6

A THREE-FACTOR MODEL IN THEORY, TRADE, AND HISTORY*

1. Introduction

One of the fundamental results in the pure theory of international trade is the factor-price equalization theorem. This result has wider applicability than to the area of trade, for fundamentally it is a statement of the relationship between any economy's commodity prices and the returns to its productive factors, whether or not that economy is engaged in trade. It is not surprising that the prices of commodities into which factors enter as productive agents influence the returns earned by those factors in a competitive market. What *is* surprising is that (under appropriate conditions) the quantities of the factors available for employment in the economy – the factor endowments – have no independent role to play in influencing factor prices. This dependence of factor prices *only* upon commodity prices is the essence of the theorem.

Of course even under the stringent assumptions of the two-commodity, two-factor case, it is not really correct to say that factor endowments have no effect on factor prices independently of commodity prices, for factor prices are uniquely determined by commodity prices only for some *range* of the factor endowments. Should the endowment bundle lie outside this range, the economy would be driven to specialize completely in one of the commodities; with fewer commodities being produced than factors employed, the basis for the theorem disappears.

The two-factor, one-commodity case provides the simplest example of general equilibrium in which factor endowments bear directly upon factor returns.[1] To

*Reprinted from: *Trade, Balance of Payments, and Growth* (North-Holland Publishing Company, Amsterdam, 1971) ch. 1, pp. 3–21.

[1] The main field in which such a model is used is obviously not that of international trade but of neoclassical growth. In the one-sector growth model, changing capital/labor ratios over time affect the real wage and the rate of profit.

reach a wider variety of possible applications, however, it is necessary to introduce more than one commodity. In this chapter I analyze a restricted version of the three-factor, two-commodity case. The restriction is that although three factors of production are employed, only *two* enter into the production of any one commodity. This still allows the straitjacket of the factor-price equalization theorem to be removed, while preserving most of the simple methods of analysis characteristic of the two-by-two model. Furthermore, it is precisely this form of the three-by-two model that has served as the basis for two interesting recent contributions to the literature in the fields of economic history (Temin [13]) and the theory of capital and international trade (Kenen [7]).

The basic structure of this three-by-two model is developed in the next section, using the framework I employed in Chapter 4 in analyzing the two-commodity two-factor model. Following that, in section 3 I discuss the concept of a *factor-price frontier* for this extended model, as a basis for interpreting Peter Temin's remarks concerning American and British technology in the mid-nineteenth century. In section 4 I turn to a question embedded in Peter Kenen's new concept of the role of capital in production and trade, namely, what is the influence of the rate of interest on relative commodity prices (and therefore on the patterns of comparative advantage). Finally, in section 5, I briefly discuss possible extensions of the model.

2. Basic structure of the model

Let X_1 and X_2 denote the two commodities produced. Sector i makes use of a factor specific to that sector, V_i, and a factor shared with the other sector, the mobile factor, V_N. If a_{ij} represents the quantity of factor i required per unit output of X_j, the basic competitive equilibrium relations can be set out as in eqs. (1)–(5). These fall into two groups. The first set, eqs. (1)–(3) states that the endowment of each factor is fully employed in one or more productive sectors. The second set, eqs. (4) and (5), is a statement of the competitive profit relationships. Here R_i is the 'rental' return for the use of one unit of factor i, and p_j is the price of commodity j.

$$a_{11}X_1 = V_1, \tag{1}$$

$$a_{22}X_2 = V_2, \tag{2}$$

$$a_{N1}X_1 + a_{N2}X_2 = V_N, \tag{3}$$

$$a_{11}R_1 + a_{N1}R_N = p_1, \tag{4}$$

$$a_{22}R_2 + a_{N2}R_N = p_2. \tag{5}$$

I assume throughout that both commodities are produced in positive amounts so that costs per unit of output are reflected exactly in market prices.

In the examples I discuss later in the chapter the V_i represent physically different factors of production. However, the model is also capable of reinterpretation as a two-factor, two-commodity model where one of the factors is completely immobile occupationally. For example, V_1 and V_2 may represent capital goods installed in each sector and incapable of being transferred. The crucial consideration is not physical identity but economic identity. With immobilities, the returns to specific factors V_1 and V_2 need not be equalized in the market.

Eqs. (1)–(5) could be taken to represent *all* the equilibrium relationships for a competitive economy with fixed factor endowments facing fixed commodity prices only if techniques of production are invariant.[2] Otherwise more information is required to determine which set of a_{ij}, out of all the ones available (shown by the unit isoquants), is chosen in the competitive equilibrium. With competition ensuring that unit costs are minimized, each a_{ij} depends upon the ratio of factor prices in industry j, as shown in eq. (6):

$$a_{ij} = a_{ij}\left(\frac{R_N}{R_j}\right). \tag{6}$$

The basis for the factor-price equalization theorem is to be found in the competitive profit relations. Consider eqs. (4) and (5). If this were a model for two commodities and two perfectly mobile factors, R_1 and R_2 would be driven to equality. With the a_{ij} depending upon factor prices, two relationships to determine two factor prices are given once commodity prices are known.[3] However, if V_1 and V_2 are different factors, or specific factors, the profit conditions are insufficient to determine factor returns solely from a knowledge of commodity prices. Use must be made also of the full-employment conditions, with the information they contain as to factor endowments. Solve eqs. (1) and (2) for each X_j and substitute into eq. (3) to obtain eq. (,3′):

$$\frac{a_{N1}}{a_{11}} V_1 + \frac{a_{N2}}{a_{22}} V_2 = V_N. \tag{3'}$$

Since the a_{ij} depend on factor prices, eqs. (4), (5) and (3′) provide a set of three

[2] With fixed coefficients, however, the resource constraints, eqs. (1)–(3), are overdetermined unless inequalities are introduced. I do not pursue this matter as in general I assume sufficient variability in the a_{ij} to allow all resources to be fully absorbed in productive use.

[3] Of course a factor intensity condition is required as well. It is sufficient in the 2 × 2 model to have factor proportions *different* in the two sectors. The classic source for a discussion of the intensity conditions, and especially for a general treatment of the case of uneven numbers of goods and factors, is the 1953 paper by Samuelson [10].

relationships in the three factor prices and, as parameters, the two commodity prices and *all* the factor endowments.

The structure of this 3×2 model is best revealed by considering the way in which the equilibrium is disturbed by arbitrary small changes in commodity prices and factor endowments. First I shall examine the equations of change that are derived from eqs. (4), (5) and (3′) to focus on the impact of parametric changes upon the returns to factors of production. Following that I shall make use of relationships (1) and (2) to discuss the effect of changes on the composition of outputs.

The basic equations of change, revealed by differentiating eqs. (4), (5) and (3′), are given in eqs. (7)–(9):

$$\theta_{11}\hat{R}_1 + \theta_{N1}\hat{R}_N = \hat{p}_1, \tag{7}$$

$$\theta_{22}\hat{R}_2 + \theta_{N2}\hat{R}_N = \hat{p}_2, \tag{8}$$

$$\lambda_{N1}\sigma_1\hat{R}_1 + \lambda_{N2}\sigma_2\hat{R}_2 - \{\lambda_{N1}\sigma_1 + \lambda_{N2}\sigma_2\}\hat{R}_N = \{\hat{V}_N - \lambda_{N1}\hat{V}_1 - \lambda_{N2}\hat{V}_2\}. \tag{9}$$

A '$\hat{\ }$' over a variable denotes the relative change in that variable (e.g. $\hat{R}_1$ is $\mathrm{d}R_1/R_1$). The θ_{ij} refers to the distributive share of factor i in industry j, while λ_{Nj} is the fraction of the mobile factor, V_N, absorbed by the jth industry. In deriving eqs. (7)–(9) use has been made of two simple relationships involving the relative changes in the input-output coefficients $\hat{a}_{ij}$. Consider the first industry. With a_{i1} chosen so as to minimize unit cost, the distributive-share weighted average of the changes in the a_{i1} coefficients, $\{\theta_{11}\hat{a}_{11} + \theta_{N1}\hat{a}_{N1}\}$, must be zero.[4] This directly yields, in eq. (7), the statement that the change in the market price of X_1 must be a positively weighted average of (and therefore trapped between) the changes in individual factor prices. In addition, the *definition* of the elasticity of substitution between factors in the first industry, σ_1, relates the change in the a_{N1}/a_{11} ratio to the change in the factor price ratio. This, and the comparable definition of σ_2, suffice to yield eq. (9).

Formal solutions for the effects on factor returns of changes in commodity. prices and factor endowments are provided in eqs. (10)–(12):

$$\hat{R}_1 = \frac{1}{\Delta}\left\{\left[\lambda_{N1}\frac{\sigma_1}{\theta_{11}} + \frac{1}{\theta_{11}}\lambda_{N2}\frac{\sigma_2}{\theta_{22}}\right]\hat{p}_1 - \frac{\theta_{N1}}{\theta_{11}}\lambda_{N2}\frac{\sigma_2}{\theta_{22}}\hat{p}_2 + \frac{\theta_{N1}}{\theta_{11}}\left[\hat{V}_N - \lambda_{N1}\hat{V}_1 - \lambda_{N2}\hat{V}_2\right]\right\}, \tag{10}$$

[4] Geometrically this states that the slope of the isoquant equals the slope of the factor-cost line. For a more detailed treatment of these relationships, see Chapter 4.

$$\hat{R}_N = \frac{1}{\Delta}\left\{\lambda_{N1}\frac{\sigma_1}{\theta_{11}}\hat{p}_1 + \lambda_{N2}\frac{\sigma_2}{\theta_{22}}\hat{p}_2 + \left[\lambda_{N1}\hat{V}_1 + \lambda_{N2}\hat{V}_2 - \hat{V}_N\right]\right\}, \tag{11}$$

$$\hat{R}_1 - \hat{R}_2 = \frac{1}{\Delta}\left\{\left[\frac{1}{\theta_{22}}\lambda_{N1}\frac{\sigma_1}{\theta_{11}} + \frac{1}{\theta_{11}}\lambda_{N2}\frac{\sigma_2}{\theta_{22}}\right](\hat{p}_1 - \hat{p}_2) + \frac{1}{\theta_{11}\theta_{22}}(\theta_{N1} - \theta_{N2})\left[\hat{V}_N - \lambda_{N1}\hat{V}_1 - \lambda_{N2}\hat{V}_2\right]\right\}, \tag{12}$$

where

$$\Delta = \lambda_{N1}\frac{\sigma_1}{\theta_{11}} + \lambda_{N2}\frac{\sigma_2}{\theta_{22}}.$$

The solution for $\hat{R}_2$ is not explicitly shown, as it can be obtained by permuting subscripts in the solution for changes in the other specific factor R_1. Note that the expression σ_i/θ_{ii} occurs frequently. This is the elasticity of the marginal product curve of the mobile factor in industry i.[5] Thus, Δ is a weighted average of these elasticities.

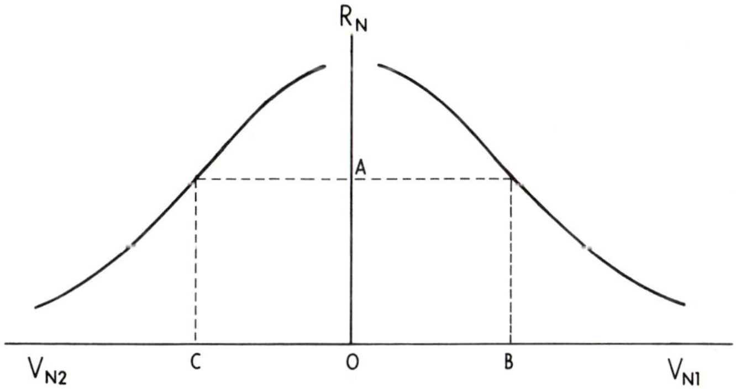

Figure 6.1

[5]Consider the first industry. The marginal physical product of the mobile factor is given by R_N/p_1. This declines as a_{N1}/a_{11}, the ratio of mobile to fixed factor use, rises. The elasticity of the marginal product curve (defined so as to be positive) is $(\hat{a}_{11} - \hat{a}_{N1})/(\hat{R}_N - \hat{p}_1)$. But by eq. (7) $(\hat{R}_N - \hat{p}_1)$ equals $\theta_{11}(\hat{R}_N - \hat{R}_1)$. Given the definition of σ_1, the result follows.

With the model characterized by each sector having a specific factor not used by the other sector, it is not surprising that it is the elasticities of the marginal product curves for the mobile factors that assume importance. A simple graphical device, fig. 6.1, could be employed to derive some of the results in this model. The marginal product curves for the mobile factor are put back to back. With

With more factors employed than commodities produced, factor endowments exercise an influence over factor returns independent of commodity prices. The relationships are simple. With commodity prices held constant an increase in the endowment of the mobile factor lowers the return to that mobile factor and raises the return to both specific factors. By contrast, an increased endowment of either specific factor raises the return to the mobile factor and lowers both R_1 and R_2. Changes in endowments always alter the returns to the mobile factor in a direction *opposite* to the returns to *both* specific factors. This is true because with commodity prices constant, any increase in the return to a factor of production must lower the return to the other factor used in that industry. Thus, in eqs. (7) and (8) an increase in R_N with p_i constant must lower both R_1 and R_2. Although R_1 and R_2 move in the same direction as endowments change, eq. (12) explicitly shows that R_1 will undergo a greater *relative* change than R_2 if the share of the mobile factor used in the first industry (θ_{N1}) exceeds its share in the second industry (θ_{N2}).

Turn now to the influence of commodity price changes on factor prices. Clearly an equiproportionate rise in both commodity prices (a 'pure' inflation) changes all factor prices by the same proportionate amount. Of more interest is the case in which the system is disturbed by a change in *relative* commodity prices. Suppose the price of commodity 1 rises relatively to that of commodity 2. Then the following relationships hold:

$$\hat{R}_1 > \hat{p}_1 > \hat{R}_N > \hat{p}_2 > \hat{R}_2.$$

The change in each commodity price must be trapped between the changes in the returns to factors used to produce that commodity. Furthermore, the changes in the returns to specific factors are more pronounced than in the return to the mobile factor. Indeed, as the solution in eq. (11) shows, $\hat{R}_N$ is a positively weighted average of the changes in each commodity price, a feature of the model that I shall require in section 4.

Factor-price/commodity-price relationships in the standard two-commodity, two-factor model are characterized by what I have called the *magnification effect*. With two mobile factors (and no specific factors), a relative rise in the price of commodity 1 would cause the return to one factor (the factor used more intensively in producing commodity 1) to rise by more (relatively) than either

Footnote 5 continued
given commodity prices and factor endowments the diagram directly gives the solution for $R_N(OA)$ as dependent upon the total quantity of the mobile factor available to the two sectors (*OB* plus *OC* equals V_N). A change in V_i or p_i shifts the appropriate marginal product schedule. An increase in V_N moves both *OB* and *OC* outwards and lowers R_N.

commodity price, and the return to the other factor to rise by less than either commodity price (or perhaps to fall). This is the basis for the Stolper–Samuelson theorem [12], whereby the *real* return to the factor used intensively in a tariff-protected industry is unambiguously raised, regardless of consumption patterns. This magnification effect is preserved in the present model for the specific factors but *not* for the mobile factor. Thus, if labor is the single mobile factor, wages calculated in terms of one of the commodities might rise with protection but not in terms of the other commodity.

Note that whereas the fortunes of the specific factors wax or wane together with changes in factor endowments, they move in opposite directions (relative to any other prices) in the face of alterations in relative commodity prices.

Turning to the composition of outputs note from eqs. (1) and (2) that $\hat{X}_i$ equals $\hat{V}_i - \hat{a}_{ii}$. It would be an easy matter to solve for the change in each output, but consider, instead, the change in the *ratio* of outputs produced. This is given directly by eq. (13):

$$\hat{X}_1 - \hat{X}_2 = (\hat{V}_1 - \hat{V}_2) + (\hat{a}_{22} - \hat{a}_{11}). \tag{13}$$

If coefficients of production are highly inflexible, output changes are limited to a large extent by changing available quantities of the specific factors. But the intensity with which the specific factors are used depends upon elasticities of substitution and upon changes in all the factor prices, which, by eqs. (10 and (11), are linked to commodity price and endowment changes. Substitution yields eq. (14) for the change in the ratio of outputs produced:[6]

$$(\hat{X}_1 - \hat{X}_2) = (\hat{V}_1 - \hat{V}_2) + \frac{1}{\Delta}\left[\theta_{N1}\frac{\sigma_1}{\theta_{11}} - \theta_{N2}\frac{\sigma_2}{\theta_{22}}\right](\hat{V}_N - \lambda_{N1}\hat{V}_1 - \lambda_{N2}\hat{V}_2)$$

$$+\frac{\lambda_{N1}\theta_{N2} + \lambda_{N2}\theta_{N1}}{\Delta}\frac{\sigma_1}{\theta_{11}}\frac{\sigma_2}{\theta_{22}}(\hat{p}_1 - \hat{p}_2). \tag{14}$$

For given endowments the coefficient of $(\hat{p}_1 - \hat{p}_2)$ shows the elasticity of substitution along the transformation schedule. Of course this must be positive, and the transformation schedule exhibits the usual bowed-out shape. In the 2×2 case (both factors mobile), this result is also obtained *unless* the two industries use factors in the same proportion, in which case the production-possibilities curve is linear. Should this same proviso be applied to the present model? The first question that comes up in this connection is how to compare factor proportions when

[6] To solve for $\hat{a}_{ii}$ use two relationships: (1) the θ-weighted average of the changes in input coefficients in the ith industry is zero, and (2) the definition of σ_i. This yields $\hat{a}_{ii} = -\theta_{Ni}\sigma_i(\hat{R}_i - \hat{R}_N)$.

the two industries each use a factor not employed by the other industry. The answer is found by observing that both industries use the same mobile factor, and the distributive shares of that mobile factor in the two industries can be compared. Consider X_1 to be N-intensive if and only if θ_{N1} exceeds θ_{N2}.[7] As eq. (14) shows, even if factor intensities in the two industries are, in this sense, equal, the coefficient of $(\hat{p}_1 - \hat{p}_2)$ still remains finite and, indeed, can be quite small for low values of the elasticities of substitution. When both factors are mobile, the element leading to increasing opportunity costs is the fact that resources initially released by one industry are required in different proportions by the other industry. With some factors specific to an industry, however, expansion of output in that industry must entail adding more of the mobile factor to a fixed quantity of the specific factor (and less of the mobile factor in the other industry), which, by the law of diminishing returns, drives up relative costs in the expanding industry.

A question of great interest to trade theory and to the neoclassical theory of growth involves the way in which changes in factor endowments *shift* the transformation curve. The *magnification effect* discussed earlier in connection with price changes is also a feature of the dual relationship between endowment and output changes at constant commodity prices in the traditional 2×2 case.[8] For example, an increase in the endowment of only one productive factor would, at constant prices, raise the output of the commodity using that factor intensively by relatively a greater amount than the factor has increased, and reduce the output of the other commodity. To see how much of this relationship survives in the present 3×2 model, it is necessary to make a distinction between increases in the endowment of the mobile factor V_N and increases in the supply of either specific factor.

Consider the latter effect first. An increase in V_1 would result in greater production of X_1. Unlike the 2×2 case, however, factor prices are adjusting to this change even when commodity prices are being held constant. In particular, the return to the mobile factor rises relative to the return to either specific factor, and this serves to lower the ratio of mobile to specific factor used in the first industry. That is, $\hat{V}_{N1}$, although positive, would be less than $\hat{V}_1$, and therefore $\hat{X}_1$ must fall short of $\hat{V}_1$, thus invalidating this aspect of the magnification effect. However, it is still the case that the output of the other commodity falls, as V_2 is assumed un-

[7] Thus, referring to eq. (12), an increase in the endowment of the mobile factor at constant commodity prices raises, relatively, the return to the specific factor used in the industry making intensive use of the mobile factor. In Chapter 4, I showed that factor proportions in the 2×2 case are uniquely related to the size of θ_{ij} compared with θ_{ik} where $k \neq j$.

[8] This relationship is usually referred to as the Rybczynski theorem. See Rybczynski [9], Jones [4] and Chapters 4 and 5.

changed and some of the mobile factor has been drawn into the expanding industry.

A less extreme change in the composition of outputs results from an increase only in the endowment of the mobile factor (at constant commodity prices). The relative cost of using the mobile factor is cut in both industries and, since V_1 and V_2 are unchanged, more intensive use of factor N must increase outputs of both X_1 and X_2. As eq. (14) shows, this output expansion may not be uniform in the two industries. Two influences operate to alter the relative composition of output. (1) Differences between the two industries in the intensity with which the mobile factor is used. This effect is similar to the *only* explanation for changes in the composition of outputs in the 2 × 2 case. Other things equal, X_1 expands relatively to X_2 when V_N rises if the distributive share of the mobile factor in the first industry, θ_{N1}, exceeds θ_{N2}. By 'other things equal' is meant (2) the elasticities of substitution in the two sectors. Even if factor intensities (as defined in terms of the θ's) are equal as between industries, high values for σ_1 relative to σ_2 allow X_1 to expand relatively to X_2. That is, to preserve the same value for R_N in the two sectors, most of the increase in N must go into the sector where large increases are required to lower the marginal product of N.

3. The factor-price frontier

This model can be used to shed light on some queries suggested by Peter Temin's [13] recent discussion of technology in Britain and America in the mid-nineteenth century.[9] The key question I wish to explore is whether one economy can be operating with the same production functions as another and still have higher real wages *and* higher interest rates. An examination of the factor-price frontier for the standard 2 × 2 model suggests a negative answer to this question. But what can be said if technology makes use of three factors of production with the restriction that each sector only uses two factors? This is precisely the model used by Temin; the general properties were discussed in the preceding section. My purpose in this section is to construct factor-price frontiers appropriate to Temin's model.

For this historical interpretation, let labor be the mobile factor, capital be represented by V_1, and land by V_2. Interpret X_1 as the output of manufacturing goods

[9] I am indebted to Robert Fogel for bringing my attention to this literature. I have had many useful conversations with Fogel and with Stanley Engerman on the material covered in this section. For comments on Temin's article see Drummond [2] and Fogel [3].

(including machines) and X_2 as the output of the agricultural sector. The special assumptions made are that no land is used in manufacturing activity and no capital is used in agriculture. The interest rate can be associated with the ratio between the returns to capital, R_1, and the price of new machines p_1. How the 'real wage' is defined makes a considerable difference to the results. To begin with, I make the extreme assumption that only agricultural goods enter into workers' consumption, so that wages, R_N, need be deflated only by the price of agricultural goods, p_2.

A factor-price frontier is a locus of all combinations of factor prices allowed by an economy's given technology.[10] It is not an unambiguous concept. For example, if both factor prices are deflated by the price of the same commodity, the factor-price frontier is dependent only upon the production function for that sector. Thus, in eq. (7), a relationship between R_1/p_1 and R_N/p_1 is implicitly given – a downward sloping curve whose elasticity is the ratio of distributive shares. If 'real' wages were interpreted as R_N deflated by the price of manufactured goods, an economy employing only labor and capital to produce manufactured goods can raise real wages only at a sacrifice of lower rates of interest (rates of profit), regardless of how many factors are used in the rest of the economy. The mid-nineteenth century American economy must have had a superior technology *in manufacturing* if real wages, in this sense of the word, and the rate of interest were higher than in the United Kingdom. This is one extreme, and it is more interesting (and perhaps relevant) to look at the other – letting real wages be defined as R_N/p_2.[11]

In a standard 2×2 model with capital and labor mobile, a downward sloping locus relates the wage rate deflated by the price of the consumption good to the rental on capital deflated by the price of the capital good.[12] Each point on the frontier corresponds to a particular commodity price ratio. An increase in the relative price of the labor-intensive commodity would raise the real wage and lower the rate of interest. However, such a locus in the 3×2 model of this paper, is *upward sloping*. Suppose the relative price of manufactures rises, and consider the

[10] For an early discussion of the concept of a factor-price frontier see Samuelson [11].

[11] To the extent that workers also consumed manufactured goods, the appropriate deflator would be an index of both p_1 and p_2, with weights determined by the share of the two goods in the total budget. The appropriate factor-price frontier would lie somewhere between the polar extremes considered in the text.

[12] Although the frontier must be negatively sloped, it *may* be bowed-out (concave to the origin). The condition for this to occur is similar to the conditions under which convergence to balanced growth is jeopardized in two-sector growth models, namely the capital good (manufactures) is capital intensive and elasticities of substitution are 'sufficiently' low. For a discussion of this and related matters see the paper by Michael Bruno [1]. In the text, nothing hinges on the concavity of the frontier, only the slope.

chain of inequalities for commodity and factor prices exhibited in the preceding section. The interest rate has risen ($\hat{R}_1 > \hat{p}_1$) as has the real wage ($\hat{R}_N > \hat{p}_2$). Two countries could have the same technology, but if transport costs or other impediments allowed a higher relative price for manufacturing goods in one of them (say America), both the rate of interest and real wages would have to be higher in that country.[13]

But this is not the end of the story for, unlike the standard 2 × 2 case, differences in factor endowments exert an independent influence on factor prices. At constant commodity prices, another factor price frontier is traced out if endowments change, and this frontier is negatively sloped. Suppose the supply of one of the specific factors, land, should rise.[14] At constant commodity prices this must raise the real wage and lower the rate of interest – the returns to mobile and specific factors are affected in opposite direction. In fig. 6.2 I have shown this second kind of factor-price frontier by the downward sloping dotted curve. If the relative price of food was low in America, and if America was land (and capital) abundant (relative to the labor endowment) compared with Britain, both the real wage and rate of interest in America (say at A) could have been

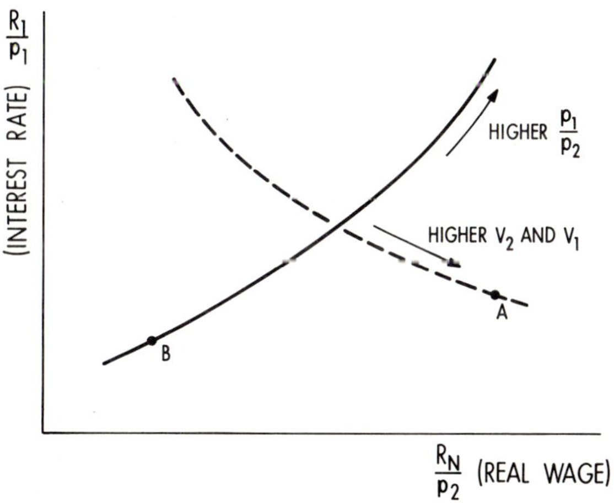

Figure 6.2

[13] Of course *all* factor returns cannot be higher in one country than in another if technologies are identical. In the present example land rents would unambiguously be lower in America.

[14] From eq. (9) it is clear that a more complicated endowment change can just as easily be considered. A pure increase in the endowment of land would have the same kind of impact on factor prices as an increase in the weighted average of land and capital that exceeded any increase in the labor force.

higher than in Britain (say at B). These stylized facts are consistent, in this model, with both countries having available the same basic technology.

4. Influence of the rate of interest

In Kenen's treatment of 'Nature, Capital, and Trade' [7] the mobile factor is capital. At first glance Kenen's model seems rather complicated: five different productive activities are considered. However, all this activity can be decomposed into three groupings: (1) a standard 2×2 model of the Heckscher–Ohlin variety; (2) a standard two-factor, one-commodity process whereby the capital good is created, and (3) a three-factor, two-commodity model of the type with which this paper is concerned.

Consider, first, the 3×2 section of his model, where he introduces his novel theory of capital. Two factors of production exist in nature, land, and labor (V_1 and V_2). But these factors are inert until and unless they are made productive by an act of investment. In real terms this can be thought of as, say, the addition of fertilizer to the land or education to the labor. In terms of the abstract model, Kenen posits two production functions ('factor service supply' functions), each of which combines a homogeneous kind of capital (let N equal K) with the specific inert factor (and none of the other factor). In Kenen's treatment, this interaction yields a stream of factor services for a finite number of periods, after which the 'improved' factor reverts to its 'inert' state unless further investment is undertaken. It is convenient for the present discussion to limit this amount of time (before sudden death depreciation) to one period. Thus, at any point of time the economy has the factor endowment bundle (V_1, V_2, V_K) and has, as outputs, the bundle (X_1, X_2), the quantities of 'educated' labor and 'fertilized' land.[15]

Of course the 'output' bundle (X_1, X_2) is really the input bundle for other productive activities. On the one hand, educated labor and improved land are each required to produce both of two commodities (say Y_1 and Y_2) that represent final consumer goods that enter into international trade. Capital is not directly required in these processes, although indirectly it is embodied in X_1 and X_2. On the other hand, the two improved factors are used to produce the capital good.

Kenen is especially concerned with the application of his model to the theory

[15] Kenen makes stringent assumptions about the form of the factor-service supply function: each is a Cobb–Douglas function ($\sigma_i = 1$) with equal shares of capital ($\theta_{K1} = \theta_{K2}$, a constant). See [7, p. 451, n. 46] as corrected in the 'erratum', p. 658. I am considering the general case.

of international trade. Suppose that two countries have identical technologies and engage in free trade in the two goods Y_1 and Y_2. This serves to equalize the returns to the two factors X_1 and X_2 via the usual Heckscher – Ohlin theory. But equal p_1 and p_2 (the returns to the improved factors) do *not* imply the same returns to capital or the inert factors in both countries. As eqs. (10) and (11) illustrate, differences in factor endowments have an independent bite on R_1, R_2 and R_K. Other things equal, the country with relatively large quantities of capital will have lower values for R_K and lower interest rates. The latter follows since the cost of producing the capital good is equated as between countries despite the fact that capital does not enter into trade.

Perhaps the most subtle relationship embedded in Kenen's model connects the rate of interest to the relative price of commodities that enter into trade, and it is this aspect of his model I wish to discuss in this section. To erase the effects of differences in factor endowments *per se* suppose there exist two countries with identical endowments. Nevertheless, suppose that, before trade, one of the countries has a lower rate of interest than the other. With the opening up of trade, which commodity is exported by the low interest rate country? That is, in Kenen's model, what bias in comparative advantage is imparted by differences in the rate of interest? Equivalently one could reverse the procedure and ask about the effect of a change in the commodity terms of trade upon the rate of interest.

By introducing a make-believe production function, it is possible to get at this relationship and explain the link between relative commodity prices and interest rates using the standard Heckscher – Ohlin factor proportions account of relative prices valid for the 2×2 case. The improved factors X_1 and X_2 produce the traded goods Y_1 and Y_2 in a competitive setting. Therefore the relative price of Y_1 and Y_2 is determined in standard fashion by the relative factor-price ratio p_1/p_2 or vice versa. It is as if the traded goods were really the improved factors. The hard question concerns the link between the factor-price ratio p_1/p_2 and the rate of interest.

The price of the capital good p_K is determined in a competitive model by the cost of production and thus by the technology used and the factor prices p_1 and p_2. Considering small changes, relationship (15) connects $\hat{p}_i$ with $\hat{p}_K$, in the same fashion as eqs. (7) and (8) linked the $\hat{R}_i$ with the $\hat{p}_i$:

$$\theta_{1K}\hat{p}_1 + \theta_{2K}\hat{p}_2 = \hat{p}_K. \tag{15}$$

Now the rate of interest in this kind of model is the ratio of the returns for the use of capital R_K, and the price of the capital good p_K. If there existed a production process whose output was the 'services' of capital, and using X_1 and X_2 as inputs, a relationship such as (15) for $\hat{R}_K$ could be obtained. Clearly no such physical process exists, but the pricing relationship connecting $\hat{R}_K$ with $\hat{p}_1$ and $\hat{p}_2$ that would be relevant for such a make-believe process *does* exist!

Consider the solution for $\hat{R}_K$ (replace N by K) in eq. (11). If endowments are held constant, relationship (16) emerges:

$$\theta_{1s}\hat{p}_1 + \theta_{2s}\hat{p}_2 = \hat{R}_K. \tag{16}$$

where

$$\theta_{is} \equiv \frac{\lambda_{Ki}\,(\sigma_i/\theta_{ii})}{\Delta}$$

and

$$\Delta = \lambda_{K1}\frac{\sigma_1}{\theta_{11}} + \lambda_{K2}\frac{\sigma_2}{\theta_{22}}.$$

The symbols θ_{1s} and θ_{2s} have been used to suggest the distributive shares that would be appropriate in such a make-believe production process. The point is that any increase in the returns to the improved factors filters down and affects, favorably, the return for the service of capital. Of course, by eq. (15) such a change would also raise the cost of capital. The change in the interest rate is $(\hat{R}_K - \hat{p}_K)$, and the link between this change and the change in p_1/p_2 (and therefore also the relative prices of the traded commodities). is given simply by comparing θ_{1s} and θ_{1K} (or θ_{1s}/θ_{2s} with θ_{1K}/θ_{2K}). An increase in the rate of interest raises the relative price of the commodity using educated labor relatively intensively (compared with improved land) if and only if educated labor is relatively more important in contributing to the rental on capital goods than it is in contributing to the costs of producing capital goods.[16]

The feature of the 3 × 2 model that permits the financial counterpart of the make-believe production function for the services of capital is clearly (by eq.

[16] As remarked in footnote 15, Kenen considers only the special case in which σ_1 is unity and θ_{K1} equals θ_{K2}. The appropriate comparison in the general case is θ_{1K}/θ_{2K} with θ_{1s}/θ_{2s}. With Kenen's special assumptions, the former exceeds the latter if and only if p_1X_{1K}/p_2X_{2K} exceeds K_1/K_2. But if θ_{K1} equals θ_{K2}, K_1/K_2 must equal p_1X_1/p_2X_2. Therefore in Kenen's case the direction of change in commodity prices given by a change in the interest rate is linked to the comparison between the ratio of the two educated factors in producing $K(X_{1K}/X_{2K})$ and in the economy's endowment bundle (X_1/X_2). As is easily seen, this physical relationship as between factor proportions does not generalize. See Kenen [7, p. 449], and especially eq. (21).

Kenen's special assumptions as to the form of the factor-service supply functions also affect the way in which his transformation curve between X_1 and X_2 (his 'gross factor-service frontier', [7, p. 445] shifts with the accumulation of capital. With $\sigma_1 = \sigma_2$ and θ_{K1} equal to θ_{K2} (and therefore θ_{11} also equal to θ_{22}), the coefficient of $\hat{V}_N$ in my eq. (14) is zero. An increase in K shifts the $X_1 - X_2$ transformation schedule uniformly outwards from the origin, as Kenen demonstrates.

(11)) that the return to capital is derived from the market returns of the improved factors – and that changes in R_K must be a *positively* weighted average of changes in the p_i.[17] It is as if X_1 and X_2 were actually used to produce the services of capital in a competitive market, so that the zero-profit relationship appropriate to such a process would be given by eq. (16).

5. Possible extensions of the model

The preceding two sections have served to illustrate two uses that have been made of the model analyzed in Section 2. In this concluding section I suggest briefly how this model might be extended, still falling short of a completely general model in which all three factors can continuously be substituted for each other in producing each of the two commodities.

One suggestion involves allowing all three factors to be used in each industry but a pair of these to be fixed in proportion to each other – always the same pair, but not necessarily in the same proportion as between sectors.[18] Let a_{21} always equal αa_{11} and a_{12} equal βa_{22}. The a_{Ni} can be varied continuously with the bundle of (a_{1i}, a_{2i}). If $\alpha\beta$ is less than unity, the first commodity is distinguished from the second by a more intensive use of factor 1 relative to factor 2 (but not necessarily relative to factor N). The model of section 2 is the special case in which $\alpha = \beta = 0$. Consider the other extreme: if $\alpha\beta = 1$, the model reduces to the familiar two-factor, two-commodity model, where the two factors are N and a particular bundle of factors 1 and 2 (always in the ratio $1/\alpha$ or, equivalently, β). From the production side of the model alone, it is not possible to determine R_1 and R_2 separately, only the return to the composite factor.

For intermediate cases, where $\alpha\beta < 1$, consider the two *different* composite factors: $(a_{11}, \alpha a_{11})$ and $(\beta a_{22}, a_{22})$, with returns R_1^* and R_2^*. In terms of these composite factors the special form of the 3 × 2 model in section 2 is applicable.[19]

[17] In either this 3 × 2 models, or in the standard 2 × 2 model, every factor-price change is a weighted average of the changes in all commodity prices. However, except for the mobile factor in the 3 × 2 model, one of the weights in each case is *negative* (this is the magnification effect). Therefore such a pricing relationship could not be interpreted as having come from a productive process in which the two commodities are inputs and the service of the particular factor is the output.

[18] I am indebted to Murray Kemp for this suggestion.

[19] For the concept of elasticity of substitution consider factor N in relation to the composite bundle. For example, define σ_1 as the relative change in (a_{11}/a_{N1}) divided by the relative change in (R_N/R_1^*). Eq. (3′) changes to

$$\frac{a_{N1}}{a_{11}}\frac{(V_1 - \beta V_2)}{(1 - \alpha\beta)} + \frac{a_{N2}}{a_{22}}\frac{(V_2 - \alpha V_1)}{(1 - \alpha\beta)} = V_N.$$

R_1^* is merely $R_1 + \alpha R_2$, the cost of the bundle (a_{11}, a_{21}).

For example, a change in commodity prices at unchanged endowments has a determinate effect on R_i^* and R_N (as given by a reinterpretation of eqs. (10) and (11)). These changes in the R_i^*, in turn, determine the changes in the R_i via a set of relationships equivalent to the zero-profit factor-price, commodity price equations of change in the standard 2 × 2 model:

$$\theta'_{11}\hat{R}_1 + \theta'_{21}\hat{R}_2 = \hat{R}_1^*,$$

$$\theta'_{12}\hat{R}_1 + \theta'_{22}\hat{R}_2 = \hat{R}_2^*,$$

where

$$\theta'_{ij} \equiv \frac{\theta_{ij}}{\theta_{1j} + \theta_{2j}}.$$

Thus, by introducing the notion of composite factors it is possible to decompose a more general 3 × 2 case to the special form of the 3 × 2 model discussed in this paper and the standard 2 × 2 pricing relationships.

An alternative extension focuses on the relationship between V_1 and V_2 instead of introducing all three factors into the production process for any one commodity. Throughout the chapter I have assumed that endowments of the specific factors are given as parameters. Suppose, instead, they are outputs of a productive process whereby V_2 can be 'converted' into V_1 at increasing opportunity costs. Let the factor endowment ratio V_2/V_1 respond positively to relative returns, R_2/R_1.[20] The basic set of relations (7)–(9) is altered only in having $\lambda_{N1}\hat{V}_1 + \lambda_{N2}\hat{V}_2$ now depend upon the extent of the change in factor returns R_2/R_1 and the elasticity of substitution σ_V along the transformation locus connecting V_2 and V_1.[21]

The model in this chapter is the special case $\sigma_V = 0$. As the transformation curve between V_1 and V_2 becomes more elastic, the result of section 2, whereby the change in the return to the mobile factor is trapped between the changes in the

[20] In [8], Howard Petith analyzes a two-sector vintage model. Each sector employs a different kind of machine, and these machines, in turn, are jointly produced subject to increasing opportunity costs.

[21] If R_1/R_2 rises, V_1/V_2 also increases. The sign of $(\lambda_{N1}\hat{V}_1 + \lambda_{N2}\hat{V}_2)$ turns out to depend on a comparison of the distributive shares of the mobile factor V_N in the production of commodities X_1 and X_2. The implication of this is given by eq. (12). If the first commodity is N-intensive (in the sence that θ_{N1} exceeds θ_{N2}), compare the impact on the ratio R_1/R_2 of an increase in the endowment of the mobile factor (with constant commodity prices) under the alternative assumptions (1) that V_1 and V_2 remain constant, and (2) that V_1 and V_2 respond to changes in R_1/R_2. In both cases R_1/R_2 rises since X_1 is N-intensive. But in case (2) $\lambda_{N1}\hat{V}_1 + \lambda_{N2}\hat{V}_2$ is positive, thus damping the increase in R_1 and R_2, and in their spread. The possibility of having V_i respond to prices reduces the required extent of the change in prices. For a brief discussion in another context of the importance of terms such as $\lambda_{N1}\hat{V}_1 + \lambda_{N2}\hat{V}_2$ see Jones [6, p. 330].

commodity prices, is altered to conform more closely with the 'magnification' effect of the standard 2×2 model. That is, for sufficiently large σ_V, an increase in the relative price of the N-intensive commodity increases R_N by a proportionately greater amount.

These extensions serve to illustrate how more general cases can be decomposed into the kinds of results familiar from the 2×2 model and the results characteristic of the special form of the 3×2 model examined in this chapter.

References

[1] Bruno, M., 'Fundamental Duality Relations in the Pure Theory of Capital and Growth', *Review of Economic Studies* (January 1969).

[2] Drummond, I.M., 'Labor Scarcity and the Problem of American Industrial Efficiency in the 1850s: A Comment', *The Journal of Economic History* (September 1967).

[3] Fogel, R.W., 'The Specification Problem in Economic History', *The Journal of Economic History* (September 1967).

[4] Jones, R.W., 'Duality in International Trade: A Geometrical Note', *Canadian Journal of Economics and Political Science* (August 1965); also Chapter 5, this volume.

[5] Jones, R.W., 'The Structure of Simple General Equilibrium Models', *The Journal of Political Economy* (December 1965); also Chapter 4, this volume.

[6] Jones, R.W., 'Comments on Technical Progress', *The Philippine Economic Journal*, Second Semester (1966).

[7] Kenen, P.B., 'Nature, Capital, and Trade', *The Journal of Political Economy* (October 1965).

[8] Petith, H., 'Vintage Capital, Joint Production and the Theory of International Trade', *International Economic Review*, 13 (February 1972) 148–159.

[9] Rybczynski, T.M., 'Factor Endowments and Relative Commodity Prices', *Economica* (November 1955).

[10] Samuelson, P.A., 'Prices of Factors and Goods in General Equilibrium', *Review of Economic Studies*, 21 (1953–1954).

[11] Samuelson, P.A., 'Parable and Realism in Capital Theory: The Surrogate Production Function', *Review of Economic Studies*, 29 (1962).

[12] Stolper, W.F. and P.A. Samuelson, 'Protection and Real Wages', *Review of Economic Studies*, 9 (November 1941).

[13] Temin, P., 'Labor Scarcity and the Problem of American Industrial Efficiency in the 1850's', *The Journal of Economic History* (September 1966).

Chapter 7

OUTPUTS AND PRICES IN SIMPLE TRADE MODELS

1.

Two basic production models have been examined in the preceding three chapters. In Chapters 4 and 5 two completely mobile productive factors were combined in different proportions to produce two tradeable goods – the simple Heckscher–Ohlin model. In Chapter 6 each of two sectors employed a factor specific to that sector as well as a factor common to both sectors and sufficiently mobile to earn the same return in each. With technology typified by constant returns to scale, in each model the transformation schedule was bowed-out so that an increase in a relative commodity price causes that industry's output to expand.[1]

This chapter analyzes more closely the flexibility of output response to price changes in these two models. In the preceding chapters an expression was developed for each model for the elasticity of substitution between commodities along the transformation curve, σ_s. This literally was defined as the relative change in the ratio of outputs produced (x_1/x_2) divided by the (small) change in the ratio of output prices (p_1/p_2). In the two-factor Heckscher–Ohlin model the expression for σ_s, as developed in Chapter 4, is reproduced as eq. (1):

$$\sigma_s = \frac{Q_1\sigma_1 + Q_2\sigma_2}{|\lambda||\theta|}, \tag{1}$$

where

$$Q_1 \equiv \theta_{L1}\lambda_{K1} + \theta_{K1}\lambda_{L1} > 0; \qquad Q_2 \equiv \theta_{L2}\lambda_{K2} + \theta_{K2}\lambda_{L2} > 0.$$

As before, σ_i denotes the elasticity of substitution between labor and capital in the ith sector. λ_{ij} is the fraction of the economy's supply of factor i used in the jth

[1] I am ignoring the limiting case of fixed coefficients.

industry-while θ_{ij} refers to factor is distributive share in the jth sector. The determinants $|\lambda|$ and $|\theta|$ refer, respectively, to the expressions $(\lambda_{L1} - \lambda_{K1})$ and $(\theta_{L1} - \theta_{L2})$, and will each be positive if, as I now assume, industry 1 is relatively labor intensive. In the specific-factor model of Chapter 6, σ_s is the coefficient of $(\hat{p}_1 - \hat{p}_2)$ in eq. (14), rewritten now as eq. (2):

$$\sigma_s = \left\{ \frac{\lambda_{N1}\theta_{N2} + \lambda_{N2}\theta_{N1}}{\theta_{22}} \right\} \frac{\sigma_1/\theta_{11}}{\{\lambda_{N1}(\sigma_1/\theta_{11}) + \lambda_{N2}(\sigma_2/\theta_{22})\}} \sigma_2. \tag{2}$$

The λ_{Nj} refer to the fraction of the mobile factor used in each sector. θ_{11} and θ_{22} refer, respectively, to the distributive share received by the specific factor in industries 1 and 2.

Section 3 of this chapter introduces some inessential simplifying assumptions to facilitate a comparison between (1) and (2). But first I turn, in section 2, to a 'global' version of the concept of elasticity of substitution along a transformation curve for the Heckscher – Ohlin model. As expression (1) reveals, two basic features of the technology determine the size of σ_s; the elasticities of factor substitution in each industry, σ_i, and the extent to which factor proportions differ between industries, as captured by the size of $|\lambda|$ or $|\theta|$ or, more particularly, their product, $|\lambda||\theta|$. This must be a positive fraction and is smaller the closer the two industries are in the ratio of capital to labor employed. Several recent articles have discussed the role of elasticities and factor proportions in affecting the shape of the transformation schedule.[2] Section 2 of this chapter discusses this issue with different geometric tools familiar from earlier literature on Heckscher – Ohlin theory

2.

Fig. 7.1 illustrates two bowed-out transformation schedules. Curve (II) is, in some obvious way, more bowed-out than is curve (I). In particular, production along curve (II) is associated with an unambiguously wider range of commodity price ratios than is production along curve (I); curve (II) is steeper as it hits the horizontal axis than is (I), and flatter as it hits the vertical axis. If such a comparison between two transformation schedules can be made, I shall refer to transformation curve (I) as having, in a 'global' sense, a higher elasticity of sub-

[2] See Melvin [3], Scarth and Warne [4], and Krauss, Johnson and Skouras [2].

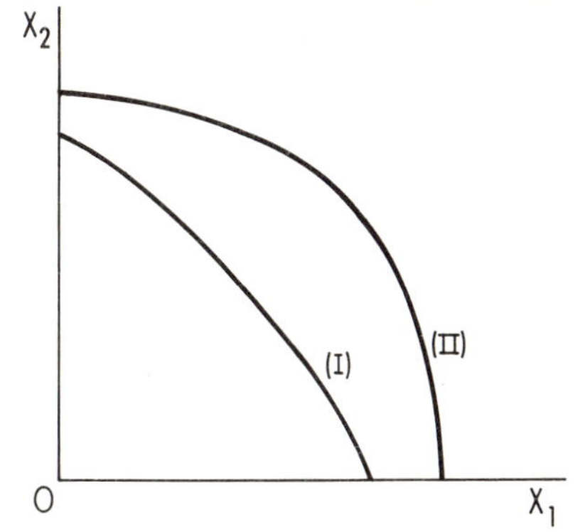

Figure 7.1

stitution between commodities.[3] I shall argue that in this global sence the elasticity of substitution along a transformation curve is reduced either by a reduction in σ_i in the two industries or by an increased disparity in factor proportions.

The argument is carried out by means of a diagram made popular by Harry Johnson.[4] The assumption that commodity 2 is capital intensive is captured in the upper part of fig. 7.2, showing capital/labor ratios in each industry rising as the wage/rental ratio rises. The lower half of fig. 7.2 confirms this factor intensity ranking by illustrating that an increase in the p_1/p_2 price ratio (measured downwards from the origin) drives up (by a magnified relative amount) the wage/rent ratio as long as both commodities are produced. The economy's transformation curve is not shown in fig. 7.2, but once the factor endowment proportions are specified, say at ρ, so also is the range of possible factor price ratios (*AB*), which serves to delimit the range of commodity price ratios (*A'B'*) that can be observed along the transformation curve. Now pick some 'interior' factor-price ratio, say *OC*, and the corresponding commodity price ratio, *OC'*. Two exercises are suggested. First, change the technology such that the elasticity of factor substitution is lowered in each sector, with the proviso that at wage/rent ratio *OC* factor proportions are unaltered at *EC* and *DC* for the two commodities and so also the commodity price ratio (*CF*). The second exercise keeps the σ_i's unchanged and instead alters the technology by increasing the optimal capital/labor ratio for capital-intensive commodity 2 and reducing it for commodity 1, at any factor-

[3] Note that a locally calculated σ_s for curve (I), as per eq. (1), might not exceed that calculated for curve (II) at every possible point of comparison. One might require such a comparison along any ray from the origin, but this is stronger than I wish to adopt.

[4] See Johnson [1]; also see Chapter 1.

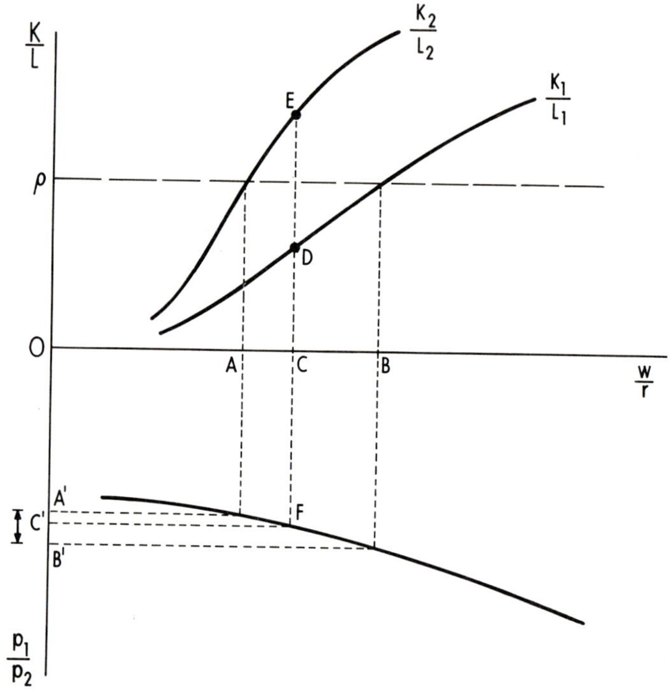

Figure 7.2

price ratio, in such a way that at initial wage/rent ratio *OC* the terms of trade remain at *CF*.[5] In each case the object of the exercise is to see what impact the suggested change in technology has on the possible commodity price range, *A'B'*.

The elasticity of factor substitution for commodity 2 at point *E* in fig. 7.2 is by definition given by the elasticity of the curve at *E*.[6] If this curve is rotated clockwise around *E*, the value of σ_2 would be reduced. In similar fashion rotate clockwise around *D* the factor proportions curve for the first industry. Fig. 7.3 illustrates how such a reduction in σ_1 and σ_2 serves to increase the range of commodity prices for which production of both commodities can be positive. That is,

[5] This involves sliding unit value isoquants further apart along a downward sloping tangent line whose slope is the factor-price ratio.

[6] As drawn, σ_2 is greater than unity at *E* since a tangent line at *E* cuts the vertical axis below the origin.

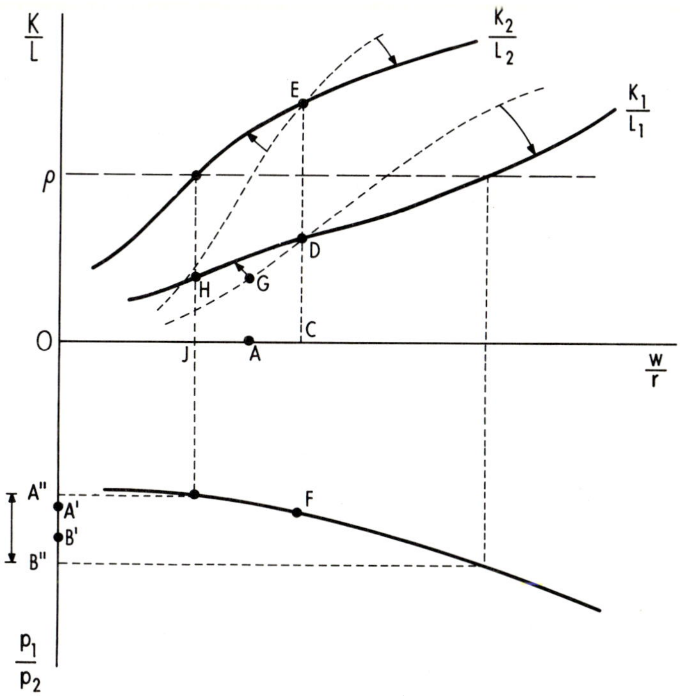

Figure 7.3

the 'global' elasticity of substitution between commodities along the transformation curve would be reduced.[7]

Fig. 7.4 illustrates the alternative type of change in technology. At any given factor-price ratio let capital-intensive x_2 become more capital intensive and

[7]Note that the factor-price, commodity-price locus in the bottom half of fig. 7.3 may change its shape. But at point F it would maintain its slope. The elasticity of the curve is given by $|\theta|$ since $(\hat{p}_1 - \hat{p}_2) = |\theta|(\hat{w} - \hat{r})$. At initial factor-price ratio, OC, factor intensities are presumed not to change, leaving the value of $|\theta|$ undisturbed. Thus, if the curve in the bottom half of fig. 7.3 shifts as the σ_i are reduced, this invokes a second-order small in the neighborhood of F. Also, compare relative commodity costs in the neighborhood of near-specialization in commodity 2. Before the shift in technology, the factor-price ratio was in the neighborhood of OA, with factor proportions in x_2 near the endowment ratio, ρ, and in x_1 near AG. After the σ_i's have been lowered, the minimal w/r drops to OJ, but factor proportions in x_2 remain near ρ and for x_1, HJ is approximately the same as GA. Thus, the paramount influence on costs is the reduction in the wage/rent ratio (rather than changes in factor proportions), and this implies a reduction in the relative cost of producing labor-intensive commodity 1. Therefore any shift in the schedule in the lower half of fig. 7.3 would still preserve a lower value for OA'' than for OA'. A similar argument could be applied to the comparison of OB' and OB''.

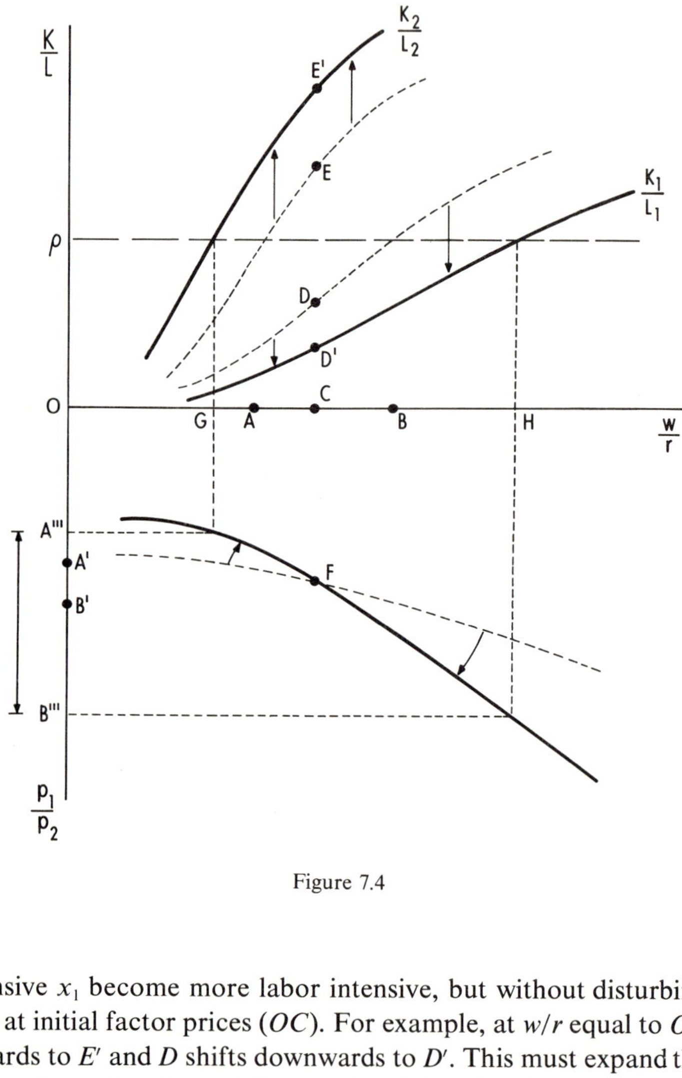

Figure 7.4

labor-intensive x_1 become more labor intensive, but without disturbing the cost ratio (*CF*) at initial factor prices (*OC*). For example, at w/r equal to *OC*, point *E* shifts upwards to *E′* and *D* shifts downwards to *D′*. This must expand the range of commodity-price ratios from *A′B′* to *A‴B‴*. Note that there are two reasons for this. The shifts in the factor proportions curves have expanded the range of possible factor prices, from *AB* to *GH*. But the curve linking factor and commodity prices in the bottom half of fig. 7.4 rotates clockwise around initial point *F*. As factor proportions become more widely separated, the value of $|\theta|$ is increased and any change in factor prices leads to a greater change in commodity prices than before the alteration in technology. This double-edged role played by having the increased spread in factor proportions cause the 'global' elasticity of substitution between commodities along the transformation curve to shrink is picked up in the 'local' formula (1) for σ_s by the fact that both $|\lambda|$ and $|\theta|$ in the denominator increase.

3.

The expressions for σ_s, both in the Heckscher–Ohlin model (1), and the specific factor model (2), can be greatly simplified by making appropriate assumptions. Note that both in (1) and (2) it is the general size of the σ_i that effect the value of σ_s rather than any discrepancy between sectoral σ_i's. That is to say, large σ_i's cause σ_s to be large, and little damage to the logic of the argument is introduced by assuming that $\sigma_1 = \sigma_2$.[8] Note how this alters σ_s in eq. (1). The numerator becomes $(Q_1 + Q_2)\sigma_i$. But, as Chapter 4 discusses, $Q_1 + Q_2$ is the fraction $\{1 - |\lambda||\theta|\}$. Therefore σ_s simplifies to the expression given by (3):

$$\sigma_s = \frac{1 - |\lambda||\theta|}{|\lambda||\theta|}\sigma_i. \tag{3}$$

The simplification leading to (3) allows the role of factor intensities and elasticities of factor substitution in influencing the flexibility of output response to commodity prices to stand out clearly. Increases in each sector's σ_i increase σ_s proportionally. And $|\lambda||\theta|$, always lying between zero and unity, becomes an unambiguous index of the difference between factor proportions used in the two industries. At one extreme each sector uses just one factor (labor for good 1, say, and capital for good 2). $|\lambda||\theta|$ becomes unity, and σ_s reduces to zero. By contrast, as factor proportions become more alike, $|\lambda||\theta|$ approaches zero and the transformation curve approaches a downward sloping straight line.

In the specific-factors case, leading to expression (2) for σ_s, the curvature of the transformation curve stems not from factor intensity differences but from the fact that diminishing returns describe the effect on output in one sector as it attracts labor from the other but cannot also attract more of the specific factor. Of course, the higher are the σ_i's, the less pronounced is the tendency for returns to diminish. In simplifying (2) I assume not only that $\sigma_1 = \sigma_2$, as before, but that factor proportions are identical between sectors. By this I mean that the share of

[8] Compare with the criterion for the transfer problem, discussed in Chapter 9. There the difference between each country's marginal propensity to consume each commodity is crucial. Assuming away such differences would not represent an inessential simplification.

the mobile factor (θ_{Ni}) is the same for the two sectors. In the Heckscher–Ohlin model differences in factor intensities are crucial, and all factors possess the same degree of mobility (i.e. are perfectly mobile). By contrast, the specific-factors model stresses the difference in degree of mobility between one type of factor and another, and to focus on the importance of mobility it seems appropriate completely to abstract from any intersectoral differences in factor intensities.

With this assumption the specific factor shares, θ_{11} and θ_{22}, are also equal. Call their common value θ_s, the share of the specific factors in the national income. The first bracketed term in (2) then becomes $(1 - \theta_s)/\theta_s$. With $\sigma_1 = \sigma_2$ as well, the middle of the three terms in (2) goes to unity. That is, σ_s in (2) simplifies to the expression given in (4):

$$\sigma_s = \frac{1 - \theta_s}{\theta_s}\sigma_i. \tag{4}$$

These simplifications show that the form for σ_s in the two models is quite similar. In each case a common role is played by σ_i.

Technology that is more flexible in allowing factors to substitute for each other contributes to more elastic responses of outputs to price changes, regardless of other specifications of the economy having to do with factor mobility and factor intensities. But each model separately shows how these other specifications influence the price-output responses in the economy. Eq. (4) shows that the greater the lack of mobility for factors (i.e. the higher the share of specific factors in the national income), the lower will output flexibility be. The role played by factor intensities in the Heckscher–Ohlin model, captured by the $|\lambda||\theta|$ term, is taken over in exactly analogous fashion in the specific factors model by the θ_s term.

References

[1] Johnson, H.G., 'Factor Endowments, International Trade and Factor Prices', *The Manchester School of Economic and Social Studies*, 25 (September 1957) 270–283; reprinted in: H.G. Johnson, *International Trade and Economic Growth* (Harvard University Press, 1958).

[2] Krauss, M., H.G. Johnson and T. Skouras, 'On the Shape and Location of the Production Possibility Curve', *Economica* (N.S.), 40 (1973) 305–310.

[3] Melvin, J., 'On the Derivation of the Production Possibility Curve', *Economica* (N.S.), 38 (1971) 287–294.

[4] Scarth, W. and R.D. Warne, 'The Elasticity of Substitution and the Shape of the Transformation Curve', *Economica* (N.S.), 40 (1973) 299–304.

Chapter 8

THE STRUCTURE OF THE GENERAL PRODUCTION MODEL IN TRADE THEORY*

Earlier chapters in Part II have analyzed the structure of the two-factor, two-commodity model within a general activity analysis framework, and have extended these concepts to the 'specific-factors' version of a three-factor, two-commodity model. Although relationships among factor and commodity prices and endowment changes and the composition of outputs might be expected to be (and indeed are) vastly more complicated in general cases with lots of commodities and productive factors, the analytical framework developed for the simpler models can be adapted to the more general case in order to develop basic structural properties.

Two key assumptions of the simple models are retained in the more general case. The first of these posits that the number of productive primary factors[1] is at least as great as the number of commodities. Note that if, by contrast, the number of commodities exceeds the number of factors, the transformation surface is *ruled.*[2] That is, flats of varying dimensions on the surface prevent its being strictly concave. The most simple example is provided by the Ricardian two-commodity, one-factor (labor) case in which the transformation schedule is a downward sloping straight line. Such an example illustrates a general point: if commodity prices are arbitrarily chosen, the number of commodities actually produced will not typically exceed the number of factors. Alternatively phrased:

*Based on 'The Relevance of the Two-Sector Production Model in Trade Theory', *Journal of Political Economy* (October 1977), authored jointly with José Scheinkman.

[1] Throughout I ignore the existence of intermediate products.

[2] A simple discussion of this problem is found in Melvin [11]. A more general treatment of the case in which the number of commodities exceeds the number of factors is provided by Chang [2]. An early classic source of the importance of the number of commodities versus the number of factors is Samuelson [14].

a country that faces a set of prices for traded commodities determined by the outside world (and bearing no relationship to the country's own technology) will usually be forced to specialize in production so that at most the same number of traded commodities is produced as factors of production exist.[3]

As the Ricardian example amply illustrates, it is quite possible for a country to produce a larger number of commodities than the number of primary factors, as long as commodity prices adjust to equal marginal rates of transformation. More formally put, the competitive profit conditions state that in equilibrium the unit value of any activity undertaken at positive levels must equal the unit cost of the activity. Unit costs depend upon factor prices. If commodities (or, strictly speaking, activities) exceed factors in number, the competitive profit equations outnumber the primary factors. For any set of factor prices it is possible to determine unit costs and therefore commodity prices that would allow all commodities to be produced, but it would in general not be possible to reverse this procedure and start with arbitrary commodity prices and solve for the set of factor prices. In addition, if commodity prices are so chosen as to allow more commodities to be produced than the number of factors, the composition of outputs would not be unique at that set of prices. To avoid these problems I assume that the number of commodities in the model, n, is less than or equal to the number of productive factors, r.

The second key assumption is that each productive activity yields an output of only one commodity. That is, these models assume no joint production. To catch the flavor of this assumption more explicitly, I assume that each activity (producing a single output) combines as inputs at least two productive factors. This basic asymmetry in technology is commonly assumed, though not always made explicit. It is the key ingredient in explaining the *magnification effects* discussed in Chapter 4 for the 2×2 model, with the Stolper–Samuelson theorem on the one hand, and the Rybczynski theorem on the other, as special cases.

Let technology be summarized by an $r \times n$ non-negative matrix of input–output coefficients, A. As already assumed, the number of productive factors, r, is greater than or equal to the number of commodities, n. For a given technology, I assume each element of A, a_{ij}, is a unique, smoothly differentiable, zero homogeneous function of all factor prices:

$$a_{ij} = a_{ij}(w_1, \ldots, w_r). \tag{1}$$

Its differential is given in (2):

$$\mathrm{d}a_{ij} = \sum_{k=1}^{r} a_{ij}^{k} \mathrm{d}w_k, \tag{2}$$

[3] The many-commodity, two-factor case was discussed in Chapter 2.

where a_{ij}^k is defined as $\partial a_{ij}/\partial w_k$. Furthermore, (i) each a_{ij}^i must be negative since it is an 'own' substitution term, and (ii) $\Sigma_k w_k a_{ij}^k$ equals zero, a reflection of the zero homogeneity of a_{ij}.

The simple 2×2 and 3×2 versions of the production model were developed by analyzing in turn the full employment conditions and the competitive profit conditions. Let x represent the vector of outputs and V the vector of factor endowments. If, as I assume, the technology possesses sufficient flexibility to allow full employment of all factors to be maintained, then

$$Ax = V. \tag{3}$$

Now consider a small change in the endowment vector. Commodity outputs and techniques adjust to maintain full employment. For the ith factor this entails

$$\sum_j x_j \mathrm{d}a_{ij} + \sum_j a_{ij}\mathrm{d}x_j = \mathrm{d}V_i. \tag{4}$$

The changes in the a_{ij} depend on factor prices as in (2), so that

$$\sum_k s_{ik}\mathrm{d}w_k + \sum_j a_{ij}\mathrm{d}x_j = \mathrm{d}V_i, \tag{5}$$

where s_{ik} is defined as $\Sigma_j x_j a_{ij}^k$. That is, s_{ik} shows how the economy's demand for factor i would respond *at unchanged outputs* to a change in the return to factor k. Techniques would change along the appropriate isoquant in each industry and s_{ik} sweeps together these changes over all industries. Of course each s_{ii} is negative and $\Sigma_k w_k s_{ik}$ equals zero.

In matrix notation the differentiated full employment conditions can be written as

$$S\mathrm{d}w + A\mathrm{d}x = \mathrm{d}V. \tag{6}$$

S is the $r \times r$ matrix of s_{ik} coefficients, $\mathrm{d}w$ is the r-element column vector of factor price changes, $\mathrm{d}x$ is the n-element column vector of output changes, and $\mathrm{d}V$ the r-element column vector of changes in factor endowments.

Assume that all industries operate at positive levels so that the dual competitive profit conditions are shown by

$$A'w = p. \tag{7}$$

With technology sufficiently flexible to yield full employment, assume all factor prices and commodity prices are strictly positive. As in the simple models, cost minimization in each industry ensures that

$$\sum_i w_i \mathrm{d}a_{ij} = 0,$$

so that in matrix notation the equations of change are

$$A'\mathrm{d}w = \mathrm{d}p. \tag{8}$$

Eqs. (6) and (8) contain the structure of the general model. It proves convenient to write them together as

$$\begin{bmatrix} S & A \\ A' & 0 \end{bmatrix} \begin{bmatrix} \mathrm{d}w \\ \mathrm{d}x \end{bmatrix} = \begin{bmatrix} \mathrm{d}V \\ \mathrm{d}p \end{bmatrix}. \tag{9}$$

The properties of this partitioned matrix and its inverse reveal what can be said in the general model about the trade theorems discussed in the earlier chapters in Part II, For easy reference, let

$$B \equiv \begin{bmatrix} S & A \\ A' & 0 \end{bmatrix}. \tag{10}$$

Consider, first, the properties of the S-matrix. In each industry I assume the cost function has a regular minimum so that for the corresponding substitution matrix in the jth industry, S^j, $u'S^ju$ is strictly negative for every nonzero vector u not proportional to w. This latter restriction on u is required since homogeneity implies that $\Sigma_k\, w_k a_{ij}^k$ is zero. Thus,

$$u'Su < 0, \quad \text{for } u \text{ not proportional to } w, \qquad u \neq 0. \tag{11}$$

Since w is strictly positive, S has a negative diagonal and rank equal to $r - 1$. S is symmetric and negative semidefinite.

Turn now to the B matrix. I assume that the rank of A is n, so that all commodities are produced by linearly independent techniques. Note that should any nonzero u take $A'u$ into the zero vector, u could not be proportional to w since, by (7), $A'w$ equals the commodity price vector, which is assumed strictly positive. Thus, for any such u, $u'Su$ must be strictly negative. In other words, B is a bordered symmetric matrix representing a quadratic form which is *negative definite* under constraints. With $r > n$, and with the rank of A equal to n, B has full rank $n + r$. Write its inverse as in (12):

$$B^{-1} \equiv \begin{bmatrix} S & A \\ A' & 0 \end{bmatrix}^{-1} \equiv \begin{bmatrix} K & G \\ G' & L \end{bmatrix}. \tag{12}$$

Solving explicitly for $\mathrm{d}w$ and $\mathrm{d}x$:

$$\begin{bmatrix} \mathrm{d}w \\ \mathrm{d}x \end{bmatrix} = \begin{bmatrix} K & G \\ G' & L \end{bmatrix} \begin{bmatrix} \mathrm{d}V \\ \mathrm{d}p \end{bmatrix}. \tag{13}$$

The inverse of B has some known properties.[4] The K matrix answers the following question: What is the impact of a change of factor endowments on factor prices if commodity prices are held constant? In the case in which the number of commodities (n) equals the number of factors (r), the factor-price equalization result applies and the K matrix is the zero matrix. More generally, K is symmetric, negative semidefinite, with rank $r - n$. If $r > n$, an increase in a factor endowment at constant commodity prices can never raise that factor's return.[5] Although generally speaking endowment changes alter factor prices when commodity prices are constant and $r > n$, some combinations of endowment changes can be accommodated by output changes with no factor-price alterations. For example, if endowments expand precisely in the proportions required by the jth sector, full employment can be maintained just by letting x_j expand at initial techniques (and factor prices). Indeed, endowment changes that are linear combinations of the columns of A do not require factor-price changes. More formally, at constant commodity prices dw equals KdV by (13). But BB^{-1} is the identity matrix, so that the product of the second row of B, $(A', 0)$, and the first column of B^{-1}, (K, G'), is zero. That is, $KA = 0$.

The $n \times n$ submatrix L relates output changes along a given transformation surface to commodity price changes. To see what is required of L, write $BB^{-1} = I$ as in (14):

$$\begin{bmatrix} S & A \\ A' & 0 \end{bmatrix} \begin{bmatrix} K & G \\ G' & L \end{bmatrix} = \begin{bmatrix} I & 0 \\ 0 & I \end{bmatrix}. \tag{14}$$

Multiplying the first row of B by the second column of B^{-1},

$$SG + AL = 0.$$

Therefore, $AL = -SG$, or $G'AL = -G'SG$. But by (14), $A'G = I$ or, what is the same thing, $G'A = I$. Therefore,

$$L = G'SG.$$

Pre- and postmultiply by a vector x to obtain

$$x'Lx = -(Gx)'S(Gx).$$

[4] See Caratheodory [1, pp. 195–196] and Samuelson [13, pp. 378–379].

[5] Cf. Jones and Scheinkman [8], for conditions sufficient to guarantee that K has a strictly negative diagonal.

Since S is a negative, symmetric, semidefinite matrix, L must be a *positive, symmetric, semidefinite* matrix.[6]

The off-diagonal blocks of B^{-1}, G and G', are transposes of each other since B^{-1} is symmetric. This reveals what Samuelson has called the *reciprocity* relationship.[7] With reference to eq. (13) this states:

$$\frac{\partial x_j}{\partial V_i}=\frac{\partial w_i}{\partial p_j}. \tag{15}$$

In words, the left-hand term shows the impact on the output of commodity j of a unit increase in the endowment of factor i when all other factor endowments and *commodity* prices are being held constant. The reciprocity relationship says nothing about the sign or size of this derivative. Instead, it states that, whatever its value, it will be the same as the impact a unit increase in the price of commodity j would have on the return to factor i when all other commodity prices and factor endowments are held constant.[8]

The two partial derivatives in (15) are linked to the Stolper–Samuelson and Rybczynski theorems. However, these theorems deal directly with *relative* changes, so that the reciprocity relationship can be rewritten as

$$\left\{\frac{V_i}{x_j}\frac{\partial x_j}{\partial V_i}\right\}=\frac{\alpha^i}{\alpha_j}\left\{\frac{p_j}{w_i}\frac{\partial w_i}{\partial p_j}\right\}, \tag{16}$$

where α^i denotes the share of the national income, Y, received by factor i, and α_j reveals the fraction of Y represented by the value of sector j's output. Fig. 8.1 illustrates relationship (16) for some industry, j, and two alternative factors, i_1 and i_2. It is assumed that the share of factor i_2 in the national income exceeds that of commodity j, while α^1 is smaller than α_j.

The reciprocity relationship, either in the form of (15) or (16), is quite general. It applies to cases with joint production and intermediate products.[9] For commodity j and factor i_1, it states that the pair of Stolper–Samuelson and Rybczynski terms lies somewhere along line i_1 in fig. 8.1. The *distribution* of these terms depends on further details of the technology. In particular, I seek the appropriate generalization of the Stolper–Samuelson and Rybczynski theorems for the case in which joint production is ruled out.

[6] Unless there is only one output, L can be shown to have a *positive* diagonal since the rank of S is $r - 1$. Cf. Jones and Scheinkman [8].

[7] See Samuelson [14, p. 10].

[8] Of course if $n = r$ this latter proviso is unnecessary as K becomes the zero matrix.

[9] For a proof in the more general case see Jones and Scheinkman [8], or, for even more detail, see Diewert and Woodland [4].

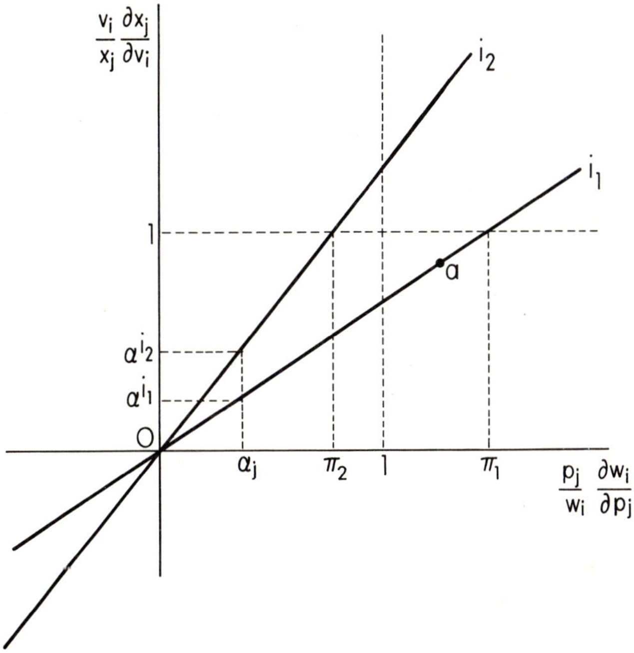

Figure 8.1

Since the Stolper–Samuelson and Rybczynski theorems deal with *relative* changes, it proves convenient to rewrite the basic equation set (9) as in (17):

$$\begin{bmatrix} \sigma & \lambda \\ \theta' & 0 \end{bmatrix} \begin{bmatrix} \hat{w} \\ \hat{x} \end{bmatrix} = \begin{bmatrix} \hat{V} \\ \hat{p} \end{bmatrix}. \tag{17}$$

As in previous uses, a '^' over a variable denotes the relative change in that variable. σ_{ij} is the element $w_j s_{ij}/V_i$, a substitution elasticity that shows the percentage change in the economy's demand for factor i (at unchanged outputs) associated with a 1% increase in the return to factor j. The matrix, σ, has a negative diagonal and zero row sums. The λ and θ matrices maintain their earlier interpretation: λ_{ij} is the fraction of the economy's supply of factor i employed in the j_{th} industry while θ_{ij} is factor i's distributive share in producing x_j. Since λ and θ' are each row stochastic, so is the entire matrix in (17). It is nonsingular (since B is nonsingular), and can be solved for relative wage and output changes:

$$\begin{bmatrix} \hat{w} \\ \hat{x} \end{bmatrix} = \begin{bmatrix} M & N \\ Q & R \end{bmatrix} \begin{bmatrix} \hat{V} \\ \hat{p} \end{bmatrix}. \tag{18}$$

The M and R matrices put factor-price/factor-endowment and commodity-output/commodity-price relationships, already described by the K and L matrices, into elasticity form. Generalizations of the Stolper–Samuelson theorem linking commodity-price changes to changes in factor prices are contained in the structure of the N matrix, while Q displays Rybczynski-type results of endowment changes on outputs at constant commodity prices. I now assume not only that each output requires positive amounts of at least two factors, but also that each factor is employed by at least two industries.

What should one expect to find in the Stolper–Samuelson matrix, N? Earlier attempts to generalize the Stolper–Samuelson theorem sought conditions (in the case where $n = r$) on the original input–output A matrix that would guarantee that N had a diagonal all of whose elements were positive and exceeded unity, and negative off-diagonal elements.[10] These conditions turned out to be rather strict.[11] Whereas an N-matrix of this type suggests that if one commodity price rises there will be one unambiguous winner (the factor used 'intensively' in that industry), while all other factors suffer a decline in their returns, it is possible to ask how the A-matrix must look to ensure that when p_j rises only one factor unambiguously loses whereas all other factors find their returns increased.[12] Inada [6] has initiated this question. As Ethier [5] has suggested, it might be more useful to ask what general properties the Stolper–Samuelson N matrix possesses without imposing such strict requirements on the original input–output matrix.

The basic extension of the Stolper – Samuelson theorem states that if p_j alone rises, at least one factor must find its real reward enhanced and at least one other factor must suffer. In the 2×2 case this exhausts the factors, but in cases where $r > 2$ other factor returns may rise, but by more or less than $\hat{p}_j$, or may fall. This depends on the fine details of the original A-matrix. But the basic extension follows simply from the assumption of no joint production.[13] Consider a change only in p_j. From (17) it is clear that if x_j is produced, $\hat{p}_j$ is a non-negative weighted

[10] In terms of fig. 8.1 the distribution of Stolper–Samuelson terms along the horizontal axis would display, for each j, one term greater than unity and all other elements to the left of the origin. The Inada example, described below, would indicate that for each j there exists one element less than zero and all other elements positive.

[11] See, for example, the contributions of Chipman [3], Uekawa [15], and Kemp and Wegge [10]. To illustrate how strict these conditions are (in the 'even' $n = r$ case), they exclude the possibility that some factor of production might not be employed by some industry.

[12] However, an increase in w_i when p_j rises is not sufficient to ensure that factor i unambiguously gains, since $\hat{w}_i$ may not exceed $\hat{p}_j$. The term 'unambiguous' has been used by Ethier [5] in discussing these issues.

[13] The logic of the argument is spelled out for the 2×2 case in the discussion of the magnification effect in Chapter 4.

average of all the $\hat{w}_i$, where the weights are the distributive shares of factors in the jth industry. If all $\hat{w}_i$ are the same, they will equal $\hat{p}_j$. But if the $\hat{w}_i$ (for i used in j) are not all identical, at least one must exceed $\hat{p}_j$. Other commodity prices are being held fixed, so that a similar argument establishes that some $\hat{w}_k$ must be negative.[14]

A more formal matrix proof has been employed by Ethier [5] in the case where $n = r$. Suppose, more generally, that $r \geqq n$. Explicitly:

$$\begin{bmatrix} \sigma & \lambda \\ \hline \theta' & 0 \end{bmatrix} \begin{bmatrix} M & N \\ \hline Q & R \end{bmatrix} = \begin{bmatrix} I & 0 \\ \hline 0 & I \end{bmatrix}. \tag{19}$$

Multiply the second row of the first matrix by the second column of the second:

$$\theta' N = I. \tag{20}$$

The jth column of N refers to the impact of a rise in p_j on all factor prices. Previous reasoning suggests that (except in special cases – see footnote 14) at least one element of the jth column of N exceeds unity and at least one other element is negative. By (20) the jth column must be nonzero, so that for some k, N_{kj} does not vanish. The trick is to find some row, i, of θ' such that the element θ'_{ik} is strictly positive and such that i does not equal j. The assumption that every factor, k, is used in at least two industries guarantees that some $\theta'_{ik} > 0$ for $i \neq j$. Now multiply the ith row of θ' by the jth column of N to obtain: $\Sigma_h \theta'_{ih} N_{hj} = 0$ for $i \neq j$. Since $\theta'_{ik} N_{kj}$ is nonzero, N_{kj} is either negative or positive. If it is positive, there must exist at least one other element of the jth column of N, N_{qj}, $q \neq j$, such that $N_{qj} < 0$ since the product of the ith row of θ' and the jth column of N is zero. Therefore at

[14] Special cases push this basic extension to its limit. For example, suppose (contrary to our assumption) that some industry uses only one factor. If that industry price rises, that factor price must rist exactly by the same amount. If that factor is used in no other industry, no factor price need fall. Another example is provided in Jones–Scheinkman [8]. Suppose the distributive share matrix in a 3 × 3 case is given by

$$\theta' = \begin{bmatrix} 0 & \frac{1}{2} & \frac{1}{2} \\ \frac{1}{2} & 0 & \frac{1}{2} \\ \frac{1}{2} & \frac{1}{2} & 0 \end{bmatrix}.$$

In such a case the N-matrix (the inverse of θ') is

$$N = \begin{bmatrix} -1 & 1 & 1 \\ 1 & -1 & 1 \\ 1 & 1 & -1 \end{bmatrix}.$$

Therefore if p_j rises no factor return rises by a greater relative amount. All factors used in the jth sector benefit by the same relative extent as $\hat{p}_j$.

least one element in every column of N must be negative. If joint production is ruled out, an increase in only one commodity price must force at least one factor return to fall.

Multiplying the jth row of θ' by the jth column of N yields unity. If all elements of θ' were positive, this would suffice to establish that some element of the jth column of N must exceed unity since it has been shown that some other element is negative and θ' is row stochastic. Footnote 14 shows how the argument can break down if some elements of θ' are zero. However, either the jth column of N has an element exceeding unity *or* the factor whose wage goes down when p_j rises (and there must be at least one such factor which loses) is not used in the production of commodity j. Ignoring the latter possibility, the absence of joint production guarantees a distribution along the horizontal axis in fig. 8.1 for given industry j that contains at least one factor to the left of the origin and one factor exceeding unity.

Whereas each column of N traces out how all factor prices are disturbed by a rise in one commodity price, each row of N focuses upon a particular factor and suggests how that factor's return is altered by a change in each commodity price separately. *If* some element in each row exceeds unity, it would be possible to find some commodity for which a price increase would unambiguously benefit that factor. Every factor would, in such a case, have at least one 'natural friend'. Similarly, *if* every row of N contained at least one negative entry, every factor would have at least one 'natural enemy'. Must every row of N contain such elements?

The case in which the number of productive factors exceeds the number of commodities illustrates that the answer to this question on both counts must be negative. Consider the 'specific-factors' model of Chapter 6, in which each of two sectors employed a factor used only in that industry. In addition, another factor (call it labor) is mobile between the two industries. If either commodity price rises, the wage rate rises, but relatively not by as much. That is, the row of N corresponding to the impact of price changes on the return to mobile labor would contain no elements greater than unity nor any negative elements.[15] By contrast, each specific factor has one natural friend and (in the two sector model) one natural enemey.

More structure is possessed by the Stolper–Samuelson N matrix in the 'even' case in which the number of factors equals the number of commodities. This $n \times n$ case is the most natural extension of the 'even' 2×2 case in which the Stolper-

[15] As is shown in Jones [7], the properties of the $n + 1$ factor, n sector version of the specific factors model parallel precisely those of the 3×2 model of Chapter 6. See also the discussion in Ruffin and Jones [12].

Samuelson theorem was first discussed. To see what can be said in this case about the rows of N, rewrite (19) as

$$\left[\begin{array}{c|c} M & N \\ \hline Q & R \end{array}\right]\left[\begin{array}{c|c} \sigma & \lambda \\ \hline \theta' & 0 \end{array}\right] = \left[\begin{array}{c|c} I & 0 \\ \hline 0 & I \end{array}\right]$$

and note that with $r = n$, the M matrix becomes the zero matrix–the factor-price equalization result. Multiply the first row of the first matrix by the first column of the second:

$$N\theta' = I.$$

Now consider the ith row of N. Postmultiply it by the kth column of $\theta'(k \neq i)$. The product is zero. By the previous kind of argument, as long as every commodity uses at least two factors, some element of the ith row of N must be negative since the elements of θ' are non-negative. That is, in the 'even' case each factor has at least one 'natural enemy'. In search of 'natural friends', multiply the ith row of N by the ith column of θ'. This yields unity. But since θ' is *not* column stochastic this result cannot be used to establish that every row of N must have at least one element exceeding unity. The ith column of θ' refers to factor i's share in each industry, and the column sum could greatly exceed unity if the factor is important enough in the economy. However, if the ith column sum of θ' falls short of unity, an argument similar to that used previously can establish that some element of the ith row of N must exceed one. That is, if a factor is 'unimportant' enough,[16] it must possess at least one natural friend in the sense that some commodity can be found for which an increase in price raises w_i by a greater relative amount.

The properties of the Q matrix in (18) reveal the extent to which the Rybczynski theorem generalizes. Although obvious similarities with the Stolper–Samuelson N matrix are suggested, the Q matrix is less tightly structured if the number of factors exceeds the number of commodities. The reason lies in the asymmetry in the two equation sets captured by (17). Whereas the competitive profit conditions of change assume the simple form

$$\theta'\hat{w} = \hat{p}$$

because of the envelope result expressed by the cost-minimization condition, $\Sigma_i w_i da_{ij} = 0$, the full employment conditions are more complicated:

$$\sigma\hat{w} + \lambda\hat{x} = \hat{V};$$

Factor prices can change even with commodity prices constant if $r > n$.

[16] Note that with $n = r$, the average column sum in θ' is unity. Thus, being 'unimportant' is a property shared, on average, by half the factors.

Each column of Q indicates how all outputs respond to an increase in a particular factor. In general little can be said. For example, in the 3×2 model of Chapter 6 an increase in mobile labor at constant commodity prices would raise all (both) outputs, but perhaps neither by a greater relative extent than the growth in labor supply. The basis for the generalization of the Rybczynski result is reflected in the *rows* of Q. Each row must contain at least one negative element. In words, for any output, x_j, there exists at least one factor endowment, V_i, such that at constant commodity prices an increase in V_i would cause x_j production actually to fall. A simple matrix proof is at hand, but application of the reciprocity relationship (15) is more direct. Pick any commodity, j, and ask what would happen to factor prices if p_j rises, keeping constant all other commodity prices and factor endowments. As established earlier, some w_i must fall. By (15), if all commodity prices are constant and V_i is raised (for this same i), output of commodity j must fall.

The reciprocity relationship in form (16) and fig. 8.1 can be used to show why it may *not* be possible to establish that some element in every row of Q must exceed unity. Suppose p_j alone increases, and endowments are fixed. For some factor i, $\hat{w}_i$ must exceed $\hat{p}_j$. But suppose this factor is like i_1 in fig. 8.1, where i_1's share in the national income, α^{I_1}, falls short of sector j's output share, α_j. Then

$$\left\{\frac{V_{i_1}}{x_j}\frac{\partial x_j}{\partial V_{i_1}}\right\}$$

might not exceed unity.[17]

As these remarks, and eq. (16), suggest, a value for $(\hat{w}_i/\hat{p}_j)$ greater than unity provides no guarantee that $(\hat{x}_j/\hat{V}_i)$ would also exceed unity, or vice versa. But, as Kemp and Ethier [9] have shown, a value for $(\hat{w}_i/\hat{p}_j)$ greater than unity does indicate a strong positive relationship between factor i and commodity j, interpreted in terms of output responses to endowment changes. That is to say, if $\{\hat{w}_i/\hat{p}_j\}$ exceeds unity, it must be the case that an increase in V_i at constant commodity prices would raise output x_j so much that the *net* value of the aggregate of all other outputs must fall. To see this note than an increase in the endowment of factor i at constant commodity prices by one unit must raise national income by an amount indicated by

[17]That is, the Stolper–Samuelson term, $\hat{w}_i/\hat{p}_j$, may lie between unity and π_1 along the horizontal axis in fig. 8.1.

that factor's return. That is,[18]

$$w_i = p_j \frac{\partial x_j}{\partial V_i} + \sum_{h \neq j} p_h \frac{\partial x_h}{\partial V_i} \,. \tag{21}$$

But, by reciprocity relationship (15), this can be rewritten as

$$w_i \left\{ 1 - \frac{p_j}{w_i} \frac{\partial w_i}{\partial p_j} \right\} = \sum_{h \neq j} p_h \frac{\partial x_h}{\partial V_i}, \tag{22}$$

from which the Kemp–Ethier result follows. As Kemp and Ethier point out, relationships such as (21) are derived from extremely basic properties of the technology that have nothing to do with the presence or absence of joint production.[19]

If the number of factors equals the number of commodities, the Rybczynski Q matrix assumes as much structure as the Stolper–Samuelson N matrix for $r = n$. In general every column of Q now has at least one negative element and one element greater than unity. If only one endowment rises, and with factor prices uniquely linked to fixed commodity prices, some output must fall and some other output expands by a greater relative amount than does the factor endowment.

To conclude, consider the possible impact which some one-commodity price rise ($\hat{p}_j > 0$) at constant endowments may have on the relative return to factor i.

(i) The return to factor i could fall. If joint production is ruled out, there must be at least one such factor.

[18] More generally,

$$\sum_i w_i \mathrm{d}V_i = \sum_h p_h \mathrm{d}x_h$$

on the one hand and

$$\sum_i V_i \mathrm{d}w_i = \sum_h x_h \mathrm{d}p_h$$

on the other. For details see Jones and Scheinkman [8] or Chapter 4.

[19] A similar kind of argument establishes that

$$x_j \left\{ 1 - \frac{V_i}{x_j} \frac{\partial x_j}{\partial V_i} \right\} = \sum_{h \neq i} V_h \frac{\partial w_h}{\partial p_j},$$

since the reciprocity result can be applied to the observation that if only commodity j's price rises, $x_j \mathrm{d}p_j$ must equal $V_i \mathrm{d}w_i$ plus

$$\sum_{h \neq i} V_h \mathrm{d}w_h.$$

This states that if an increase in i's endowment at constant commodity prices causes x_j to rise by a greater proportional amount, an increase in p_j by itself would raise w_i so much that the net income accruing to the aggregate of all other factors must fall.

(ii) The return to factor i might rise, but by less, relatively, than the national income. With other commodity prices constant,

$$\hat{Y} = \sum_h \alpha^h \hat{w}_h = \alpha_j \hat{p}_j.$$

Therefore if $\hat{w}_i/\hat{p}_j$ is less than output share α_j, industry j is not biased in favor of factor i.[20]

(iii) The return to factor i might rise by the same relative amount as the average of all factors. For given j, α_j represents an average of all the $\hat{w}_i/\hat{p}_j$ – the average which uses as weights the factor shares in the national income.[21]

(iv) If $\hat{w}_i/\hat{p}_j$ exceeds α_j, industry j is said to be biased towards factor i. There are two alternative ways in which this bias might be deemed to be 'strong'. If $\hat{w}_i/\hat{p}_j$ exceeds unity, clearly factor i has an unambiguous 'friend' in industry j. If joint production is ruled out, there must be at least one such factor. Alternatively, industry j may be strongly biased towards factor i in the sense that an increase in p_j *lowers* the net amount received by the aggregate of all factors other than i. Even if joint production is ruled out, such a factor may not exist. For example, in the 3 × 2 specific-factors version discussed in Chapter 6, any commodity price rise never raises the return to the factor specifically used in that sector by more, in absolute terms, than the national income, although $\hat{w}_j$ does exceed $\hat{p}_j$.[22]

In fig. 8.1 the cut-off points π_1 and π_2 reveal that for an 'important' factor such as i_2, an increase in p_j may lower the aggregate return to the rest of the economy without unambiguously raising w_{i_2} relative to p_j, while for a factor such as i_1, whose share in Y is smaller, $\hat{w}_{i_1}$ might exceed $\hat{p}_j$ without absorbing all the increase in Y.[23]

[20] This notion of bias is developed in Ruffin and Jones [12].

[21] If, instead, the distributive factor shares in the jth industry are used as weights, the $\hat{w}_i/\hat{p}_j$ average to unity. Or, if any of the sets of distributive shares in the $n - 1$ other industries, $\theta_{ik} (k \neq j)$ are used, the weighted average,

$$\sum_i \theta_{ik} \frac{\hat{w}_i}{\hat{p}_j}$$

is zero.

[22] This is readily seen from fig. 8.1. No specific factor earns more than is produced in the single sector it is employed, so that relative price and output changes lie along a line like i_1 rather than i_2. Since an increase in the endowment of a specific factor cannot raise output in its sector by relatively more at constant commodity prices (as the mobile/specific factor proportion falls), the appropriate point on the i_1 line is a, lying to the left of π_1.

[23] If the number of factors, r, exceeds the number of commodities, n, on average α^i will be smaller than α_j, so that, as fig. 8.1 illustrates, it may be easier to find factors, i, such that $(\hat{w}_i/\hat{p}_j)$ exceed unity for given j than to find commodities, j, for which $(\hat{x}_j/\hat{V}_i)$ exceed unity.

This chapter has developed the general model where joint production is ruled out and factors are at least as numerous as commodities. The structure of this model, as set out in absolute form in (9), or in relative form in (17), reveals some of the basic relationships already familiar from 2×2 and 3×2 versions. Of particular relevance is the role of the asymmetry between factors and commodities in technology (implied by the absence of joint production) in supporting magnification effects whereby commodity price changes eventuate in more radical spreads in the factoral distribution of income and endowment changes at constant commodity prices call for significant alterations in the composition of output. Finally, structure in the 'uneven' case in which factors outnumber commodities has been related to the classic Heckscher–Ohlin case in which the number of commodities produced matches exactly the number of factors employed.

References

[1] Caratheodory, C., *Calculus of Variations and Partial Differential Equations of the Frist Order, Part II, Calculus of Variations* (Holden-Day, San Francisco, 1967).

[2] Chang, W., 'Some Theorems of Trade and General Equilibrium with Many Goods and Factors', unpublished.

[3] Chipman, J., 'Factor Price Equalization and the Stolper–Samuelson Theorem', *International Economic Review*, 10 (October 1969) 399–406.

[4] Diewert, W.E. and A.D. Woodland, 'Frank Knight's Theorem in Linear Programming Revisited', *Econometrica* (March 1977) 375–398.

[5] Ethier, W., 'Some of the Theorems of International Trade with Many Goods and Factors', *Journal of International Economics*, 4 (May 1974) 199–206.

[6] Inada, K., 'The Production of Coefficient Matrix and the Stolper–Samuelson Condition', *Econometrica*, 39 (March 1971) 219–240.

[7] Jones, R.W., 'Income Distribution and Effective Protection in a Multi-Commodity Trade Model', *Journal of Economic Theory*, 11 (1975) 1–15.

[8] Jones, R.W. and J. Scheinkman, 'The Relevance of the Two-Sector Production Model in Trade Theory', *Journal of Political Economy*, 85 (October 1977) 909–935.

[9] Kemp, M.C. and W. Ethier, 'A Note on Joint Production and the Theory of International Trade', in: M.C. Kemp, *Three Topics in the Theory of International Trade* (North-Holland, Amsterdam, 1976) ch. 7, pp. 81–84.

[10] Kemp, M.C. and L. Wegge, 'On the Relation Between Commodity Prices and Factor Rewards', *International Economic Review*, 10 (October 1969) 407–413.

[11] Melvin, J., 'Production and Trade with Two Factors and Three Goods', *American Economic Review*, 58 (1968) 1248–1268.

[12] Ruffin, R. and R.W. Jones, 'Protection and Real Wages: The Neo-Classical Ambiguity', *Journal of Economic Theory* (April 1977) 337–348.

[13] Samuelson, P.A., *Foundations of Economic Analysis* (Harvard University Press, 1947).

[14] Samuelson, P.A., 'Prices of Factors and Goods in General Equilibrium', *Review of Economic Studies*, 21 (1953) 1–20.

[15] Uekawa, Y., 'Generalization of the Stolper-Samuelson Theorem', *Econometrica*, 39 (March 1971) 197–218.

PART III

THE TRANSFER PROBLEM

INTRODUCTION TO PART III

Whereas the first two parts of this book concentrate on the details of the production structure, the classical transfer problem gives at least equal weight to demand. The impact which a transfer of real income from one country to another has on the terms of trade depends in large part on the nature of the dissimilarity in tastes in the two countries. Indeed, the *direction* of change in the terms of trade in simple models depends only upon a comparison of marginal propensities to consume the same commodity in each country or, alternatively, a comparison of the sum of marginal propensities to import with unity.

The transfer literature is a branch of trade theory in which there is 'orthodoxy' and 'antiorthodoxy'. Most earlier writers on the subject subscribed to the orthodox doctrine whereby a country that is called upon to make a transfer – whether voluntarily in the form of loans, or involuntarily in the form of reparations or tribute – will suffer a 'secondary burden' in the form of worsened terms of trade. As Samuelson [6,7] stressed in his now classic early 1950s pieces on the transfer problem, the question is one of presumption and much depends on the form of the model. Samuelson found no grounds for othodoxy (or its opposite) in simple 2×2 trade models. Instead, orthodoxy could be defended, he argued, only in cases in which natural or man-made impediments to trade existed, and even then supporting assumptions as to the nature of taste patterns are important. In Chapter 9 the issue is analyzed in the context of a simple exchange model with no impediments and I argue the antiorthodox presumption that a transfer is more likely to improve than to deteriorate a country's terms of trade. The rationale is extremely simple: if two countries differ in their taste biases, the country with the greater marginal propensity to consume commodity j is likely to end up importing commodity j. Trade patterns may not be independent of tastes, and this provides the antiorthodox presumption in the simple model.[1]

[1] I owe an apology to Fritz Machlup for usurping in Chapter 9 the title he had previously used in [4]. I had originally chosen a different title, 'The Transfer Problem Reconsidered', but found that Lloyd Metzler had pre-empted my choice in his 1942 paper [5]. In a subsequent piece [2], John Chipman avoided my problem with titles.

If the Samuelson of the early 1950s shot down many of the orthodox arguments, the Samuelson of the early 1970s provided a more robust orthodox platform of his own (Samuelson [8]). What is the presumption as to transfer and the terms of trade if, in each country, leisure provides a desirable alternative to work? This is a model in which nontraded commodities (leisure in Samuelson's case) provide an essential link in the argument: the transferor decreases his demand for nontradeables and thus releases resources for production of tradeables. If production is concentrated along export lines, the transferor's terms of trade are apt to deteriorate. In Chapter 10 I discuss the transfer problem in the context of a model with two tradeables and one nontradeable in each country and show how Samuelson's correct argument concerning production or supply biases in favor of orthodoxy may be qualified by demand biases in the opposite direction. I also mention briefly the argument advanced in Caves and Jones [1] that, if resources are transferred, the transferor is likely to contract instead of expand tradeables production, thus reversing the impact of the Samuelson presumption.

The treatment in the text of Chapter 10 is kept deliberately nonmathematical in order to expose the bare arguments supporting each camp. A brief Appendix (I) was originally added to provide the basis for the core criterion. To this I have now added a more general Appendix (II) on the question of stability in the trade model with nontraded goods. This serves both to illustrate how the transfer criterion is related to the stability issue and offers an analytical treatment of the general model with nontraded goods that is alternative to (but consistent with) my analysis in [3] which aimed to link up with the Robinson–Bickerdike–Metzler literature.

Chapter 11 attempts to relate the transfer literature to recent problems faced by LDCs in adjusting to the oil crisis and the severe commodity price changes of the early 1970s. As I emphasize there, the transfer literature lies at the core of the theory of international trade. The essence of trade is that countries are exchanging bundles of commodities with each other so that any changes in relative prices must cause an international *transfer* of real incomes. The transfer problem may refer explicitly to outright grants or loans, but the phenomenon of transfer is more deeply imbedded in the existence of trade and changes in the terms along which it is conducted.

References

[1] Caves, R.E. and R.W. Jones, *World Trade and Payments: An Introduction* (Little Brown, 1973, 1977).

[2] Chipman, J., 'The Transfer Problem Once Again', in: Horwich and Samuelson, eds., *Trade, Stability, and Macroeconomics* (Academic Press, 1974), ch. 2, 19–78.
[3] Jones, R.W., 'Trade with Non-traded Goods: The Anatomy of Inter-connected Markets', *Economica* (May 1974) 121–138.
[4] Machlup, F., 'The Transfer Problem Revisited', in: Machlup, *International Monetary Economics* (Allen & Unwin, 1966) ch. 19, pp. 433–446.
[5] Metzler, L., 'The Transfer Problem Reconsidered', *Journal of Political Economy* (June 1942) 397–414.
[6] Samuelson, P.A., 'The Transfer Problem and Transport Costs: The Terms of Trade When Impediments are Absent', *Economic Journal* (June 1952) 278–304.
[7] Samuelson, P.A., 'The Transfer Problem and Transport Costs, II: Analysis of Effects of Trade Impediments', *Economic Journal* (June 1954) 264–289.
[8] Samuelson, P.A., 'On the Trail of Conventional Beliefs about the Transfer Problem', in: Bhagwati, Jones, Mundell and Vanek, *Trade, Balance of Payments, and Growth* (North-Holland, Amsterdam, 1971) pp. 327–351.

Chapter 9

THE TRANSFER PROBLEM REVISITED*

1.

Since the early 1950s little has been written on the effect of income transfers between countries on the terms of trade of the transferor. In large part this is explained by the fact that the issue of transfer in the context of a standard two-country, two-commodity model of trade was so comprehensively treated by Samuelson in two papers in the *Economic Journal* in 1952 and 1954.[1] The primary purpose of Samuelson's two articles was to focus intensively on the 'orthodox' doctrine whereby there is a presumption that the terms of trade will deteriorate for the country making the unilateral transfer, the 'paying' country. After an exhaustive study of arguments that had previously been put forth to support the orthodox doctrine, Samuelson concluded that in the absence of transport costs, tariffs or other impediments to trade, '... there is no presumption that the terms of trade will deteriorate rather than favour the paying country' [5, p. 299]. In his second paper [6], Samuelson showed how the orthodox presumption could, in certain cases, be restored once impediments to trade are explicitly introduced.

In this chapter I intend to suggest that in a wide variety of cases there is a presumption as to the way in which the terms of trade will move with transfer, even in the no-impediments model. However, the bias is antiorthodox: there is a pre-

* *Economica* (May 1970) 178–184. I am indebted to the National Science Foundation for support of this research and to Richard Caves, Paul Samuelson, and Jagdish Bhagwati for useful discussion on a number of points.

[1] See Samuelson [5,6]. These have since been abridged and brought together (see Samuelson [7]). Samuelson's two articles were followed by a piece by Johnson [2]. There has been more recent interest in the transfer problem within the context of models more complicated than the standard two-commodity case, for example McDougall [4].

sumption that the terms of trade move in favor of the transferor. That is, the real income loss represented by the transfer at initial prices may be mitigated by the 'secondary' effects of an improvement in the terms of trade.[2] Furthermore, my argument for the antiorthodox bias in the no-impediments case is best illustrated by making the same explicit assumption about tastes and Engel's curves as does Samuelson in the impediments case to support the orthodox position. Although this may seem paradoxical, these two positions are consistent with each other because my argument about bias rests essentially upon possibilities implicitly ruled out by Samuelson.

It should be emphasized that in this model transfer may turn the terms of trade in either direction or leave them unaltered. What is at issue is the semantically tricky question of dealing with presumption and bias. More crudely put, would a 'betting man' have any reason to predict which way the terms of trade would turn without detailed knowledge of taste and production patterns in each country?

2.

One of the virtues of Samuelson's treatment is the emphasis placed on the fact that the criterion for establishing which way the terms of trade are altered by transfer involves only the income propensities. Johnson [2] is even more explicit in suggesting that in a stable market it is sufficient to analyze the effect of transfer on world demand for one of the commodities at the initial pretransfer prices. Since an adjustment of production patterns would normally not take place unless prices change, the direction of the price change can be analyzed without loss of generality by using a model of pure exchange, a procedure I shall adopt throughout. In the no-impediments case, the transfer at initial prices raises demand for both commodities in the receiving country (I assume neither good is inferior) and lowers demand for both commodities in the paying country. If the marginal propensity to consume the imported commodity in the paying country is less than the marginal propensity to consume that same commodity in the receiving country, net world demand for the commodity increases and, once the market is cleared, the terms of trade will have turned against the transferor. This is the orthodox position. I now turn to a case in which this outcome would be 'less likely' than the alternative.

A basic assumption I wish to make is that a country's taste pattern is indepen-

[2] Of course this 'secondary' effect can never outweigh the primary loss in a stable market. The paying country suffers a net loss of real income.

dent of its commodity endowment (production) pattern.[3] The pattern of trade is determined both by the relation between the two countries' taste patterns and by the relation between their production patterns. Therefore, in the general case the export – import pattern is *not* independent of differences in tastes. It is this connection which lies at the heart of my argument.

The assumption about tastes most conducive to my results about bias in that in each country tastes are homothetic; that is, taste patterns satisfy what Samuelson refers to as the Viner convention:[4] income elasticities are unity, making relative prices, and not income, the sole determinant of the ratio of the two commodities consumed.[5] If the two countries have identical taste patterns, the contract curve is given by the diagonal of a box whose dimensions represent aggregate world endowments of the two commodities. Suppose tastes differ. Without loss of generality the contract curve can be illustrated as in fig. 9.1, showing country 1 with a bias in its taste pattern for commodity B: at any common terms of trade, country 1 consumes a higher ratio of B to A than does country 2. With homothetic indifference curves the contract curve must lie entirely on one side of the diagonal if it does not coincide with the diagonal.

Now consider picking an endowment point for each country (such that world totals correspond to the dimensions of the box in fig 9.1). I assume that the distribution of endowment points is independent of the taste pattern. One possibility is

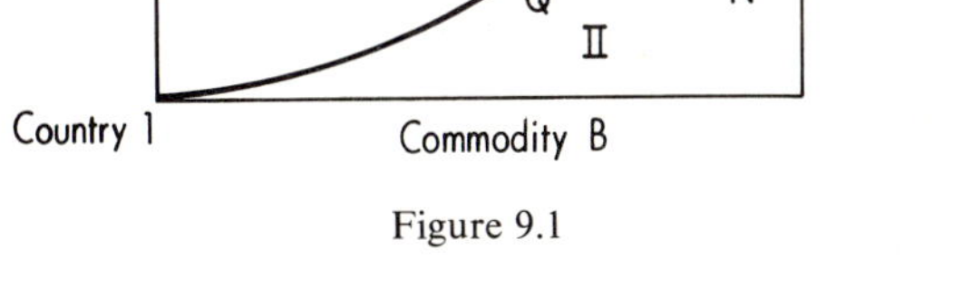

Figure 9.1

[3] This, of course, may not be the case. In some countries, it may be argued, tastes are biased towards the consumption of the commodity that bulks larger in domestic production. On the other hand, it may be that the 'snob' appeal of imported goods biases tastes away from local production. Samuelson assumes [5, p. 298] that there is '... no *a priori* correlation between regional patterns of production and tastes', which is the assumption I am making.

[4] For example, see Samuelson's extended discussion [5, pp. 295–298].

[5] Note that this is the assumption most frequently made about individual demands in justifying the construction of community indifference curves.

a uniform distribution over the entire box. Another is a normal distribution centered on the diagonal. All that I require is that there is a greater likelihood that the endowment point lies in the (larger) region I than in region II. If the endowment point lies in region I, say at M, country 1 must be an importer of commodity B. A transfer from country 1 to country 2 would move the equilibrium trading point down the contract curve towards 1's origin, as the new budget line for country 1 would run southwest of M. This must lower the relative price of B: homotheticity ensures that the indifference curves become flatter and flatter with a movement along the contract curve from 2's origin to 1's origin. The terms of trade have moved in favor of the transferor.

If the endowment point had, instead, been in region II, say at point N, a transfer from 1 to 2 would still result in a movement along the contract curve towards country 1's origin, and the relative price of B again would fall. However, the trading pattern is reversed in this case: country 1, the transferor, is now the exporter of B and thus suffers a deterioration in its terms of trade. This is the orthodox result which, on the basis of my assumptions, is 'less likely'.

The direction of trade depends on a comparison of A/B in each country's endowment bundle and A/B in each country's consumption pattern. If endowments and tastes are independent we would expect, in half the cases, for the country with the taste bias in favor of consuming B to have a relatively high A/B ratio in its endowment. For example, this is the situation in which the endowment point lies above the diagonal in fig. 1. Both the endowment difference and the taste difference conspire to make country 1 an importer of B. In the other half of possible cases, endowment and taste differences conflict in their influence on the trading pattern. In fig. 9.1, that part of region I below the diagonal but above the contract curve corresponds to a situation in which the differences in tastes are more pronounced than the differences in endowments, so that the trading pattern reflects the taste bias. For the endowment point to lie in region II requires both a conflict between endowments and tastes *and* a more pronounced difference in endowments. With homotheticity in demand, only with endowments in region II will the 'orthodox' position as to the effect of transfer on the terms of trade emerge.

These remarks serve to introduce one of the major ways in which my 'presumption' can be removed. Much of the modern Heckscher–Ohlin theory of trade links trade patterns to differences in factor endowments or, in the context of this exchange model, differences in the ratio of commodities produced at common price ratios. This assumption – that endowment differences 'outweigh' demand differences – is sufficient to re-establish Samuelsons's conclusion that in the no-impediments case there is no presumption as to the effect of transfer on the terms of trade. As a special case, consider a model in which each country is completely specialized in a different commodity. Which corner of the box in fig. 9.1 (north-west or south-east) contains the endowment point may be completely independent of demand patterns, and yet the directional pattern of trade then becomes independent of taste differences. This, implicitly, is the kind of situation Samuelson had in mind and, therefore, no argument about bias in the effect of a transfer on the terms of trade based on my argument could possibly emerge.[6]

Whether endowment (or production) differences are more pronounced than taste differences is ultimately an empirical question. The point is that in theory it may be useful to avoid pronouncing *a priori* which blade of the scissors is the more important.[7]

Even if taste differences may be more pronounced, thus dominating the trading pattern, the argument I have presented may disappear, or be reversed, if taste patterns are not homothetic. The reason for this is that the transfer problem relates to relatively marginal transfers of real income, and thus involves only marginal propensities to consume. The question as to which country is an importer of which commodity involves, on the demand side, the aggregate (or average) spending propensities. Thus, a crucial link is the relationship between marginal and average propensities to consume the two goods in each country. The assumption of homotheticity I have employed is much too strong for my purposes. All that is required is a positive relation (correlation?) between average and marginal propensities. The fact that country 1 imports commodity B lends a presumption to 1's having a relatively high average propensity to consume B. Unless this also implies a presumption as to a relatively high marginal propensity to consume B, there emerges no presumption as to the effect on the terms of trade.

In discussing the effects of transfer when impediments are present, Samuelson explores the case in which marginal utilities are independent and linear (an assumption attributed to Pigou). In this case a high average propensity is associated with a low marginal propensity [6, pp. 271–280]. In terms of fig. 9.1, it now becomes region I that leads to the orthodox result. Once again, however, the presumption about bias that emerges in Samuelson's treatment is different from my own. Pigou's case of independent utilities leads to the antiorthodox bias in Samuelson's discussion. Although I am not primarily concerned with the case of

[6] For example, Samuelson states: 'If we like, we can think of Europe as producing little (or no) food and much clothing; of America as producing little (or no) clothing and much food' [5, p. 281].

[7] This Marshallian phrase is not altogether suitable since it is the differences in the positions of the two 'blades' between countries that is relevant.

impediments to trade, it may be useful to sketch, in the next section, why the arguments about bias seem to move in opposite directions in our two treatments. In the concluding section I revert to the no-impediments case to discuss the consequence of possible bias for the question of market stability.

3.

In [6] Samuelson considers two types of impediments to trade–real impediments (transport costs) and artificial impediments (tariffs). Here I consider only the case in which, before transfer, each country has levied a tariff on imports.[8] The tariff rates are held constant throughout the transfer. To highlight the bias in transfer introduced by the existence of tariffs, I shall follow Samuelson in assuming that taste patterns are identical between countries so that, in the no-impediments case, the contract curve is the diagonal and transfer involves no change in the terms of trade. I am also assuming initially that taste patterns satisfy the Viner convention (homotheticity).

Fixed tariff rates in both countries imply a constant wedge between the relative prices in the two countries. A contract curve can be drawn, linking points in the box where the indifference curves differ by this constant wedge, but only after the endowment point is known.[9] The trade pattern, which in this case of identical tastes depends just upon endowment differences, dictates the country in which the relative price of B is higher (the B-importing country). Suppose the endowment point is the extreme south-east corner of the box in fig. 9.1 – country 1 has no A in its endowment bundle and must therefore be an A-importer. In each country, everywhere along the contract curve, the relative price of its import good must be higher than in the no-impediments case (shown by common slopes of indifference curves along the diagonal); that is, with impediments the contract curve is drawn towards the endowment point – the A/B consumption ratio in each country will, after tariffs, more closely resemble its endowment proportions. Thus, the contract curve looks as drawn in fig. 9.1, with the endowment point in region II. Since marginal and average propensities correspond, the

[8]The analysis of transport costs is inherently more difficult as Samuelson assumes they take the form of a loss of commodities in shipment. This implies that the dimensions of the box depend upon the quantities traded.

[9]Given the tariff wedge, there will be two curves, one on each side of the diagonal, along which marginal rates of substitution differ between countries by exactly the wedge. But only the curve closer to the endowment point corresponds to possible post-tariff equilibrium positions. Along the other curve, the price of imports would be lower in the importing country.

existence of tariffs with homothetic indifference curves lends a presumption (a certainty if tastes are identical) that transfer worsens the terms of trade for the transferor. This is Samuelson's result. It does not contradict the argument about bias presented in the preceding section, for by assumption it was the difference in endowments that was the sole determinant of the trade pattern.

The Pigou case leads to different results. Again, the tariff wall in each country serves to raise the ratio of the physical amounts of the export good to the import good consumed in that country, relatively to the no-impediments case; that is, the situation is once more as portrayed in fig. 9.1, with the endowment point in region II. However, higher average propensities imply lower marginal propensities in Pigou's case, and thus transfer tends to improve the terms of trade of the transferor.

4.

To conclude, I return to the case in which there are no impediments to trade and in which taste patterns are either homothetic or at least exhibit a positive relationship between average and marginal propensities to consume. In the preceding sections I have concentrated on the impact of transfer on the terms of trade. But, as is well known, the criterion for the transfer problem is directly relevant to the criterion for market stability. (See, for example, Johnson [3] and Hahn [1].) In a two-commodity model of exchange, the market is stable if and only if a rise in price from the equilibrium level reduces aggregate market demand. Substitution effects for buyers and sellers both work to effect such a reduction. But any price rise also serves to redistribute real income from the net importer to the net exporter. The net income effect on aggregate demand depends upon the difference between the marginal propensities to consume the commodities of the net buyers and net sellers. Income effects are destabilizing if and only if the marginal propensity to consume the commodity whose relative price has risen is greater for exporters than for importers.

Therefore, if average and marginal propensities are positively linked, and if endowment differences may be less pronounced than taste differences, there is a presumption that income effects overall are stabilizing. The case for market stability is even stronger than usually implied by the statement that substitution effects (always stabilizing) must outweight income effects (about which no presumption is made).[10] Just as in the transfer argument, the possibility that the

[10]Consider fig. 9.1 once again. Rule out substitution effects by assuming each country has right-

import of a commodity betrays an underlying taste bias for that commodity lends a presumption as to which way net income effects operate.

References

[1] Hahn, F., 'The Balance of Payments in a Monetary Economy', *Review of Economic Studies* (February 1959).

[2] Johnson, H.G., 'The Transfer Problem: A Note on Criteria for Changes in the Terms of Trade', *Economica* (May 1955).

[3] Johnson, H.G., 'The Transfer Problem and Exchange Stability', *Journal of Political Economy* (June 1956); reprinted in: Caves and Johnson, eds., *Readings in International Economics* (Homewood, Ill., 1968) ch. 9.

[4] McDougall, I.A., 'Non-Traded Goods and the Transfer Problem', *Review of Economic Studies* (January 1965).

[5] Samuelson, P.A., 'The Transfer Problem and Transport Costs: The Terms of Trade when Impediments are Absent', *Economic Journal* (June 1952).

[6] Samuelson, P.A., 'The Transfer Problem and Transport Costs, II: Analysis of Effects of Trade Impediments', *Economic Journal* (June 1954).

[7] Samuelson, P.A., 'The Transfer Problem and Transport Costs', in: Caves and Johnson, eds., *Readings in International Economics* (Homewood, Ill., 1968) ch. 8.

(footnote 10 continued)
angled, homothetic indifference curves. The contract curve will not be as illustrated. Instead, the rays from each origin going through the corners of that country's indifference map will meet at some point such as Q. The contract 'curve' becomes two conical bands joined at Q and confined by the rays from the two origins. If the endowment point lies in that part of region I north-west of Q, the market must be stable. If it lies in II south-east of Q (a smaller region), it must be unstable. Only income effects are involved.

Chapter 10

PRESUMPTION AND THE TRANSFER PROBLEM*

Is there any presumption as to which way a country's terms of trade change if it makes a transfer of purchasing power to other countries? This question, presumably laid to rest by Samuelson [10, 11] and Johnson [4] in the early 1950s, has enjoyed a burst of renewed interest in recent years, as shown in the work of McDougall [6, 7], Pearce [8], Jones ([5] and Chapter 9), Samuelson [12], Caves and Jones [1] and, in a recent extremely detailed treatment, Chipman [3]. Most of this new literature has been concerned with a model of trade that includes non-traded commodities, an important extension of the earlier trade model only lightly touched upon in the original Samuelson and Johnson papers.[1]

In the present chapter I wish to focus upon the issue of presumption with transfer in the context of a model with nontraded goods, in order to expose in a relatively simple fashion what issues are involved. For this purpose formal analysis in the body of the chapter is kept to a minimum, with two appendixes supplying the required proofs. Two unifying themes emerge. First, the question of presumption hinges in large part on the underlying causes of trade. In particular, the presumed direction of change in the terms of trade depends upon whether demand differences between countries are more or less pronounced than supply differences. Secondly, if trade is explained by differences both in demand and supply, much

**Journal of International Economics*, 5 (1975) 263 – 274. I am indebted to the National Science Foundation and to Monash University for support of this research, and to Rudiger Dornbusch, Paul Samuelson, Ted Sieper, and John Chipman for useful conversations and correspondence on this topic.

[1]Chapter 9 and the treatment of this issue in Caves and Jones [1] do not deal with nontraded goods. Samuelson's recent article [12] can, as Chipman has pointed out, be considered a special case in which the nontraded good is leisure. In this chapter I ignore all impediments to trade in the form of tariffs or transport costs (except for nontraded goods), considerations discussed in the earlier Samuelson and Johnson analyses.

depends upon the degree of sensitivity to price changes of demanders, on the one hand, and producers, on the other.

The home country makes a transfer of purchasing power to the foreign country. If commodity markets satisfy the Hicks conditions for perfect stability, as I assume they do, the impact of a transfer on the terms of trade can be determined by the sign of world excess demand for the home country's import commodity at the initial prices for traded goods, with prices for nontradeables adjusting to clear the local market in each country. If an excess world demand for home importables is created, the home country suffers a 'secondary burden', in the form deteriorating terms of trade, in addition to the primary burden of the transfer itself. This is what Samuelson and Ohlin have termed the 'orthodox' result, and the question of 'presumption' involves an analysis of those forces tending to raise world excess demand for the commodity imported at home and those tending to reduce excess demand.

In a general model in which both countries produce and consume two different tradeable commodities and a commodity which, by virtue of high transport costs, cannot be traded on world markets, the balance of forces affecting the excess world demand for the home country's importables, and therefore the terms of trade, seems on the surface to be fairly even. In the home country there is a direct income effect of the transfer, tending to reduce home demand for importables. Abroad the increase in purchasing power tends in part to flow into increased demand for this same commodity. In a model with no nontradeables, these are the only factors affecting the world market at the initial terms of trade – no substitution effects in production or consumption would appear as all (one) relative prices are given. But the story becomes more complicated in the presence of nontraded commodities. At the initial terms of trade home demand for its own nontradeable falls, serving to lower the price of nontradeables relative to both traded commodities. Such a price change tends to drive resources away from the nontradeable good and, in the general case of substitution in production (an assumption which I maintain throughout), the supply of both tradeables rises. On the demand side there is a substitution effect away from both tradeables towards greater home consumption of the nontradeable commodity.

In the general case of substitutables, the secondary repercussion of the change in the price of nontradeables at home is to reduce excess world demand for home importables.[2] But an opposite reaction occurs abroad. The price of nontradeables

[2]The argument could alternatively have focussed upon the market for the home country's exportable. The transfer reduces net home demand for its exportable as well as its importable.

in the foreign recipient country is bid up, production of both tradeables is cut and consumption of both tradeables rises due to a substitution effect.

The ingredients are thus clear. Reactions in the home country all conspire to reduce its demand for imports: the direct income effect, and the indirect substitution effect both in demand and supply. Abroad there is an opposite reaction on all counts, raising foreign net demand for the home country's importables. As proved in the appendixes, these forces are all brought together in the following statement: In a stable market the terms of trade of the transferor (the home country) worsen if and only if

$$m_2^* + \omega^* m_3^* > m_2 + \omega m_3.\text{[3]} \tag{1}$$

Commodity 2 is the home country's importable, commodity 1 represents the home country's exportable, and commodity 3 is the nontraded good in each country. m_j is the marginal propensity to consume commodity j at home, and m_j^* the marginal propensity to consume j abroad. The ω^* and ω terms are positive fractions, embodying the substitution effects in consumption and production triggered by the alteration in the price of nontradeables versus tradeables in each country. Specifically,

$$\omega \equiv \frac{[\theta_2 E_2^3 + \alpha_2(-e_2^3)]}{[\theta_2 E_2^3 + \alpha_2(-e_2^3)] + [\theta_1 E_1^3 + \alpha_1(-e_1^3)]} \tag{2}$$

and ω^* is the same term for the foreign country. E_j^3 represents the substitution elasticity in demand of a rise in the price of nontradeables on consumption of the jth commodity. With all commodities assumed to be substitutes in consumption, E_2^3 and E_1^3 are both positive. e_j^3 is the substitution elasticity in production: the effect of a 1% increase in the price of nontradeables on the production of commodity j. If all goods are substitutes in production, e_1^3 and e_2^3 are both negative. Finally, θ_j represents the fraction of national income represented by the *demand* for good j at home, and α_j the fraction of national income represented by *production* of good j.

One element in the analysis of presumption with transfer can be stated at the outset. A comparison of the size of ω and ω^* involves a general comparison between the degree of substitutability (in both consumption and production) between nontradeables and importables, on the one hand, and nontradeables and exportables, on the other. This was clearly enunciated by McDougall.[4] Recall that commodity 2 is the home country's importable and the foreign country's

[3] This condition is not new. See for example, Chipman [3, p. 41, eq. 56].
[4] Cf. McDougall [7, p. 74]. It is also discussed by Jones [5] and, for the production side, suggested by Samuelson [11, p. 289].

exportable. Therefore ω^* will exceed ω, leading to an orthodox presumption that the transferor will suffer a worsening of its terms of trade if, on average, exportables are better substitutes for nontradeables (in both consumption and production) than are importables.[5] Suppose this is the case. Then in the home country, as the price of nontradeables falls (at initial terms of trade), some reduction in net import demand takes place, but not as much relatively as the lowering in its demand for (and increase in production of) its exportables, since nontradeables and exportables are by assumption better substitutes than nontradeables and importables. In the foreign country, by contrast, relatively large reductions in production of commodity 2 and increases in demand for commodity 2 (its exportable) are called forth. Thus on this account (neglecting any difference in marginal propensities) world excess demand for the home country's importables rises and the transferor's terms of trade deteriorate.

Should one expect, *a priori*, that this is the case? At this point we leave this an open question, but will return later to an examination of the 'likely' ranking of ω and ω^*. Much depends on further assumptions which need to be made explicit.

It is perhaps tempting to pursue an analogy to these remarks and, with reference to the basic criterion (1), suggest that if nontradeables bulk larger in the national income of the foreign country (in both average and marginal terms), an orthodox presumption emerges. More precisely, is it possible to state that if the marginal propensity to consume nontradeables is higher in the recipient country ($m_3^* > m_3$), the terms of trade are likely to deteriorate for the transferor? The pitfall in this argument is that a high value of m_3^* must imply a low value for ($m_1^* + m_2^*$), the foreign marginal propensity to consume tradeables. And, although an increase in m_3^* may only result in a smaller reduction in m_2^* (since m_1^* might also be presumed to fall), m_3^* is premultiplied in criterion (1) by a positive fraction, ω^*. In short, we ignore any presumption about transfer linked to the relative importance of the nontradeable sector.[6]

With this in mind we shall henceforth assume that $m_3 = m_3^*$, and $\theta_3 = \theta_3^*$.[7] Are there limits to this kind of before-the-fact presumption of equality between

[5] That is, ω^* exceeds ω if and only if $[\theta_2^* E_2^{3*} + \alpha_2^*(-e_2^{3*})][\theta_1 E_1^3 + \alpha_1(-e_1^3)]$ exceeds $[\theta_2 E_2^3 + \alpha_2(-e_2^3)][\theta_1^* E_1^{3*} + \alpha_1^*(-e_1^{3*})]$. As is discussed below, this criterion reduces for a simple model to the Robinson criterion for a devaluation to worsen the terms of trade: that the product of export supply elasticities exceeds the product of import demand elasticities. Cf. Robinson [9] and Jones [5].

[6] This is correct except for the fact that low values for m_3 and m_3^* imply a greater weight attached to the direct income effect as expressed by m_2 and m_2^*. As m_3 and m_3^* approach zero in the limit, the classical criterion $(m_2^* - m_2) > 0$ is reached.

[7] If marginal and average propensities are functions of commodity prices, note that for traded goods these are equated between countries, while for nontraded goods there is no presumption as to the initial ranking.

countries? The answer which Chapter 9 tried to suggest is a decided 'yes'. The transfer question is posed for *open economies*, engaged in trade. Therefore one cannot presume an identity between countries in all those factors affecting trade: demand functions, production functions and factor endowments. For then there would be no trade! The point, instead, is to analyze what presumption, if any, the existence of those differences between countries that lead to trade has for the question of how the terms of trade behave with transfer. In Chapter 9 I suggested that for two countries producing only two tradeable commodities, the marginal propensity to consume importables by the home country might be expected to exceed the marginal propensity of the foreign country to consume the same commodity, if marginal propensities in general are positively related to average propensities. The home country imports commodity 2 either because its taste pattern is biased towards its consumption, or its production pattern is biased away from its local availability, or in any case because compared with its supply of commodity 2 its demand is relatively strong versus the situation abroad. As a betting man with no *a priori* knowledge about supply, I would be willing to gamble on the other ingredient, demand, sometimes determining the trade pattern.

This kind of argument for the presumed greater value of m_2, compared with m_2^*, remains, for what it is worth, in a more complicated model with nontraded goods. The question that needs probing is whether the assumed trade pattern lends any presumption that ω exceeds or falls short of ω^*.

To proceed with this question, consider the value of E_1^3 compared with E_2^3, or e_1^3 compared with e_2^3. I have already discussed a case in which there may be a systematic bias – the case in which exportables and nontradeables are better substitutes for each other than are importables and nontradeables, both in demand and production. By this is meant that, with the home country importing commodity 2, E_2^3 falls short of E_1^3, and $(-e_1^3)$ exceeds $(-e_2^3)$. (A comparable bias abroad would have E_2^{3*} exceeding E_1^{3*}, etc.) Suppose there is no such bias, in either direction. This is tantamount to assuming that demand and supply functions for tradeable goods are *separable* relative to the price of nontradeables. More explicitly, it is an assumption that a change in the price of nontradeables (p_3) will not affect the *ratio* of tradeables consumed or produced. That is, separability implies that $E_1^3 = E_2^3$ and $e_1^3 = e_2^3$. With such an assumption the expression for ω (and, by analogy, for ω^*) can be greatly simplified. Let $E \equiv E_1^3 = E_2^3$, and $e \equiv e_1^3 = e_2^3$, so that E and e reflect the extent of substitutability in demand and supply for tradeables with respect to a change in the price of nontradeables. Then

$$\omega = \frac{E}{\{E + (-e)\}} \frac{\theta_2}{(\theta_1 + \theta_2)} + \frac{(-e)}{\{E + (-e)\}} \frac{\alpha_2}{(\alpha_1 + \alpha_2)}. \tag{3}$$

That is, ω is a positively weighted average of the share of consumption of tradeables represented by the demand for good 2 $[\theta_2/(\theta_1 + \theta_2)]$ and the share of production of tradeables represented by the production of good 2 $[\alpha_2/(\alpha_1 + \alpha_2)]$. The weights reflect the relative degree of substitutability in comsumption $[E/(E + (-e))]$ versus that in production $[(-e)/(E + (-e))]$.

In this expression for ω (and the comparable expression for ω^*), the θ_j and α_j reflect directly the pattern of trade. With the home country importing commodity 2, θ_2 must exceed α_2, and θ_2^* must fall short of α_2^*.

Suppose the pattern of trade reflects primarily a difference in demand conditions between countries so that θ_2 exceeds θ_2^* but α_2 is roughly equal to α_2^*. By itself this serves to raise the value of ω compared with ω^* and leads to an antiorthodox presumption: The terms of trade will tend to move in favor of the transferor. The case is re-enforced if the presumed excess of θ_2 over θ_2^* spills over to the direct *marginal* propensities to consume the transferor's importable, m_2 and m_2^*. That is, if the existence of trade primarily reflects a difference in demand patterns, there is a presumption in favor of a terms of trade improvement for the country making a transfer.

If, on the other hand, demand conditions are roughly comparable between countries, and supply differences underlie the trading pattern, α_2 will be smaller than α_2^*, and this tends to raise ω^* as compared with ω. In such a case an orthodox presumption can emerge: The terms of trade tend to deteriorate for the transferor. Much of the pure theory of trade concentrates on supply differences as providing the main source for international trade.

This kind of exercise helps to reveal how demand and supply differences between countries, in terms of the aggregate consumption and production patterns, each might lend a presumption to the transfer question. But suppose both operate. That is, suppose that the home country imports commodity 2 both because its demand pattern is biased towards consumption of commodity 2 and its production pattern is biased away from supply of commodity 2. The net impact on the size of ω and ω^* then depends upon the general comparison of substitution elasticities in demand with those in supply. More precisely, an antiorthodox presumption occurs if, generally speaking, consumers (with real incomes constant) are more responsive to price changes than is production. If $E > (-e)$ (and with similar values abroad), ω must exceed ω^* because the share of commodity 2 in the home country's consumption bundle exceeds that for the foreign country ($\theta_2 > \theta_2^*$), and the share of commodity 2 in production at home (α_2) falls short of α_2^* by a roughly comparable amount. Conversely, those who believe that production is generally more elastic to price changes than consumption find some argument in favor of the orthodox presumption. However, if demand differences relative to incomes still favor commodity 2 in the home, importing country, the direct antiorthodox effect of a negative $(m_2^* - m_2)$ must be set against this.

These relationships can easily be illustrated in a diagram showing demand and supply for traded commodities. Fig. 10.1 illustrates the situation for the home country. Initial equilibrium in the traded goods' sector is shown by production point A_1 and consumption point B_1 along budget line 1, whose slope indicates the terms of trade. The fact that the consumption point lies north-west of the production point reflects the assumption that the home country is an importer of commodity 2. Suppose the home country transfers purchasing power to the foreign country of amount T, measured in units of commodity 1. Before any price changes occur there is a direct impact of the transfer on consumption of tradeables at home: the budget line shifts inwards to line 2, the horizontal value of the shift being given by $(m_1 + m_2)\,T$. Consumption of tradeables shifts from point B_1 to point B_2. If income elasticities are unity (so that average and marginal propensities to consume correspond), the B_1B_2 arrow would point towards the origin. This is the direct effect of the transfer in the home country. There is a comparable direct effect abroad which, if income elasticities there are also unity and if the foreign average propensity to consume its exportables (good 2) is smaller than the home propensity to consume importables (also good 2), leads to an antiorthodox excess world supply of good 2.

The indirect effects of the transfer, working through the change in the price of nontradeables, can also be shown. In the home, transferring country the price of nontradeables must fall. At the initial prices for traded goods this must shift demand away from tradeables (from point B_2 to point B_4 in fig. 10.1) and

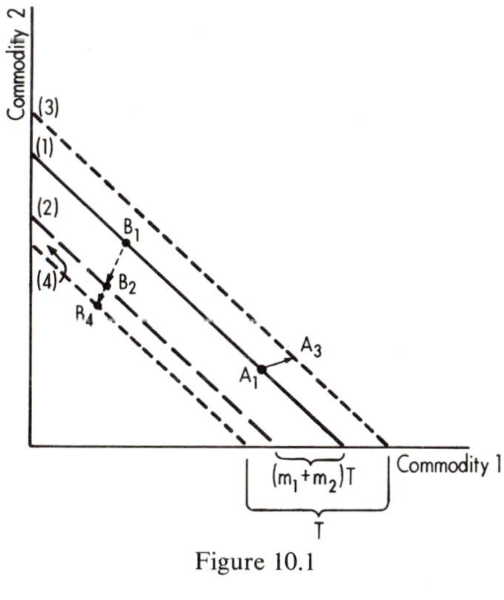

Figure 10.1

push resources into tradeables, expanding the production point from A_1 to A_3. If separability prevails, the B_2B_4 arrow points towards the origin and the A_1A_3 arrow away from the origin. The length of the B_2B_4 arrow, as opposed to the A_1A_3 arrow, reflects the degree of substitutability in demand (E) as opposed to production ($-e$). The horizontal distance between lines 3 and 4 is the total transfer T. An antiorthodox bias for these indirect effects follows if B_2B_4 is steeper than the comparable $B_2^*B_4^*$. By contrast, an orthodox bias is created if the home A_1A_3 arrow is flatter than the corresponding, inward-pointing $A_1^*A_3^*$ arrow. The diagram illustrates the importance for the presumption issue of the causes of trade and the extent of substitutability in demand relative to supply.

All these remarks are of a general nature. It may prove useful to see how they relate to various special models that have been discussed in the transfer literature.

(1) *The pure exchange model.* In each country production is invariant with respect to prices. The transformation surface is a three-dimensional box. All the supply elasticities, the e_j^3 and e_j^{3*} vanish. What emerges? If trade takes place solely because of a difference in the commodity endowment pattern between countries, no presumption can be made. There is no reason to think that m_2 differs from m_2^* or that ω differs from ω^*. This is consistent with Chipman's [3] finding in this case, as well as that of Chapter 9. But if demand differences favor the home country importing the second commodity, both in terms of the marginal and average propensities to consume, the presumption is decidedly antiorthodox. With reference to the basic criterion (1), m_2 exceeds m_2^* and ω exceeds ω^* (because θ_2 exceeds θ_2^*). In the separable case ω reduces to the share of commodity 2 in the consumption of all tradeables.

(2) *Each country specializes in the production of its export and nontradeable commodities.* Chipman has analyzed this case in detail. He is quite correct in pointing to the orthodox bias imparted by such a case. Given the assumed pattern of production, the home country must import commodity 2, and no presumption about demand differences can be inferred from the trade pattern. With transfer the home country contracts its consumption of commodity 2 but, as the price of nontradeables falls, it does not expand its production (since it produces none of commodity 2). The foreign country expands its demand for good 2, both because of an income effect and substitution effect, as its price of nontradeables rises at the initial terms of trade. But it also contracts production of its exportable, commodity 2, and this asymmetry biases the result in favor of an eventual rise in good 2's price (the home country's import).

(3) *Each country consumes only its importable and nontradeable.* Although intuitively perhaps less appealing, this assumption is the opposite of assumption 2. In this case the numerator of ω consists of $\{\theta_2E_2^3 + \alpha_2(-e_2^3)\}$, while that of ω^*

only holds the production term $\alpha_2^* (-e_2^{3*})$, so that ω tends to exceed ω^*. More importantly, m_2^* is zero so that the antiorthodox presumption is clear.

(4) *Each country produces only its nontraded good and its exportable and consumes only its nontraded good and its importable.* This is the model, [5], I recently explored in detail, and represents a combination of assumptions 2 and 3. The direct income effects are strongly antiorthodox since m_2^* vanishes. However, the indirect effects working through substitution between traded and nontraded goods depend on the balance between supply and demand elasticities. The forms for ω and ω^* reveal that an antiorthodox presumption for the indirect effects emerges only if $(\theta_2 E_2^3)$ $(\theta_1^* E_1^{3*})$ exceeds $(\alpha_1 e_1^3)$ $(\alpha_2^* e_2^{3*})$. As discussed in detail in Jones [5] this can be translated into the Robinson [9] criterion that the product of demand elasticities for importables (and imports) exceeds the product of supply elasticities for exportables (and exports). The weight that should be attached to this term depends in large part on how significant the nontraded sectors in the two economies are (in the sense of m_3 and m_3^*). If tradeables loom large in national incomes, the antiorthodox presumption prevails.

Throughout this discussion no explicit details of each country's productive technology and resource base have been assumed other than that transformation surfaces (or curves if only two commodities are produced) are strictly bowed-out from the origin and that all goods are substitutes in production. Chipman examines a case in which transformation surfaces are 'ruled' in the sense that many combinations of three commodities may be produced at a given set of relative prices. This is a phenomenon that can occur if a country produces more commodities than it has factors of production, and all production functions exhibit constant returns to scale. Any hint of indeterminacy is dispelled once the requirement is made that production of nontradeables in each country must balance local demand. Nonetheless, the mechanism whereby this is achieved in each country differs from that spelled out above.

Consider the home country and imagine it possesses two factors of production, capital and labor, and produces all three commodities. At given terms of trade, factor prices are uniquely determined and, of necessity, the cost and price of the nontraded commodity as well. Therefore with transfer *at the initial given terms of trade*, no relative prices change and the terms ωm_3 and $\omega^* m_3^*$ in criterion (1) disappear. However, output of commodity 2 can change, not because price changes shift resources about, but because the fall in home demand for nontradeables (the direct income effect of the transfer) causes resources to be released to the tradeable goods sector at constant prices. The crucial feature about teachnology that dictates the direction and extent of change in production of importables is the comparison of capital/labor requirements in the three industries. In the earlier argument (where a transfer led to a fall in the price of nontradeables at home) production of importables at home increased. In the case of *diversification* (Chipman's term for all three goods being produced in a two-factor setting) production of commodity 2 could actually fall. This would certainly be the case if, say, the home good were more labor intensive than either traded good, and exportables at home were more labor intensive than importables. For then the tradeables goods sector would have to absorb a bundle of newly released labor and capital that was more labor intensive than either traded commodity, and this can be accommodated only by an increase in labor-intensive exportables and an actual reduction in production of importables. Not surprisingly, this leads to a strong orthodox presumption that p_2/p_1 will have to rise to clear markets.

Chipman presents a series of theorems applicable to cases in which one or both countries diversifies to all three commodities. Of these I comment on only one: suppose both countries have identical homothetic utility functions and, as well, identical production functions. Then a transfer leaves the terms of trade unaffected. The only way in which trade can exist is if factor endowments differ. But with relative prices constant, output changes in one country exactly balance and counteract output changes in the other. With demand conditions also identical, the transfer does not change the world excess demand for the second commodity. Perhaps this result is not surprising, but note that it depends on the assumption that each country produces all three commodities in a two-factor world. If, instead, there were a third factor, insuring strictly bowed-out transformation surfaces, the theorem need not hold. Despite the assumption that utility and production functions are identical, factor endowments must be different or else there would be no trade. This implies that the transformation surfaces also differ, and there is no reason to suspect, say, that e_2^3 and e_2^{3*} would be the same.

One feature common to all these models (except the exchange model) is that production of tradeable commodities can change at the initial terms of trade. This complication is absent in the model without nontraded commodities, leading to the especially simple form of criterion (1) whereby only differences in taste patterns are involved. Two types of production changes have been discussed: those called forth by changes in the price of nontradeables in each country and, in the case of ruled surfaces, those called forth by a change in resources required by the nontraded sector at constant prices. But in either case the thrust of change is in the direction of greater production of tradeables in the transferring country and lower production of tradeables in the recipient country. If exportables in each country bear the main impact of these production changes, as would of necessity be the case if each country specialized to exportables and nontradeables, the orthodox bias in these production changes is clear: world supply of the transferor's exportable rises. To balance such a picture, the discussion in Caves and Jones [1] suggested that a transfer may involve resources as well as purchasing power. Thus even if all prices are constant, the recipient country may *expand* production of all goods, including tradeables, and the transferor *contract* production of all goods. The bias imparted by any tendency to concentrate resources in the commodity exported then runs in the opposite, antiorthodox direction.

My objective in this chapter is not to come down firmly in the antiorthodox camp. Instead it is to explore the ways in which asymmetries between countries may prejudice the issue. The essence of trade is that there are asymmetries, and to the extent that the trade pattern reflects taste differences, the anti-orthodox presumption is supported both in the direct income effects and the indirect effects working through substitution terms. If there exist direct production effects as well, as in the case of a transfer of resources, such an antiorthodox bias may be enhanced. The orthodox bias leans on a presumption of supply differences explaining trade patterns, as well as a judgement that production generally responds more sensitively to price than does demand.

Appendix I: The transfer criterion

The first task in deriving criterion (1) is to solve for the change in the price of nontraded goods in each country *at the initial terms of trade* when the home country makes a transfer ($\mathrm{d}T$ in units of its exportables) to the foreign country. Let D denote demand and x production. Let commodity 1 serve as numeraire so that its price p_1 remains constant. Since the terms of trade are being held fixed, p_2 is also constant. Therefore only p_3 can vary, and the market-clearing equation for nontradeables at home can be written as

$$D_3(p_3, y) = x_3(p_3).$$

The term y denotes real income measured in units of commodity 1. Differentiating,

$$E_3^3\hat{p}_3 + \frac{1}{D_3}\frac{\partial D_3}{\partial y}\,\mathrm{d}y = e_3^3\hat{p}_3,$$

where E_3^3 is the own substitution elasticity in demand (negative) and e_3^3 is the own substitution elasticity for nontradeables in supply (and must be positive). (A circumflex over a variable denotes a relative change in that variable.) At unchanged terms of trade the change in real incomes at home, $\mathrm{d}y$ in units of exportables, equals $-\mathrm{d}T$, and $(p_3/p_1)(\partial D_3/\partial y)$ is the marginal propensity to consume nontradeables, m_3. Solving for $\hat{p}_3$,

$$\hat{p}_3 = -\frac{m_3}{p_3 D_3\{-E_3^3 + e_3^3\}} p_1 \mathrm{d}T.$$

The price of nontradeables falls at home. By analogy it rises abroad, and $\hat{p}_3^*$ is given by

$$\hat{p}_3^* = \frac{m_3^*}{p_3^* D_3^*\{-E_3^{3*} + e_3^{3*}\}} p_1 \mathrm{d}T.$$

World excess demand for the home country's importable, commodity 2, is given by $\{D_2 + D_2^* - x_2 - x_2^*\}$. At given prices for traded goods each change in demand depends on the change in the price of nontradeables and real income, and production changes (along transformation surfaces) depend only upon the price of nontradeables. Thus the *value* of the change in world excess demand for commodity 2 is

$$\{p_2 D_2 E_2^3 \hat{p}_3 - m_2 p_1 \mathrm{d}T\} + \{p_2 D_2^* E_2^{3*} \hat{p}_3^* + m_2^* p_1 \mathrm{d}T\}$$
$$-p_2 x_2 e_2^3 \hat{p}_3 - p_2 x_2^* e_2^{3*} \hat{p}_3^*.$$

Substitute the solutions for $\hat{p}_3$ and $\hat{p}_3^*$ to obtain

$$p_2 \mathrm{d}\{D_2 + D_2^* - x_2 - x_2^*\} = p_1 \mathrm{d}T \left\{ (m_2^* - m_2) + \frac{[\theta_2^* E_2^{3*} - \alpha_2^* e_2^{3*}]}{[-\theta_3^* E_3^{3*} + \alpha_3^* e_3^{3*}]} m_3^* - \frac{[\theta_2 E_2^3 - \alpha_2 e_2^3]}{[-\theta_3 E_3^3 + \alpha_3 e_3^3]} m_3 \right\}.$$

For substitution effects in consumption, $\Sigma p_j \mathrm{d}D_j = 0$, which implies that $\Sigma_j \theta_j E_j^3 = 0$. Along the transformation surface $\Sigma_j p_j \mathrm{d}x_j = 0$ so that $\Sigma_j \alpha_j e_j^3 = 0$ as well. Recall that θ_j is the share of income spent on commodity j, and α_j is the share of income represented by the production of commodity j. Therefore if all goods are substitutes, the coefficients of m_3 and m_3^* are positive fractions, the ω and ω^* terms shown in the text. Inequality (1) emerges as the condition for a transfer to result in an excess world demand for the home country's importable at the initial terms of trade.

Appendix II: The stability criterion

The concept of Hicksian imperfect stability, whereby an increase in p_j causes excess supply to be created in the jth market when markets other than the jth market (and the numeraire market) are cleared, is appropriate to this model with its distinction between traded and nontraded goods. Still retaining the home country's export commodity (1) as numeraire, the market for traded commodity 2 is deemed to be imperfectly stable if a rise in p_2 creates world excess supply of commodity 2 assuming the prices of nontradeables in each country, p_3 and p_3^*, adjust to clear nontraded goods markets. This appendix derives this condition for stability in order (i) to illustrate how the transfer criterion (eq. (1) of the text) is imbedded in the criterion for market stability, and (ii) to demonstrate how the criterion for the model with nontraded goods can easily be related to the form of the stability expression for the classic 2-traded goods model exhibited in Caves and Jones [2].

Stability requires the derivative of world excess demand for commodity 2, $\{(D_2 + D_2^*) - (x_2 + x_2^*)\}$, to be negative with respect to p_2. Cast in relative changes, stability in the world market requires:

$$\left\{\lambda\left(-\frac{\hat{D}_2}{\hat{p}_2}\right) + \lambda^*\left(-\frac{\hat{D}_2^*}{\hat{p}_2}\right)\right\} + \left\{\rho\left(\frac{\hat{x}_2}{\hat{p}_2}\right) + \rho^*\left(\frac{\hat{x}_2^*}{\hat{p}_2}\right)\right\} > 0, \qquad \text{(A1)}$$

where

$$\lambda \equiv \frac{D_2}{D_2 + D_2^*}, \qquad \lambda + \lambda^* = 1,$$

$$\rho \equiv \frac{x_2}{x_2 + x_2^*}, \qquad \rho + \rho^* = 1.$$

In words, the sum of two weighted averages – of relative demand changes and relative production changes – must be positive, the weights reflecting consumption shares and production shares for each country. If no nontraded goods were included in the model, criterion (1) would reduce to:

$$\{\lambda(-E_2^2) + \lambda^*(-E_2^{2*})\} + \{\rho e_2^2 + \rho^* e_2^{2*}\} > \mu(m_2^* - m_2) \qquad \text{(A2)}$$

where

$$\mu \equiv \frac{M}{D_2 + D_2^*} \quad \text{and} \quad M \equiv D_2 - x_2.$$

All the income effects are swept together in the right-hand expression. The substitution terms of the left-hand side must be positive, so that stability is guaranteed if $m_2 > m_2^*$, the criterion in this simple model for the antiorthodox result in the event of transfer. If the orthodox result prevails, the term μ, which is a fraction that is small if trade represents a small part of total world production or consumption, dampens the potentially destabilizing aggregate of the income effects when the marginal propensity to consume a commodity is greater for the exporter than for the importer.

As I now proceed to demonstrate, the condition for market stability when nontraded goods markets exist, with prices always adjusting to clear markets, is shown by

$$\{\lambda[(-E_2^2) - \omega E_2^3] + \lambda^*[(-E_2^{2*}) - \omega^* E_2^{3*}]\} + \{\rho[e_2^2 - \omega(-e_2^3)] + \rho^*[e_2^{2*} - \omega^*(-e_2^{3*})]\} > \mu\{[m_2^* + \omega^* m_3^*] - [m_2 + \omega m_3]\}. \tag{A3}$$

The terms, ω and ω^*, are as defined in the text. Once again, the net income effects are shown in the right-hand side, and this must be negative if, in the context of the model with nontraded goods, a transfer would improve the terms of trade for the transferor – the antiorthodox result. As previously, the left-hand side averages the substitution effects of price changes on the demand and production of commodity 2 in the two countries. But the substitution terms now include not only the direct impact of a change in the terms of trade, but the indirect effect of the change in the price of nontradeables. For example, when p_2 rises, home substitution effects cut back demand for import commodity 2 – this is what E_2^2 captures. But if the price of nontradeables, p_3, is forced to rise some demand is deflected back towards the second commodity if, as I assume, all goods are net substitutes. This indirect effect is expressed by ωE_2^3 and, as will be shown, the term ω refers to the fractional rise in the price of nontradeables relative to the rise in tradeable p_2 assuming away all income effects. Since ω is a fraction, and E_2^3 and E_2^1 (both assumed positive) add up to $(-E_2^2)$ (by homogeneity), the coefficient of λ in (A3) must still be positive: a rise in p_2 causes a substitution away from commodity 2.

The derivation of (A3) from basic stability expression (A1) depends on the specification of demand and output functions. Consider just the home country. With commodity 1 the numeraire, let

$$D_2 = D_2(p_2, p_3, y) \tag{A4}$$

so that

$$\hat{D}_2 = E_2^2 \hat{p}_2 + E_2^3 \hat{p}_3 + \frac{p_1}{p_2 D_2} m_2 \mathrm{d}y. \tag{A5}$$

Similarly, for outputs,

$$x_2 = x_2(p_2, p_3) \tag{A6}$$

so that

$$\hat{x}_2 = e_2^2 \hat{p}_2 + e_2^3 \hat{p}_3. \tag{A7}$$

With this breakdown all that remains is (i) to determine real income changes ($\mathrm{d}y$ and, abroad, $\mathrm{d}y^*$) and (ii) to solve for market-clearing $\hat{p}_3$ (and $\hat{p}_3^*$) relative to the terms of trade change, $\hat{p}_2$.

The existence of nontraded commodities does not alter the basic relationship given in (A8) to show that a deterioration

$$\mathrm{d}y = -\frac{p_2 M}{p_1}\hat{p}_2 \tag{A8}$$

in the terms of trade worsens real income by an amount proportional to the value of trade (and $\mathrm{d}y^* = -\mathrm{d}y$). The market-clearing condition for nontradeables, shown by (A9),

$$D_3(p_2, p_3, y) = x_3(p_2, p_3) \tag{A9}$$

can be differentiated to yield

$$\frac{\hat{p}_3}{\hat{p}_2} = \frac{\{E_3^2 - e_3^2\}}{\{-E_3^3 + e_3^3\}} - \frac{p_2 M m_3}{p_3 D_3\{-E_3^3 + e_3^3\}}. \tag{A10}$$

With commodities assumed net substitutes, the first term is a positive fraction ('own price' p_3 has a stronger impact on nontradeables than does p_2). That is, if income effects could be ignored, a rise in p_2 would cause p_3 to rise, but relatively not by as much. Indeed, since, for example, $\theta_3 E_3^2$ always equals $\theta_2 E_2^3$, the first term is precisely the ω-term defined in eq. (2) of the text.

Final confirmation that expression (A3) correctly states the condition for market stability can be obtained by substituting the breakdowns of $\hat{D}_2$ and $\hat{x}_2$ (eqs. (A5) and (A7)), together with (A8) and (A10), into (A3), with comparable substitutions for foreign terms.

References

[1] Caves, R.E. and R.W. Jones, *World Trade and Payments* (Little, Brown, Boston, 1973) ch. 22.

[2] Caves, R.E. and R.W. Jones, *World Trade and Payments: An Introduction*, 2nd edn. (Little, Brown, Boston, 1977) p. 426.

[3] Chipman, J.S., 'The Transfer Problem Once Again', in: G. Horwich and P.A. Samuelson, eds., *Trade, Stability, and Macroeconomics* (Academic Press, New York, 1974).

[4] Johnson, H.G., 'The Transfer Problem: A Note on Criteria for Changes in the Terms of Trade', *Economica* (May 1955).

[5] Jones, R.W., 'Trade with Non-Traded Goods: The Anatomy of Inter-Connected Markets', *Economica* (May 1974).

[6] McDougall, I., 'Non-Traded Goods and the Transfer Problem', *The Review of Economic Studies* (January 1965).

[7] McDougall, I., 'Non-Traded Commodities and the Pure Theory of International Trade', in: McDougall and Snape, eds., *Studies in International Economics* (North-Holland, Amsterdam, 1970).
[8] Pearce, I., *International Trade* (Macmillan, London, 1970).
[9] Robinson, J., 'Beggar-My-Neighbor Remedies for Unemployment', in: A.E.A., *Readings in the Theory of International Trade* (Blakiston, Philadelphia, 1949).
[10] Samuelson, P.A., 'The Transfer Problem and Transport Costs: The Terms of Trade when Impediments are Absent', *Economic Journal* (June 1952).
[11] Samuelson, P.A., 'The Transfer Problem and Transport Costs, II: Analysis of Effects of Trade Impediments', *Economic Journal* (June 1954).
[12] Samuelson, P.A., 'On the Trail of Conventional Beliefs About the Transfer Problem', in: Bhagwati, Jones, Mundell and Vanek, eds., *Trade, Balance of Payments, and Growth* (North-Holland, Amsterdam, 1971).

Chapter 11

TERMS OF TRADE AND TRANSFERS: THE RELEVANCE OF THE LITERATURE*

1. Introduction

There are occasional periods in modern history when actual or contemplated international transfers of income and purchasing power assume significant proportions: the post World War I reparations imposed on Germany after the Treaty of Versailles; Marshall Plan aid to Europe after World War II; private international capital movements to Canada and the United States in the nineteenth century or to Israel in the past two decades. To these classic examples the early 1970s have added the redistribution of income and wealth involved in the striking rise in prices of some raw materials and foodstuffs and, especially, of oil, and the attendant problem of 'recycling'. Over the years there has developed a large literature in the theory of international trade dealing with the 'transfer problem', in part prompted by these historical episodes. My purpose in this chapter is to discuss the relevance of some of this literature to the current world situation.

The 'transfer problem' has many guises. Basically the literature asks about the consequences of country A making a unilateral payment (loan, reparation, or gift) to country B. What happens to international prices, to domestic prices, to real incomes or consumptions, to the internal distribution of income in each country (to real wages, rents)? How is the payment financed at home or redistributed abroad? Is the transfer actually made, or is it under-affected – or over-affected?

* Chapter 4 in Leipziger, D., ed., *The International Monetary System and the Developing Nations* (A.I.D., Washington, D.C., 1976) 99–114. I wish to thank Eitan Berglas and Michael Mussa for helpful discussions. This chapter was prepared for the Agency for International Development's Conference on the International Financial System and the Concerns of Developing Nations, 4 June 1975, in Washington, D.C.

Are aggregate employment levels disturbed? What happens to the volume of goods and services produced in each country? in the world? Some models have been designed to capture some of these features, others to ignore some while concentrating on alternative questions.

Most treatments of the transfer process begin their stories by asking how markets are disturbed by one country making a payment to another assuming the *terms of trade remain constant*. This is a useful assumption, even when the question ultimately being asked deals with the effect of a transfer on changing the terms of trade, for in a stable market this question depends on whether the transfer creates an excess world demand for the transferor's import commodity at the initial prices. Nonetheless, recent events have been dominated by significant changes in the terms of trade, *not* because of transfer payments, but for reasons having to do with the success of the OPEC cartel and the general changes in world demands and supplies of basic commodities. These changes in the prices of internationally traded commodities are themselves the *instigators* of the transfer.

To elaborate, any change in a relative price implies a transfer of real income from the net buyer of the commodity that has risen in price to the net seller. Thus the core of the 'transfer problem' can be found in the analysis of price changes. I therefore begin my discussion of the relevance of the transfer literature by analyzing the impact on an economy of an exogenous change in its terms of trade, assuming that the economy adjusts its spending fully to the new circumstances. If the price of oil rises to a country that is a net importer of oil, I ask how prices and production are affected assuming the country's real spending fully adjusts to the loss of real income imposed on it by the adverse movement in its terms of trade. Such adjustment has typically *not* taken place recently in some oil-importing states. Instead, countries hit by rising oil prices have tended to resist the decline in living standards by running trade deficits. These deficits have in part been made possibly by the failure of OPEC countries to expand their current expenditure levels to match higher incomes. This 'restraint' may in some cases be involuntary. However, it does represent another form of *transfer*: from the countries who have gained (from previous improvements in their terms of trade) to those who have lost. Therefore I follow the analysis of the impact of a change in the terms of trade assuming full adjustment with a succeeding analysis of the transfer problem *per se* – with this transfer really moderating the extent to which the 'losing' countries need cut their current living standards.

The picture which emerges is a stereotype of a two-country world: country A gets hit by a deterioration in its terms of trade, but has its required adjustment cushioned by a transfer from country B. If A is a Western Europe plus the United States (and Japan?) and B the Middle East oil-producing states, perhaps not too much violence is done to the facts. But what about other countries? I conclude the chapter with some remarks on how other countries may be affected indirectly by the fall-out from adjustments made by countries A and B as they adjust both to the terms of trade change and the transfer.

2. The impact of a change in the terms of trade

A rise in import prices relative to export prices causes an aggregate real income loss that is proportional both to the extent of the deterioration in the terms of trade ($-\Delta p_m$, where p_m is the price of imports and p_x is the assumed constant price of exports) and the volume of affected imports (M). In relative terms call the fall in real income, as a fraction of overall income, $\hat{y}$. Then

$$\hat{y} = -\frac{p_m M}{Y}\tilde{p}_m.$$

That is, if imports are approximately 10% of incomes, and if import prices rise 50%, real incomes fall by roughly 5%. This is the 'transfer' brought about by the change in the terms of trade.

Of course all sectors of the community need not suffer the same loss of real income. Factors of production which are used only in domestic import-competing sectors can expect a rise in incomes.[1] Factors specific to other sectors will have higher than average real income losses, while factors of production mobile between sectors might find their real incomes relatively unaffected (with incomes in terms of importables falling, but rising in terms of exportables).[2]

Trade literature has recently shown a revived interest in economies in which some goods are produced and consumed locally but cannot enter international trade because transport costs are too high. In such a world it is legitimate to ask what effect a rise in import prices may have on local prices of nontradeables. For a small country unable to influence directly the price of tradeables, the answer to this question helps reveal the extent to which price disturbances from abroad are

[1] Assuming the price of that kind of import rises. If some import-competing prices remain constant or fall, factors specific to that industry must suffer. McKinnon [11] has made this point on the export side: if some exportables go up in price, other exportables are likely to be hurt.

[2] A formal model for the specific-factors case was developed in Jones [6]. Recently Ruffin and Jones [17] have suggested there is a presumption that the mobile factor may lose real income if the commodity that rises in price is imported. Further comments on income distribution in the context of the oil crisis are found in Mussa [14].

transmitted in magnified or diluted form to the price level as local prices react. One difficulty in analyzing the problem is that the familiar two by two world is left behind if one wishes explicitly to have an importable sector, an exportable sector, and a sector producing non-tradeables. In a recent article [7] I tried to circumvent this problem by making an assumption that may have relevance for some LDCs: production is concentrated in exportables and nontradeables and consumption is confined to importables and nontradeables.

In such a case would a rise in import prices, assuming export prices constant, serve to raise or lower the price of nontradeables? The answer is ambiguous. It depends on the relative strength of income and substitution effects. As the price of importables rises, some demand is deflected towards nontradeables, and this serves to push up their price. However, the deterioration in the terms of trade has served to lower real incomes. Indeed, the expression for the real income loss is precisely the same as previously stated – the relative fall in real income is given by the share of income devoted to importables times the percentage deterioration in the terms of trade. This loss in real income will in part be transmitted to the market for nontradeables via the marginal propensity to consume nontradeables.

In this model there is a simple criterion that nets out the substitution and income effects: a rise in the price of importables (with the prices of other tradeables constant) serves to *depress* the local price of nontradeables if and only if the uncompensated demand for imports is inelastic. The logic is simple: the price of nontradeables will fall if an excess supply is created at the initial price of nontreadeables. At the initial price, production remains constant as only exportables and nontradeables are produced and their prices are held fixed. Also, money income from production remains constant. But the price of imports has risen, and this entails a greater expenditure on imports if the uncompensated elasticity of demand for imports is less than unity. If so, less is available for spending on nontradeables. That is, supply would be unchanged but demand for nontradeables would fall at the initial prices for nontradeables. To clear their market, the price of nontradeables would have to fall in a stable market.

The lines of the argument are not altered in fundamental forms in the more general case in which exportables are also consumed and some import-competing production takes place. The fate of the price of nontradeables hinges on a comparison of substitution and income effects.[3]

Note the crucial role played in the above by the assumption that the loss of real income is transmitted to current consumption. The budget constraint underlying

[3]This is set out in Jones [7, p. 136].

demand behavior was of the classic form: all income derives from current production and is currently spent. Thus in equilibrium the country experiencing the rise in import prices nonetheless adjusts to a balance of trade equilibrium: expenditures are cut in real terms to match the loss of real income. This is clearly not the stereotype of the typical Western European oil-importing country, for whom a rise in oil prices was matched by balance of payments deficits. In part, of course, this reflects the accompanying 'transfer' from OPEC to the oil-consuming countries, and this will be discussed below. But first consider what a simple monetary story might reveal about the impact of higher import prices on the balance of payments. To begin the analysis, return to the case of an economy with fixed export prices and producing only tradeable goods.

Let the demand for money, Z, depend upon real income, y, and the price level, P.[4] Real income is defined as the value of production, Y, deflated by the price level, which weights the importable and exportable prices by the consumption weights. Thus,

$$Z = f(y, P).$$

Let E_Z^y be defined as the elasticity of money demand with respect to real income at a constant price level, $f_y \cdot (y/Z)$. I assume that a doubling of the price level at constant real income will double the demand for money. Thus, taking relative changes,

$$\hat{Z} = E_Z^y \hat{y} + \hat{P}.$$

(A ˆ over a variable denotes a relative change.)

With p_x remaining constant and p_m, the price of importables, rising,

$$\hat{P} = \theta_m \hat{p}_m,$$

where θ_m is the share of aggregate consumption devoted to the importable good. By contrast,

$$\hat{y} = -(\theta_m - \alpha_m)\hat{p}_m,$$

where α_m is the share of income devoted to production of importables. This is precisely the same expression as set out previously for $\hat{y}$, $-(p_m M/Y)\hat{p}_m$. Therefore two forces react on the demand for money balances: the rise in the price level, P, serves by an equal relative amount to raise the demand for money. The deterioration in real income, however, lowers the demand for money. If unity is a reason-

[4] To keep the explanation simple, money is assumed to be the only asset. Thus no interest rate considerations are involved.

able value for the elasticity of the demand for money with respect to real income at constant price level, netting the two effects yields

$$\hat{Z} = \alpha_m \hat{p}_m.$$

The demand for money rises.[5] The price level rises proportionately to the share of *importables* in consumption, whereas real income falls proportionately to the share of *imports* in consumption (or income). If any local production of importables takes place the demand for money rises.

The monetary approach to the balance of payments stresses that if local supply of credit (money) is held constant, an increase in demand can only be met by running a surplus in the balance of payments. Thus this version of the monetary approach predicts that oil-importing countries will either run surpluses or, if no local production takes place, at least not have a balance of payments deficit.[6]

This analysis is moderated if the economy also produces nontradeables. If all incomes are spent, and the price of imports (p_m) rises with the price of exportables (p_x) constant, the price of nontradeables (p_n) may either rise or fall. In the simple model (in which no importables are produced and no exportables consumed), p_n rises if substitution effects are strong enough to make demand for imports elastic. In the general case (all goods produced and consumed), p_n rises if substitution effects in favor of increased demand for nontradeables (in both consumption and production) outweigh income effects (from the deterioration in the terms of trade) working to reduce p_n. If p_n does rise, the general level of prices rises unambiguously, and the story proceeds much as in the case uncomplicated by nontradeables. However, if substitution effects are relatively weak, p_n may fall and, as well, the general price index may fall. That is,

$$\hat{P} = \theta_m \hat{p}_m + \theta_x \hat{p}_x + \theta_n \hat{p}_n$$

and $\hat{p}_m$ is positive, $\hat{p}_x$ is zero, and $\hat{p}_n$ is, in this case, negative. Is there any limit to the relative fall in p_n? No – this can be exceedingly sharp if substitution possibilities are very limited.

If the price level falls for a country faced with a rising price of imports, the monetary view of the balance of payments suggests a deficit. The fall in real in-

[5]More directly, the demand for money, Z, could be written as $Z = kY$, where Y is the money value of income produced.

[6]Note the similarity to the analysis of devaluation for a small country, e.g. in Dornbusch [3]. In that case also the price level rises (all tradeables go up in price). But the terms of trade remain constant, so there is not the loss of real income as in the present case. What the present analysis shows, however, is that the real income loss lowers the demand for money by less than the rise in the price level has raised it if any production of importables takes place.

come (as the terms of trade deteriorate) encourages a decline in the demand for money balances, and this is no longer outweighed or nullified by a rise in demand for monetary balances to cope with a rising price level. Assuming control over the supply of money, the fall in monetary demand eventuates in deficits in the balance of payments.

Two final comments need to be added to this monetary version of a rise in oil prices. First, the monetary adjustment is transitory. Even if the prices of some imports rise and stay higher, a relatively short period of surpluses may be all that is required to raise money stocks to the new higher level. After that the monetary impact vanishes. And, for countries not producing any oil, the price level and real income effects may cancel. Second, note that if *all* countries attempted to keep money supplies constant, so that the world money supply is not allowed to expand, a rise in the price of some goods (oil) must eventually be matched by a fall in other prices. The world economy is a closed economy, and the price level depends endogenously on the world money supply.

3. The transfer process

The preceding account of adjustment to a terms of trade change does not capture the essence of recent disturbances, for it ignores the attempt of some countries whose terms of trade have worsened nonetheless to keep current real expenditures from falling commensurately as well as the failure of countries whose terms of trade have improved to expand current expenditures by the full amount. This is like a transfer, running counter to, and moderating the influence of, the initial real income transfer embedded in the terms of trade change. In this section I discuss the transfer literature in search of criteria of relevance to the current situation.

The most simple, classic, case has country *B* transferring purchasing power to country *A*, assuming all incomes (including the transfer) are spent, full employment is maintained, and each country produces and consumes only importables and exportables. The key question concerns the extent of dissimilarities in the two countries' taste patterns. If the receiving country were to expand its consumption in precisely the same form as the paying country contracts its spending, no world excess demand or supply is created at the initial prices for traded goods. Thus no relative prices change, the receiving country spends more than its produced income by precisely the amount of the transfer and overall balance of payments equilibrium is maintained with no price or exchange rate changes required.

The 'orthodox' presumption[7] posited a difference in spending behavior, with each country having a higher marginal propensity to spend on its own export good than did the other country for that same good. This would tend to create a 'secondary burden' for the transferor. Let T denote the amount of purchasing power transferred from B to A, and concentrate on the impact of such a transfer on the market for B's export good at the initial terms of trade. No production changes occur along either country's transformation curve (since the relative price is given). Demand in A for both goods rises. In particular, A's demand for B's export good rises by the marginal propensity to import A, m_A, times the amount of transfer, T. In country B, demand for B's export good falls. Let m_B indicate B's marginal propensity to consume its own import good. Thus B's demand for B's export good falls by $(1 - m_B)T$. The 'orthodox' presumption is based on the biased assumption about tastes – that $(1 - m_B)$ exceeds m_A. Therefore at initial prices the transfer lowers net world demand for B's exports, and in order to have commodity markets clear, the transferor (B) must suffer a deterioration in its terms of trade. A transfer entails a 'direct burden', the transfer itself, and a 'secondary burden', the deterioration of the terms of trade.

This is the classic theme picked up by Keynes in arguing about German reparations. He worried about the required deterioration in the German relative export price in order to encourage the export surplus that would match the transfer. On theoretical grounds he was challenged by Ohlin,[8] and on practical grounds by the concurrent transfer of private funds to Germany during the 1920s and the subsequent cessation of payments.

An alternative phrasing of the transfer criterion asks about the changes in the trade balance that would be induced by the transfer itself without any changes in the terms of trade. Thus B's imports fall by $m_B T$ and A's imports rise by $m_A T$. Both changes contribute towards a trade surplus for country B. Is it enough? That depends on whether $(m_A + m_B)T$ exceeds or falls short of T, the amount of the transfer. Equilibrium requires B's trade surplus to match the transfer. In the 'orthodox' case, with $m_A + m_B$ less than unity, B's trade surplus is insufficient and the transfer is 'underaffected'. If prices are flexible, the solution previously cited is applicable: B suffers a deterioration in its terms of trade.

If prices are not responsive to market disequilibria the situation is more difficult to analyze. The popular story has country B suffering a deficit in its overall balance of payments, with reserves running down in B and up in A. What is left out of

[7] For a discussion of 'orthodoxy' as to presumption with the transfer problem see Samuelson [18], and Jones [5].

[8] See the two basic papers by Keynes [9], and Ohlin [15].

account is the commodity market disequilibrium and its connection to the budget constraint. It is implicitly assumed that country B actually spends an amount equal to what its received income would be if it could sell all the exports it desires at the initial (and sticky) prices, despite the fact that it cannot (there is, by assumption, excess supply of B). Similarly, there must exist inventories of country A's exports that are being sold to country B, but the receipts from which in country A do not get currently spent.[9] Variations on this story are quite possible.[10]

Recent interest in trade models with nontraded goods has spilled over to the transfer literature.[11] The setting is similar in most respects to the classical model just cited, except that an analysis of the impact of transfer at initial terms of trade is now complicated by endogenous movements in the prices of nontraded commodities in each country. The ambiguity in the direction of change of nontraded goods' prices, found for a terms of trade change in section 2, is absent in this case. If country B is the transferor, then at unchanged prices for tradeables, the price of nontradeables in B must fall – a consequence of the loss of spending in country B. In the recipient country there is an opposite effect: the rise in purchasing power contained in the transfer drives up the price of nontradeables in country A.

Putting these two parts together, suppose that country A suffers a worsening in its terms of trade (in the form of higher import prices at given export prices), but its suggested real spending cut is moderated by a subsequent transfer from country B. The substitution effect of the rise in import prices pulls the price of nontradeables upwards in country A. The real income effect works counter to this. But this should really be labelled the 'real spending' effect, and the transfer from B mitigates the cut in real spending. The upshot is that with the transfer receipt, country A is more likely to experience a rise in the price of nontradeables than without the receipt.

One consequence of the transfer-inflicted change in the relative price of nontradeables (compared to tradeables) in each country is that demand changes are no longer captured only by simple marginal propensities to consume. Rather, price elasticities of demand must also be compared. Perhaps a more striking contrast with the simple classical case is that at unchanged terms of trade there is nonetheless a shift of resources between tradeables and nontradeables in each country. World markets for tradeables are disturbed both by changes in demand

[9] This was the kind of assumption I made in an early paper [4] and it has recently been attacked by Mussa [13].

[10] See, for example, the discussion in Caves and Jones [1, ch. 4].

[11] For example, see McDougall [10], Pearce [16], Samuelson [19] Chipman [2], and Jones [8].

and supply, and the criterion for the impact of transfer on the terms of trade becomes more complicated.[12]

The direction of change in demands and supplies in the two countries can be stated quite easily in the (typical) case in which all three classes of commodities (importables, exportables, and nontradeables) are substitutes for each other in consumption and production. In the transferor (B), the fall in the price of non-tradeables deflects demand away from both importables and exportables and attracts resources to both tradeable goods. That is, net supply to the world of each kind of tradeable good rises as a consequence of reactions in the transferor. In receiving country (A), the opposite reaction takes place. With the price of non-tradeables bid upwards, country A's demand for both classes of traded goods rises, while resources are bid away from both importables and exportables. What is left unclear, of course, is the net impact on world markets.

Is there a presumption as to the transfer-induced change in the terms of trade that would be required to clear markets? One answer is that it might not matter much with these induced changes likely to be small. However, if the terms of trade do change, I have argued in Chapter 10 that any 'orthodox' presumption depends upon: (i) supply differences between countries being more pronounced than demand differences, and/or (ii) production being more responsive to price changes than is consumption. On the antiorthodox side would be any presumption that a country imports a commodity in part because of a relatively high marginal propensity to consume the commodity. For example, is the marginal propensity to consume oil greater in the United States (or England, or Italy) or in Saudi Arabia (or Kuwait or Nigeria)? This comparison, of course, is the basic one cited in the classical model without nontraded goods.

The transfer model that incorporates nontraded commodities illustrates that production of traded goods can be disturbed even at the initial terms of trade. But note the direction of change: the receiving country cuts down its production of both tradeables and the transferor expands production of importables and exportables. These changes in production are inspired by the rise in the price of non-tradeables in the receiving country and fall in the lending country. These results depend as well on a key assumption of the model: the transfer of purchasing power is for the purpose of expenditure on consumer goods instead of for the purpose of investment (or in the form of capital goods transfer, as from Germany to the Soviet Union in 1945 and 1946). Consider the alternative whereby productive capacity rises in the recipient country and falls (at least compared to what it would have been) in the transferor. These changes could encourage *greater*

[12] This issue is discussed in much more detail in Chipman [2], and in Chapter 10.

output of tradeables in the receiving country. Indeed, in Caves and Jones [1] it was argued that a transfer of real resources could be likened to a mixture of growth in the recipient country and decline in the transferor. Furthermore, this might yield an 'antiorthodox' presumption that the terms of trade could turn against the recipient, just as growth can damage a country's terms of trade.

All the models discussed so far have been characterized by the assumption that full employment is maintained. Any disturbance caused by a transfer affects spending patterns and perhaps production, but not employment. To conclude this discussion of transfer models I consider the Keynesian variant with rigid prices, unemployed resources, and positive marginal propensities to save.[13] It is a model in which outputs and employment are demand determined. Let Y^A and Y^B represent each country's level of output, as distinct from the level of disposable income in each country ($Y^A + T$, $Y^B - T$), where T represents a transfer of purchasing power from B to A. Outputs and disposable income are each distinguishable from expenditure levels, E^A and E^B. Finally, let R represent country A's trade surplus.

The basic equilibrium relationships, set out in the following pair of equations,

$$Y^A = E^A(Y^A + T) + R(E^A, E^B),$$

$$Y^B = E^B(Y^B - T) - R(E^A, E^B),$$

state that output in each country equals the sum of home and foreign demand for that country's output. What is the impact of a transfer from B to A? Formally the above equations can be differentiated totally with respect to T (assuming T is initially zero). Solutions would, of course, depend upon behavior relations in each country, such as the marginal propensity to save (e.g. $s^A \equiv 1 - \mathrm{d}E^A/\mathrm{d}(Y^{A_2} + T)$) and the marginal propensity to import out of an increase in expenditure (e.g. $m^A = -\partial R/\partial E^A$).

Certain features of the classical model survive in this Keynesian model. In the classical model the 'orthodox' presumption was that $(1 - m^A)$ exceeded m^B in which case the transfer from B to A would raise world demand for A's export product at the initial terms of trade. In the Keynesian model one can ask about the impact of the transfer on demand for A's product at initial levels of output. This increases if and only if

$$(1 - m^A)(1 - s^A) > m^B(1 - s^B).$$

The difference in the two criteria reflects the fact that in the Keynesian model, of

[13] For references see Metzler [12] and Swoboda and Dornbusch [20].

any increase in A's disposable income only the fraction $(1 - s^A)$ spills over into increased expenditures.

If the propensities to save in the two countries are not equal, nonclassical results can emerge. For example, at initial output levels the transfer reduces world demand for B's good (the 'orthodox' presumption) if and only if

$$(1 - m^B)(1 - s^B) > m^A(1 - s^A).$$

This criterion is the same as the criterion for the demand for A's output to rise if and only if s^A equals s^B. Pursuing this point, consider the impact of transfer on the sum of outputs in the two countries. The solution is

$$[\mathrm{d}Y^A + \mathrm{d}Y^B] = [s^B - s^A]\frac{\mathrm{d}T}{\Delta}$$

where $\Delta \equiv s^A s^B + m^A(1 - s^A)s^B + m^B(1 - s^B)s^A > 0$. The new element that the Keynesian model introduces is that the transfer may increase or reduce world levels of output and employment. As the expression shows, if the transfer is from a country with a high marginal propensity to save (OPEC?) towards a region with a lower marginal propensity to save (Western Europe?) levels of employment in the world rise. (Of course this neglects the original transfer embedded in the rise in oil prices, which works the other way.)

Note the two-layer set of questions introduced in the Keynesian transfer model. First, what does the transfer do to world levels of output and employment? This depends on the discrepancy between savings behavior at the margin between the lending and borrowing regions. Secondly, what does the transfer do to the *-allocation* of the world's demand between the two regions? Suppose savings propensities are equal so that world output levels are constant. A comparison of taste patterns at the margin discloses how individual output levels are affected, and the criterion is purely classical. For example, in the orthodox case in which $(1 - m^A)$ exceeds m^B, the transfer involves not only disposable income in the recipient country (A) rising and in the transferring country (B) falling (this it must do in any case),[14] but also output levels and employment rising in A and falling in B. By contrast, in the antiorthodox case in which the sum of marginal import propensities exceeds unity, when B makes a transfer to A world demand shifts towards B's product (since B's propensity to consume its own goods is less

[14]The formal solution is

$$[\mathrm{d}Y^A + \mathrm{d}T] = \frac{s^B}{\Delta}\mathrm{d}T \quad \text{and} \quad [\mathrm{d}Y^B - \mathrm{d}T] = -\frac{s^A}{\Delta}\mathrm{d}T.$$

than A's propensity to import), and there is no 'secondary burden' on B's level of employment. In A, disposable income rises but employment falls.[15]

4. Transfer, the terms of trade, and the position of LDCs

A search of the literature on transfers and terms of trade changes, some of which has been described in this chapter, fails to reveal that separate models are applicable to developed countries, on the one hand, and LDCs on the other. To conclude I sketch briefly my own views as to how and why this literature is of relevance to less developed countries.

The impact of a deterioration of a country's terms of trade on real incomes is no respector of income levels; higher import prices hurt regardless of whether *per capita* incomes are high or low. If the price of oil rises and the country produces no oil, real income in the LDC falls by approximately the fraction of national income devoted to oil consumption times the relative deterioration in the terms of trade. Of course other basic commodities have also changed in price. Has real income fallen for a country exporting sugar and importing oil? Here a comparison of the extent of price changes is not enough. For a small country facing changes in the prices of many commodities,

$$\hat{y} = \sum_{i} (\alpha_i - \theta_i)\hat{p}_i,$$

where, as before, α_i is the fraction of national income represented by the production of good i and θ_i the consumption share.[16] For many LDCs α_i is zero and θ_i positive for $i =$ oil. However, if the price of some other commodity, j, has risen and if j is exported, α_j exceeds θ_j and real income rises on that account. In many LDCs the pattern of production of exportables is highly concentrated. In this example the share of income represented by exports of sugar, say, could easily exceed by a multiple the share of income represented by imports of oil.

Some might emphasize that the possibilities for substitution between oil and other sources of energy (or out of energy into other inputs or commodities) are

[15] These remarks assume equal savings propensities in the two countries. In the general case

$$\frac{dY^A}{dT} = \frac{1}{\Delta}\left[(1 - m^A)(1 - s^A)\cdot s^B - m^B(1 - s^B)\cdot s^A\right],$$

with the comparable expression for country B. If savings propensities differ, a transfer may cause employment in both countries to rise (or to fall).

[16] This expression assumes competitive pricing and full employment so that resource reallocation has a negligible impact on real incomes.

more limited for LDCs than for developed countries. If so, is this reflected in the foregoing expression for real income changes? Yes. For finite price changes the expression for $\hat{y}$ is an approximation in which the share fractions α_i and θ_i should reflect an average of the shares before and after prices have changed. Compare two countries, each initially spending 10% of national income on oil imports. If in the LDC demand for oil is quite inelastic, while in the developed country demand is elastic, the θ_i appropriate for the LDC is greater than 10% and for the developed country less than 10%.

The discussion in section 2 on the impact of a change in the terms of trade on the local price of nontradeables is as applicable to LDCs as to developed countries. The crucial criterion weighed substitution against income effects. Again, if LDCs are typically represented by low substitution elasticities (for nontradeables *vis-à-vis* imports), the depressing effect of income losses on the price of nontradeables may dominate. As for the transitory monetary effects, these may be negligible if oil production is absent, assuming no local expansion of the credit base.

Section 3 of the paper, on the classical and Keynesian transfer mechanisms, seems to be more suited to the analysis of two large countries than to the situation of the LDCs. Such an impression would be superficial. It would be possible to alter the traditional two-country framework and, instead, deal with a tripartite LDC.DC.OPEC model. But this is probably not necessary. For any given LDC it is of importance to ask what net effect on world demand and supply of all tradeables is brought about by the transfer between the block of large developed countries and OPEC. In a sense, the LDCs are bystanders in the world market. The transfer mechanism is of relevance to them in that if taste and production patterns differ between DCs and OPEC, relative prices of all sorts of tradeables can change. An LDC producing exports demanded more heavily by OPEC countries than by the Western developed world can expect an induced terms of trade improvement. The transfer literature suggests that these issues are important – a redistribution of income and spending can affect world markets, including those commodities imported and exported by a small LDC.

Although the transfer literature concentrates on the composition of commodity expenditures and production, it is tempting to apply the spirit of the analysis to capital flows. In a sense the Keynesian model of transfer attempts this – it suggests that if the net transfer has been from oil-consuming states to OPEC, and if the marginal propensity to save in OPEC countries is relatively high, there will be a tendency for world unemployment to rise, the distribution among countries depending on the world pattern of spending and import propensities. But more directly, if OPEC is the gainer, how does the pattern of its aid and capital placement differ from those of the United States and Western Europe? Is it the case that LDCs are not allowed to run current account deficits to help cushion the import of higher oil prices? Any increase in OPEC aid to LDCs allows current deficits to be run.

Direct aid is one matter, commercial loans and investment another. Many commentators suggest that OPEC plans to recycle its new earnings primarily in the capital markets in New York and Europe, with LDCs left out. It is as if, for commodity expenditures, the OPEC marginal propensity to import from LDCs were negligible. But the analogy from commodity to capital markets has its limitations. An inflow of funds to Western capital markets can spill over and, through a lowering of interest rates, make funds more available and on better terms for the LDCs. This is not to deny that LDCs may have to pay higher rates or find it difficult to borrow at all commercial rates. This was probably the case before the oil crisis. The relevant question deals with the impact of the rise in oil price and the transfers on the state of world capital markets as viewed by LDCs. And the answer may consist broadly of (i) an increased 'need' or demand by LDCs for financing as an alternative to a real drop in current consumption levels, coupled with (ii) on balance more direct aid made available to at least some LDCs and (iii) perhaps marginal changes in the availability of private capital. For oil-importing LDCs, (i) may dominate; a deterioration in the terms of trade usually does involve some current loss in real spending as well as incomes.

The simple theme of the transfer literature runs throughout: a reallocation of world income affects prices, interest rates, and markets generally if tastes and production responses differ between gainers and losers. Even though oil-importing LDCs may count themselves among the relatively heavy losers, the taste and production differences that count may well be not their own (if these countries are small relative to world markets), but rather those of OPEC countries versus the larger developed countries. The transfer literature is of relevance to these LDCs, even at one stage removed.

References

[1] Caves, R. and R. Jones, *World Trade and Payments* (Little, Brown, 1973).

[2] Chipman, J., 'The Transfer Problem Once Again', in: Horwich and Samuelson, eds. *Trade, Stability, and Macroeconomics* (Academic Press, 1974) ch. 2.

[3] Dornbusch, R., 'Devaluation, Money and Non-traded Goods', *American Economic Review* (December 1973).

[4] Jones, R., 'Stability Conditions in International Trade: A General Equilibrium Analysis', *International Economic Review*, (May 1961).

[5] Jones, R., 'The Transfer Problem Revisited', *Economica* (May 1970) 178–184; also Chapter 9, this volume.

[6] Jones, R., 'A Three-Factor Model in Theory, Trade and History', in: Bhagwati *et al.*, eds., *Trade, Balance of Payments, and Growth* (North-Holland, Amsterdam, 1971); also Chapter 6, this volume.

[7] Jones, R., 'Trade with Non-traded Goods: The Anatomy of Interconnected Markets', *Economica* (May 1974).

[8] Jones, R., 'Presumption and the Transfer Problem', *Journal of International Economics*, 5 (1975) 263–274; also Chapter 10, this volume.

[9] Keynes, J., 'The German Transfer Problem', *Economic Journal* (March 1929).

[10] McDougall, I., 'Non-traded Goods and the Transfer Problem', *Review of Economic Studies* (1965).

[11] McKinnon, R., 'International Transfers and Nontraded Commodities: The Adjustment Problem', in: Leipziger, ed., The International Monetary System and the Developing Nations (A.I.D., 1976).

[12] Metzler, L., 'The Transfer Problem Reconsidered', *Journal of Political Economy* (June 1942).

[13] Mussa, M., 'Tariffs and the Balance of Payments: A Monetary Approach', in: Frenkel and Johnson, eds., The Monetary Approach to the Balance of Payments (Toronto, 1976).

[14] Mussa, M., 'Oil, Relative Prices and Macroeconomic Policy in an Open Economy', unpublished.

[15] Ohlin, B., 'The Reparation Problem: A Discussion', *Economic Journal* (June 1929).

[16] Pearce, I., *International Trade* (Macmillan, 1970).

[17] Ruffin, R. and R. Jones, 'Protection and Real Wages: The Neo-Classical Ambiguity', *Journal of Economic Theory*, 14 (April 1977) 337–348.

[18] Samuelson, P., 'The Transfer Problem and Transport Costs: The Terms of Trade When Impediments are Absent', *Economic Journal* (June 1952).

[19] Samuelson, P., 'On the Trial of Conventional Beliefs about the Transfer Problem', in: Bhagwati, Jones, Mundell and Vanek, eds., *Trade, Balance of Payments, and Growth* (North-Holland, Amsterdam, 1971).

[20] Swoboda, A. and R. Dornbusch, 'Adjustment, Policy, and Monetary Equilibrium in a Two-Country Model', in: Connolly and Swoboda, eds., *International Trade and Money* (Toronto, 1973) ch. 12.

PART IV

INTERNATIONAL FACTOR MOBILITY

INTRODUCTION TO PART IV

Ricardo's initial discussion of the concept of comparative advantage highlighted the second-best nature of free trade in commodities when factors of production are immobile internationally. The solution in which English labor produces cloth with technological methods inferior to those available to Portuguese labor is optimal only if English labor and/or Portuguese technology (or climate) is prevented from, or incapable of, moving across national boundaries. The Heckscher–Ohlin theory is similarly directed to showing how movements of commodities can substitute for international movements of productive factors. Of course if technologies are everywhere identical and if production is sufficiently diversified, factor prices become equalized between countries and the assumption that factors are trapped behind their national frontiers matters little in the analysis of world output patterns. Should production functions differ between countries, however, no presumption as to factor price equalization remains.

Chapter 12, based on earlier work of G.D.A. MacDougall [5] and Murray Kemp [2, 3], analyzes a model in which technology differs between countries and in which physical capital is free to locate globally where its return is maximized, subject to whatever taxes or subsidies on repatriated earnings of capital are imposed. The paramount question deals with the optimal combination of trade taxes and taxes on capital flows when both goods and capital are internationally mobile. The treatment in Chapter 12 encompasses not only the case in which one country has free exercise with the two tax instruments in maximizing its own real income subject to passive behavior abroad, but also two second-best situations in which international agreement precludes the use of one tax or the other. For example, a commitment to free trade puts additional stress on the tax on repatriated earnings from home capital located abroad. An increase in such a tax that serves to cause some capital to return home may drive up the return earned by remaining units of capital abroad but would also have an impact on commodity markets. Should an increase in the tax on capital income cause greater world production of the commodity exported by the tax-levying country, there may be a conflict between the two 'terms-of-trade' of welfare significance – the relative price of commodities and the return to exported capital. In such a case subsidies to capital exports may prove optimal.

Although production technology is assumed in Chapter 12 to differ between countries, the Heckscher–Ohlin assumption that capital earns the same return in both sectors of the economy (because it is mobile and nonspecific in its form) is maintained. This sets the basic technological relationship between the return to capital located abroad and the home country's commodity terms of trade. If the foreign country is completely specialized, these two prices can independently be altered, whereas if the foreign country is incompletely specialized, these two prices are locked together by the nature of foreign technology. This difference leads to the two strands of analysis pursued side-by-side in Chapter 12. Not considered there is the type of model analyzed in Chapter 6, in which capital is specific to the sector in which it is employed. In such a case the return to capital sent abroad depends *both* on the quantity of capital exported and upon the commodity terms of trade. Although details are not provided here, it is interesting to note that the general results described in Chapter 12 are robust with respect to the underlying assumption as to occupational specificity of capital.

To pursue this point briefly, consider the relationship between the return to capital exported abroad and the relative price of the home country's exports in the Heckscher–Ohlin model. Everything depends upon factor intensities abroad. If home exports are produced by capital-intensive techniques in the foreign country, an increase in the relative price of the capital-intensive commodity (the home exportable) drives up (by a magnified amount) the return to home-owned capital located abroad. In the alternative specific-capital model, will an improvement in the home country's commodity terms of trade tend to increase the return to home capital placed in the foreign country? A positive answer to this question requires the home country to export the commodity which uses the type of capital equipment that is also exported. Must this be the case? Obviously not, for the home export of capital used in producing good *j* promotes foreign production of good *j*. In terms of Ray Vernon's concept of the product cycle [7], a country may eventually import the commodity whose production abroad has been supported by previous exports of capital. So also, in a Heckscher–Ohlin world in which capital is not specific, an export of capital may so increase foreign production of the capital-intensive commodity that the home country may eventually export the labor-intensive good. Regardless of the underlying productive structure, the key question concerns the complementarity, or lack of it, between a nation's exports of commodities and capital.

In the original published version of Chapter 12 I claimed that if technologies differed between countries, it would be unusual to find both countries incompletely specialized in both commodities. For this remark I was properly taken to task by Murray Kemp and Ken-ichi Inada in [4] and by John Chipman in [1]. The issue is taken up in Chapter 13, in which taxes and tariffs are assumed away and, instead, the analysis focuses upon the world production pattern and capital location as the terms of trade are altered. If the world supply of mobile capital is within the proper bounds, and if the character of technology permits the relative costs of producing both commodities to be equated at a common return to capital (without assuming technologies are identical), there will exist a range of world outputs all corresponding to this particular terms of trade. In John Chipman's phrase [1], the world production-possibilities schedule will possess a 'flat'.[1]

The entire analysis in Part IV ignores the questions of economic growth associated with current production of capital goods. (One example of such an analysis is that of Negishi [6].) The reason for this omission is found not in the belief that current investment activity is unimportant, but rather in the desire to separate out the question of geographical *location* of an existing capital stock. This distinction between stocks and flows has its analogue in the balance of payments literature.

References

[1] Chipman, J., 'International Trade with Capital Mobility: A Substitution Theorem', in: Bhagwati, Jones, Mundell and Vanek, eds., *Trade, Balance of Payments, and Growth* (North-Holland, Amsterdam, 1971) pp. 201–237.

[2] Kemp, M., 'Foreign Investment and the National Advantage', *Economic Record*, 38 (March 1962).

[3] Kemp, M., 'The Gain from International Trade and Investment: A Neo-Heckscher-Ohlin Approach', *American Economic Review*, 56 (September 1966) 788–809.

[4] Kemp, M. and K. Inada, 'International Capital Movements and the Theory of International Trade', *Quarterly Journal of Economics* (August 1969).

[5] MacDougall, G.D.A., 'The Benefits and Costs of Private Investment from Abroad: A Theoretical Approach', *Economic Record*, 36 (March 1960).

[6] Negishi, T., 'Foreign Investment and the Long-Run National Advantage', *Economic Record*, 41 (December 1965).

[7] Vernon, R., 'International Investment and International Trade in the Product Cycle', *Quarterly Journal of Economics* (May 1966) 190–207.

[1] I also remark upon the matter of a Chipman 'flat' in Chapter 15.

Chapter 12

INTERNATIONAL CAPITAL MOVEMENTS AND THE THEORY OF TARIFFS AND TRADE*

1.

The main body of the pure theory of international trade is characterized by the assumption that commodities are mobile between countries while factors of production are not. Modifications of this extreme assumption must be made to allow an investigation of such questions as the consequences of the movement of labor from one country to another in response to differential awards or the possibility of foreign investment. In this latter connection interesting work has recently been undertaken by Murray Kemp and others[1] on the gains to a country to be derived from interfering with the free international flow of capital, especially in conjunction with an optimal strategy with regard to interference in the international flow of commodities via a tariff. This chapter represents an extension of this work and investigates the manner in which traditional trade theory must be modified to allow for capital movements.

The model to be discussed is the standard two-country, two-commodity model of trade in which labor is immobile internationally but either some of the capital resources of the home country are invested abroad or the home country's capital stock is augmented by foreign-owned capital. I shall be interested both in the case

* *Quarterly Journal of Economics*, 81 (February 1967) 1–38 (pp. 31–34 of section 7 have been deleted). I am indebted to the National Science Foundation and to the Social Science Research Council for support of this work. My interest in the subject was greatly stimulated by having access to early drafts of the paper by M.C. Kemp [9]. I have benefited from conversations with Nobuo Minabe, Winston Chang, Richard Caves and June Flanders.

[1] See Kemp [5, 6, 7]. See also MacDougall [10] and Balogh and Streeton [3]. In an interesting analysis of factor movements and the terms of trade, Akihiro Amano [1] compares the case of labor migration with that of capital movements.

in which capital flows are unimpeded and in the case in which the government of the home country controls the amount of net foreign investment by a tax on international capital movements. The government in the foreign country is assumed to remain passive in always following a policy of noninterference in commodity and factor markets. Competitive conditions and full employment prevail in the private sector in each country.

Several patterns of specialization are allowed. The case in which both countries are completely specialized is in some respects the easiest to analyze and served as a useful assumption in the earlier literature. However, as Kemp has suggested, the analysis of optimal tariff and tax policy changes significantly if, instead, the foreign country is incompletely specialized (see Kemp [9]). Much less importance in his analysis of optimal tariff and tax policy changes significantly if, instead, the foreign ized.[2] If capital is mobile between countries, whether or not impeded by a tax, complete specialization is apt to occur in at least one of the countries, regardless of the similarities or differences in technical knowledge as between the two countries.[3]

In the following three sections of this Chapter I shall be concerned with the case of *full optimization* – the home country is free to choose any tariff and tax rate it pleases with the aim of maximizing home welfare. This is the situation considered by Kemp. It turns out, however, that one reason usually cited for interfering with the free flow of capital – that restricting (or encouraging) foreign investment may alter the commodity terms of trade in the home country's favor – has no role to play in the case of full optimization. Partly for this reason I shall, in Section 5, discuss the case in which the tariff rate cannot be altered (say because of commercial agreements) but the home country is free to interfere with the movement of capital. The analysis at this point is focused on the way in which taxation of foreign investment might accomplish some of the same results as could be obtained by changing tariff rates. The role of capital movements in affecting real incomes is brought out by comparing this case with the one in which both tariffs and taxes can be levied.

Section 6 treats the case in which capital flows are not subject to regulation so that the rates of return to capital in the two countries (in this 'riskless' model of trade) must be equal. In some preliminary comments I shall discuss the new conditions for market stability that are appropriate to this model and the pos-

[2]As is explained later, in sections 5 and 6, there are cases in which the degree of specialization in the home country is important.

[3]In the original version of this paper the reasons for this were taken up in the last section. These have been deleted, since incomplete specialization in both countries is not the rare possibility suggested here. See the Introduction to Part IV and Chapter 13.

sibility that a tariff may worsen a country's terms of trade. Finally, I analyze the possibility that optimal tariff strategy in this model with free capital flows may lead to conclusions differing radically from the standard results for the traditional closed (no factor movements) model.

Such terms as 'capital movements' and 'export of capital' are used throughout the chapter in a specific sense that differs from traditional balance-of-payments terminology. In the subsequent analysis debits and credits on current account are always considered in balance. Foreign investment involves a change in location, but not in ownership, of real capital equipment. Generally two kinds of items appear in the current account: exports and imports of consumer goods and dividend or interest payments on foreign-owned capital or home-owned capital invested abroad.

2.

Because the early part of this chapter rests heavily on Kemp's analysis I shall adopt most of his notation. Thus D_i and X_i represent consumption and production of commodity i, and E_i, the excess demand, in the home country. Starred variables, such as D_i^* and X_i^* refer to quantities in the foreign country. With commodity 1 serving as numeraire, p and p^* represent home and world price, respectively, of commodity 2, and r and r^* denote the (rental) return to capital in each country.

In this section I develop a general expression to represent the dependence of real income in the home country upon the two variables (the terms of trade and the quantity of foreign investment) it hopes to influence by commercial and tax policies. But first consider the determinants of real income abroad. Assume an index of foreign social welfare, U^*, to depend only upon the bundle of goods consumed abroad:

$$U^* = U^*(D_1^*, D_2^*). \tag{1}$$

Furthermore, assume that no satiation or specialization in consumption takes place. Then total differentiation of (1) yields:

$$\frac{\mathrm{d}U^*}{U_1^*} = \mathrm{d}D_1^* + \frac{U_2^*}{U_1^*}\mathrm{d}D_2^*,$$

where U_i^* is the marginal utility of commodity i. $\mathrm{d}U^*/U_1^*$ is the change in foreign real income measured in units of commodity 1. Call this $\mathrm{d}y^*$. With the foreign price ratio equal to the marginal rate of substitution, obtain:

$$dy^* = dD_1^* + p^* dD_2^*. \tag{2}$$

The change in real income is the price-weighted change in the quantities consumed.

The budget constraint in the foreign country links the value of consumption to the value of production, with an adjustment made for repatriation of dividends or interest earned on that portion of the capital stock (K) owned by residents of the home country but invested in the foreign country. (If K is negative the foreign country is a net investor in the home country.) Thus:

$$D_1^* + p^* D_2^* = X_1^* + p^* X_2^* - r^* K. \tag{3}$$

The quantity of each commodity produced, X_i^*, depends upon the foreign price, p^*, and upon K. By differentiating (3) and using (2), it is possible to express the dependence of foreign real incomes on price changes, as in (4):

$$dy^* = -\{E_2^* dp^* + K dr^*\}. \tag{4}$$

To derive (4) use has been made of two simple kinds of aggregate relationships: (i) the price-weighted sum of changes in production along the transformation curve

$$\left\{ \frac{\partial X_1^*}{\partial p^*} + p^* \frac{\partial X_2^*}{\partial p^*} \right\},$$

is zero,[4] and (ii) the price-weighted sum of changes in production (at constant prices) resulting from an inflow of an extra unit of capital,

$$\left\{ \frac{\partial X_1^*}{\partial K} + p^* \frac{\partial X_2^*}{\partial K} \right\},$$

must equal the foreign rate of return to capital, r^*. Thus the change in foreign real income depends upon (a) its net trading position with the home country, as expressed by the quantity of foreign imports of goods (E_2^*) and of capital (K), and (b) changes in the commodity terms of trade (p^*) and the return to capital (r^*).

If the same procedure were attempted in order to derive an expression for the change in *home* real incomes, dy, difficulties would emerge in dealing with the

[4] If specialization is complete and p^* is not equal to the slope of the transformation schedule, each $\partial X_i^* \partial_p^*$ is zero. Otherwise the statement asserts that for small changes in price, changes in real income resulting from movements along the transformation schedule involve second-order smalls. Cf. Jones [4].

budget constraint. Home incomes are derived not only from production and dividends (or interest) on net capital invested abroad, but also from revenues flowing from taxation of capital and goods flows. These revenues depend partly on demands which are, in turn, linked to real incomes. Explicit concern with this element of mutual interdependence is avoided in Kemp's use of the market-clearing equation for goods. Each D_i is, in equilibrium, equal to world production $(X_i + X_i^*)$, less foreign demand, D_i^*. Since $\mathrm{d}y$ is the home-price-weighted sum of consumption changes, $\{\mathrm{d}D_1 + p\mathrm{d}D_2\}$, it can be expressed as in eq. (5):

$$\mathrm{d}y = \{\mathrm{d}X_1 + p\mathrm{d}X_2\} - \{\mathrm{d}E_1^* + p\mathrm{d}E_2^*\}. \tag{5}$$

The two simple kinds of aggregate relationships exploited in deriving $\mathrm{d}y^*$ are, with suitable modification, of use here as well. The domestic price-weighted sums of production changes along the home transformation curve,

$$\left\{\frac{\partial X_1}{\partial p} + p\frac{\partial X_2}{\partial p}\right\},$$

must go to zero, while the home rate of return to capital, r, must reflect the gain in income, at constant prices, that would accrue from an increment at home of one unit of capital,

$$-\left\{\frac{\partial X_1}{\partial K} + p\frac{\partial X_2}{\partial K}\right\}.$$

Thus the first bracketed expression in (5) reduces to $-r\mathrm{d}K$. Rewrite the second bracketed term as the *foreign-price*-weighted sum of excess demands, $\{\mathrm{d}E_1^* + p^*\,\mathrm{d}E_2^*\}$, plus a correction factor $(p - p^*)\mathrm{d}E_2^*$, to allow for any difference between home and foreign relative valuation of commodities. Now $\{\mathrm{d}E_1^* + p^*\,\mathrm{d}E_2^*\}$ is the difference between $\{\mathrm{d}D_1^* + p^*\,\mathrm{d}D_2^*\}$, which is $\mathrm{d}y^*$, and $\{\mathrm{d}X_1^* + p^*\,\mathrm{d}X_2^*\}$, which is just $r^*\,\mathrm{d}K$. With these simplifications, the expression for $\mathrm{d}y$ reduces to eq. (6):

$$\mathrm{d}y = \{E_2^*\mathrm{d}p^* + K\mathrm{d}r^*\} + \{(p^* - p)\mathrm{d}E_2^* + (r^* - r)\mathrm{d}K\}. \tag{6}$$

Two sets of changes can alter real income in the home country. The first is a favorable movement in the relative price of any commodity or factor exported by the home country. This is shown by the first bracket and represents, as well, an unfavorable change of the same amount in foreign real income (see eq. (4)). If home and foreign prices are identical, representing a case of noninterference in goods and factor markets, the second bracket disappears. However, with positive taxes and tariffs this latter term shows the gain in the home country's real income that can be obtained by an incremental shipment abroad of any item (good or factor) for which the world price or return exceeds the home price (or return).

The decomposition of the factors affecting real income at home shown by (6) is useful in exposing these two sets of influences. However, it does not take into account two types of interdependence which affect policy. E_2^* is the foreign country's excess demand for commodity 2 and thus depends upon the foreign relative commodity price ratio, p^*, and the quantity of net foreign investment, K. Similarly, the rate of return abroad, r^*, depends in general upon these same two variables, p^* and K. By stating the nature of these two relationships explicitly it is possible to consider $\mathrm{d}y$ as dependent upon $\mathrm{d}p^*$ on the one hand and $\mathrm{d}K$ on the other, and thus to examine the influence of commercial and fiscal policy upon real incomes.

Consider, first, the relationship between r^* and (p^*, K). If production is incompletely specialized abroad, r^* is determined uniquely by p^* and not at all by K.[5] To put the relationship into relative terms, define γ^* as $(p^*/r^*)(\partial r^*/\partial p^*)$. Clearly the sign of γ^* depends upon the factor-intensity ranking of industries in the foreign country, and will be positive if and only if X_2^* is capital-intensive. But more can be said: if γ^* is positive it must exceed unity. This is an example of what I have called the *magnification effect*,[6] whereby a change in commodity prices brings about a relatively greater change in factor prices.[7]

If the foreign country is completely specialized in the first commodity,[8] the foreign rate of return in units of commodity 1 (r^*) is capital's marginal physical product in commodity 1. With fixed labor and 'own' capital supply, this depends only upon the extent of investment from abroad, K. Let δ^* be defined as (K/r^*) $(\partial r^*/\partial K)$. Then δ^* is negative if the home country is a net lender (so that $K > 0$).[9] In general, $r^* = r^*(p^*, K)$ so that, by total differentiation, $\mathrm{d}r^*/r^*$ is given

[5] This is the kind of relationship underlying the factor-price equalization theorem. Of course, a substantial change in K might bring about complete specialization, in which case further (small) changes in K *do* affect r^*.

[6] See Chapter 4.

[7] The fact that γ^* must exceed unity if it is positive is a reflection of the Stolper-Samuelson [15] tariff theorem.

[8] I follow Kemp in assuming that the foreign country either produces both commodities or is specialized in commodity 1.

[9] $\partial r^*/\partial K$ must be negative with complete specialization. It shows how much capital's marginal product in commodity 1 is driven down as more capital is put into producing 1 (as of a fixed labor endowment). Of course, this is linked to the elasticity of substitution between capital and labor in producing commodity 1 in the foreign country (σ_1^*). Specifically, it can be shown that δ^* equals $-\beta^*\theta_L^*/\sigma_1^*$, where β^* is the fraction of total capital used in the foreign country that is owned by the home country and θ_L^* is labor's distributive share in the foreign country.

by[10]

$$\frac{\mathrm{d}r^*}{r^*} = \gamma^* \frac{\mathrm{d}p^*}{p^*} + \delta^* \frac{\mathrm{d}K}{K}. \tag{7}$$

E_2^* is also a function of p^* and K. For given amounts of foreign investment and fixed resources, the dependence of E_2^* on p^* is of the kind described by the foreign offer curve for imports. Let η_2^* be the elasticity of demand along this curve, so that $\eta_2^* \equiv (\partial E_2^*/\partial p^*)(p^*/E_2^*)$. Assuming no inferior goods, η_2^* is negative as long as the foreign country imports commodity 2. For given world terms of trade the manner in which E_2^* is affected by changes in K depends upon the pattern of specialization. If foreign specialization is complete, a change in K does not affect foreign production of commodity 2 (since X_2^* is zero) but does affect demand, as an increase in K forces r^* down, thus reducing the burden of indebtedness in the foreign country. From (4) and (7), $\partial y^*/\partial K$ (with p^* constant) equals $-r^*\delta^*$. This, in turn, changes demand at constant prices so that $\partial D_2^*/\partial K$ equals $-(m_2^*/p^*)r^*\delta^*$, where m_2^* is the marginal propensity to consume the imported commodity in the foreign country. If foreign specialization is incomplete, (4) and (7) indicate that changes in K at constant p^* cannot change r^* and thus cannot affect y^* or D_2^*. Production, however, is affected as an inflow of capital at constant prices raises production of the capital-intensive commodity. By a basic reciprocity theorem due to Samuelson,[11] $\partial X_2^*/\partial K$ equals $\partial r^*/\partial p^*$. Let μ^* denote the ratio of annual rental payments on home capital invested in the foreign country to foreign imports of commodity 2. Then $\partial X_2^*/\partial K$ equals $(E_2^*/K\mu^*\gamma^*)$ and the decomposition of $\mathrm{d}E_2^*$ can be given as

$$\mathrm{d}E_2^* = E_2^* \left\{ \eta_2^* \frac{\mathrm{d}p^*}{p^*} - \mu^*[m_2^*\delta^* + \gamma^*]\frac{\mathrm{d}K}{K} \right\}. \tag{8}$$

Again, if one of the components of the coefficient of $\mathrm{d}K/K$ is nonzero, the other must vanish.

The basic expression for $\mathrm{d}y$ was given in (6). With both r^* and E_2^* dependent upon p^* and K, y can be considered a function of p^* and K. Eq. (9) then gives

[10] Note that either γ^* is zero or δ^* is zero, so that in any particular situation $\mathrm{d}r^*$ depends only upon $\mathrm{d}p^*$ or $\mathrm{d}K$ but not both. If specialization is incomplete $\partial r^*/\partial p^*$ is the same as $\mathrm{d}r^*/\mathrm{d}p^*$, and if the foreign country produces only commodity 1, $\partial r^*/\partial K$ equals $\mathrm{d}r^*/\mathrm{d}K$.

[11] See Samuelson [14] and Kemp [9]. See also the discussion of duality and reciprocity given in Chapters 4, 5 and 8.

the general solution for a change in home real income:

$$dy = \frac{\partial y}{\partial p^*} dp^* + \frac{\partial y}{\partial K} dK, \tag{9}$$

where

$$\frac{\partial y}{\partial p^*} = E_2^* \left\{ 1 + \mu^* \gamma^* + \frac{(p^* - p)}{p^*} \eta_2^* \right\}$$

and

$$\frac{\partial y}{\partial K} = \left[1 + \left(m_1^* + \frac{p}{p^*} m_2^* \right) \delta^* - \frac{(p^* - p)}{p^*} \gamma^* \right] r^* - r.$$

3.

The objective of policy in the (active) home country is taken to be the maximization of home real income. In this and the following section I assume no constraints are set upon this maximization, so that the expressions for $\partial y/\partial p^*$ and $\partial y/\partial K$ in (9) are each set equal to zero (for an internal maximum position).[12] The results for this case of *full optimization* when the foreign country is completely specialized have been analyzed by Kemp [5] and can be discussed briefly.

The basic simplification is that with the foreign country completely specialized to the first commodity, γ^* is zero. A change in the price of the second commodity in terms of the first has no effect on the rate of return in the foreign country. The formulae for the optimal tariff on goods flows and the optimal tax on capital are then derived by setting $\partial y/\partial p^*$ and $\partial y/\partial K$ each equal to zero and noticing: (i) the tariff rate, τ, links home and foreign commodity price ratios so that $p^* = p(1 + \tau)$, and (ii) the tax rate, t, levied on income earned at home on foreign investments allows the foreign rate, r^*, to differ from the home rate, r, but competition ensures that $r = r^*(1 - t)$. Thus if the tax rate is positive, the foreign rate of return must be higher than that prevailing at home if any of the home country's capital is to be invested abroad. Of course, this link between rates is reversed if the home country is a borrower, in which case, (iii) the tax rate, t^*, levied on the income from foreign capital invested at home serves to align home and foreign rates so that $r(1 - t^*) = r^*$.

[12] Kemp discusses special boundary cases where, for example, the home country invests all its capital abroad.

The formulae for *optimal* tax and tariff rates are set out in (10) and (11):

$$\tau = -\frac{1}{1+\eta_2^*}, \tag{10}$$

$$t = -\left\{m_1^* + \frac{p}{p^*}m_2^*\right\}\delta^*. \tag{11}$$

The expression for τ is familiar from the standard case in which no capital movements are considered. Referring to eq. (9) it is clear that full optimization requires $\partial y/\partial p^*$ equal to zero (and therefore the relationship shown by (10) if the foreign country is completely specialized) whether or not $\mathrm{d}K$ is zero. Similarly, $\partial y/\partial K$ going to zero in the case of full optimization requires a rate of income tax on foreign investments given by (11).[13] The basic conclusion is simple: It always pays the home country to levy a positive tax on capital flows, whether on balance it is a lender or borrower.

4.

If the foreign country is incompletely specialized, a small change in capital flows does *not* alter the rate of return to capital unless the foreign commodity price changes. That is, δ^* is zero, and r^* is linked uniquely to p^* instead of to K. This difference is important, for a tariff policy that attempts to affect real incomes by altering the commodity terms of trade must take account of the accompanying changes in rates of return to foreign investment. It is this phenomenon that underlies the possibility of 'paradoxical' results discussed by Kemp.

It would be possible to compute the formulae for optimal tariff and optimal tax by setting $\partial y/\partial p^*$ and $\partial y/\partial K$ in (9) each equal to zero – the procedure used in the last section. An alternative method, which more clearly reveals the source of 'paradoxical' patterns of tariffs and taxes, is to examine the sign of $\partial y/\partial p^*$ and $\partial y/\partial K$ in an initial situation of free trade and unimpeded capital flows. $\partial y/\partial p^*$ reduces to E_2^* $(1 + \mu^*\gamma^*)$, and if this is positive the home country can raise its income by raising its relative export price by imposing a tariff.[14] That is, in the optimal situation the tariff rate would be positive.

[13] If K is negative, the home country is faced with the possibility of taxing foreign investments in the home country at rate t^*. In the optimum position t^* equals $1/(1 + x)$ where x is $[m_1^* + (p/p^*)m_2^*]\delta^*$. Notice that with K negative, δ^* is positive, so that optimal t^* is also positive.

[14] I am assuming that a tariff serves to improve a country's terms of trade. In Section 6 I shall investigate this question more carefully.

Assume the home country exports commodity 2 so that E_2^* is positive. If the home country is also a capital exporter, μ^* is positive. Then raising p^* from the initial situation (via a positive tariff) clearly raises home real income if, in the foreign country, commodity 2 is capital-intensive (γ^* positive). y increases both because the relative price of the home country's export good rises and because the rate of return earned on capital invested abroad rises. In a sense there are two terms of trade to be considered (p^* and r^*), and if X_2^* is capital-intensive a tariff improves them both.

A conflict arises if commodity 2 is labor-intensive abroad, for any improvement in p^* must be associated with a reduction in the return on foreign investment, r^*. Whether, in these circumstances, a tariff should be imposed depends on the relative magnitudes of capital exports and commodity exports of the home country. If μ^* is small, so that exports of capital are minor compared with exports of commodity 2 (in value terms), $(1 + \mu^*\gamma^*)$ will be positive and it pays to raise p^*. However, with γ^* negative, there is some value for μ^* high enough so that $\partial y/\partial p^*$ becomes negative. That is, the home country is in this case primarily an exporter of capital, and should alter p^* so that its return on foreign capital, r^*, is increased, even though this requires an export subsidy (as it will if X_2^* is labor-intensive.) Pushing this line of reasoning further, consider the case where the home country exports *only* capital, importing both commodities. It will wish to raise p^* if and only if X_2^* is capital-intensive.[15]

The case in which the home country is a capital importer is symmetrical. The home country now wishes to lower r^*, the amount it must pay out per unit of foreign capital invested at home. If X_2^* is labor-intensive this can be accomplished by improving its commodity terms of trade (raising p^*). The possibility of conflict arises if X_2^* is capital-intensive, in which case r^* and p^* move in the same direction, and an improvement in the commodity terms of trade can be obtained only at the expense of an increase in the interest burden on foreign capital invested at home. Again, the value of μ^* is important in suggesting whether on balance it is to the borrowing country's advantage to improve its commodity terms of trade (μ^* a small negative number) or lower the cost of borrowing capital (μ^* a larger negative number). It cannot have it both ways.[16]

The conclusions regarding the optimal pattern of tariffs can be stated simply. Two terms of trade are involved: p^* and r^*. With incomplete specialization

[15]In this case μ^* is negative and less than -1. Since γ^* must be greater than unity if it is positive, and E_2^* is negative, $E_2^*(1 + \mu^*\gamma^*)$ is positive if and only if X_2^* is capital-intensive.

[16]Note that if the home country exports both commodities, μ^* must be less than -1 and $\partial y/\partial p^*$ is positive if and only if X_2^* is labor-intensive.

abroad p^* and r^* are linked via the foreign technology. For the home country 'paradoxically' to levy a subsidy on its natural export good (2) would require (i) a conflict between a favorable movement in p^* and an unfavorable movement in r^*, together with (ii) the earnings from capital flows being relatively important compared with commodity flows in the balance of payments.

Consider, now, the sign of the optimal tax on capital flows. In an initial situation of free movement in goods and capital, $\partial y/\partial K$ is zero. This stands in sharp contrast to the case in which the foreign country is completely specialized. In the latter event a movement of K can serve directly to force changes in r^*. But with the foreign country producing both commodities, a change in K at constant commodity terms of trade can affect home real incomes only if the valuation on either capital or commodities differs between the two countries. Referring to eq. (6), with p^* constant it is only via the second bracketed expression that a change in K can change home real incomes.

The implication of full optimization for the sign of the tax on capital flows can be deduced from setting $\partial y/\partial K$ equal to zero in (9). Suppose the home country is a capital exporter. Then the optimal tax rate is given by

$$t = \frac{(p^* - p)}{p^*}\gamma^*, \tag{12}$$

where the rates of return at home and abroad are linked by t such that $r^*(1 - t) = r$ Clearly the optimal tax rate is positive if and only if (i) p^* exceeds p (i.e. the tariff rate, τ, is positive) and X_2^* is capital-intensive, or (ii) p exceeds p^* (i.e. exports are subsidized so that τ is negative) and X_2^* is labor-intensive.

The common sense behind these relationships can be illustrated in fig. 12.1,

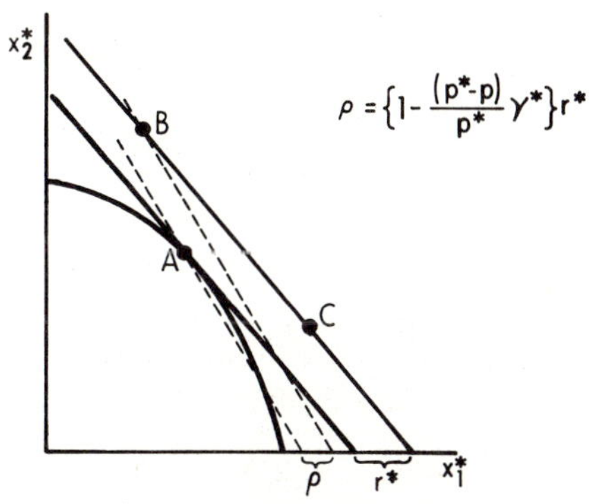

Figure 12.1

which shows the foreign country's production-possibilities schedule. Suppose the initial equilibrium is at A, with the slope of the line tangent at A representing the inverse of the fixed *foreign* commodity price ratio, p^*. Consider the impact of an inflow of capital abroad by one unit at constant p^*. The foreign transformation schedule is shifted outwards, such that it is tangent to the line through BC (parallel to the line tangent at A) either at a point northwest of A (such as B) or southeast of A such as C).[17] The value to the foreign country of the increased production made possible by the postulated increase of one unit of capital is r^* in units of commodity 1. At constant p^* foreign consumption is unaltered, so that the extra bundle of goods produced (shown either by vector AB or AC) accrues to the home country. The question then arises: what is this bundle worth to the home country? If it is worth r^* to the home country then no tax should be levied, so that the opportunity cost of capital at home, r, is equated to its marginal worth invested abroad. However, if home and foreign prices differ, this bundle at home will *not* be worth r^*, as it is in the foreign country. The output of one commodity has risen and of the other has fallen. If the relative valuation of the good whose output has increased is higher at home than abroad, the value to the home country of the extra bundle would exceed r^*. In these circumstances it would pay the home country to subsidize capital exports, so that capital would flow abroad even when r^* is below r. However, if the home country's valuation of the good that has increased in supply is relatively lower than abroad, the value at home of the changed bundle of goods will fall short of the foreign value, r^*. In fact, it may be *negative*. For example, suppose X_2^* is capital-intensive so that an extra unit of capital abroad shifts production from A to B. If the relative price of commodity 1 at home is greater than the slope of a line through B and A, B actually has a lower valuation at home than does A. That is,

$$\left\{1 - \frac{(p^* - p)}{p^*}\gamma^*\right\} r^*$$

is negative. In these circumstances it would always pay the home country to cut back its capital exports.[18] The case illustrated by the dotted line in fig. 12.1 is less extreme. It has X_2^* capital-intensive, a higher relative price for commodity 1

[17] This is a reflection of the magnification effect. See Rybczynski [13].

[18] Kemp [9] argues that the optimal tax should not exceed 100%. The point is that if the extra bundle of goods (say AB) has negative value, the only way $\partial y/\partial K$ could be brought to zero would be for t to exceed 1. An analogy is to be found in the traditional argument about optimal tariffs (e.g. see eq. (10)). If the foreign offer curve is inelastic, the formula suggests a negative duty. Clearly this is a misinterpretation stemming from the attempt to set $\partial y/\partial p^*$ equal to zero by a tariff in a region where $\partial y/\partial p^*$ must be positive.

at home, and thus a net value for the extra bundle, ρ, falling short of r^*. ρ represents the marginal return to the home country of capital invested abroad at constant commodity prices, and is set equal to r by a positive tax on capital exports.

Consider the possible combinations of optimal tariff and optimal tax. For the case in which the home country is a capital exporter there are three possibilities. (i) Both tax and tariff rates are positive. This occurs if and only if the two terms of trade move together, i.e if X_2^* is capital-intensive. (ii) If X_2^* is labor-intensive, but nonetheless commodity 2 bulks 'larger' in the home country's balance of payments than does its earnings on capital invested abroad,[19] the optimal tariff is still positive, but capital exports should be subsidized as increased capital exports increase foreign production of the good with a relatively high valuation at home. (iii) If X_2^* is labor-intensive but capital exports are 'more important' than commodity exports in the home country's balance of payments, its commodity exports are subsidized in order to raise r^*. But the commodity whose production is increased abroad with capital flows now has a relatively lower valuation at home. Thus capital exports should be discouraged by a positive tax. This exhausts the possibilities. Notice that it never pays to subsidize both goods and factor exports.[20]

Similar results hold for the case in which the home country is a capital importer. (i) If the home country's export good, commodity 2, is labor-intensive abroad, the tariff rate must be positive as this serves to improve both terms of trade. By also levying a tax on capital imports, the home country manages to increase foreign production of the commodity (1) with a relatively higher valuation at home. Both τ and t^* are positive.[21] (ii) If X_2^* is capital-intensive and the capital inflow into the home country is relatively small, it pays, again, to levy a positive tariff, despite the fact that r^* is also driven up. A tax on capital inflows would encourage foreign production of commodity 2, which has a lower relative valuation at home. Therefore it would be optimal, instead, to subsidize foreign investment at home. τ is positive but t^* is negative. (iii) The sign of both tariff and tax are

[19] In the sense that $(1 + \mu^*\gamma^*)$ is positive.

[20] Notice that in cases (ii) and (iii) the foreign country exports its capital-intensive commodity (1), but nonetheless is an importer of capital. As Professor June Flanders has commented, this seems to be a surprising trade pattern in view of the Heckscher–Ohlin theory. However, it can be made consistent if either (a) factor intensity reversals are present, or (b) technology differs as between the two countries such that the home country has a technological superiority in producing commodity 2. For an interesting discussion of the possibility that trade in commodities and capital movements might be complementary instead of substitutive, a possibility suggested in cases (ii) and (iii), see Amano [2].

[21] The formula for optimal tax is now $t^* = x/(1 + x)$, where x equals $-[(p^* - p)/p^*]\gamma^*$.

reversed if X_2^* is capital intensive but capital inflows are more 'important' than commodity exports in the sense that $(1 + \mu^* \gamma^*)$ is negative. It now becomes optimal to lower r^*, at the expense of lowering p^*. With commodity 2 being valued relatively higher at home than abroad, foreigners should be encouraged to keep more of their capital at home (and thus increase output of X_2^* at constant prices) by means of a positive tax.

It thus emerges that the lending and borrowing cases are essentially symmetrical, and that although a tax rate or a tariff can be negative, they can never both be negative.[22]

The magnification effect, whereby the returns to factors of production change by a relatively greater amount than do commodity prices, has a key role to play in the foregoing results. As regards the question of whether a tariff or subsidy on commodity trade is optimal, a possible conflict arises only if the home country either exports capital *and* a commodity (commodity 2, by assumption), or imports capital *and* a commodity. In these cases the two terms of trade may move in opposite directions, and the sign of the tariff depends on the relative composition of the balance of payments. However, should capital stand alone, either as an export or import, no such conflict can arise. For example, suppose the home country exports capital and imports both commodities. Tariff policy should always be directed towards raising r^*. By contrast, suppose it exports commodity 2 and imports capital and commodity 1. It does not always pay to raise p^*.

Secondly, the magnification effect in its dual (Rybczynski) form asserts that at constant p^* a change in K results in an increase in one commodity and a decrease in the other commodity produced abroad. This is what allows the possibility that this extra bundle of goods available to the home country, with a positive valuation abroad (r^*), could actually have a negative value when home prices are used.

Finally, the magnification effect allows a comparison of the rates of the optimal tariff and the optimal tax, assuming both are positive. Let the home country be a capital exporter. Then *the optimal tax rate must always exceed the optimal tariff rate*, in the sense of $(1 + \tau)(1 - t)$ having to be less than unity. For $\partial y / \partial K$ equal to zero implies that $(r^* - r)/r^*$ equals $[(p^* - p)/p^*]\gamma^*$ or

$$\gamma^* = \frac{1 - r/r^*}{1 - p/p^*}$$

The case considered, where tax and tariff are positive, requires a positive γ^*. But

[22] This position contradicts the claim made by Kemp [9] that both tax and tariff may be negative in the optimal position if the home country is a capital exporter.

then γ^* must exceed unity, by the magnification effect. Therefore $r/r^* < p/p^*$ or $(1 + \tau)(1 - t) < 1$.[23]

5.

The discussion in the preceding sections dealt with the case of full optimization. Both the duty or subsidy on commodity flows and the tax or subsidy on capital flows could be adjusted by the home country so as to maximize its real income. But this freedom to maneuver is not always available. A tariff agreement might restrict the use of commercial policy for national objectives. Or a tax convention might guarantee noninterference in capital markets. In either event the home country, in its attempt to increase its real income, would have to rely on only one method.

In this section I analyze the case in which the home country is prohibited from changing the duty or subsidy on commodity flows. To make the analysis simpler, I shall assume that the tariff is fixed at the zero level, i.e. that free trade in *commodities* is guaranteed. The basic question then concerns the role of taxes or subsidies on *capital* flows in altering home real income. Can a tax on capital improve real income in the manner of a tariff on commodities? Of special interest is the comparison between optimal tax strategy in the case of full optimization and in the 'second-best' case to be analyzed here.

The general expression for a change in home real income was given by eq. (9), in which it was suggested that p^* and K could be altered independently in maximizing y. To do this requires the use of a policy instrument like a tariff so that p^* can be altered as of given K. However, with no spread between home and foreign commodity prices allowed, p^* depends upon K. The procedure I shall follow is to inquire as to the sign of $\mathrm{d}y/\mathrm{d}K$ from an initial position of umimpeded capital flows (r initially equal to r^*). Rewrite (9) as (9′):

$$\frac{\mathrm{d}y}{\mathrm{d}K} = \frac{\partial y}{\partial p^*}\frac{\mathrm{d}p^*}{\mathrm{d}K} + \frac{\partial y}{\partial K}, \tag{9'}$$

[23] As already noted, Kemp [9] asserts that the tax rate and tariff rate might both be negative. In his diagrams, this is illustrated in Region VI′ in fig. 4b. In this case $\mu^*\gamma^*$ (his ϵ_2^*) must lie between zero and minus one. But for this case, $\mu^* < -1$, and X_2^* is capital-intensive. By the magnification effect, γ^* must, therefore, be greater than unity and it is impossible for $\mu^*\gamma^*$ to lie between zero and minus one. That is, the region in which Kemp finds both tax and tariff negative is empty. By the same reasoning his region II′ in fig. 4d is empty.

where

$$\frac{\partial y}{\partial p^*} = E_2^*(1 + \mu^* \gamma^*) \quad \text{and} \quad \frac{\partial y}{\partial K} = \delta^* r^*.$$

A change in the amount of foreign investment, K, in general alters real income directly, as of given commodity terms of trade, and indirectly, through requiring a change in these terms of trade. p^* is the price ratio that clears commodity markets, and in general there exists a different equilibrium p^* for each value of K. That is, to preserve equilibrium, $d(E_2 + E_2^*)$, the change in the world excess demand for commodity 2,[24] must be zero. This requires a change in p^* to offset any change directly invoked by a change in capital flows.

Consider the factors affecting home excess demand for commodity 2. Demand is determined by the terms of trade and by real income. Production is determined by the terms of trade and factor endowments. Let $\bar{\eta}_2$ collect the pure substitution elasticities on the side of demand and production, and let γ represent the ratio between the relative change in the return to capital in the home country and the relative change in the commodity terms of trade.[25] The three determinants of dE_2 can be set out as in eq. (13):

$$dE_2 = E_2^* \left\{ \bar{\eta}_2 \frac{dp}{p} + \frac{m_2}{p^* E_2^*} dy + \mu^* \gamma \frac{dK}{K} \right\}. \tag{13}$$

An increase in p must decrease E_2 via the substitution effects in consumption and production. In addition any increase in real income spills over to increase E_2 through m_2, the home country's marginal propensity to consume commodity 2. Finally, account must be taken of the shift in supply of X_2 brought about by any change in capital flows. By the basic duality relationship in this general equilibrium model, the change in production at constant homes prices is given by γ. It is important to note that since, by assumption, the home country always produces commodity 2, γ reduces to unity if the home country is completely specialized (to commodity 2).[26]

[24] Of course, commodity I could have been chosen instead. If one market is cleared, so must the other be.

[25] Explicitly, $\bar{\eta}_2$ is defined as

$$\frac{p}{E_2^*} \left\{ \left. \frac{\partial D_2}{\partial p} \right|_y - \left. \frac{\partial X_2}{\partial p} \right|_K \right\},$$

so that $E_2^* \bar{\eta}_2$ must be negative. Similarly, γ is $(p/r)(\partial r/\partial p)$.

[26] In general, r equals the *value* of capital's marginal product in producing commodity 2. If the home country is specialized to commodity 2, an increase in p at constant endowments cannot alter the marginal physical product of capital. Therefore r rises in the same proportion as p. In the foreign country complete specialization implies all resources are used to produce commodity 1, and therefore that γ^* reduces to zero.

A similar expression is obtained for the foreign country. Since initially prices and rates of return are equal in the two countries, $-\mathrm{d}y^*$ must equal the gain in home real income, $\mathrm{d}y$. Therefore $\mathrm{d}(E_2 + E_2^*)$ is given by

$$\mathrm{d}(E_2 + E_2^*) = E_2^* \left\{ \bar{\eta}_2 \frac{\mathrm{d}p}{p} + \bar{\eta}_2^* \frac{\mathrm{d}p^*}{p^*} + \frac{(m_2 - m_2^*)}{p^* E_2^*} \mathrm{d}y + \mu^*(\gamma - \gamma^*) \frac{\mathrm{d}K}{K} \right\}. \tag{14}$$

All substitution effects work to reduce world excess demand for commodity 2 if the relative price of commodity 2 rises. There is, in addition, the net impact on demand of any transfer of real income, and the net impact on world production of any transfer of capital. Two further simplifications are possible. From eq. (9) the expression for $\mathrm{d}y$ in terms of $\mathrm{d}p^*$ and $\mathrm{d}K$ can be obtained, noting that initially $p = p^*$ and $r = r^*$. Secondly, the values for the home and foreign commodity terms of trade *stay* the same by the free trade assumption made in this section. That is, $\mathrm{d}p = \mathrm{d}p^*$. Therefore the change in world excess demand for commodity 2 can be expressed as a function of the change in p^* and the change in K as in (15):

$$\mathrm{d}(E_2 + E_2^*) = E_2^* \left\{ -\Delta \frac{\mathrm{d}p^*}{p^*} + \mu^*[(\gamma - \gamma^*) + (m_2 - m_2^*)\delta^*] \frac{\mathrm{d}K}{K} \right\}, \tag{15}$$

where

$$\Delta = -\{\bar{\eta}_2 + \bar{\eta}_2^* + (m_2 - m_2^*)(1 + \mu^*\gamma^*)\}.$$

I assume that commodity markets are stable. By this I choose to mean that for any given allocation of the world's capital a rise in the relative price of commodity 2 reduces world excess demand for commodity 2. That is, the coefficient of $\mathrm{d}p^*$ is negative, or $E_2^*\Delta$ is positive. The coefficient of $\mathrm{d}K$ represents the shift of the excess world demand curve for the second commodity at the initial set of prices that is brought about by a capital flow. Any change in K must change p^* so as to clear markets. The value for $\mathrm{d}p^*/\mathrm{d}K$ is therefore given by

$$\frac{\mathrm{d}p^*}{\mathrm{d}K} = \frac{r^*}{E_2^*\Delta}\{(\gamma - \gamma^*) + (m_2 - m_2^*)\delta^*\}. \tag{16}$$

Passing over directly to the ultimate effect of a change in capital flows on home real income, substitute the terms of trade impact shown by (16) into (9′) to obtain eq. (17) for $\mathrm{d}y/\mathrm{d}K$:

$$\frac{\mathrm{d}y}{\mathrm{d}K} = \frac{r^*}{E_2^*\Delta} E_2^*\{(1 + \mu^*\gamma^*)(\gamma - \gamma^*) - (\bar{\eta}_2 + \bar{\eta}_2^*)\delta^*\}. \tag{17}$$

This is the general result used to analyze optimal tax strategy in this free trade world. If, from the initial position of unimpeded capital flows, an increase in K should increase y, foreign investment should be encouraged by a subsidy if the home country is a net lender, and discouraged by a tax if on balance foreigners are investing in the home country. As in the case of full optimization, the optimal tax pattern varies depending upon the degree of specialization.

Consider, first, the case in which the foreign country is incompletely specialized. Let the home country concentrate its resources in commodity 2. A striking result emerges for this case: the sign pattern of the optimal tax on capital flows is *identical* to that in the case of full optimization. Although the process through which interference in the international flow of capital affects home real incomes differs in these two cases, the qualitative nature (but not the specific rates) of optimal tax strategy is independent of whether commercial (tariff) policy can be pursued!

To check this assertion formally note that in (17) δ^* goes to zero and γ reduces to unity. That is, the sign of $\mathrm{d}y/\mathrm{d}K$ is the same as that of $-\{E_2^*(1+\mu^*\gamma^*)\}\{\gamma^*-1\}$. For the case in which the home country is a net lender compare this expression with eq. (12) for the optimal tax if full optimization is pursued. The first bracketed expression above is familiar: if this is positive it would pay the home country to levy a positive tariff on goods if tariff policy could be pursued. That is, $E_2^*(1+\mu^*\gamma^*)$ has the same sign as (p^*-p) in formula (12) for t. And, by the magnification effect, a positive γ^* requires, as well, a positive (γ^*-1), the second bracketed expression above. In other words, $\mathrm{d}y/\mathrm{d}K$ is negative (and therefore a tax on capital flows is optimal when the home country is a net lender), if and only if the tax rate in the case of full optimization would be positive.

Less formally, return to eq. (9′). Note that the *direct* effect of capital flows on home income, $\partial y/\partial K$, disappears in the obligatory free trade case of this section. Capital flows can affect real income only via the indirect effect they have on the terms of trade. Two issues are involved. (i) Does an increase in K raise or lower p^*? As (16) shows, this depends uniquely on whether X_2^* is labor- or capital-intensive. (ii) Does an increase in p^* raise or lower home real incomes? As the earlier analysis shows, this depends uniquely on the sign of $E_2^*(1+\mu^*\gamma^*)$. In the case of full optimization the sign of the tax is positive (in the lending case) if the commodity whose production would be increased abroad by an increase in K at constant world prices (which depends only on factor intensities abroad, as in (i)) has a lower valuation at home than abroad (which would be the case if an optimal tariff is called for, as it would be if an increase in p^* would raise y, as in (ii)).

The argument and the results are similar in the case in which the home country is a borrower.

If the foreign country is completely specialized (to commodity 1, by assumption), rather different results emerge. Recall that in the case of full optimization it was always in the home country's interest to restrict capital flows, as this would tend to raise r^* if the home country is a lender, and reduce r^* if it is a net borrower. But this result depends sensitively on the assumption that an optimal tariff policy is consistently being pursued. In the general expression for dy given by eq. (9), $\partial y/\partial p^*$ is zero if an optimal tariff is in force, so that any small change in p^* that would result from a change in capital flows has no effect on y. Therefore only $\partial y/\partial K$ matters in tax policy, and if the foreign country is specialized, y can be altered by changing K so as to drive up or down the rate of return on foreign investment. An alternative framework that guarantees the traditional result does not necessarily require an *optimal* tariff. Rather, any tariff policy that serves to stabilize world prices (i.e. that keeps dp^* zero) also leads to the simple result that $\partial y/\partial K$ in (9) is the only relevant consideration in the analysis of tax policy. With complete specialization, of course, this alternative is important, for fixing p^* does not fix r^*, as the latter depends only upon K. But if tariffs *cannot* be altered, and the assumption in this section of guaranteed free trade is a special case of this, a change in K generally alters p^*, so that (in the case of complete specialization) there exist both direct and indirect influences of restriction of capital flows. With this in mind, it turns out that it may pay the home country to subsidize capital exports.

Expression (16) suggests that with δ^* nonzero the task of determining which way the commodity terms of trade change when K changes is more complicated than in the case of incomplete specialization abroad. Not only are pure supply effects involved (the first expression in the brackets, $(\gamma - \gamma^*)$, which in this case reduces to γ since γ^* is zero); also, the change in the rate of return on capital necessarily involves a transfer of real income from one country to another, which spills over to affect net world demand for commodities if taste patterns at the margin (m_2 and m_2^*) differ between countries. And, as is clear from the literature on the transfer problem, this real income transfer can push the terms of trade in either direction.

However, the primary concern here is not with the direction of change in the terms of trade, but with the ultimate impact on real incomes. And here a familiar result from the transfer literature helps to simplify matters: regardless of the impact on the terms of trade, the real income of the transferor must decline if the market is stable. This can be checked by referring to the second term in brackets in (17). At unchanged terms of trade, $\partial y/\partial K$ is $r^*\delta^*$. This real income transfer affects p^*, which further affects y. The net effect on real income, ignoring supply effects, is $-[(\bar{\eta}_2 + \bar{\eta}_2^*)/\Delta]r^*\delta^*$, which must be the same sign as $r^*\delta^*$, and which will be larger or smaller than $r^*\delta^*$ in absolute value depending upon which way the terms of trade move. Of course, this is not the whole story, for an increase in K not only (i) transfers real income (and thus affects prices) by causing r^* to change, but also (ii) changes world production of commodity 2 as capital is drawn out of the home country – by an amount indicated by γ. It is this second aspect of capital flows, and only this aspect, that introduces the possibility that the traditional results of tax strategy discussed in section 3 may be overturned.[27] Once again, as in the case of incomplete specialization, the crucial question concerns factor intensities. Except now it is the structure of production in the home country that dominates.

Referring again to (17) it is clear that the sign of $E_2^*\{\gamma - (\bar{\eta}_2 + \bar{\eta}_2^*)\delta^*\}$ determines optimal tax strategy in this free trade world. Take the case in which the home country is a lender, so that δ^* is negative. Without supply effects dy/dK would be negative and it would be optimal to tax capital outflows. But such a tax brings capital back to the home country and, at constant p^*, serves to increase production of the commodity that is capital-intensive at home. If this should be commodity 2 (γ positive), pressure for p^* to fall is introduced, and this serves to erode the gains brought about by raising r^*. If δ^* is small in absolute value, r^* will not be greatly raised by restricting K. Also, if substitution elasticities of demand are small, any increases in world supply of commodity 2 will bring about a large,

[27] A parallel is to be found in the literature on immiserizing growth. There it is pointed out that the recipient of new goods (i.e. the growing country) may on balance suffer thereby because of a possible consequent deterioration in its terms of trade. This could never happen if the goods were *not* newly produced, but *transferred* from somewhere else in the world so that world supply remains unchanged. Alternatively put, it might pay Brazil to dump coffee into the ocean; it would never pay her to give that coffee away.

It is important to be clear about the nature of the transfer discussed in the text. Capital goods are not being 'transferred' in the sense of being given away from the home country to the foreign country (or vice versa). Instead, the 'initial transfer' is $r^*\delta^*$, or $\partial y/\partial K$, the change in real income at the initial commodity terms of trade. The classical theorem then states that changes in p^* required to clear markets that are disturbed only by this change in real income (and not by any change in world supply of any commodity) cannot induce further real income changes to such an extent that the country that gains at initial commodity terms of trade ends up with a loss in real income. But now consider the case in which capital goods *are* given away. Let dk represent a marginal gift of capital goods from the home country to the foreign country – no annual r^* payment required in return on this marginal bit of capital. Can the real income of the 'capital transferor', the home country, actually increase as a consequence? The answer is yes, and this differs from the 'classical theorem' alluded to above for two reasons. (1) Perhaps most obviously, the world supply of *commodities* can change at initial p^* even though the world supply of capital does not. But there is a second factor as well. (2) Even if the world production of all commodities remains unaltered, the donor of capital can be made better off because the rate of return on capital is affected. To be sure, the 'paradoxical' case in which the home country ends up with a larger real income could only occur if it were initially a net borrower (δ^* positive). Then, if δ^* is large enough (greater than unity), the home country would gain by giving capital away (and thus driving down r^*) if supply effects (1), could be ignored. But note that this does not violate the 'classical theorem', because at initial p^* the transferor is really the foreign country. The expression for dy/dk is as in (17) for dy/dK with δ^* replaced by $(\delta^* - 1)$.

rather than small, drop in p^*. That is, the terms of trade effect of the supply changes brought about by the change in K outweigh the beneficial effects in manipulating r^* if condition (18) is satisfied:

$$\gamma > (\bar{\eta}_2 + \bar{\eta}_2^*)\delta^*. \tag{18}$$

If it is, it would pay the home lending country to subsidize foreign investment.

As a final comment, note the asymmetry between borrowing and lending cases if the home country is completely specialized. γ reduces to unity and (18) can still be satisfied. But if the home country is a net borrower, a subsidy is optimal only if $\mathrm{d}y/\mathrm{d}K$ is negative. This would require $(\hat{\eta}_2 + \hat{\eta}_2^*)\delta^*$ to exceed unity. But δ^* is positive when $K < 0$, so that this expression must be negative. The 'paradoxical' result cannot arise. If the home country is a borrower, it wants to lower r^*, and does this by discouraging borrowing. This also has the effect of reducing the supply of its export good (the only good it produces by assumption), without increasing foreign supply (since the foreign country is specialized to the other commodity). In the best traditions of protectionism the borrower can use the tax on capital imports to lower the rate it has to pay to obtain funds and to restrict world production of its export good.[28]

6.

It remains to consider the case in which tax policy cannot be used to control capital movements. The home country has only commercial policy available in order to raise its real income. Of course, if capital is immobile internationally there is little new to be said – this is the domain of the traditional theory of the optimal tariff. The interesting question concerns the theory of tariffs and trade when capital is mobile internationally. For simplicity I assume that the fixed tax on capital movements is zero – capital is completely mobile.

In each country the rate of return to capital depends either upon the local commodity price ratio or upon the level of the capital stock. The requirement that rates of return always be equalized leads to

$$r(p, K) = r^*(p^*, K). \tag{19}$$

Any price changes in general throw these rates out of line, necessitating a capital

[28] Note that I have refrained from saying '*and* to improve its commodity terms of trade', for p^* may not rise even with the reduction in world supply of commodity 2. However, if it falls, it would not fall as much as if world supply were unaffected.

movement to restore equality. Following the spirit of eq. (7), requirement (19) implies a relation (20), among commodity-price changes in the two countries and the capital flow.

$$\gamma\frac{\mathrm{d}p}{p} - \gamma^*\frac{\mathrm{d}p^*}{p^*} = (\delta^* + \delta)\frac{\mathrm{d}K}{K}. \tag{20}$$

In (20) it has been assumed that the *initial* situation is one of free trade in commodities. The new term, δ, is defined as $-(K/r)(\partial r/\partial K)$ so that both δ and δ^* are negative (or zero, if the country is incompletely specialized) when the home country is a net lender.

Before turning to the analysis of the impact of tariffs on real incomes for this model it is necessary to consider two preliminary questions that have only been dealt with in the traditional framework in which factors are immobile internationally. The first is the question of stability and the second raises anew the possibility that a tariff may have 'paradoxical' effects on the commodity terms of trade, either in the world market or the protected market.

Taking these in turn, note that the condition for market stability invoked in the last section pertained to the effect of a change in world price on world excess demand for any *given* disposition of capital resources. This led to the requirement that $E_2^* \Delta$ in eq. (15) be positive. But this is no longer appropriate if capital moves endogenously in *response* to changes in prices and rates of return.

There is a sense in which capital movements are stabilizing. Suppose the tariff rate is fixed (say at zero) so that $\mathrm{d}p$ equals $\mathrm{d}p^*$ and consider relationship (20). If p^* should rise, either r^* or r or both change, depending upon the pattern of specialization. Suppose $(\gamma - \gamma^*)$ is positive, i.e. that the increase in p^* has raised the home rate of return, r, relative to the foreign rate, r^*. Then (20) suggests that a flow of capital from the foreign country to the home country is required in order to bring rates into line.[29] Since r exceeds r^* this is precisely the movement of capital to be expected in competitive world markets.[30] Furthermore, the sign of $(\gamma - \gamma^*)$ indicates the change in world output of commodities that would be forthcoming because of the induced changes in K when p^* rises. If $(\gamma - \gamma^*)$ is positive, I have just argued that capital flows from the foreign country to the home country ($\mathrm{d}K$ is negative), which must increase net world output of commodity 2. By contrast, if $(\gamma - \gamma^*)$ is negative, an increase in p^* raises the foreign return to capital relative

[29] Note the importance of having at least one country specialized, as I have been assuming. Otherwise the change in K cannot influence rates of return (to correct the imbalance caused by the initial price changes).

[30] I am, of course, ignoring the possibility of destabilizing speculation as to the future course of rates.

to the home return, inducing an increase in K and (because γ is less than γ^*) an increase in world output of commodity 2. That is, the sign of $(\gamma - \gamma^*)$ indicates the alignment of home and foreign rates of return to capital and, in its dual capacity, the effect of an increase in K on each country's output. The net effect is that the changes in K induced by a change in commodity prices always serve to increase world output of the commodity that has risen in price. However, it is still possible that the capital movements add an unstable element to the commodity markets.

To pursue this question of stability in commodity markets re-examine expression (15) for the change in world excess demand for commodity 2 in a free trade world. With capital completely mobile, the $\mathrm{d}K$ and $\mathrm{d}p^*$ shown there are linked by the requirement that rates of return on capital stay in line. Solve (20) for $\mathrm{d}K/K$ and substitute into (15) to obtain[31]

$$\mathrm{d}(E_2 + E_2^*) = -E_2^*\Delta'\frac{\mathrm{d}p^*}{p^*}, \tag{21}$$

where

$$\Delta' = \Delta - \frac{\mu^*}{(\delta + \delta^*)}(\gamma - \gamma^*)[(\gamma - \gamma^*) + (m_2 - m_2^*)\delta^*].$$

For stability it is required that $E_2^*\,\Delta'$ be positive. Consider here only the case in which the foreign country imports commodity 2 so that E_2^* is positive. Then $\mu^*/(\delta + \delta^*)$ must always be negative, whether the home country is a lender or a borrower. In comparing the new stability condition (the positivity of Δ') with the old (the positivity of Δ) it thus becomes crucial to consider the sign of $(\gamma - \gamma^*)$ $[(\gamma - \gamma^*) + (m_2 - m_2^*)\delta^*]$. If this is positive, the new conditions for market stability are even weaker than previously.

It turns out that the only possible destabilizing factor is, once again, the redistribution-of-income term. Regardless of supply conditions $(\gamma - \gamma^*)^2$ must be positive, so that a bias exists towards having Δ' exceed Δ.[32] But it is only a bias, as the following example shows. Suppose the home country to be a net lender and the foreign country to be completely specialized, so that γ^* is zero and δ^* is negative. Suppose, furthermore, that γ is positive (commodity 2 is capital-intensive in the

[31] Note that I have assumed that p^* and p remain equal to each other. That is, to investigate stability I inquire as to the slope of the excess demand curve for commodity 2 as of *given* tariff rates – which for simplicity have been chosen initially zero. Solving yields

$$\frac{\mathrm{d}K}{K} = \frac{(\gamma - \gamma^*)}{(\delta^* + \delta)}\frac{\mathrm{d}p^*}{p^*}.$$

[32] This is the formal expression of the dual role played by $(\gamma - \gamma^*)$ discussed previously.

home country). Then as p^* (and p) rise, r rises, and capital flows back towards the home country, causing an equilibrating rise in r^* abroad. This increase in r^* transfers real income from the foreign country to the home country, and if m_2 exceeds m_2^* this has a *de*stabilizing influence on commodity markets. To be set against this, of course, can be counted not only the substitution effects in demand and production but the increased world supply of commodity 2 occasioned by the capital flow back to the home country. It is conceivable, however, that the former effect dominates. Henceforth I assume that both $E_2^*\Delta$ and $E_2^*\Delta'$ are positive.

Turn, now, to the possibility that, in a stable market, a tariff may (a) worsen rather than improve world terms of trade (p^*), and (b) raise, instead of lower, the relative domestic price of exports (p). Once $\mathrm{d}y$ is broken down into its dependence on $\mathrm{d}p^*$ and $\mathrm{d}K$ in eq. (14) there emerges a relationship, (22), connecting the change in world prices, home prices, and capital flows. That is, (22) shows how these three terms must be balanced in order to clear commodity markets:

$$\{\bar{\eta}_2\}\frac{\mathrm{d}p}{p} + \{\bar{\eta}_2^* + (m_2 - m_2^*)(1 + \mu^* y^*)\}\frac{\mathrm{d}p^*}{p^*} + \mu^*\{(y - y^*) + (m_2 - m_2^*)\delta^*\}\frac{\mathrm{d}K}{K} = 0. \tag{22}$$

The traditional results for the impact of tariffs on prices, extended to allow for the existence of *past* capital flows, can readily be derived by setting $\mathrm{d}K$ equal to zero. Since the procedure to be used in the general case is the same, it is useful to set out these results for purposes of comparison. The tariff rate, τ, links the home and world relative prices of commodity 2 by the relationship: $p^* = p(1 + \tau)$. Therefore $(\mathrm{d}p^*/p^* - \mathrm{d}p/p)$ is itself a measure of the change in the tariff, $\mathrm{d}\tau$, if trade is initially free (as I shall continue to assume). Subtract $\bar{\eta}_2(\mathrm{d}p^*/p^*)$ from the first term in (22) and add this same expression, $\bar{\eta}_2(\mathrm{d}p^*/p^*)$, to the second term. With $\mathrm{d}K$ assumed zero this yields

$$\{\bar{\eta}_2\}\left(\frac{\mathrm{d}p}{p} - \frac{\mathrm{d}p^*}{p^*}\right) - \Delta\frac{\mathrm{d}p^*}{p^*} = 0.$$

Since $\bar{\eta}_2$ and Δ have opposite signs $(\mathrm{d}p/p - \mathrm{d}p^*/p^*)$ and $\mathrm{d}p^*/p^*$ must have opposite signs. That is, a tariff must improve the world terms of trade, p^*.

By a similar kind of argument add $\mathrm{d}p/p$ times the coefficient of $\mathrm{d}p^*/p^*$ to the first term in (22) and subtract it from the second to obtain

$$-\Delta\frac{\mathrm{d}p}{p} + \{\bar{\eta}_2^* + (m_2 - m^*)(1 + \mu^* y^*)\}\left(\frac{\mathrm{d}p^*}{p^*} - \frac{\mathrm{d}p}{p}\right) = 0.$$

If a tariff is imposed $(\mathrm{d}p^*/p^* - \mathrm{d}p/p)$ is positive. Since $-\Delta$ is negative (assuming, still, that $E_2^* > 0$), $\mathrm{d}p$ must have the same sign as $\{\bar{\eta}_2^* + (m_2 - m_2^*)(1 + \mu^* \gamma^*)\}$. This is a slight generalization of Metzler's classic result [11]. An alternative form of expression is that p can be raised (the 'paradoxical' result) only if $-\eta_2^*$, the elasticity of the foreign country's offer curve (defined here so as to be positive), falls short of $m_2(1 + \mu^* \gamma^*)$.

How are these standard results affected by taking into account the endogenous nature of capital flows? Instead of setting $\mathrm{d}K = 0$ it is necessary to recognize that the price changes induced by the tariff cause r and r^* to get out of line, calling forth capital flows as described in relation (20). Solve (20) for $\mathrm{d}K/K$ and substitute this value into (22) to obtain

$$\{\bar{\eta}_2 + \alpha\gamma\}\frac{\mathrm{d}p}{p} + \{\bar{\eta}_2^* + (m_2 - m_2^*)(1 + \mu^*\gamma^*) - \alpha\gamma^*\}\frac{\mathrm{d}p^*}{p^*} = 0, \tag{23}$$

where

$$\alpha = \frac{\mu^*}{(\delta + \delta^*)}\{(\gamma - \gamma^*) + (m_2 - m_2^*)\delta^*\}.$$

By exactly the same kind of reasoning as just used, and assuming that Δ' is positive (the stability condition appropriate in a world of free international movement of capital), a tariff improves the world terms of trade only if the coefficient of $\mathrm{d}p$ is negative and lowers the domestic price of exports, p, only if the coefficient of $\mathrm{d}p^*$ is negative. These are the 'generalized' results which are seen to depend upon the signs of $\alpha\gamma$ on the one hand and $\alpha\gamma^*$ on the other.

Taking these in reverse order, consider $\alpha\gamma^*$. The conclusion is simple: with at least one country driven to specialize completely, $\alpha\gamma^*$ must be non-negative. If the foreign country is specialized, γ^*, and therefore $\alpha\gamma^*$, is zero. Suppose, instead, that the home country is specialized ($\gamma = 1$) and the foreign country is not ($\delta^* = 0$). Then $\alpha\gamma^*$ is $(\mu^*/\delta)\gamma^*(1 - \gamma^*)$. Since E_2^* is assumed positive, $\alpha\gamma^*$ must be positive since the magnification effect assures that a positive γ^* implies a negative $(1 - \gamma^*)$. That is, with capital responsive to rate differences, there is an even stronger case for supposing that a tariff will be 'protective' of local industry than if capital were not responsive. However, the 'paradoxical' Metzler result could still occur.

No such simple results are available for the effect of a tariff on world terms of trade, for $\alpha\gamma$ may be of either sign. If $\alpha\gamma$ is sufficiently positive, a tariff may worsen a country's world terms of trade, which does violate the accepted doctrine. Examine, first, the situation in which the foreign country is completely specialized, so that $\alpha\gamma$ reduces to

$$\frac{\mu^*}{(\delta + \delta^*)}\gamma\{\gamma + (m_2 - m_2^*)\delta^*\}.$$

Once again it is the possible effect of the income-redistribution term that is the only source for the 'paradoxical' result. If this is 'weak' enough so that the expression in brackets has the same sign as γ, $\alpha\gamma$ must be negative and a tariff improves a country's world terms of trade.

If the foreign country is incompletely specialized, δ^* is zero, and at unchanged p^* there is no redistribution of income. However, $\alpha\gamma$ can become positive now for a different reason. It equals $(\mu^*/\delta)(1 - \gamma^*)$, which is positive if X_2^* is capital-intensive. Suppose this to be the case. At initial p^* a tariff reduces p. By substitution effects in the home country, net demand for commodity 2 rises. (This is what $\bar{\eta}_2$ summarizes.) However, with the home country specialized, the decrease in p brings about a proportionate decrease in r. This, in turn, causes capital to flow to the foreign country (where r^* is linked to p^* and therefore is unchanged at constant p^*). Although this capital flow serves to reduce the home country's production of commodity 2, the foreign country's production rises by an even greater amount if X_2^* is capital-intensive (again, by the magnification effect). That is, at the initial value for p^* the tariff causes an increase in the *world* supply of commodity 2 if X_2^* is capital-intensive, and this could conceivably outweigh the increased home demand for commodity 2. If so, p^* will fall in a stable market.

These results are useful in exploring the question of the impact of tariffs on home real incomes when capital movements are free and endogenous. Again, it is a variation of the basic eq. (9) that is required. Consider (9″):

$$\frac{\mathrm{d}y}{\mathrm{d}\tau} = \left\{ \frac{\partial y}{\partial p^*} + \frac{\partial y}{\partial K}\frac{\mathrm{d}K}{\mathrm{d}p^*} \right\} \frac{\mathrm{d}p^*}{\mathrm{d}\tau}, \tag{9″}$$

where $\partial y/\partial p^*$ and $\partial y/\partial K$ are as shown in (9′). With initial free trade, an increase in p^* has a direct and indirect effect on real income. If specialization abroad is incomplete, a simple result emerges: the effect of a price change in stimulating capital movements and, through this mechanism, affecting the foreign rate of return and thus real income can be ignored. For with specialization incomplete abroad, movements of capital cannot, apart from price changes, affect r^*; $\partial y/\partial K$ is zero. The tariff discussion of section 4, with full optimization, is appropriate here, with the proviso that a tariff does indeed improve the country's terms of trade.

The remaining case is the one in which the foreign country is completely specialized. This is the case that led to strong conclusions if both tax and tariff policies could be optimally used: if foreign demand is not infinitely elastic it is always optimal to levy a tariff. With an optimal tax wedge between r and r^* ruled out, this conclusion needs to be revised.

The first task is to derive an expression for the impact of a change in p^* on capital flows. This can most readily be done by considering the effect of a change in p on K, via eq. (20), and linking that with the relationship between changes in home and world prices shown by (23). With complete specialization abroad, γ^* is zero; and (20) can be solved for $\mathrm{d}K/\mathrm{d}p$:

$$\frac{\mathrm{d}K}{\mathrm{d}p} = \frac{K}{p^*}\frac{\gamma}{(\delta + \delta^*)}. \tag{20'}$$

The sign of this expression depends only upon γ. If X_2 is capital-intensive, an increase in p must reduce the amount of foreign investment if the home country is a lender and increase the flow to the home country if it is a borrower. For a rise in p raises r if γ is positive, and this reduces K (which has the effect of raising r^*, serving to equalize rates of return). In the 'usual' case a tariff drives up p^* and pushes down p. That is $\mathrm{d}p/\mathrm{d}p^*$, as given by (23′), is negative:

$$\frac{\mathrm{d}p}{\mathrm{d}p^*} = -\frac{B}{A}, \tag{23'}$$

where $A = \bar{\eta}_2 + \alpha\gamma$ and $B = \{\bar{\eta}_2^* + (m_2 - m_2^*)\}$. It is possible, however, for a tariff to worsen the world terms of trade (if A is positive) or raise the domestic export price (if B is positive), but not both, for $-(A + B) = \Delta'$ which, by considerations of stability, is positive (assuming $E_2^* > 0$). Therefore $\mathrm{d}K/\mathrm{d}p^*$ is given as in (24):

$$\frac{\mathrm{d}K}{\mathrm{d}p^*} = -\frac{K}{p^*}\frac{B}{A}\frac{\gamma}{(\delta + \delta^*)}. \tag{24}$$

The effect of a tariff on world prices was discussed previously. The formal expression for $\mathrm{d}p^*/\mathrm{d}\tau$ is given in (25), and is usually positive:

$$\frac{\mathrm{d}p^*}{\mathrm{d}\tau} = -p^*\frac{A}{\Delta'}. \tag{25}$$

All the ingredients of (9″) are at hand, and can be combined in (26):

$$\frac{\mathrm{d}y}{\mathrm{d}\tau} = E_2^* \left\{1 - \mu^*\gamma\frac{B}{A}\frac{\delta^*}{\delta + \delta^*}\right\} \left\{-\frac{p^*A}{\Delta'}\right\}. \tag{26}$$

The impact of a tariff differs depending upon: (i) its effect on prices, p^* and p, as determined by the signs of A and B, (ii) whether the home country is a lender or borrower, which affects the sign of μ^*, and (iii) factor intensities in the home country or the degree of specialization at home, which affects the sign of γ.

Many cases are possible. Consider here only the 'normal' case where A and B are both negative so that the tariff raises p^* and lowers p. From a position of initial free trade has y increased? Depending upon factor intensities at home, the indirect effect of capital movements on r^* either supports the beneficial effect on y of the increase in p^* or does not. In the case of conflict, it is possible for the indirect effect to outweigh the direct.

If the home country is a lender, μ^* is positive. Therefore if X_2 is capital-intensive, the indirect effect runs counter to the direct. The upshot of the tariff is to lower r^*, since the lowering of p reduces r, encouraging a further capital flow abroad. If capital exports from the home country are sufficiently large relative to commodity exports (large μ^*), the optimal tariff strategy is to subsidize goods exports in order to induce the capital flow back to the home country (that serves to raise r^*) that in different circumstances could be achieved by a tax on capital movements. The case for the borrower is similar, except that the object is then to reduce r^*. This is a by-product of the tariff if X_2 is capital-intensive. On the other hand, if γ is negative, it may be optimal for the borrower to subsidize commodity exports, which raises p (by the assumption that B is negative) and therefore lowers r, inducing a lowering of r^* through cutting down capital imports.

Other cases call for fairly obvious modifications in the argument.

7.

This has been a long chapter. Because results have depended upon the pattern of specialization and the degree of freedom available in manipulating tax and tariff rates it has been necessary to develop the argument in a somewhat taxonomic, case-by-case manner. Nonetheless, some general conclusions can be stated.

The source of the 'paradoxical' result wherein a tax on goods or factors is *negative* in the optimal solution is the linkage between the two terms of trade in the model, p^* and r^*. If specialization is incomplete abroad, r^* depends directly upon p^* via the foreign technology and therefore the situation can arise in which a favorable movement in one price ratio is always associated with an unfavorable movement in the other. Thus in the case of full optimization a negative tariff is possible if capital flows (literally the flow of interest or dividend payments) are important enough in the balance of payments.

This direct link between r^* and p^*, and with it the possibility of a negative tariff or tax in the optimal solution, disappears if specialization abroad is complete *and* *full* optimization is pursued. Thus the optimal tariff rate is unequivocally positive *if* an optimal tax is levied so that $\partial y/\partial K$ is zero. And, a positive tax on capital flows is optimal *if* any resultant change in the commodity terms of trade has no effect on real income (because the tariff has been chosen so that $\partial y/\partial p^*$ is zero). However, in the 'second-best' situations considered in Sections 5 and 6, the removal of one lever of policy introduces an indirect link between the commodity terms of trade (p^*) and the foreign rate of return (r^*) even with complete specialization abroad. And with this indirect link there re-emerges the possibility that it may pay to subsidize, instead of to tax, commodity flows or capital flows. Thus if capital flows are relatively small, it may pay to subsidize capital flows in a free trade world to benefit from a possible favorable movement in the commodity terms of trade. Or, if capital is completely mobile internationally and tariffs can be levied, it may pay to subsidize commodity flows if capital flows are relatively important. In the former case a subsidy on capital flows induces a change in the commodity terms of trade in order to clear markets (which will have been disrupted by the change in world demand and supply conditions by the change in K). In the latter case the change in commodity terms of trade throws the home rate of return out of line, necessitating equilibrating capital flows, which induce changes in the foreign rate of return. And in either case these changes (in p^* or r^*) have effects on real income which must be weighed against the direct effects of the tax or tariff.

The strong conclusions that are available with full optimization and complete specialization abroad are therefore seen to be the exception rather than the rule. In general 'paradoxical' results are possible. Even without the direct link between p^* and r^* provided by the technology if specialization abroad is incomplete, the repercussion of a change in one terms of trade upon the other via the requirement that markets be cleared or rates of return be equilibrated introduces the possibility that a seemingly unfavorable movement in one price ratio is justified by the corresponding favorable turn in the other. If specialization abroad is incomplete, p^* and r^* are linked directly via the technology, and this becomes the dominant consideration, which is operative whether full optimization is possible or only one policy lever can be manipulated. This explains the similarity in the results for the case of incomplete specialization between section 5 or section 6 and section 4.[33]

[33] One difference between the case of full optimization and the second-best cases should be noted. Kemp discusses the possible sign of total government revenue, from taxing trade and capital movements. If foreign production is completely specialized, government revenue must be positive. In the case of incomplete foreign specialization, the expression for total government revenue is easily derived. By definition it equals $(p^* - p)E_2^* + (r^* - r)K$, which can be rewritten as

$$p^*E_2^*\left\{\frac{(p^*-p)}{p^*}+\frac{(r^*-r)}{r^*}\mu^*\right\}.$$

One difference between the cases of complete and incomplete specialization persists. Consider just the case in which $K > 0$, i.e. in which the foreign country is an 'importer' of capital. As noted earlier the foreign country could nonetheless be an exporter of its capital-intensive commodity if technology differs sufficiently between countries. However, the 'normal' Heckscher–Ohlin pattern calls for the 'exporter' of capital also to export its capital-intensive commodity. With *incomplete* specialization in the foreign country, technology requires the two terms of trade, p^* and r^*, to move together in the 'normal' case, thus disallowing the possibility of 'conflict' that leads either to negative tax or negative tariff. With *complete* specialization abroad, and with the indirect link between r^* and p^* that emerges from the market-clearing or rate-equating conditions in the cases of sections 5 and 6, the possibility of 'conflict' between p^* and r^* is associated with the 'normal' case. Thus in section 5 a tax on capital flows could help by raising r^* but hurt by lowering p^* if the home country exports its capital-intensive commodity. And, in section 6, a tariff that raises p^* and lowers p encourages capital to flee to the foreign country (thus lowering r^*, which works counter to the rise in p^*) if X_2 is capital-intensive.

As a final comment consider some of the assumptions of the model. Neither country is engaged in *current* capital accumulation. That is, savings are assumed to be zero. This rules out many of the interesting phenomena associated with models of growth. But this is deliberate, for the primary concern of the chapter is with a static question: what is the optimal location of already existing capital equipment? This is a question that would not disappear in models of growth, but its analysis would be made more complicated by phenomena involved in the growth process that do not bear directly on this static question. By the same token, classic questions of optimal tariff strategy do not disappear in a dynamic setting, but they are thereby made more difficult to analyze.[34] Some objection might be

(footnote 33 continued)
But in the case of full optimization, $(r^* - r)/r^*$ equals $[(p^* - p)/p^*]\gamma^*$, and $(p^* - p)/p^*$ equals $-(1 + \mu^*\gamma^*)/\eta_2^*$. Therefore total government revenue is

$$-p^*E_2^*\frac{(1 + \mu^*\gamma^*)^2}{\eta_2^*},$$

which is always positive (or zero), even when one tax or the other is negative. (Kemp's incorrect expression for government revenue allowed for a negative result, which tended to support his incorrect conclusion that both tax and tariff could be negative.) However, in section 5 it was shown that the tax on capital flows could be negative when the tariff was zero and, in section 6, that the duty on imports could be negative when capital flows were unimpeded. In both cases, obviously, government revenue is negative.

[34] In a recent article Negishi [12] has discussed the question of benefits from foreign investment in the context of a world in which capital goods are currently produced. Some of his conclusions seem

raised to the assumption that capital goods can be physically moved from one country to another. If depreciation and current capital accumulation were allowed this objection would be weakened. But note that the spirit of this assumption is the same as in general neoclassical models of production allowing for the transfer of resources (including capital) from one occupation to another. More importantly, if capital is *not* mobile from one country to another, the classical theory of trade comes back into its own, and this theory has been well developed. Thus the model in this paper can be considered an extreme case, with 'realistic' situations representing a blend of this with already known results.

Finally, note that in a sense this model has 'on the cheap' broken away from the two-commodity restriction characterizing most of trade theory. That is, the variety of results obtainable in models in which more than one terms of trade exist, and the necessity of balancing off effects in one market with those in another, are introduced by allowing capital to be mobile internationally *without* introducing more than two commodities in consumption (since the services of capital do not enter the utility function) or in production. A more general model (with more than two commodities or factors) would introduce questions of possible complementarity in consumption or production that are avoided here

References

[1] Amano, A., 'International Factor Movements and the Terms of Trade', unpublished.

[2] Amano, A., 'The Relation Between International Movements of Goods and Factors', unpublished.

[3] Balogh, T. and P. Streeton, 'Domestic versus Foreign Investment', *Bulletin of the Oxford University Institute of Statistics*, 22 (August 1960).

startling: under certain circumstances (savings linked to earnings of capital instead of to national income) it pays to subsidize, instead of to tax, foreign investment. The additional element in the analysis, ruled out in the present paper and in the earlier treatments (Kemp [5, 6, 9], MacDougall [10]) is the possibility that changes in foreign investment may induce a rise in the level of savings and capital endowment and thus a rise in future maintainable levels of consumption. Consider the general expression (6) of this paper. For his 'paradoxical' results, Negishi simplifies by assuming (i) no commodity trade, so that E_2^* and dE_2^* vanish, and (ii) no change in the foreign return to capital, so that dr^* goes to zero. This leaves only $(r^* - r)dK$ in (6), which is small near the initial state of unimpeded capital flows. But an extra term is added to (6) – the effect of an increase in K in stimulating further capital accumulation at home. This term must dominate near the initial point of zero tax or subsidy and thus must be the sole determinant of whether taxes or subsidies on capital flows are optimal. But note the 'second-best' flavor of Negishi's results: interfering in the level of foreign investment is profitable because the overall capital/labor ratio was not 'optimal' to begin with. If it were, a change in the capital/labor ratio would have no further effect on maintainable levels of real consumption. For a further discussion of Negishi's model see Kemp [8].

[4] Jones, R.W., 'Stability Conditions in International Trade: A General Equilibrium Analysis', *International Economic Review*, 2 (May 1961).

[5] Kemp, M.C., 'Foreign Investment and the National Advantage', *Economic Record*, 38 (March 1962).

[6] Kemp, M.C., 'The Benefits and Costs of Private Investment from Abroad: Comment', *Economic Record* 38 (March 1962).

[7] Kemp, M.C., *The Pure Theory of International Trade* (Prentice-Hall, New York, 1964) ch. 13, 14.

[8] Kemp, M.C., 'A Guide to Negishi', *Economic Record*, 41 (December 1965).

[9] Kemp, M.C., 'The Gain from International Trade and Investment: A Neo-Heckscher–Ohlin Approach', *American Economic Review*, 56 (September 1966).

[10] MacDougall, G.D.A., 'The Benefits and Costs of Private Investment from Abroad: A Theoretical Approach', *Economic Record*, 36 (March 1960).

[11] Metzler, L., 'Tariffs, the Terms of Trade, and the Distribution of National Income', *Journal of Political Economy*, 57 (February 1949).

[12] Negishi, T., 'Foreign Investment and the Long-Run National Advantage', *Economic Record*, 41 (December 1965).

[13] Rybczynski, T.M., 'Factor Endowments and Relative Commodity Prices', *Economica*, 22 (November 1955).

[14] Samuelson, P.A., 'Prices of Factors and Goods in General Equilibrium', *Review of Economic Studies*, 21 (1953–1954).

[15] Stolper, W.F. and P.A. Samuelson, 'Protection and Real Wages', *Review of Economic Studies*, 9 (November 1941).

Chapter 13

PRODUCTION PATTERNS WITH CAPITAL MOBILITY*

1. Introduction

The present chapter is concerned with some aspects of trade theory with internationally mobile real capital, not in the context of an optimal commercial and investment strategy, but in the framework of a free-trade, no-impediments-to-capital-movements model. Two countries with different technologies are engaged in trading two commodities, each produced with homogeneous labor and capital subject to constant returns to scale. The pattern of production in each country depends sensitively upon the terms of trade. Indeed, the main task in this chapter is to investigate how production patterns and the location of real capital change as the terms of trade run the gamut from very low to very high values and, in the background, real capital moves from country to country as required to equalize rentals.[1] Recent work of Chipman [2] has suggested that the world production-possibilities schedule may possess a 'flat' if, in a world of real capital mobility, it is possible for both countries to be diversified in producing both commodities. I shall investigate both the Chipman case and the case in which the world's transformation schedule is strictly bowed out in order to ascertain what specialization patterns can be expected, whether capital flows get reversed as the terms of trade change, and the type of relationship that exists between the terms of trade and the return to capital.

*Abridged version of 'Trade Patterns with Capital Mobility', jointly with Roy Ruffin, in: M. Parkin and A.R. Nobay, eds., *Current Economic Problems* (Cambridge, 1975) pp. 307–332. Jones's research was supported by the National Science Foundation.

[1] I avoid the use of 'interest rates' in the model of this chapter as dynamic considerations of time preference are absent. With free trade in commodities and unimpeded mobility of real capital equipment, the rental on a machine will be equated between sectors and between countries.

2. Comparative advantage uniquely defined

The most simple case to consider is the one in which the technological difference between countries confers upon each one a unique comparative advantage in one of the two commodities. But care must be taken in interpreting this in the case of international capital mobility. In the standard Heckscher–Ohlin model it is differences in factor endowment proportions that lead to positions of comparative advantage. In a model of capital mobility, the concept of a country's factor proportions becomes more ambiguous, and it makes more sense to compare relative costs when countries earn the same return on their capital.[2]

Let p denote the relative price, or cost, of commodity 2 in units of commodity 1 ($p \equiv p_2/p_1$), and let R indicate the rental return of capital (r) deflated by the price of the first commodity ($R \equiv r/p_1$). Suppose in both countries the second commodity is capital-intensive. Fig. 13.1 illustrates for this case the situation in which for any common return to capital (R) the foreign country would, if both commodities were produced, possess a comparative advantage in the second commodity. Indeed the vertical distance between the two curves would reflect the *relative* foreign superiority in producing the second commodity in Harrodian terms. The assumption made in this first section is that the foreign curve is lower than the home curve throughout.

Two remarks can be made about the technological relationship between the terms of trade (p) and the return to capital (R) illustrated in fig. 13.1. First, if a country is producing both commodities, its curve indeed shows its (p–R) combination and, furthermore, its curve is flatter at any point than a ray drawn from

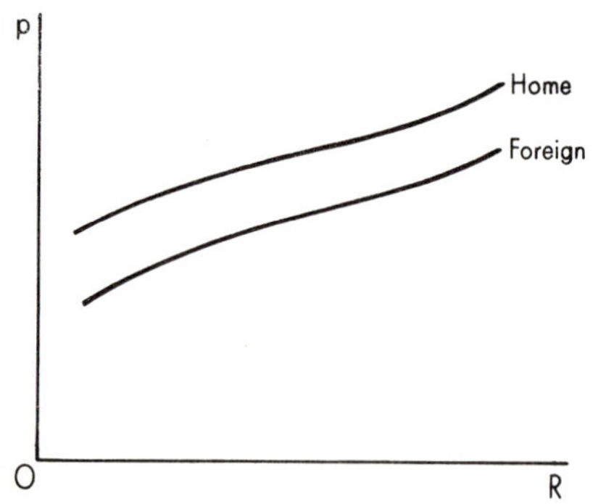

Figure 13.1

[2]For a brief discussion of the concept of factor abundance in a model of capital mobility, see Chapter 15.

the origin to that point. This reflects the assumption that commodity 2 is capital-intensive, requiring a magnified increase in R for any given increase in the relative commodity price, p. Secondly, a country's (p–R) combination will generally *not* be shown by a point on its curve in fig. 13.1 if that country is specialized in producing only one commodity. The question of specialization depends both upon its technology and upon the aggregate bundle of factors used in local production. For any given resource base there is only a finite range of price ratios (shown by slopes of its transformation schedule) for which that country can be incompletely specialized. For values of p above a certain value, all resources would be devoted to producing the high-priced second commodity. For values of p below a certain level only commodity 1 would be produced.

Fig. 13.2 illustrates for the home country the three-section breakdown of the relationship between the return to capital and the commodity-price ratio for some given value of its resource base. Incomplete specialization, along section II (a piece of the technological determined curve shown in fig. 13.1), takes place if the terms of trade lie in the range ($\underline{p} - \bar{p}$). For $p \leqq \underline{p}$, the country would be forced to specialize in the first commodity. With a given quantity of capital and labor (the entire endowment bundle) devoted to the first commodity, R, the marginal product of capital in the first commodity, is uniquely determined. This is shown by the vertical segment I in fig. 13.2. At the other extreme, for $p \geqq \bar{p}$, all resources are devoted to commodity 2, thus fixing capital's marginal product in terms of the second commodity, r/p_2. But R equals this marginal product, r/p_2, times the terms of trade, p_2/p_1. Therefore the (p–R) relationship when only commodity 2 is produced is shown by section III – a line segment which, if extended, would go through the origin.

The fact that the relationship between the terms of trade and the return to

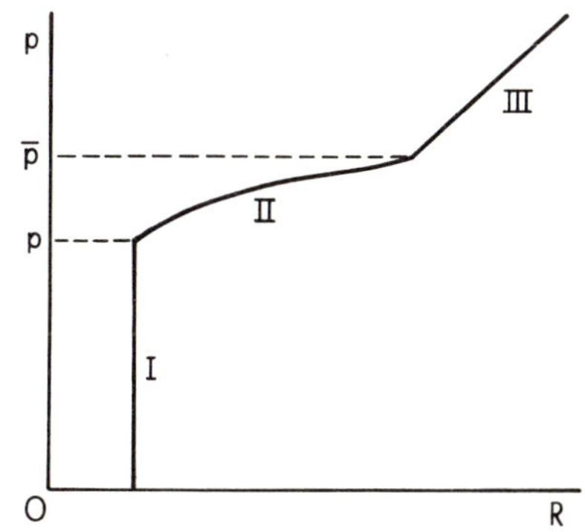

Figure 13.2

capital depends not only upon a country's technology but also upon its resource base is vital for a trade model with capital mobility between countries because each nation's resource base keeps changing as capital flows are required to maintain a uniform rate of return. Referring again to fig. 13.2, suppose the home country experiences an inflow of capital. This has the effect of shifting the vertical section I line leftwards and rotating (around the origin) the section III line counter-clock-wise. That is, for any commodity-price ratio for which the country is specialized (before and after the capital flow) an inflow of capital will lower the return to capital. For any price ratio at which production remains incompletely specialized, there is no change in the R associated with a given p as the capital stock rises; this is a reflection of the unique relationship between commodity and factor prices, independent of factor endowments, when there is incomplete specialization.

If the foreign country has a comparative cost advantage in the second commodity for any common rate of return to capital, as fig. 13.1 illustrates, both countries cannot be incompletely specialized in a world of perfect capital mobility. Literally, the curves do not intersect. Free trade implies a common p; capital mobility implies a common R. This is possible only if at least one of the countries is on a section I or section III type curve (as in fig. 13.2).

To trace out the production patterns for the world transformation curve consider, first, the two extremes for which both countries are specialized in the *same* commodity. For example, suppose p is so low (or the relative price of the first commodity is so high) that both produce only commodity 1. The requirement that the rental on capital be equated between countries determines the division of the world's fixed capital stock between them. Fig. 13.3 illustrates the point. Both the home $R(K)$ curve (reading left to right) and the foreign $R^*(K^*)$ curve (reading right to left) show each country's return to capital falling as that country obtains more capital (with each country's labor supply always fixed). The distribution of the world's capital stock that would be observed when both countries specialize in commodity 1 is shown by the intersection point of the two curves, where 0 and 0* are separated by the total world supply of capital.

The other extreme has both countries specializing in commodity 2 because p is sufficiently high. Capital mobility now ensures that R/p is equated to R^*/p (the marginal product of capital in commodity 2 for each country). A diagram similar to fig. 13.3, except with R/p and R^*/p on the axes, could be drawn. Again, some allocation of the world's capital stock is determined. However, nothing that has so far been specified about the technology in each country necessarily determines whether the home country would have more or less capital at very high p than a low p. The world transformation schedule will exhibit slopes that lie

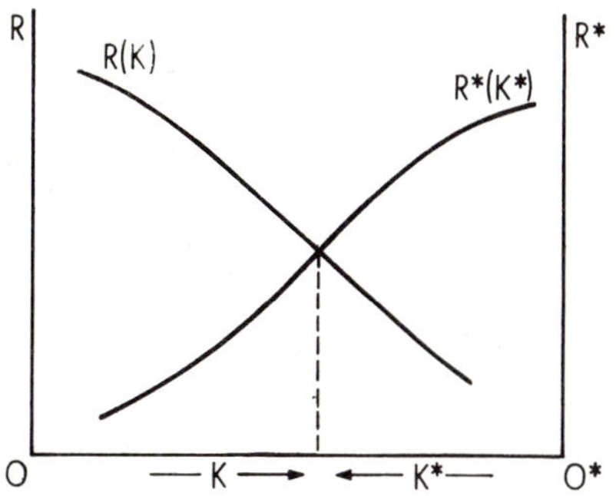

Figure 13.3

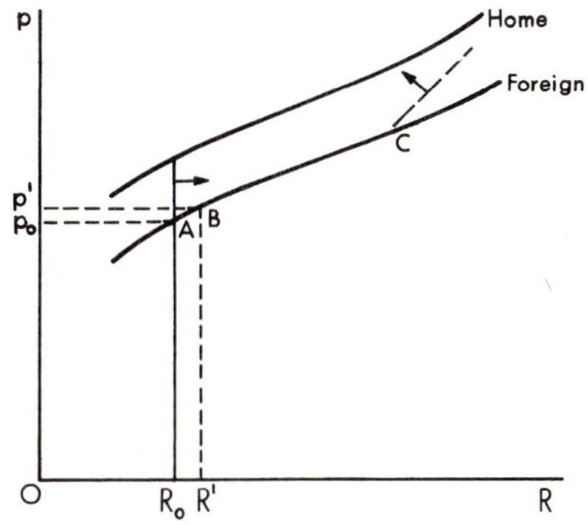

Figure 13.4

between the highest value of p for which both countries remain specialized in commodity 1 and the lowest value for p that drives both into producing just commodity 2.

Trace out the world production-possibilities schedule by treating the terms of trade as a parameter and letting p vary from low to high values. Referring to fig. 13.4, both countries specialize completely in the first commodity for all $p \leqq p_0$, and the world return on capital is given by R_0. At p_0 the foreign country is an incipient producer of the second commodity; p_0 reflects the relative cost of producing the first unit of commodity 2 abroad. Suppose commodity 2's relative price rises to p'. If capital were immobile internationally, its return would be driven up by a magnified amount abroad (to R'), while remaining at the R_0 level at home. In a world of capital mobility this discrepancy is a signal for relocation of capital in the foreign country from the home country. Such a movement would continue until the vertical home country section I segment shifts sufficiently to the right to intersect the foreign country's section II segment at point B. Thus in a world of capital mobility both points A and B would lie on the locus of all world pairs of p and R.

This capital movement from the home country to the foreign country shifts rightwards the vertical section I segment for the home country because of the increasing capital shortage at home. But it also shifts leftwards (counter-clockwise) the section I segment (section III segment) for the foreign country. This is illustrated by fig. 13.4's counter-clockwise arrow for the section III segment commencing at point C. This is significant, for as p rises and as capital flows from the home country abroad, the world (p–R) response is traced out by points like B on the foreign country's section II segment, as long as B remains to the left of points like *C*. Once *B* and *C* pass each other, the pattern of specialization must change. In particular, the foreign country can no longer remain incompletely specialized.

To pursue this point, note that as capital flows into the foreign country as p rises, less and less commodity 1 is being produced abroad, and this for two reasons. First, for any given allocation of the world's capital stock, the rise in p encourages foreign output of commodity 2 at commodity 1's expense. Secondly, by the Rybczynski theorem, for any given value of the terms of trade a capital inflow results in a lower output of labor-intensive commodity 1. Therefore eventually the foreign country becomes specialized in producing commodity 2, and this happens when point *C* in fig. 13.4, moving down the foreign (p–R) curve, hits point *B* moving up.

Fig. 13.5 illustrates a terms of trade, p'', at which both countries are completely specialized, the home country in commodity 1 and the foreign country in commodity 2, and share a common rental on capital, R''. If p should rise, the foreign return on capital (shown along the *CDF* segment above *D*) would exceed the home rate (shown by R''), once again attracting capital from the home country to the foreign. The economic reasoning is clear; a rise in 2's relative price must coax out greater production of 2 somewhere in the world. In this range, with both countries specialized, only the foreign country can produce commodity 2, and so it receives another influx of capital.

This capital flow serves again to shift the home country's vertical section I DBR'' curve rightwards (as increasing capital scarcity at home drives up the return to capital for any terms of trade) and the foreign *CDF* section III ray counterclockwise. Thus for slightly higher $p > p''$, the new world (p–R) combination would be shown by a point such as *E*. But since *CDF* extended would pass through

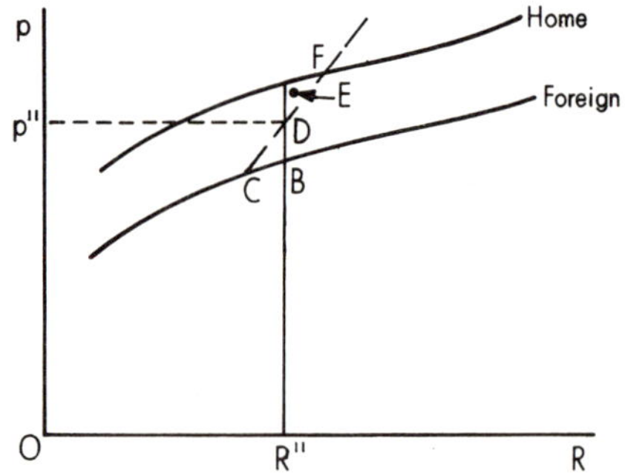

Figure 13.5

the origin, the world's return to capital (R) has increased, in going from D to E, by a smaller proportion than has the terms of trade (p). This reverses the typical magnification effect connecting commodity and factor prices (exhibited by the two curves in fig. 13.1) whereby a given change in relative commodity prices calls forth a more than proportionate change in factor prices if there is no joint production.

The reason why the magnification effect gets reversed when each country is specialized in a different commodity is easy to state. First, note that a typical magnification effect depends upon the existence of some economy (such as the foreign economy for lower values of p) producing both commodities with two mobile factors. But consider the world economy when each country is specialized to a different good. It resembles a three-factor, two-sector economy in which each sector uses some factor specific to that sector (that country's labor force) and some factor used in common by both sectors (the world's mobile capital). For such a model any change in relative commodity prices must cause a change in the return to the mobile factor (capital) that is a positive weighted average of (and therefore trapped between) the commodity price changes.[3] Such an analogy between a three-factor, two-commodity (world) economy with one mobile and two specific factors does not apply if either country is incompletely specialized, for in that case that country cannot be identified with a productive sector producing just one commodity. Instead it would be analogous to a sector typified by joint production, in which case the standard relationship breaks down.

As p rises, eventually the home country can start producing the second commodity. This is illustrated by point D in fig. 13.6: the foreign country is specialized in commodity 2 along its CD-extended section III segment, while at R''' the world terms of trade, p''', correspond to the relative costs of producing the second commodity at home. This is a crucial point, for it designates the high-water mark in terms of foreign location of capital. For any $p > p'''$ in fig. 13.6, the home return on capital would exceed the foreign return, serving to attract capital back to the home country, thus shifting the home country's vertical DR''' segment to the left and the foreign CD segment clockwise to the right (so that CD-extended still passes through the origin). After such a capital flow fig. 13.6 would look much like fig. 13.5, with one important difference in interpretation: the world's (p–R) combination would be shown by point F (in fig. 13.5) instead of point D. The home country, for p high enough, produces some of commodity 2.

The direction of the capital flow for p greater than p''' in fig. 13.6 may seem paradoxical. The foreign country's technology imparts to it an unambiguous

[3]For proofs of details concerning such a three factor, two commodity model, see Chapter 6.

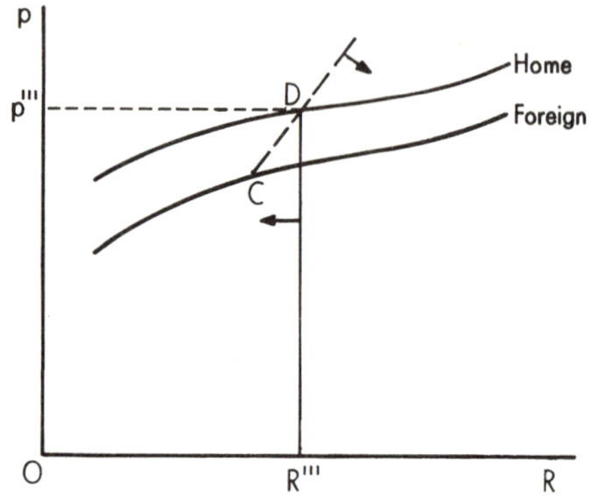

Figure 13.6

comparative advantage in producing the second commodity, and yet, for $p > p'''$ an increase in the relative price of the second commodity pulls capital out of the foreign country and into the home country. Two observations may help to explain this: (i) since capital is internationally mobile, its rate of return must be the same in both countries despite the presumed difference in their technologies. This means that an extra unit of capital in either country would increase the *aggregate* national production in that country by the same value, R, measured in units of the first commodity. With the foreign country specialized in producing the second commodity, any loss of capital must come entirely out of its production of the second commodity. But production changes at home can be more dispersed than this once the home country is incompletely specialized. An increase in one unit of capital employed at home raises aggregate production by R, but can raise the production of an individual commodity by a greater value if it also serves to contract output of the other commodity. This leads to the second observation: (ii) commodity 2 is the capital-intensive commodity. Therefore an inflow of capital serves to increase the production of commodity 2 by a magnified amount at home, an amount greater than the reduction in the completely specialized foreign country.

Underlying these remarks is the 'reciprocity theorem' enunciated some years ago by Samuelson [3]. Applied to this two-sector model it states that

$$\partial R/\partial p = \partial x_2/\partial K$$

for any country in which x_2 denotes that country's output of the second commodity and K that country's capital stock. It is a relationship that holds whether or not there is incomplete specialization. In terms of the diagrams it states that if, from the point of intersection of the two countries' (p–R) curves (including the specialized segments I and III), the home curve is steeper than the foreign curve (i.e. $\partial R/\partial p$ is lower at home than abroad), a flow of capital from the home to the foreign country will increase world output of commodity 2 since it will increase foreign output by more than it reduces home output. This condition was satisfied at point A in fig. 13.4, or point D in fig. 13.5, but *not* at point D in fig. 13.6 or point F in fig. 13.5. As p rises, capital moves from low to high rates of return (and serves to equalize them). Samuelson's theorem states that such a capital flow will always raise world output of the commodity that has risen in price. Alternatively phrased, the possibility of capital mobility must, through these production effects, serve to make world outputs more responsive to world prices.

To complete the story, further increases of p about p''' serve continuously to attract capital back to the home country and the world (p–R) movement is along the home country's curve. The home country remains incompletely specialized until its section III specialization segment, which is moving to the left as capital flows into the home country, reaches the foreign country's section III segment (i.e. CD-extended in fig. 13.6), which is shifting clockwise to the right. When these match up, there is a world capital allocation that remains for any further rise in p; the world is specialized completely to commodity 2.

Several diagrams serve to sum up the relationships that have been discussed. The locus of possible world terms of trade and rates of return to capital are illustrated in fig. 13.7. In regions *1* and *5* the world is completely specialized in commodities 1 and 2, respectively. Region *2* reflects the foreign technological link between p and R when the foreign country produces both commodities and region *4* reflects, in the same fashion, the home technology. In region *3* each country is completely specialized to the commodity in which it has a comparative advantage,

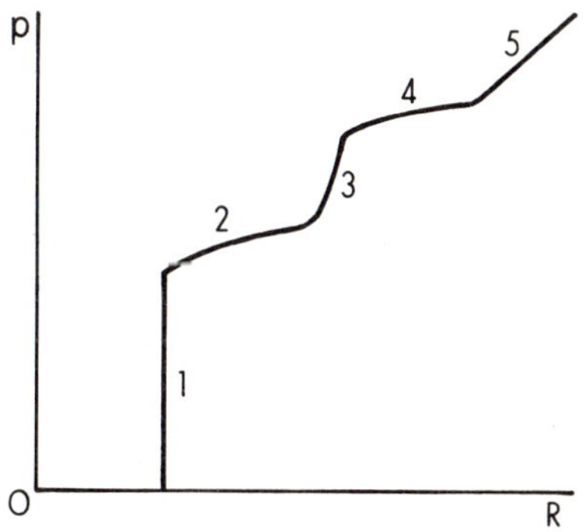

Figure 13.7

and the typical magnification effect whereby a given change in commodity prices results in a greater than proportional change in factor prices gets reversed.

The world transformation curve is drawn in fig. 13.8, where the numbers correspond to those used in fig. 13.7. At no point can both countries be incompletely specialized since the technologies exhibited in fig. 13.1 grant each a unique position of comparative advantage. Note how similar this is to a Ricardian world transformation curve, in which region *3*, with both countries specialized to different commodities, shrinks to a point, and regions *2* and *4* are straight lines with different slopes.[4] Near the axes it is always the country with the comparative advantage in a commodity that will be the first to produce it, and the slope of the world transformation curve must reflect the cost ratio of the country that is incompletely specialized.

Fig. 13.9 displays the quantity of capital employed in the home country, and how this varies with the terms of trade. It reflects, in regions *2* and *3*, the flow of capital abroad as p rises, but also illustrates that there must of necessity be a reverse flow of capital back home in region *4* as, with further increases in capital-intensive commodity 2's relative price, the home country becomes a 'better' source to obtain extra production of commodity 2 since it is incompletely specialized and therefore can release capital and labor from x_1 to join an inflow of capital from abroad in producing more x_2. The foreign country, being already completely specialized, is denied this source of advantage. The quantity of capital at home when p is very low (region *1*) is arbitrarily drawn as the same as that for very high p (region *5*) because nothing has been specified in the technology that requires it to be higher (or lower).

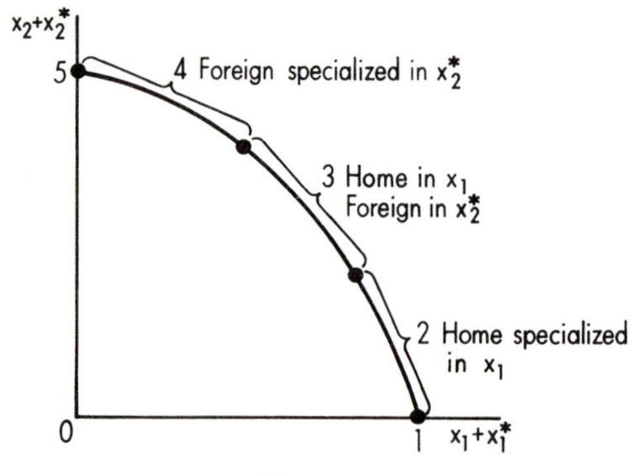

Figure 13.8

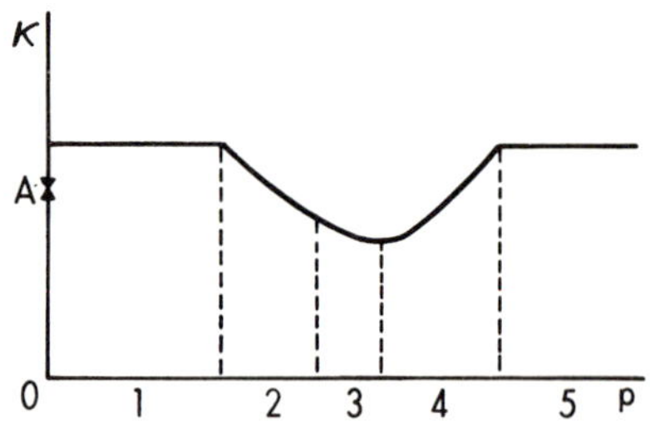

Figure 13.9

[4] See the discussion in Chapter 3.

Nothing has been said about the home country's position as net debtor or creditor or, to use different terms, whether the home country is a net investor abroad. The pattern of capital location in fig. 13.9 is assumed to be independent of the pattern of ultimate ownership. But suppose that OA represents the home country's owned level of capital; then for extreme values of the terms of trade the rest of the world has a net investment position at home, while for a middle range of p-values the home country is a net investor abroad. This contradicts what might have sounded more plausible, that a country will tend to have net investment abroad if, and only if, the relative price of the foreign country's export commodity is sufficiently high. In any case, the relationships between K and p cannot be monotonic. As the next section demonstrates, this is a general result.

Although the net position of the pattern of investment can change with the terms of trade, the pattern of trade is completely invariant. This follows immediately from the previous conclusion that both countries cannot simultaneously be producing both commodities. Therefore if any trade takes place, the foreign country must export commodity 2, in which, as fig. 13.1 recorded, it has a well-defined comparative advantage.

3. A reversal in positions of comparative advantage

There are many ways in which technologies can differ between countries, and it may be the case that the two (p–R) curves could intersect. In particular, one country may possess a superior technology to another in producing both commodities, but such that at a certain rate of profit the *relative* costs of production are equated between countries. This is illustrated for rate R_0 and the common cost ratio p_0 in fig. 13.10. The existence of this single intersection implies a reversal in the position of comparative advantage: for low rates of return to capital the foreign country, as before, possesses a technologically determined comparative advantage in producing the second commodity, while for $R > R_0$ the home country becomes the relatively superior producer of commodity 2.

The significance of the (p_0, R_0) point of intersection is that if these prices prevail, each country can be incompletely specialized in producing both commodities. This is the specialization pattern I had ruled out too hastily in Chapter 12, on the grounds that it would be unlikely that any particular individual set of prices (p_0, R_0) would prevail over any other. But as Chipman [2] has pointed out, a point such as (p_0, R_0) supports a finite range of world production combinations whereas (p, R) combinations where at least one country is specialized correspond to single world output combinations. That is, *if* a reversal in positions of com-

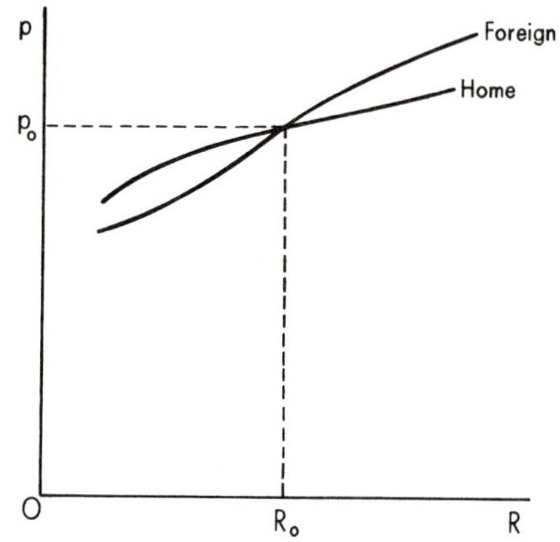

Figure 13.10

parative advantage is possible (as illustrated in fig. 13.10), and *if* the world's capital supply lies in an appropriate range (to be discussed below), the world transformation curve has a flat section along which the terms of trade are p_0 and the rate of return to capital is R_0.

The proviso about the size of the world's capital stock being appropriate is necessary because associated with each total capital supply is a range of possible returns to capital, $\underline{R} - \bar{R}$. For example, fig. 13.3 illustrated the manner in which the return to capital is determined if both countries are specialized in producing commodity 1. This the lower limit, $\underline{R}$, and the upper limit, $\bar{R}$, would be determined in analogous fashion when both countries are specialized to commodity 2. With reference to fig. 13.10, the rate R_0 could not be observed (and therefore the world production possibility curve could not possess a 'Chipman flat') if the world's capital stock is so high that $\bar{R}$ falls short of R_0 or so low that $\underline{R}$ exceeds R_0. I assume, now, that $\underline{R} < R_0 < \bar{R}$.

The logic supporting the flat can be revealed quite simply. Consider a movement of capital, say from the foreign country to the home country, when the terms of trade are p_0 and the common return to capital is R_0 (fig. 13.10). Each country's output pattern changes along a Rybczynski line, with outputs of capital-intensive commodity 2 rising at home and falling abroad. Since each Rybczynski line is just that – a *line* – the sum of the two must also be a line. And the output changes in the two countries cannot cancel each other out. At (p_0, R_0) in fig. 13.10 the home curve is flatter than the foreign curve. By Samuelson's reciprocity theorem the flow of capital to the home country must therefore on net increase the world's supply of commodity 2 (and decrease the world's supply of commodity 1). These output changes all take place at the given p_0, which is the slope of the world's transformation curve along the linear segment.

This linear segment has bounds, however. The capital flow will eventually cause one of the two countries to specialize completely in one of the two commodities. Once a country is specialized, any further capital flow must alter the rate of return to capital and, with it, the terms of trade. The flat linear segment of the transformation schedule will typically be flanked by two strictly bowed-out sections along which specialization in at least one country is complete.

As was discussed in the preceding section, the question of specialization can be analyzed by observing the movements of the type-I and type-III segments in each country as capital flows between them. Reconsider the argument used in fig. 13.4. p_0 represented the lowest relative price of commodity 2 at which some commodity 2 could be produced (by the foreign country). As p rises from p_0 the world (p–R) combination moves upwards along the foreign curve of incomplete specialization (e.g. from A to B) as the vertical section I type segment of the home country shifts to the right. In the meantime the section III type segment for the foreign country (the dashed line through C in fig. 13.4) is swinging counter-clockwise (through the origin) as capital flows into the foreign country. Eventually point C, moving leftwards, and points A or B, moving upwards to the right, pass each other and then each country becomes specialized to a different commodity (e.g. at point D in fig. 13.5). Now, suppose the value of R at which B and C meet is smaller than R_0 in fig. 13.10. This may or may not be the case, but if it is, the entire pattern of world production discussed in the preceding section (and summarized in the world transformation schedule in fig. 13.8) is traced out for values of p and R below the intersection (p_0, R_0) point in fig. 13.10.

The story is picked up at this point by fig. 13.11. The world (p R) combination is shown by point F. The foreign country is completely specialized to the second commodity and the home country is incompletely specialized, as in range *4* of fig. 13.8's production-possibilities curve. As p rises, capital is flowing to the home country from the foreign country, swinging the foreign CF ray rightwards (clockwise through the origin). Eventually point F reaches point A, the intersection point, and at this (p_0, R_0) combination the foreign country can start producing commodity 1.[5] Capital continues to flow from the foreign to the home country, serving to increase foreign production of labor-intensive commodity 1 and reduce

[5]Not shown explicitly in fig. 13.11 is the home section III type segment for specialization in the second commodity. With capital flowing to the home country this segment is shifting leftwards. Could it reach point A before point F, moving rightwards, does? The answer in general is yes, but this possibility has been explicitly ruled out by the assumption that the capital stock is such that the (p_0, R_0) combination can be observed.

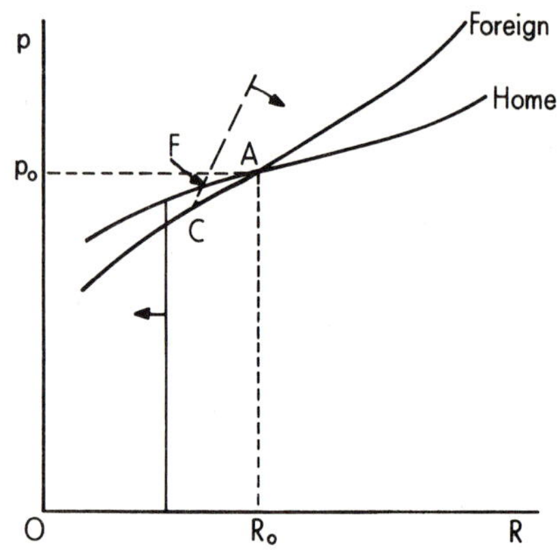

Figure 13.11

foreign x_2^* production. (At home the reverse pattern occurs, the capital inflow increases x_2 production and lowers x_1 production.)

Eventually one or the other country specializes completely. Fig. 13.12 is designed to show the situation before this happens. Both countries are incompletely specialized at point A with world terms of trade p_0 and return to capital R_0. Capital is flowing to the home country, serving to shift leftwards the home section I vertical specialization curve (from B) and the section III specialization in x_2 curve (from C). Capital is flowing out of the foreign country, serving to shift

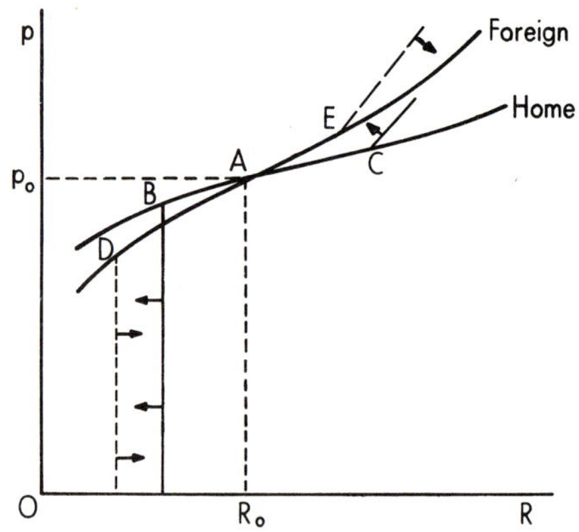

Figure 13.12

rightwards the corresponding foreign specialization segments (the dashed lines starting at D and E). The question is, does point D go through the intersection point A before C does? If it does, then the foreign country is the first to be forced into specialization in the first commodity. In such a case the position of the two countries to the right of A (i.e. for $p > p_0$ and $R > R_0$) is precisely the reverse of that shown in fig. 13.4: the foreign country would be specialized in $x_1{}^*$, the home country would be incompletely specialized, the world (p, R) point would move along the home incomplete-specialization curve in fig. 13.12 until the foreign country's vertical x_1^* specialization segment intersects the home country's point C as the latter moves leftwards. At that point each country specializes (the home country to x_2, the foreign country to x_1^*), and the story continues as before. The final specialization pattern, for sufficiently high p, has the foreign country incompletely specialized.

These patterns of specialization are indicated along fig. 13.13's world transformation locus. First, notice the interior flat, along which both countries are incompletely specialized. Secondly, note that the section *2*, *3*, *4* pattern recreates the fig. 13.8 pattern when each country uniquely has a position of comparative advantage in one commodity. By analogy, sections *6*, *7* and *8* also recreate this pattern with the two countries changing roles, as befits the fact that their positions of comparative advantage have switched. Finally, note that altogether fig. 13.13 allows all conceivable patterns of specialization: each country can be specialized in commodity 1, or commodity 2, or incompletely specialized. This leads to the nine regions of fig. 13.13.

For such a case fig. 13.14 illustrates the way in which the allocation of capital between countries is dependent upon the terms of trade. This should be compared with fig. 13.9 and the numbered ranges with fig. 13.13. For $p < p_0$ the home country

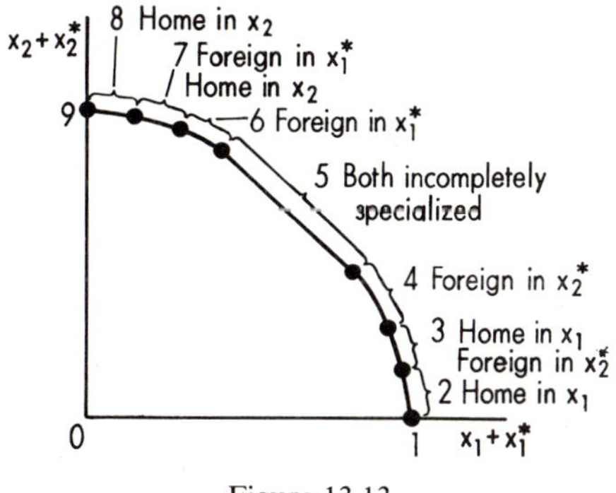

Figure 13.13

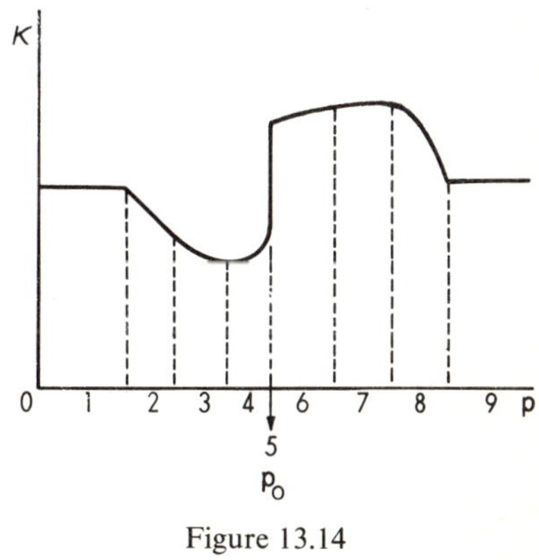

Figure 13.14

at first loses capital as the relative price of commodity 2 rises (it has a comparative disadvantage in x_2), until it starts to produce x_2 with the foreign country already specialized in x_2^* (this is region *4*). Many allocations of the world's capital are possible at p_0. World output of commodity 2 rises as capital flows into the home country, until the foreign country gets driven out of x_2^* production. As p rises a bit above p_0, world production of the second commodity rises both because x_1 production is being cut in the home country (because of the adverse price change) and because, as fig. 13.14 shows, capital is being attracted to the home country (this is region *6*). The capital flow into the home country continues when the home country becomes specialized in x_2 production (region *7*) until p reaches a sufficiently high value to attract some x_2^* production to the technologically inferior foreign country. This is the maximum point for the home country's geographical possession of capital. Region *8* is like region *4*, with the role of countries reversed. As commodity 2's relative price rises it is, paradoxically, towards the country with a comparative *dis*advantage in producing commodity 2 that the world's capital flows. The reasoning, given in more detail in discussing fig. 13.8, centered on the fact that the country with the technical comparative advantage in commodity 2 had already specialized in x_2, while the other country, incompletely specialized, was capable of combining a capital inflow with resources previously used in the first commodity to expand 2's production by more than it would be cut in the country with the comparative advantage.

The relationships between the terms of trade and the return to capital for this case is illustrated in fig. 13.15. The dotted curves correspond to the underlying

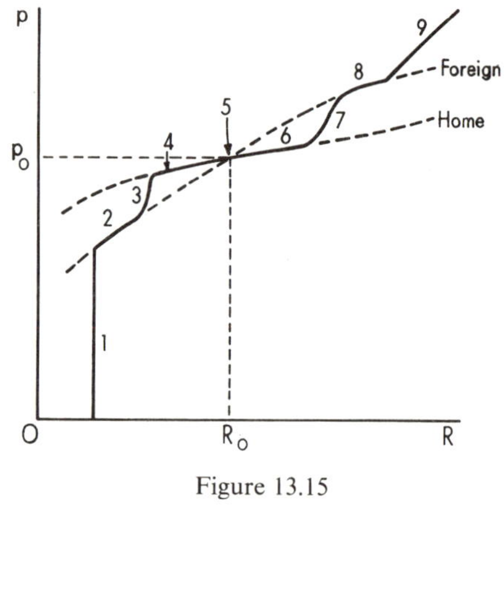

Figure 13.15

technologically determined curves of fig. 13.10, the solid curve to the world (p, R) locus. Sections *1* through *4* correspond of course to those in fig. 13.7, while sections *6* through *9* repeat the pattern with countries switching roles. The typical magnification effect is reversed in regions *3* and *7* for reasons already discussed. One feature of the specialization pattern stands out clearly in fig. 13.15: for low or high ranges of the terms of trade it is the foreign country that is incompletely specialized. The foreign technology curve is steeper than the home country's so that it has a wider range of relative cost ratios. The home country, by contrast, remains specialized except for a mid-range spread of the terms of trade (regions *4*, *5* and *6*). For any given stock of capital its transformation schedule would more closely approximate a linear Ricardian schedule than would the foreign country's.

The results summarized in figs. 13.13–13.15 represent only one of four qualitatively different outcomes of the technology reversal illustrated in fig. 13.10. The others show fewer switches in production patterns on one side or other of the 'flat', and are not illustrated here.[6]

4. Concluding remarks

This chapter has been concerned with the behavior of production patterns, capital allocation, and the return to capital in a model in which two countries with different technologies are linked not only in commodity markets through free trade but also in one of the factor markets through the assumption of capital mobility. If capital were immobile between countries – the typical assumption in standard trade theory – each country would have a unique transformation schedule and, by adding the production response of each to any common terms of trade, it would be possible to construct a world transformation curve. It would be strictly bowed out and there would be a single range of terms of trade for each country within which that country would be specialized.[7] These are results which are altered if international capital mobility is allowed.

[6]The case in which the foreign country is always unspecialized if both commodities are produced somewhere in the world is illustrated in the full Jones and Ruffin version of this chapter.

[7]The world transformation curve for the immobile capital case could have a 'kink'. Suppose one country's transformation curve were steeper everywhere than the other's; then for some range of the terms of trade the two countries would specialize in a different commodity and world outputs would be invariant to changes in p (within that range). This production pattern would resemble fig. 3.1's world production possibilities curve for the linear Ricardian model.

Variations in the conclusions were possible, depending in large part on whether the technological differences between countries impart to each a unique position of comparative advantage. However, some conclusions applied to all cases. (i) The direction of the capital flow must always be reversed as the commodity-price ratio goes from low to high values, despite the fact that the commodity trade pattern (in the no-reversal case) is unique. Thus a country may be a capital exporter for some prices, a capital importer for others, and then reverse to become a capital exporter again. (ii) A rise in a commodity's relative price may attract capital towards the country with a comparative *dis*advantage in producing that commodity. This must occur if the country is incompletely specialized while the other country is specialized. (iii) If each country is specialized to a different commodity the typical 'magnification effect' whereby a change in relative commodity prices yields a greater than proportionate change in the return to capital, is reversed. Terms of trade changes become more pronounced than changes in the common world return to capital. (iv) Despite the assumed difference in technology between countries it is possible that for one (or more) common rates of return to capital the *relative* cost of producing one commodity in terms of the other are equalized between countries. If so there may exist a range of possible capital allocations for which both countries can be incompletely specialized and both the terms of trade and the return to capital are constant. This leads to 'flats' along the world transformation schedule.

Two kinds of capital mobility have been assumed throughout this chapter. Not only can capital move from one country to another, it is also capable of moving from one sector of the economy to the other. That is, capital is neither specific in its use or geographical location. This brands the model as essentially long-run in character. The world transformation schedule should be interpreted not as an indication of the short-run response of outputs to a change in the terms of trade, but rather as an indication of world output response to various possible terms of trade that have been in existence for some time. A variation of the model that will be analyzed in Chapter 16 considers capital as being specific to a certain industrial use although mobile between countries. This 'sector-specific' model of international capital flows may more closely resemble the patterns of foreign investment undertaken by multinational firms.[8] Thus international capital flows might serve to equate rates of return to capital in the same sector in different countries but not between sectors in the same country. Such a model precisely reverses the factor market assumptions of traditional theory.

[8] See, for example, Caves [1].

References

[1] Caves, R.E., 'International Corporations: The Industrial Economics of Foreign Investment', *Economica*, 38 (February 1971) 1–27.

[2] Chipman, J.S., 'International Trade with Capital Mobility: A Substitution Theorem', in: Bhagwati, Jones, Mundell and Vanek, eds., *Trade, Balance of Payments and Growth* (North-Holland, Amsterdam, 1971) pp. 201–237.

[3] Samuelson, P.A., 'Prices of Factors and Goods in General Equilibrium', *Review of Economic Studies*, 21 (1) (1953) 1–20.

PART V

TECHNOLOGY AND TRADE

INTRODUCTION TO PART V

Trade theory has always been concerned with technology. The doctrine of comparative costs as expounded by David Ricardo presupposed that countries differed from one another in the productivity of labor in producing commodities. Whereas Ricardian theory traces through the consequence of technologies differing between countries, Heckscher–Ohlin theory asks what happens when technologies are similar.

A preliminary difficulty encountered in discussion of technology in models (such as Heckscher–Ohlin) with more than one productive factor is that technology may progress in uneven fashion – it may be biased towards one factor or towards another. Furthermore, the concept of bias or lack of bias (neutrality) is not unique. Whereas much work in trade theory has relied on a classification suggested by Hicks [2], models of economic growth have relied more heavily on the concept used by Harrod [1]. Chapter 14 and its appendix attempt to relate these two concepts, both to show how each can be illustrated with the same diagrammatic apparatus (the isoquant diagram) and to suggest that there does exist a concept of neutrality and bias common to them both.

Chapter 15 provides a survey, as of 1968, of the different roles played by the 'technology factor' in the theory of international trade. Much of the literature of the 1950s and early 1960s dealt with the consequences for trade patterns and real incomes of various kinds of technical progress, and Chapter 15 suggests how the two-sector model as set out in Chapter 4 can handle these issues. Furthermore, it stresses that if countries differ in technologies, factor prices would not tend towards equality solely as a consequence of trade in commodities. This suggests pressure for factors to migrate between countries, thus pointing up the importance for development of the theory of international factor mobility, as discussed in Part IV. This theme is further developed in Chapter 16, written jointly with Eitan Berglas. If technology is embodied in factors of production, international factor mobility is required in order to export technology. Embodiment may concern either capital, or labor, or both. The case of international capital mobility is more fully described in Chapter 16. We ask, *inter alia*, how a multinational firm's strategy in restricting technology exports might differ from that of a tax strategy devised by government in an attempt to maximize national income.

On a less formal basis Chapter 16 picks up on suggestions made in Chapter 15 that technologies adapted in one country may not be relevant for countries at earlier stages of development. In particular, differences in real wages lead to adoption of different techniques, and learning-by-doing leads to further developments unique to each economy. The transmission of technology from one country to another could be achieved by migration of personnel in the advanced country skilled in techniques acquired in an earlier era to developing regions where such technology may currently have applications. Such a process would also help to suggest why technology transfers may be more evident among countries close in their stages of development than between areas widely different in real wages and incomes.

Chapter 17 returns to the question of the impact of a change in technology on real incomes both at home and abroad and shows how a Ricardian multicommodity model (such as described in Chapter 3) possesses certain advantages for discussing this issue. One feature of a Ricardian model is that countries by-and-large do not engage in import-competing production, except for the possibility of one commodity produced in common. This means that a technical improvement introduced at home will not automatically cause difficulties for a similar industry abroad. Instead, such advances in technology may be supposed to spill over to provide real income benefits to all consuming countries. In Chapter 17 I show, nonetheless, how foreigners can be harmed by technical improvements at home. The key issue concerns the extent of world demand response to changes in relative prices. Just as low demand elasticities may convert real growth at home that is concentrated in an export sector into a fall in home real income (the case of 'immiserizing growth'), high demand elasticities in a similar situation may cause foreigners to suffer despite the initial benefit as the cost of imports to foreigners falls.

References

[1] Harrod, R., *Towards a Dynamic Economics* (London, 1948).
[2] Hicks, J.R., *The Theory of Wages* (London, 1932).

Chapter 14

'NEUTRAL' TECHNOLOGICAL CHANGE AND THE ISOQUANT MAP*

The concept of 'neutrality' in technological change that has been found most useful in models of economic growth is that offered by Harrod [5, p. 23]. According to this view technological progress is neutral if it leaves the capital/output ratio unaltered at a given rate of profit. In principle this differs from the concept of neutrality offered by Hicks [6, p. 121], in which the capital/labor ratio remains unaltered at a constant ratio of factor prices.

Since each classification has been widely used, it is only natural that the connection between the two has been analyzed.[1] The basic result for one-sector models in which capital goods are produced is that Hicks and Harrod neutrality come to the same thing only if the elasticity of substitution between capital and labor is unity. The situation is slightly more complicated in multisector models, as the *value* of the capital/output ratio in sectors not producing the capital good depends in part on the price ratio between the output of that sector and machines.

The purpose of this chapter is to show how relationships involving Harrod neutrality can be illustrated and proved by use of the isoquant diagram. Although such a diagram offers a natural means of illustrating the Hicksian classification of technological change, it does not seem to have been used heretofore to discuss the Harrod definition.[2] It turns out to be surprisingly simple to employ the iso-

* *American Economic Review* (September 1965) 848–855. The author is indebted to the National Science Foundation for support of this research in 1963–1964.

[1] Cf. Meade [11, ch. 5], Uzawa [14], Kennedy [8], Asimakopulos [3], and Amano [1].

[2] Meade [11, p. 41] uses a diagram showing total output varying with capital, with a fixed quantity of labor. Joan Robinson [12] used the average and marginal product curves of capital in discussing the definitions. This is the kind of diagram also used by Asimakopulos [3]. In more recent work [13, p. 419], Mrs. Robinson employs a diagram showing output/man against the real capital ratio (capital in wage units). Kennedy [7, p. 293] and Asimakopulos and Weldon [4] have also used this diagram.

quant map to illustrate Harrod neutrality in single and multisector models and thus also to illustrate certain key relationships in a neoclassical model in which growth proceeds at a constant rate of profit.

As a preliminary step I demonstrate how it is possible to calculate the elasticity of substitution of an isoquant diagrammatically.[3] Consider fig. 14.1, where K and L represent quantities of capital and labor. The initial equilibrium is at A with the ratio of wages to rents given by the (absolute value of the) slope of line (1) and the capital/labor ratio by the slope of (3). In moving to point B the capital/labor ratio increases to the slope of line (4), while the wage/rental ratio increases to the (absolute value of the) slope of the isoquant at B. Line (2) is drawn with the same slope. The percentage change (reduction) in the labor/capital ratio is AC/AE, while that in the rental/wage ratio is AD/AE. By definition the elasticity of substitution is the ratio of these two expressions, AC/AD. The isoquant in fig. 14.1 has elasticity of substitution less than unity.[4]

If production functions are linear homogeneous, as I assume, all the information about production is conveyed by the unit isoquant. Consider a one-sector economy producing machines (M). In fig. 14.2 the initial situation is shown at point A, where the unit isoquant is tangent to line DF, whose slope represents the ratio of factor prices (w/r). Distance OC represents a_{KM} – the amount of capital required to produce a unit of machines at point A. Similarly, the unit labor requirement at A, a_{LM}, is given by OB or CA. Since w/r equals DC/CA, DC is wa_{LM}/r. Therefore distance OD represents $(1/r)\ (wa_{LM} + ra_{KM})$ which, in a com-

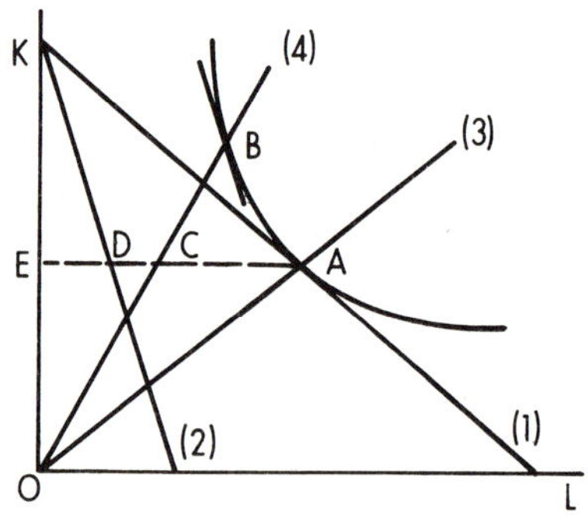

Figure 14.1

[3] An alternative representation is given by Lerner [9].

[4] For finite changes, as shown in the diagrams, assume the curves are of constant elasticity of substitution. Otherwise the graphical measure yields the arc elasticity of substitution.

petitive model, is the inverse of the rate of profit, since the price of machines, p_M, is given by $(wa_{LM} + ra_{KM})$, the unit cost of production.[5]

Technological progress is represented by an inward shift of the unit isoquant. The movement from M to M' in fig. 14.2 represents Harrod-neutral progress, for at a constant rate of profit $(1/OD)$ the capital/output ratio (OC) remains constant. Furthermore, the ratio AE/EC represents the improvement in output per man resulting from technological progress at a constant capital/output ratio.[6]

If technological progress is Harrod-neutral at the same rate for all points on the unit isoquant, it is clear that the old unit isoquant, M, could be obtained from the new by a renumbering of labor units in efficiency terms. A uniform expansion of the a_{LM} axis would put M' into M. This feature of Harrod-neutral change was noted by Joan Robinson [12] and proved by Uzawa [14]. If before technological change the production function is $M = F(K, L)$, it can be represented, after the change, by $M = F(K, \lambda L)$. In the case shown in fig. 14.2, the multiplicative factor λ is $AC/EC = 1 + (AE/EC)$, or one plus the rate of improvement of output per man.

It is well known that Hicks neutrality is shown by a radial shrinking of the unit

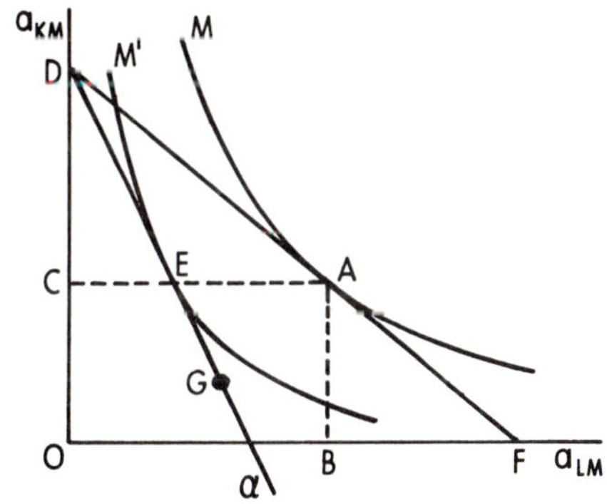

Figure 14.2

[5] By a similar argument the horizontal intercept of the factor price line (OF) is the inverse of the real wage (in machine units). Also, capital's distributive share is shown by OC/OD or AF/DF.

[6] This measure of technological progress, the improvement in output per man at a constant capital/output ratio, must be distinguished from the improvement in output/man at a constant rate of profit if technological change is not Harrod-neutral. For example, suppose the isoquant M' had been tangent to the α-line at point G in fig. 14.2. This would represent a Harrod capital-saving change, and output per man at a constant rate of profit would not rise by as much as at a constant capital/output ratio precisely because the capital/output ratio would be reduced. AE/EC would still represent the improvement in output/man at a constant capital/output ratio (except for a second-order small).

isoquant towards the origin. The slope of the isoquant is preserved along any ray from the origin. Fig. 14.3 illustrates the case in which technological change is both Hicks- and Harrod-neutral. Hicks neutrality is reflected in identical slopes at B and C. Harrod neutrality is shown by the fact that C and A represent the same capital/output ratios for the same rate of profit. Points D and C of fig. 14.1 merge (in point C of fig. 14.3), which implies that the elasticity of substitution is unity.[7]

It may be useful to think of the analogue in terms of demand theory. In fig. 14.3 envisage a series of isoquants representing successive degrees of Harrod-neutral improvements. The 'price consumption' curve would be the horizontal line AC, representing demand for labor per unit of output that would be of unit price-elasticity. If the isoquants are Hicksian-neutral as well, they represent unit income elasticity. An indifference map exhibiting unit price and income elasticity underlies the Graham demand function,[8] which, as is well known, is characterized by unit elasticity of substitution. (The constant-savings assumption often made in growth theories is equivalent to Graham demand functions for consumption and investment.)

In the one-sector model just described the capital/output ratio in physical terms is the same as the ratio in value terms. And the rate of profit is the ratio between the rental on machines and the price of the good produced in that one sector. Now consider the addition of a sector producing, say, food (the consump-

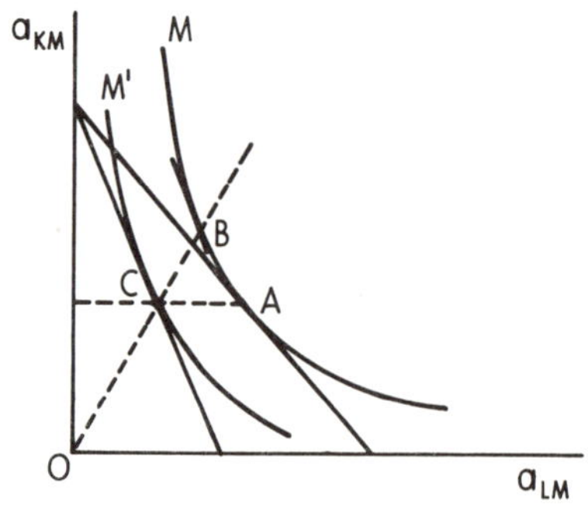

Figure 14.3

[7]Thus the assumption of unit elasticity of substitution leads to strong conclusions. A radial shrinking of the isoquant towards the origin is equivalent to a shrinkage of the labor units or, indeed, to a shrinking of the capital units. This can be seen directly by the multiplicative form of the Cobb-Douglas function.

[8]Let q be quantity demanded, Y money income, and p price. Then $q = \alpha\ (Y/p)$ in the Graham function. For example, see McKenzie [10, p. 149].

tion good). Suppose the original isoquant for food and the nature of technological change are as shown in fig. 14.2, with a_{KM} and a_{LM} replaced by a_{KF} and a_{LF}. In the special case pictured by fig. 14.2, the physical capital/output ratio in the food sector, a_{KF}, would remain constant if the 'own' rate of return to capital in the food industry (r/p_F) remained constant. Call this a case of 'own' neutrality, a definition with the advantage that it is symmetrical as between sectors and requires only information as to the nature of the change in the production function in that sector.

Only in special cases will 'own' neutrality and Harrod neutrality coincide. Harrod neutrality in the F-sector obtains if the *value* of the capital/output ratio in that sector $[(p_M/p_F)\, a_{KF}]$ remains constant at a constant rate of profit (r/p_M). It is clear from the definitions that the two versions would coincide if the relative commodity price ratio (p_M/p_F) were to remain constant at a constant rate of profit. Otherwise it is impossible to state whether the technological change occurring in the F-industry is Harrod-neutral without knowing the extent of technological progress in the M-industry.

The concept of Harrod neutrality in the consumption-goods sector (F) of a two-sector model can be illustrated in figs. 14.4 and 14.5. Let physical units be chosen so that initially both commodity prices are unity. I choose M as numeraire so that p_m is identically unity. The price of F may change as a consequence of technological progress. Assume, for convenience, that M is capital-intensive.[9]

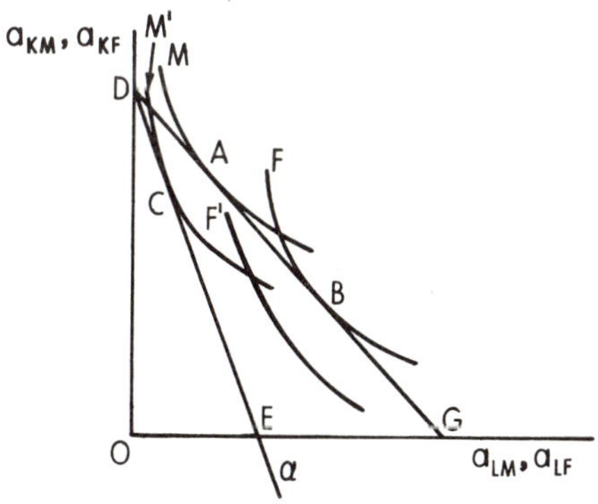

Figure 14.4

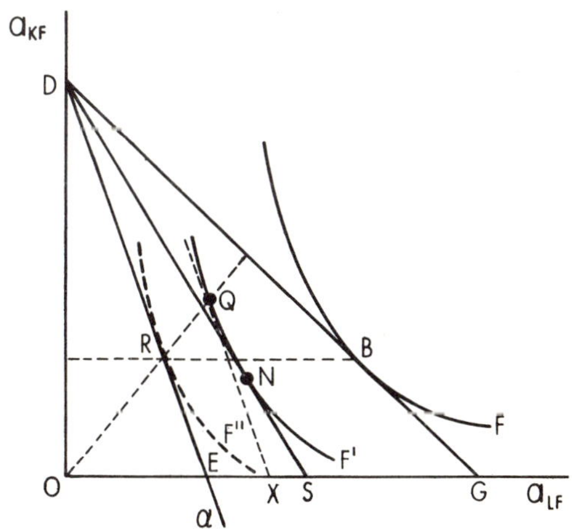

Figure 14.5

[9] Absolutely nothing in the subsequent argument depends on this.

The unit isoquants M and F in fig. 14.4 are then unit-value isoquants in the initial situation, with the factor price ratio shown by the slope of DG, and the rate of profit by $1/OD$.

Suppose technological progress takes place in the M-industry – shifting the unit isoquant to M'. As illustrated in fig. 14.4 progress is of the Harrod capital-saving variety in the M-industry. As we shall see, this is immaterial to the question of whether technological change is Harrod-neutral in the F-industry. What is relevant to that question is the *extent* of technological progress in M – the increase in output/man at a constant capital/output ratio. This is given by EG/OE.

Suppose technical improvement also takes place in the F-industry. The new unit F-isoquant may (1) still lie outside line α, (2) be tangent to line α, or (3) cut line α. In case (1) the rate of increase in output/man (at a constant capital/output ratio) in the F-industry falls short of the improvement in the M-industry. In case (2) they are equivalent and in case (3) the extent of technological progress (in Harrod's sense) in the F-industry exceeds that in the M-industry. Clearly it is only in case (2) that both goods can continue to be produced in a competitive equilibrium at the same rate of profit *without a change in the commodity price ratio.* In the case illustrated, where F' shows a smaller improvement in output per man than does M', the price of F must rise if both commodities are to be produced with $1/OD$ the rate of profit.

The argument shifts now to fig. 14.5. The α-line is given as in fig. 14.4, and is determined by the extent of the improvement in the M-industry. For F to be produced the price of F must rise. Consider deflating a_{KF} and a_{LF} by p_F. As p_F rises, this would have the effect of shifting the F' curve radially towards the origin; p_F must rise until such a shifted F' curve becomes tangent to the α-line (shown by F''). Alternatively phrased, as p_F rises, the F-isoquant showing unit-*value* becomes a radial shrinking of F'. The F'' curve in fig. 14.5 is pictured as being tangent to the α-line at point R, where the *value* of the capital/output ratio is the same as at B. This shift from F to F' thus exhibits Harrod neutrality. The capital/output ratio in quantity terms is shown at Q, and is higher as the price of F is higher. To recapitulate, draw a ray from the origin such that it intersects the α-line (showing the new factor-price ratio at the old rate of profit) at the old capital/output ratio. If the slope of F' at the capital/labor ratio shown by this ray equals the slope of α, the change is Harrod-neutral (and the appropriate radial expansion or shrinking of F' will bring F'' to a point of tangency with the α-line at the old capital/output ratio).

Several comments are suggested by this construction. First, suppose technological change is Harrod-neutral in the F-industry and of different rates in the two industries. It can then be what I have called 'own' neutral in the F-industry only if the elasticity of substitution in F is unity. (In fig. 14.5 point N would have to lie on RB.) Secondly, consider the case in which no technological change takes place in the M-industry. The α-line then corresponds to DG. If technological progress takes place in the F-industry, the unit isoquant is shifted inwards. At a constant rate of profit the price of F must fall in order that both goods be produced in a competitive equilibrium. This serves to make F'' (the unit-value isoquant) a radial expansion of F'. If F'' is to be tangent to DG (the α-line in this case) at the same value of the capital/output ratio as initially, the original movement from F to F' must have been a radial shrinking towards the origin. That is, technological change in the F-industry must be Hicksian-neutral if it is to be Harrod-neutral and no technological progress takes place in the industry producing capital goods.

Finally, consider the changes in the factor-price ratio (w/r) and the real wage (w/p_F) associated with technological progress at a constant rate of profit. The rate of increase in the wage/rental ratio is given by EG/OE, which is the rate of increase of output per man in the machine sector. At this new higher relative wage rate the real wage is given by the reciprocal of OX, where QX is parallel to α and tangent to F' at Q. Expressed in percentage terms, the rate of increase of the real wage is given by XG/OX. The rate of increase of output per man in the machine sector is approximately EG/OX, and in the other sector is approximately SG/OX.[10] Therefore the rate of increase in the real wage is a weighted average of the rates of increase of output per man in the machine sector and in the consumption (F) sector, the weights given by XS/ES and EX/ES, respectively. These weights represent the capital and labor distributive shares in the consumption sector.[11]

It may prove useful to conclude by summarizing these results: (1) Harrod neutrality in the one-sector model, and 'own neutrality' in the multisector model, lead to a change in the production function represented only by introducing a multiplicative factor for labor (the production function in 'efficiency' units remains unchanged). (2) Harrod neutrality in the one-sector model, and 'own neutrality' in the multisector model, are equivalent to Hicksian neutrality if and only if the elasticity of substitution is unity. (3) The commodity-price ratio in a two-sector model rises in favor of the consumption good, at a constant rate of profit, if and only if the rate of increase in output/man at a constant (physical) capital/output ratio is smaller in the consumption sector than in the capital-goods

[10]For small changes OE, OX, and OS are approximately equal. The formulae become exact for infinitesimal changes.

[11]XS/ES is approximately equal to NS/DS, capital's share in the F-industry. (See footnote 5.)

sector. (4) If the commodity-price ratio changes at a constant rate of profit any two of the following implies the third: (a) technological change in F is Harrod-neutral; (b) technological change in F is 'own' neutral; and (c) the elasticity of substitution is unity. (5) If no technological progress takes place in the sector producing capital goods, Harrod neutrality in any other sector is equivalent to Hicksian neutrality in that sector. (6) At a constant rate of profit, technological progress raises the real wage. The rate of increase in the real wage is the sum of the increase in output per man in the machine sector weighted by capital's share in the consumption sector and output per man in the consumption sector weighted by labor's share in the consumption sector. Should technological change occur at the same Harrodian rate in each sector, the real wage and the wage/rental ratio both increase at this rate.

Appendix: Symmetry in alternative concepts of neutrality[12]

The use of the unit isoquant diagram to illustrate the impact of technical progress may suggest that neutrality in the sense of Hicks is a more simple notion than neutrality in the sense of Harrod. This would, I would argue, be misleading. There is a concept of neutrality that underlies both the Hicks and Harrod versions as well as a third candidate which describes technical progress as neutral if the quantity of output/man is unchanged at any given real wage.

Let labor (L) and capital (K) produce machines (M) in a one-sector model. The wage, rental, and commodity price are indicated by w, r, p_M, respectively. Consider the behaviour of the ratio of any pair of physical terms to the ratio of corresponding prices. For example, fig. 14.6(a) illustrates the capital/labor ratio as falling with an increase in the rent/wage ratio. Similarly, fig. 14.6(b) shows the capital/output ratio, K/M, falling against the rate of profit, r/p_M, while fig. 14.6(c) illustrates output per man, M/L, against the inverse of the real wage, p_M/w. In each case a given technology corresponds to a given, downward sloping curve. As drawn in fig. 14.6, these curves bow in to the origin much as isoquants do. This is not necessary, although if both factors are indispensable at any price (so that isoquants do not hit the axes), these curves cannot hit the axes. By definition, the elasticity of the curve shown in fig. 14.6(a) is the elasticity of substitution.

[12] Based on section 3 of my 'Comments on Technical Progress', *The Philippine Economic Journal*, 5, Second Semester (1966) 313–332.

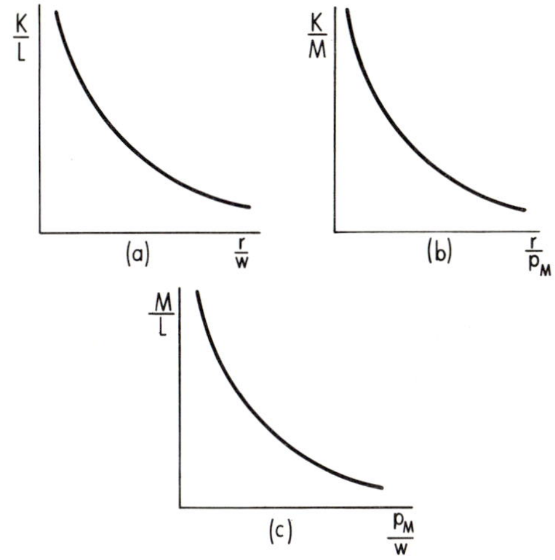

Figure 14.6

The elasticity of the other two curves is also the elasticity of substitution.[13] For example, consider fig. 14.6(b). As of given technology,[14]

$$(\hat{K} - \hat{M}) = \theta_L \sigma(\hat{w} - \hat{r}) \tag{A1}$$

But by the competitive profit conditions,[15]

$$\theta_L(\hat{w} - \hat{r}) = -(\hat{r} - \hat{p}_M). \tag{A2}$$

Therefore,

$$(\hat{K} - \hat{M}) = -\sigma(\hat{r} - \hat{p}_M). \tag{A3}$$

Each panel in fig. 14.6 is appropriate in illustrating a particular definition of neutrality. If technical change is Hicksian-neutral, the curve in fig. 14.6(a) does not shift. Similarly, Harrod neutrality leaves the curve in panel (b) invariant. An upward shift of the curve in panel (b) would show technical progress increasing the capital/output ratio at a given rate of profit. That is, it would be described as labor-saving in Harrodian terminology. So also technical change that is Hicksian

[13]The role of the elasticity of substitution-linking output/man to the real wage was pointed out in Arrow, Chenery, Minhas and Solow [2, p. 229].

[14]The proof is provided in Chapter 4. θ_L refers to labor's distributive share in this one-sector economy and σ is the elasticity of substitution.

[15]This is a rewritten form of the statement that the relative commodity price change, $\hat{p}_M$, must be the distributive share weighted average of factor price changes, $\theta_L\hat{w} + \theta_K\hat{r}$.

labor-saving shifts the curve in panel (a) upwards and, for the third alternative in panel (c), technical change could be deemed labor-saving if at a given real wage output per man had increased.

Finally, consider the algebraic representation usually given the production function:

$$M = F(L, K). \tag{A4}$$

Harrod neutrality can be captured by inserting a multiplicative term in front of the labor coefficient, while a case of Hicksian neutrality places the multiplicative term in front of both L and K. The symmetry among alternative concepts of neutrality perhaps comes out more clearly by rewriting (A4) in implicit form:

$$T(M, L, K) = 0. \tag{A5}$$

Pick any pair of arguments. For given technology the elasticity of substitution is the relative change in the ratio of the physical arguments divided by the relative change in the ratio of appropriate prices. And technical change would be neutral according to one of the three schema if and only if a multiplicative term is introduced in (A5) in front of the argument *not* included in the definition. For example, Hicks neutrality, defined as unchanged L/K ratio at given w/r, is illustrated by a multiplicative factor in front of output, M.

References

[1] Amano, A., 'Neo-Classical Models of International Trade and Economic Growth', University of Rochester, 1963, unpublished.

[2] Arrow, K., H. Chenery, B. Minhas and R. Solow, 'Capital–Labor Substitution and Economic Efficiency', *The Review of Economics and Statistics* (August 1961) 225–250.

[3] Asimakopulos, A., 'The Definition of Neutral Inventions', *Economic Journal*, 73 (December 1963) 675–680.

[4] Asimakopulos, A. and J.C. Weldon, 'The Classification of Technical Progress in Models of Economic Growth', *Economica* (November 1963) 372–386.

[5] Harrod, R.F., *Towards a Dynamic Economics* (London, 1948).

[6] Hicks, J.R., *The Theory of Wages* (London, 1932).

[7] Kennedy, C., 'Technical Progress and Investment', *Economic Journal*, 71 (June 1961) 292–299.

[8] Kennedy, C., 'Harrod on "Neutrality"', *Economic Journal*, 72 (March 1962) 249–250.

[9] Lerner, A., 'The Diagrammatical Representation of Elasticity of Substitution', in: *Essays in Economic Analysis* (London, 1953).

[10] McKenzie, L., 'On Equilibrium in Graham's Model of World Trade and Other Competitive Systems', *Econometrica*, 22 (April 1954) 147–161.

[11] Meade, J.E., *A Neo-Classical Theory of Economic Growth* (London, 1961).

[12] Robinson, J., 'The Classification of Inventions', in: A.E.A., *Readings in the Theory of Income Distribution* (Philadelphia, 1951) ch. 9, pp. 175–180.
[13] Robinson, J., *The Accumulation of Capital* (Homewood, Ill., 1956).
[14] Uzawa, H., 'Neutral Inventions and the Stability of Growth Equilibrium', *Review of Economic Studies*, 43 (February 1961) 117–124.

Chapter 15

THE ROLE OF TECHNOLOGY IN THE THEORY OF INTERNATIONAL TRADE*

1. Introduction

'Technology' refers to the way in which resources are converted into commodities. This is such a basic feature of an economic model, whether of a closed or open economy, that any discussion of the 'role' of technology in the theory of trade must be arbitrarily incomplete. In what follows I have tried to cast the net widely and deal with several aspects of technology in the theory of international trade.

2. A two-country, two-commodity, two-factor model

Some years ago the literature on trade theory was largely concerned with the analysis of the impact of technological change on the equilibrium position in a two-commodity, two-country model of trade. Although the analysis involved in discussing the role of technical change in influencing trade patterns may be in its infancy, the analysis of the impact of *exogenous* changes in techniques is basically complete. It is useful to begin by sketching out the standard trade model in a form that permits a general treatment of the exogenous case. In doing so I shall rely heavily on the procedure I developed in Chapter 4.

Consider a competitive trade model in which each of two countries is incom-

* Originally appearing in Ray Vernon, ed., *The Technology Factor in International Trade* (NBER, 1970) pp. 73–92. I am indebted to Richard Caves and Trevor Underwood for useful conversations on the topic of this paper. This research is supported in part by The Center for Naval Analyses of the University of Rochester. Such support does not imply endorsement of the content by the Navy.

pletely specialized in the production of two goods, M (manufactured goods) and F (food). Two factors of production are fully employed, L (labor) and T (land), and no international factor mobility is allowed. For the questions to be discussed in this section, it is easy to consider the general case in which production functions are allowed to differ between countries.

Even in this simple two-country case many conditions are required to describe a world trade equilibrium. It is useful to consider these conditions in smaller groups. First, examine the conditions relating to the production sector in each economy. The prevailing technology in each country can be specified by a set of input–output coefficients and their dependence upon the factor-price (wage/rent) ratio (w/r) ruling in that country at the time (t). These are shown by set (1).[1]

$$a_{ij} = a_{ij}\left(\frac{w}{r}, t\right) \tag{1}$$

For any time t the unit isoquant in the jth sector can be traced out by considering the set of a_{ij} that would be chosen over the whole range of factor-price ratios. Technical change is shown by a shifting of the unit isoquant (through a change in t). The basic (exogenous) parameters of technical change show the relative reductions in a_{ij} that would take place as of a given factor-price ratio.[2]

There remain four other relationships on the production side in each country. The requirement that both factors be fully employed is shown by (2), and the competitive profit conditions, whereby the unit cost of producing each good is equated to its price, are given by the 'dual' set (3):

$$a_{LM}M + a_{LF}F = L; \qquad a_{TM}M + a_{TF}F = T \tag{2}$$

$$a_{LM}w + a_{TM}r = p_M; \qquad a_{LF}w + a_{TF}r = p_F. \tag{3}$$

Before proceeding to complete the model, consider the impact on the production sector in each country of a change in technology. From set (1) it is clear that the methods of production change directly at the initial factor prices and indirectly through any tendency for the equilibrium set of factor prices to change. Thus the relative change in a_{ij} can be broken down into the two components shown by (1′). $\hat{b}_{ij}$ represents the relative *reduction* in an input requirement at constant factor prices, and $\hat{\underline{a}}_{ij}$ the relative change in the input–output coefficient along a

[1]Subscripts for each country are omitted where no confusion is apt to arise. Thus there is a different set (1) for each country.

[2]One input–output ratio might increase. In this case the other must be reduced if technical *progress* is to be shown.

given isoquant.[3] Furthermore, $\hat{a}_{ij}$ depends upon the extent

$$\hat{a}_{ij} = \underline{\hat{a}}_{ij} - \underline{\hat{b}}_{ij} \tag{1'}$$

of any change in the factor-price ratio, and on the elasticity of substitution in sector *j*. As I have shown in Chapter 4,[4]

$$\underline{\hat{a}}_{Lj} = -\theta_{Tj}\sigma_j(\hat{w} - \hat{r}); \qquad \underline{\hat{a}}_{Tj} = \theta_{Lj}\sigma_j(\hat{w} - \hat{r})$$

where θ_{ij} denotes factor *i*'s distribution share (e.g. wa_{LM}/p_M for labor's share in the *M* industry) and σ_j the elasticity of substitution in the *j*th industry.

Whereas the $\hat{b}_{ij}$ reflect the details of technological change, it is only certain aggregates of these parameters that are important in tracing through the impact of technical change on terms of trade, outputs, and real incomes. These aggregates are of two types. (1) The relative extent of the cost reduction in industry *j*; this is denoted by $\pi_j \equiv \theta_{Lj}\hat{b}_{Lj} + \theta_{Tj}\hat{b}_{Tj}$, the distributive-share weighted average of the direct reduction in all input–output coefficients in the *j*th industry; (2) Relative extent of the cost reduction in a particular factor's use in all industries. This is a less familiar concept. Considering labor, the relative reductions in labor use per unit output in the two industries are $\hat{b}_{LM}$ and $\hat{b}_{LF}$. Weight each by the fraction of the labor force use in that industry, λ_{Lj}, and define π_L as $\lambda_{LM}\hat{b}_{LM} + \lambda_{LF}\hat{b}_{LF}$. Now consider the effect of a general technological change on an economy with given factor endowments by differentiating (logarithmically) the sets (2) and (3) to obtain (2′) and (3′):

$$\begin{aligned} \lambda_{LM}\hat{M} + \lambda_{LF}\hat{F} &= \pi_L + \delta_L(\hat{w} - \hat{r}), \\ \lambda_{TM}\hat{M} + \lambda_{TF}\hat{F} &= \pi_T - \delta_T(\hat{w} - \hat{r}), \end{aligned} \tag{2'}$$

$$\begin{aligned} \theta_{LM}\hat{w} + \theta_{TM}\hat{r} &= \hat{p}_M + \pi_M, \\ \theta_{LF}\hat{w} + \theta_{TF}\hat{r} &= \hat{p}_F + \pi_F, \end{aligned} \tag{3'}$$

where

$$\delta_L = \lambda_{LM}(\theta_{TM}\sigma_M) + \lambda_{LF}(\theta_{TF}\sigma_F),$$

$$\delta_T = \lambda_{TM}(\theta_{LM}\sigma_M) + \lambda_{TF}(\theta_{LF}\sigma_F).$$

[3] In general a '^' over a variable denotes a relative change in that variable. Thus $\hat{a}_{ij}$ is $\mathrm{d}a_{ij}/a_{ij}$.

[4] Consider the *M* industry. Cost minimization per unit of output is shown graphically by requiring a tangency between the unit isoquant and an isocost line. Algebraically this states that the distributive share weighted average of the changes in input–output coefficients $\theta_{LM}\underline{\hat{a}}_{LM} + \theta_{TM}\underline{\hat{a}}_{TM}$, must be zero. This, together with the definition of σ_M as $-(\underline{\hat{a}}_{LM} - \underline{\hat{a}}_{TM})/(\hat{w} - \hat{r})$, is sufficient to solve separately for $\underline{\hat{a}}_{LM}$ and $\underline{\hat{a}}_{TM}$.

If there were no change in technology, (2′) and (3′) would show how any change in commodity prices would disturb factor prices (through (3′)) and how such a change in factor prices would require a change in the composition of outputs in order to maintain full employment (through (2′)). These output changes, of course, could be represented by movements along a transformation curve. Technological progress is seen to complicate matters in two ways. First, the reduction in factor requirements is seen to act like an increase in the quantity of factors available in (2′). Thus if factor prices were constant and only labor coefficients were reduced ($\pi_L > 0, \pi_T = 0$), the transformation schedule would be shifted outward and the output of the labor-intensive commodity would be increased while the output of the land-intensive commodity would be reduced. Although this sounds like the Rybczynski result [13], technical change of this kind also disturbs the relationship between commodity and factor prices through its cost-reducing impact in (3′). Therefore at the new production point the new (outer) transformation schedule need not have the same slope as at the initial point. That is, not only does any technical change act in part like an increase in factor endowments, it also acts in part like a change in commodity prices, or more accurately, like a set of industry subsidies.

With an exception I shall consider below, exogenous technical change disrupts only the production side of the model. However, it is necessary to consider the demand side in order to complete the picture of this two-country trading community. In each country demand functions must be specified. By Walras's law it would only be necessary to specify, say, that the demand for M in each country depends on that country's income and the terms of trade. Then derive a world demand function and require that, as a result of technical progress, commodity prices must adjust so as to clear markets. The relationships shown by (3′) would suffice to determine the impact on each country's factor prices.[5]

The exception I noted refers to the possibility that technical change results in an improvement in the quality of commodities instead of (or in addition to) a reduction in input coefficients. To handle this (in an exogenous fashion), introduce t as a variable in the demand functions. This would serve to capture the shift in taste patterns that would be triggered off by the quality changes.

Attention in the trade literature has sometimes centered on the impact of technical change on the real incomes of the countries participating in trade. In an extreme form the question raised concerns the possibility of immiserizing growth:

[5]It should be mentioned that this nonmonetary system will not yield a solution for the change in each commodity price. One commodity, say F, could be taken as numeraire. I have retained $\hat{p}_F$ so as not to disturb the symmetry in the expressions.

can technical progress in a country so affect the terms of trade that real income in that country is reduced? The answer, of course, is that this is a theoretical possibility. Any deterioration in a country's terms of trade (e.g. through progress in its export sector) reduces real income directly by an amount that is related both to the extent of the deterioration and the extent of the country's *imbalance* between consumption and production patterns. For example, suppose a country exports commodity M; let its real income be denoted by y measured in units of commodity F, and its consumption of M by D_M. If α_M and α_F denote the shares in national income (Y) of the *production* of each commodity, the following expression shows the change in real income:[6]

$$\mathrm{d}y = (M - D_M)\,\mathrm{d}\left(\frac{p_M}{p_F}\right) + Y[\alpha_M \pi_M + \alpha_F \pi_F].$$

Any deterioration in p_M/p_F would have to be set against the directly beneficial effect on real incomes of the improvement in technology.

This is the basic model that has been used to analyze the impact of any kind of technical change on prices, consumption, production, and real incomes of countries in a trading community. It is deficient because it does not come to grips with the *inducement mechanism* whereby the $\hat{b}_{ij}$, and therefore the π's, are linked to changes in other economic variables. I shall comment upon this in more detail in section 4. However, it is worth setting out the model in more detail because whatever inducement mechanism is considered, it is this basic model that can then be used to trace through the consequences of technical change.

3. A modification of the Heckscher–Ohlin theory

The preceding section was devoted to the question of how a *change* in technology used anywhere in the world disturbs a pre-existing trading equilibrium. In this section I discuss a closely related but separable aspect of the role of technology in trade theory, namely, how the basic Heckscher–Ohlin model of trade that assumes identical production functions must be modified to take account of *differences* in production functions between countries.

In a sense the Heckscher–Ohlin model represents a step backward from the earlier Ricardian tradition. With Ricardo, international differences in produc-

[6]This expression is derived from the budget constraint (or balance-of-payment constraint), $p_M D_M + p_F D_F = p_M M + p_F F$ and the definition of a real income change (in units of F) as the price-weighted sum of changes in consumption $(p_M/p_F)(\mathrm{d}D_M) + \mathrm{d}D_F$.

tion functions were not only allowed, but served as the basis for explaining positions of comparative advantage. Early work on the Heckscher–Ohlin model concentrated on differences in factor endowments as the source of comparative advantage and found it convenient to ignore differences in technologies between countries (and tended to minimize the influence of differences in taste patterns). This deficiency was repaired in the trade literature of the past decade.[7]

One immediate consequence for the Heckscher–Ohlin theory of allowing countries to differ in their prevailing states of technology can be inferred from eqs. (3′). The changes in factor and commodity prices exhibited there can be interpreted as reflecting the pretrade differences in these prices between two countries with slightly differing technologies. Subtract the bottom equation in (3′) from the top and rearrange to obtain

$$(\hat{p}_M - \hat{p}_F) = |\theta|\,(\hat{w} - \hat{r}) - (\pi_M - \pi_F) \tag{4}$$

where

$$|\theta| \equiv \theta_{LM} - \theta_{LF}.$$

The sign of $|\theta|$ indicates which industry is labor intensive. Suppose in both countries M is labor intensive so that $|\theta|$ is positive. A strong form of the Heckscher–Ohlin theorem states that when two countries have identical technologies, the low-wage country has a comparative advantage in producing the labor-intensive commodity. Eq. (4) suggests how easily this proposition can be modified to account for differences in technologies. The labor-intensive commodity could turn out to be relatively expensive in the low-wage country if the other country had a sufficiently strong *relative* technological superiority in producing M. In the spirit of the doctrine of comparative advantage it is only relative differences in productivity that count.

Further analysis is required if the role of technological differences between countries in determining positions of comparative advantage is to be contrasted with the bias imposed by differences in physical factor endowments. The production side of the model needs to be expanded by adding $\hat{L}$ and $\hat{T}$, respectively, to the right-hand side of eqs. (2′) to allow for differences in factor endowments as well as technologies. Solve (4) for the differences in factor-price ratios and insert into (2′). Then solve this set for the difference in the ratio of goods produced to obtain (5):[8]

[7] For a summary statement, see Amano [1].

[8] $|\lambda|$ is positive if, as assumed, M is labor intensive. σ_S is the elasticity of substitution on the supply side (along the transformation schedule).

$$(\hat{M} - \hat{F}) = \frac{1}{|\lambda|}\{(\hat{L} - \hat{T}) + (\pi_L - \pi_T)\} + \sigma_S\{(\hat{p}_M - \hat{p}_F) + (\pi_M - \pi_F)\}, \tag{5}$$

where

$$|\lambda| \equiv \lambda_{LM} - \lambda_{TM}; \qquad \sigma_S \equiv \frac{\delta_L + \delta_T}{|\lambda||\theta|}.$$

For a closed economy, this change in the ratio of outputs produced must be matched by a similar change in the ratio of quantities consumed. To wash out the separate role played by differences in tastes or income levels, I assume that both countries have identical homothetic taste patterns. Eq. (6) follows from the definition of the elasticity of substitution on the demand side:

$$(\hat{D}_M - \hat{D}_F) = -\sigma_D(\hat{p}_M - \hat{p}_F). \tag{6}$$

Equating (5) and (6) permits a solution for the difference in the relative commodity-price ratio, and this is shown as follows:

$$(\hat{p}_M \quad \hat{p}_F)$$

$$= -\frac{1}{|\lambda|(\sigma_S + \sigma_D)}\{(\hat{L} - \hat{T}) + (\pi_L - \pi_T) + |\lambda|\sigma_S(\pi_M - \pi_F)\}. \tag{7}$$

What the expression given by (7) allows is a comparison of the autarky price ratios that would rule in two economies slightly different, both in their technologies and in factor endowments. It points out that two general features of the differences in technologies are crucial in influencing positions of comparative advantage. The first, $(\pi_L - \pi_T)$, might be termed the 'differential factor effect' and it is seen that this influences commodity prices in exactly the same manner as do differences in factor endowments. The second, $(\pi_M - \pi_F)$, the 'differential industry effect', points out that technological differences between countries bias commodity prices directly to the extent that a country's technological superiority over another country is not evenly spread over both industries.[9] Elsewhere I have defined technical change (or, in this case, differences between countries) to be 'regular' if a greater aggregate reduction in labor coefficients than in land coefficients corresponds to a differential impact on costs favoring the labor-intensive industry.[10] In such a case $(\pi_L - \pi_T)(\pi_M - \pi_F) \geqq 0$,[11] and both features of the

[9] π_M and π_F are Hicksian measures of technological difference. Later in this section I shall point out how the different Harrod measures may be crucial in explaining comparative advantage positions in a world in which capital is freely mobile.

[10] See Chapter 4. Technical change need not be 'regular'. Consider a reduction in the labor coefficient only in the land-intensive industry.

[11] This assumes again that M is labor intensive.

technological differences between countries influence the commodity-price ratio in the same direction. The Heckscher–Ohlin theorem, of course, can be reversed by differences in technology. Expression (7) shows how pronounced these differences would have to be.

Perhaps the most celebrated result of the standard Heckscher–Ohlin model is the factor-price equalization theorem: with identical technologies, incomplete specialization in both countries guarantees that free trade brings about an equality in the real returns to similar factors in both countries.[12] This result disappears if technologies differ between countries.

The fact that factor prices are not equalized in the Heckscher–Ohlin model if countries have different technologies has important consequences for the standard assumption of international factor immobility underlying the body of traditional trade theory. This assumption is tolerable if goods trade is a perfect substitute for factor movements. In what follows I assume that capital and labor replace land and labor as the two explicit factors of production in the model and, for simplicity, assume that only capital is potentially mobile.[13] At initial pretrade stocks of capital, rates of return to capital in the two countries would normally not be brought into line. In such a case there is incentive to develop the theory of trade to incorporate trade in capital goods and foreign investment. For example, recent theoretical work on foreign investment has been concerned with the problem of the interconnections between impediments placed on goods trade and taxes levied on income earned on capital placed abroad, in the context of a model in which technologies in two countries are assumed at the outset to differ. (See Chapter 12 and Kemp [9].) Quite aside from the question of devising optimal tariff and tax strategy is the more general question relating to the properties of trade models in which capital is internationally mobile subject, perhaps, to certain taxes on repatriated earnings. In concluding this section I shall briefly note a few of these.

Consider, first, the question of specialization in production in a two-commodity, two-factor, two-country, competitive, riskless world in which real capital is mobile (through the possibility of foreign investment). In a recent article (see Chapter 12) I claimed it was unlikely, if technologies differed between countries, to find both countries incompletely specialized. As has recently been suggested by Kemp and Inada [10], this is an unwarranted remark. If the technological comparison between countries is such that at any common commodity price ratio the return to capital is higher in one country than another, unimpeded capital flows will drive at least one country to specialize completely. Kemp and Inada

[12] I rule out the possibility of factor-intensity reversals.

[13] It would be possible to construct a three-factor model to include land, and require land to be immobile internationally.

were concerned with another case – that in which there existed some commodity-price ratio at which rates of return to capital would be equalized with both countries incompletely specialized. As John Chipman [5] has pointed out, it is possible to derive a world transformation schedule assuming capital is freely mobile. Such a schedule has a 'flat' – a portion of the schedule is linear. This transformation schedule is shown by the solid curve in fig. 15.1. The curved sections of this schedule correspond to price ratios at which at least one country is driven to specialize completely. Thus with capital mobile it is quite possible that a free trade solution occurs along the flat and both countries are incompletely specialized. It is interesting to compare this locus with the world transformation schedule that would obtain if capital were immobile internationally, as in the traditional Heckscher–Ohlin model. This schedule is the dashed one in fig. 15.1.

In drawing this second locus I have assumed that there exists one commodity-price ratio at which rates of return to capital can be equated consistent with incomplete specialization in both countries and with the given stocks of labor and capital in the two countries. This corresponds to point A. For all other points rates of return differ between countries. Free trade in goods will then not suffice to substitute for movements of capital, either to bring about international equality in their returns or to reach the solid world efficiency frontier.[14]

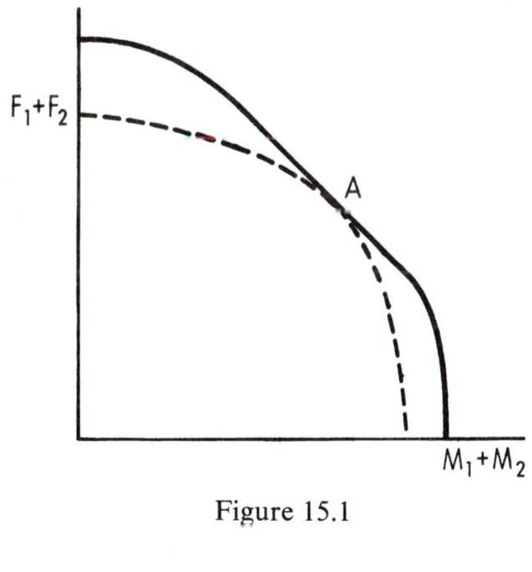

Figure 15.1

[14] Of course, with labor assumed immobile and technologies different, there will generally not be any tendency to equate real wages in the two countries. Interesting further work remains in following up Chipman's results in those cases in which taxes (or perhaps considerations of risk) serve to impede capital flows. One preliminary result may be noted: the world transformation curve will lie inside the solid curve of fig. 15.1, but will also have a linear segment. However, unlike the untaxed case shown in fig. 15.1, the slope of the transformation curve does *not* correspond to the commodity-price ratio despite the fact that no direct impediments exist to commodity movements.

Secondly, consider the determinants of comparative advantage if trade in capital goods serves to equalize rates of return to capital between countries. Let the two countries differ only slightly in their technologies. Subtract $\hat{r}$ from both sides of the first equation of (3′) to obtain (3″) as the solution for the difference in the factor price ratio between countries:

$$(\hat{w} - \hat{r}) = -\frac{1}{\theta_{LM}}(\hat{r} - \hat{p}_M) + \frac{\pi_M}{\theta_{LM}}. \tag{3''}$$

To consider equal rates of return to capital, set $(\hat{r} - \hat{p}_M)$ equal to zero in (3″) and substitute into (4) to obtain (4′):

$$(\hat{p}_M - \hat{p}_F) = \theta_{LF}\left\{\frac{\pi_F}{\theta_{LF}} - \frac{\pi_M}{\theta_{LM}}\right\}. \tag{4'}$$

In a world of capital mobility, positions of comparative advantage are determined by the Harrod, as opposed to the Hicks, measures of technical difference.[15] Now suppose that in the capital-abundant country more resources have been devoted to improving the technology and that this country has a uniform Hicksian advantage in all lines (i.e. $\pi_M = \pi_F$). In a world of capital mobility, this nonetheless biases comparative advantage in the direction of having the capital-abundant country export the capital-intensive commodity.[16] Note the sensitivity of this result to the crude inducement mechanism whereby it is the more capital-abundant country that has devoted more resources to technical improvement. If production functions in the labor-abundant country should represent superior technology, of the same Hicksian measure for each industry, and if rates of profit should be equalized between countries, the labor-abundant country would tend to have a comparative advantage in the capital intensive commodity.

Of course the entire concept of factor abundance is subject to question if capital is mobile between countries. Eq. (4′) suggests how differential rates of technical differences between countries come to dominate the determination of comparative advantage. Differences in factor endowments, in the sense of national ownership of capital per man, then get linked to commodity-price ratios through the intermediate step of affecting levels of technology through research and development.

To conclude this section consider the way in which the Heckscher–Ohlin model could be applied to Vernon's concept of the 'product cycle' (Vernon [15]). Vernon

[15] π_j/θ_{Lj} shows the improvement in output per man at a given capital output ratio (or, for small changes, at a given rate of profit), See Jones [7] and Chapter 14.

[16] If M is capital intensive the right-hand side of (4′) is negative.

argues that advanced countries tend to have a comparative advantage in producing those commodities that are newly being developed. Whereas special knowledge of the large home market and the prior existence of distribution channels imparts a bias to producing *for* the home market, the question of interest here is why the location of production should also be at home.[17] Vernon suggests that high labor costs at home may nonetheless be outweighed by the advantage of having a location in which a variety of factors of production (or special skills) is readily accessible. The role of technology is important, for what is being suggested is that the input mix at the early stages of the development of the product is different from the input mix later, when production becomes standardized. That is, in the course of the product cycle there is a systematic bias in the change in the production function required to produce the commodity.

In simplified terms, this suggests a three-factor model: capital, 'ordinary' labor, and a third factor that comprises a host of special skills on the part of labor or of capital equipment. The uncertainty associated with early stages of production, whereby the actual production process that will be required at a later stage is still not known, is thus translated into a third factor of production. Advanced countries, such as the United States, have a relative abundance of this third factor and hence a comparative advantage in producing new commodities at early stages of production. Later stages are associated with a shift in factor intensities toward a relatively greater role played by capital and labor.

To the extent that foreign production of commodities is undertaken as a form of foreign investment by firms in advanced countries, the previous remarks about trade theory in a world of capital mobility are relevant. If the rates that must be paid for the use of capital are brought into line for certain industrial activities between advanced and less advanced areas, the role of returns to capital as an explanation of comparative advantage tends to be neutralized, making it easier to conceptualize Vernon's product cycle in terms of two factors – labor and this third bundle representing various skills and amenities. That is, a comparison of labor shares with third-factor shares would be crucial in depicting a ranking of industries by comparative advantage.

One special feature of a trading world in which foreign investment is important should be noted. Capital markets within less developed countries tend to be fragmented in the sense that some industrial activities – particularly if foreign owned – yield rates on capital in line with generally low rates in the advanced countries, whereas local entrepreneurs might have to pay higher returns for the use of capital. The standard idealization in the theory of trade, whereby factor prices are equated

[17] Significant transport costs could heavily influence this decision.

within, but not necessarily between, countries (especially if technologies differ), needs to be revised to take account of differences within and similarities between countries with reference to returns to factors that may be more mobile internationally than nationally.[18]

4. Inducement mechanisms

What determines technical change? This basic question is not specific to trade theory, but any theory of the inducement mechanism has consequences for the kind of trade model discussed in the preceding sections.

A crude sort of inducement mechanism was given in section 3. It was suggested there that the rate of technical progress in any industry would increase as the economy's relative stock of owned capital (or wealth) increased. That is, wealthy countries put more resources into improving technology. Although this assumption had consequences for positions of comparative advantage in a model in which capital is mobile, it nonetheless gave no clue as to which industries would be especially favored by the input of resources to improve technology.

There is a simple inducement mechanism that discriminates between industries and is formally similar to the existence of external economies. The state of technology in any industry is linked to the level of that industry's output. In a recent article I have explored some of the ties between the Rybczynski theorem linking factor growth with the composition of outputs, the Stolper-Samuelson theorem linking commodity and factor prices, and the question of the shape of the transformation schedule, demonstrating how standard results in trade theory are altered when each a_{ij} is dependent not only upon factor prices but also upon the level of output in industry j.[19] The existence of economies of scale acts like a shift in the production function facing firms if these economies are external to the operation of the firm. If the resources devoted to R&D tend to increase with the scale of operation, further support is lent to treating each a_{ij} as a function of the output of j. Instead of pursuing the formal analysis here, I only note that the model described in sections 2 and 3 can be used with proper modification of (1).

Although the effects of economies of scale on the model may be similar to those of having knowledge improved with greater use of resources for research as output expands, they are not identical in that economies of scale may be reversible

[18] This brings up the old concept of noncompeting groups and the stimulating challenge to traditional trade theory given by Williams [16].

[19] See Jones [8]. A variation on this type of external economy is to have each a_{ij} linked to the quantity of capital employed in industry j.

whereas genuine technical progress is presumably permanent. That is, it may be useful in modifying (1) to introduce a 'ratchet' effect whereby each a_{ij} depends upon the previously attained highest level of output. A more complicated adjustment would entail having the inducement to technical change be represented by the past integral of output. In this way, the unit isoquant would still be shifting inward, even if the level of output were to remain constant.

An even better procedure might entail setting up a distinction between the use of resources to produce the commodity and the use of resources to produce new technical knowledge. That is, the $\hat{b}_{ij}$ could be considered to be outputs of a separate production process.

Any of the above alternatives falls short of capturing a realistic mechanism to explain rates of technical change. Expectations as to future sales must affect the quantity of resources devoted to improving the technology. To highlight this distinction consider, again, Vernon's model of the product cycle. It is at the early stages, where new products are being introduced, that relatively heavy use is made of resources in R&D. Reliance on current output levels as an explanation of the level of technology would fail to incorporate this phenomenon.

All these remarks deal primarily with the determinants of the *rates* of technical progress by industry and with the scale of resources devoted to shifting the production function. A small literature over the past few years has been devoted to the question of the determinants of *bias* in technical progress, *given* the inputs of resources used to improve technology [11, 14, 6, 2]. This literature derives its motivation from models of growth rather than models of trade and, in particular, attempts to demonstrate a tendency toward Harrod neutrality. Nonetheless, any inducement mechanism that serves to explain why labor coefficients are altered by different relative amounts than are capital coefficients has implications for the model set out in sections 2 and 3.

The basic concept in the literature on induced bias is that of a convex technological improvement frontier representing the maximum possible saving in the use of one factor for various prescribed levels of saving in the other factor (and given a fixed research budget). However, there are several interpretations of this frontier, depending upon which parameters are chosen to represent 'saving' for a factor of production. For example, augmenting coefficients could be used, or improvements in marginal products at given capital/labor ratios, or reductions in input-output coefficients at constant factor prices (the $\hat{b}_{ij}$ of this paper) or at a constant rate of profit. Basic to the theory in its present state is the assumption that the frontier is exogenously positioned in time.[20] This represents little advance

[20]This rules out the possibility of diminishing returns to research effort, which would cause the frontier to shrink over time, especially perhaps in the neighborhood of points previously chosen.

over a completely exogenous treatment of technical change. In addition, the assumption that a frontier specified in terms of one set of parameters is fixed in position over time in general negates the possibility that a frontier specified in terms of another set of parameters is also stationary. Furthermore, the conditions for convergence to 'neutrality' depend crucially upon which representation is chosen.

For these reasons I suspect that this literature is not now directly useful to trade theory. However, it does throw out the notion that a factor's distributive share may be a key inducement variable. That is, at the optimal point along the innovation possibility frontier, the absolute value of the slope of the frontier is equated to the ratio of distributive shares. In the language of the model in section 2, the object is to pick $\hat{b}_{ij}$ in such a way that π_j, equal to $\theta_{Lj}\hat{b}_{Lj} + \theta_{Kj}\hat{b}_{Kj}$, is a maximum.[21] Given any disturbance to a trading world (such as the imposition of tariffs or the adjustment required in the face of growth and capital accumulation), distributive shares as well as factor prices are affected, and thus indirectly the choice of new technologies. The novel element is that the question of whether the elasticity of substitution between factors is greater or less than unity becomes important because the behavior of the θ's depends upon this. Thus it might be possible that through trade there is a tendency for factor prices to get equilibrated but at the same time for factor shares to move further apart, thus stimulating more diverse developments in the technologies of the two countries.

The view that technology is improved because there is 'learning by doing' is a statement both about the inducement mechanisms for rates of change and about bias.[22] According to this concept the higher the level of production (or, in some models, the integral of past production or investment) or the more 'experience' about techniques gained by using them, the greater is the rate at which these techniques become more productive. This is similar to the external economy effect discussed earlier. But there is an important difference: the learning-by-doing hypothesis suggests that the unit isoquant gets pushed in primarily in the region where production is taking place. In the words of Atkinson and Stiglitz, technical progress is 'localized'. Although nothing is hypothesized about a 'local' tendency to 'bias' (i.e. whether learning by doing makes the production process more or less labor intensive), there is bias in a 'global' sense that rates of change are higher near the prevailing factor proportions.

The 'localization' feature of learning by doing is of interest to trade theory

[21] Implicitly it may be assumed that the model in section 2 has a right-angled innovation possibility frontier.

[22] The basic paper is Arrow [3]. See also the interesting paper by Atkinson and Stiglitz [4].

because it raises the question of how transmittable technical change is from one country to another.

5. Transmission of technology

Is the technical progress of one country readily transmittable to other countries? The discussion in section 2 presumed that it was not, but underlying the traditional Heckscher–Ohlin model is the notion that it is difficult to keep secret new techniques of production.

For some types of technical knowledge patents or licensing arrangements would allow new techniques to be sold internationally as are other commodities. The traditional view is that basic knowledge cannot be appropriated in this way, that technical knowledge takes on more the form of a public good. In this sense technical progress is freely transferable.

Even in this limiting case, however, technical progress in one country may not spill over actually to affect techniques used in other countries. Consider fig. 15.2 in which a common (solid) isoquant for two countries is shifted to the dashed isoquant again commonly available to two countries. If the high wage advanced country is producing at A, and if the low wage country is using techniques shown by B, the improvement in techniques shown by the dashed curve does not serve to lower costs in the low wage country.

Two features of this example are crucial in limiting the transference of technical improvements: (1) Factor prices differ between countries, so that different actual techniques are used along the same isoquant, and (2) technical progress in one country tends to be 'localized' in the region of existing techniques. The learning-by-doing hypothesis fits the latter category and thus serves as one basis for explaining why it is that all countries need not benefit from improvements made in

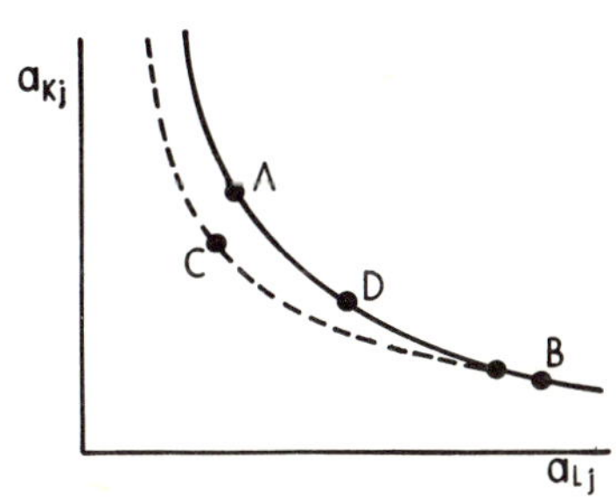

Figure 15.2

one of them, even though no secrets are kept. But the argument against the effective transmittal of new knowledge is even stronger than this. The movement from *A* to *C* in fig. 15.2 may have been the result of a technical improvement that was discovered as a consequence of time spent using the technique at *A*. On the other hand, what may be represented is that labor needs the experience of working with capital before point *C* can be reached. In this latter instance even if the low wage country is at point *D* it may not be able to benefit until its factors can adapt to the techniques at *A*.

The picture that emerges from this is that production functions may in some sense be the same between countries, but factor prices are different, and in their research efforts countries are really 'chipping away' at different points on a common production surface.

If technical progress is embodied, clearly the transmission of technical knowledge depends upon allowing trade in capital goods. The same feature also obtains with labor and the possibility of moving trained managers and special skills, perhaps through foreign investment. The view that much of the change or difference that is observed in input-output coefficients is a reflection of changes in factor skills rather than in technical knowledge leads to the position that a critical bottleneck to the international transmission of technology resides in international factor immobilities. Trade in factors is synonymous with exporting the technology.

In concluding this chapter I would like to suggest how a mixture of these views could be fitted together into the framework of a model developed recently by Kenen [12]. Kenen views capital as a resource which is used to improve the quality of uneducated labor and infertile land. That is, resources (capital) are used to raise the quality of the basic factors of production, which are then used to produce commodities that enter into trade (as well as capital). By analogy think of techniques newly developed in an advanced country. Before these can be utilized in a less developed country, resources must be devoted to the learning process. In this way, technical knowledge is not kept 'secret', but transmission is nonetheless not without cost.

With foreign-produced technology not adaptable without the use of a country's own resources, the question arises as to the proper allocation of local capital and labor to improve 'technology'. Two uses are suggested, each perhaps subject to diminishing returns: (1) adapt the foreign technology as suggested above, or (2) devote resources, partly through learning by doing, to improve local techniques that are dictated by local factor prices. These uses for resources must compete with the alternatives of raising labor productivity through capital accumulation or working directly, through education, to improve factor skills. It is not difficult to envisage a model in which the productivity of all four uses for resources gets equated at the margin.

References

[1] Amano, A., 'Determinants of Comparative Costs: A Theoretical Approach', *Oxford Economic Papers* (November 1964) 389–400.

[2] Amano, A., 'Induced Bias in Technological Progress and Economic Growth', *The Economic Studies Quarterly* (March 1967) 1–17.

[3] Arrow, K.J., 'The Economic Implication of Learning by Doing', *Review of Economic Studies* (1962) 155–173.

[4] Atkinson, A.B., and J.E. Stiglitz, 'A New View of Technological Change', *Economic Journal*, 79 (1969) 573–578.

[5] Chipman, J., International Trade with Capital Mobility: A Substitution Theorem', in: Bhagwati, Jones, Mundell, and Vanek, eds., *Trade, Balance of Payments, and Growth* (North-Holland, Amsterdam, 1971) 201–237.

[6] Drandakis, E. and E. Phelps, 'A Model of Induced Invention, Growth and Distribution', *Economic Journal* (December 1966) 823–840.

[7] Jones, R.W., 'Comments on Technical Progress', *The Philippine Economic Journal*, Second Semester, (1966) 313–332.

[8] Jones, R.W., 'Variable Returns to Scale in General Equilibrium Theory', *International Economic Review* (October 1968) 261–272.

[9] Kemp, M. C., 'The Gain from International Trade and Investment: A Neo-Heckscher–Ohlin Approach', *American Economic Review* (September 1966) 788–809.

[10] Kemp, M.C., and K. Inada, 'International Capital Movements and the Theory of International Trade', *Quarterly Journal of Economics* (August 1969).

[11] Kennedy, C., 'Induced Bias in Innovation and the Theory of Distribution', *Economic Journal* (September 1964) 541–547.

[12] Kenen, P.B., 'Nature, Capital and Trade', *Journal of Political Economy* (October 1965) 437–460.

[13] Rybczynski, T.M., 'Factor Endowments and Relative Commodity Prices', *Economica* (November 1955) 336–341.

[14] Samuelson, P.A., 'A Theory of Induced Innovation along Kennedy-Weizsacker Lines', *Review of Economics and Statistics* (November 1965) 343–356.

[15] Vernon, R., 'International Investment and International Trade in the Product Cycle', *Quarterly Journal of Economics* (May 1966) 190–207.

[16] Williams, J.H., 'The Theory of International Trade Reconsidered', reprinted in: *Postwar Monetary Plans and Other Essays* (Oxford, 1947) ch. 2.

Chapter 16

THE EXPORT OF TECHNOLOGY*

1. Introduction

Two decades after Solow's pioneering study [15] suggesting the importance of technological progress in explaining the trend of American growth, economists still find the phenomenon of technical change difficult to model. The frustration stems in large part from the difficulties in capturing in simple and general form the key variables affecting the *creation* of new technologies *de novo*. However, many problems still remain in explaining the speed and form of the diffusion of technology, and the consequences of this spread on trade patterns, income distribution, and welfare.

In this chapter I concentrate on some of the issues involved in the export of technology. Primary focus is provided by the distinction between the forms that such export may take. Section 2 discusses briefly the kind of technical knowledge that is disembodied. New knowledge can be packaged in a set of blueprints which, if applicable to other countries, can either be sold abroad or kept in local control by means of direct foreign investment. The following two sections discuss in more detail the two main ways in which technological superiority may be *embodied.* Section 3 explores the results of a model in which capital completely embodies the new technology, and this capital can be located in other countries (although not produced there). The model is a general equilibrium model, capable of expressing some depth of structural detail. Although the formal analysis of this model has not been reproduced here,[1] its main features and conclusions are discussed. Of special interest is a comparison of optimal restrictive

*Adapted from 'The Export of Technology', in: *Optimal Policies, Control Theory and Technology Exports*, Carnegie–Rochester Conference Series on Public Policy, vol. 7 (1977) pp. 159–202, jointly with Eitan Berglas. Thanks are due the National Science Foundation for support of this research.

[1] Details are found in the appendix to Berglas and Jones, *op. cit.*

policies that would be undertaken by a government wanting to maximize national income with that of a private sector (multinational) controlling the quantity of technology exports. Section 4 is concerned with the fact that much new technology is bound up with labor skills. A model is described in which technical advances in one country are not immediately applicable to countries at earlier stages of development, but become so at a later stage and require, for their implementation, international flows of skilled labor. The paper concludes, in section 5, with several related issues concerned with the export of technology.

No attempt has been made in this paper to appraise or survey the literature, much of which either ignores the international aspects of technical progress or is concerned more than we wish to be with the peculiarities of multinational corporations, or with the special plight of underdeveloped regions.

2. Disembodied technical progress

One of the major models in the theory of international economics – the Heckscher-Ohlin model – presupposes that countries all share the same technology. This does not require them to produce commodities using the same *techniques*; capital-poor countries may deliberately choose to adopt more labor-intensive factor combinations than do capital-rich countries, even though they each have knowledge of a common production function. Nor does this model preclude the analysis of technological change. It instead requires that any new knowledge created in one country is costlessly and immediately available (or made available) to all countries. Within this restriction it is still possible to ask how changes in technological knowledge disturb trading patterns, national incomes, and internal income distribution. Much of the trade literature in the 1950s and early 1960s was devoted precisely to these questions. For example, what is the consequence of Hicksian labor-saving technological progress that is confined to a labor-abundant country's export sector on this country's terms of trade? (they worsen), on its level of real income? (it may actually fall), or on the volume of trade? (probably expands).[2]

An earlier branch of international trade theory, associated with Ricardo's development of the doctrine of comparative costs, allowed countries to differ in their technological knowledge (whether disembodied or a function of climate or labor skills). Although this theory did not allow this technology to be traded

[2] For early references see Johnson [9] or Findlay and Grubert [4]. A summary statement is found in Chapter 15. Often this literature analyzes the case of technical change in just one country, but the results are quite similar.

directly, or indirectly in the form of international factor mobility, the consequences of differences in technology could be viewed in the pattern of commodity trade.

If technical knowledge can be appropriated or kept secret by its owner until sold, the basis for mutually profitable trade in technology exists. This knowledge can be exported in several forms. Internationally recognized patents would prevent foreign use of the technology except by payment of fees or through licensing devices. Alternatively, the secret might be kept but the owners of the knowledge might directly hire foreign resources for production abroad. It has often been observed that although sales of technology do occur, an export of technology through foreign investment is the more frequent form.

Several reasons have been proposed to explain why direct foreign investment may be preferred to a direct sale abroad as the channel through which technology is exported. Some of these are explicitly based on the notion of technology being embodied, if only partly, in complementary productive factors. The home country might possess superior management or skilled labor, better able to exploit the advantages of the new technology than would foreigners. But if this is the case, it is possible to argue that these skills in turn could be 'hired out' abroad. Is there more to the argument favoring foreign investment than this? Even for technological knowledge that is completely disembodied, there are two reasons why foreign investment may prove more profitable than direct foreign sales of technology.

The first reason concerns the kind of market in which the commodity is produced. Suppose the knowledge of technology involves a secret process for producing a *new* commodity so that possession of the knowledge creates a natural monopoly. Presumably foreigners would be willing to pay to obtain the technological information. But once the technology is sold, the home firm loses its natural monopoly. Even if the foreign firm has no intention of producing at competitive levels, unless it chooses to produce at a level of output that maximizes *joint* profits to all producers of this good *and* turns over all its profits to purchase the technology, the home firm would do better to retain possession.[3] In other words, the foreign firm could not afford to pay the home firm as much as the technology is worth to the home firm because it would alter the profit-maximizing level of monopoly output.

This kind of argument would disappear if the superior technological knowledge

[3] This presupposes that production costs abroad offer an advantage to producing abroad. Otherwise it would pay the home country to keep its technology and supply the foreign market directly by exports instead of foreign investment. Of course tariffs could alter this choice by providing a protected market.

lowers costs of producing a commodity that is sold worldwide on competitive markets. Even though in this situation there may be relatively little danger of 'spoiling the market', the home firm possessing the superior technology might refrain from selling it if the potential foreign producer cannot or would not pay as much as the value of the technology to the domestic firm. A superior technology is like other forms of capital in that it yields a stream of future returns. These returns are capitalized back to the present to yield the value of the new technology. If interest rates (or discount rates) are *higher* abroad, the value to *them* of the new knowledge would fall short of the value to the home firm. Rather than sell the technology, it would pay the home country to create its own production facilities abroad or, alternatively, to export from plants at home. A variation of this argument has a private firm at home, possessing new technological knowledge, dealing with a public agency abroad, an agency with a shorter time horizon than possessed by the private home firm because of local political uncertainty or forthcoming elections. In this case again the technological knowledge may be worth less to the foreign public agency than to the home private firm.

The danger of foreign expropriation would serve to counter these arguments. The value to the home firm of its production facilities abroad that adopt the new low-cost technology may prove to be less than their value would be to a foreign firm because the danger of expropriation may loom larger for the home firm than for a foreign firm.[4] I turn now to discuss a model that incorporates the risk of expropriation and the notion that the export of technology requires the export of the capital equipment which could be expropriated.

3. Technology embodied in capital

Suppose a unit of capital embodies technology in the sense that combined with a unit of *any kind of labor* its productivity is invariant. Specifically, home labor is homogeneous, and foreign labor (also homogeneous) is as productive on home machines as would be the same quantity of home labor. Each country's labor force is perfectly mobile internally, but immobile internationally. The most natural assumption to make about capital which embodies technology is that it is sector-specific. Thus, in a two-commodity world there is type-1 capital and type-2 capital. Home capital of either type is assumed to embody technology that is superior to that found in foreign capital (of comparable type).

[4] It is not always the case that a government is more likely to take over foreign firms than local domestic ones. Socialist economies may allow foreign firms a measure of freedom locally denied to their own nationals.

In such a world the export of technology is synonymous with the export of capital equipment embodying that technology. To keep matters simple, suppose type-2 capital is immobile between countries.[5] However, the home country can locate some of its type-1 capital abroad in order to take advantage of the lower real wages assumed to prevail in the (technologically) backward foreign country.

My basic concern is with the equilibrium volume of technology exports and how these are affected by changes in attitudes towards risk, by changes in the commodity terms of trade, and by changes in government tax-tariff levels. Furthermore, in a general equilibrium model one is allowed to say something about the feedback effects of a change in technology exports on the distribution of income in each country and on overall national levels of real income. Despite the focus on capital as the productive factor which embodies technology, this is not a 'vintage-capital' model of the Solow type.[6] The model is static. Not being concerned with growth and capital accumulation, I assume all incomes are consumed and none invested. This frees us to ask about the equilibrium *location* of the home country's type-1 stock of machines. It is fixed in overall supply, but its location depends upon considerations I now describe.

The superiority of home capital is illustrated in fig. 16.1 by a comparison of the two unit isoquants for producing the first commodity. The *B* isoquant shows combinations of foreign labor and *foreign* type-1 capital that can produce one unit of

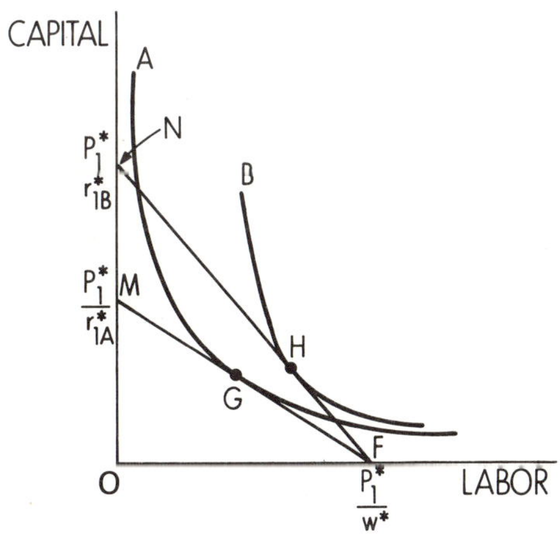

Figure 16.1

[5]This, and the assumption of home superiority throughout, rules out the possibility of two-way trade in technology (and capital). For an interesting discussion of such two-way trade see Caves [3].

[6]See Solow [16]. The next section does discuss the 'vintage' issue in connection with labor.

commodity 1. The B label suggests that these techniques belong to the 'backward' region in the foreign country, as opposed to the A (advanced) region in which superior home capital (K_A^*) is combined with foreign labor to produce the first commodity by advanced techniques. Suppose both technologies are employed abroad and that the mobility of homogeneous foreign labor ensures that each region pays the same real wage.[7] The inverse of this real wage (P_1^*/w^*) is shown by distance OF. From point F two factor-cost lines have been drawn, showing minimum-unit-cost production points G (for the advanced technology) and H (for backward techniques). The return to each type of capital is shown by the inverse of distances OM and ON for the advanced and backward sectors, respectively. The superiority of advanced technology embodied in home machines is reflected in the excess of rental return to home machines (r_{1A}^*) over that to foreign machines (r_{1B}).[8]

Whereas fig. 16.1 shows that home type-1 capital embodies superior technology and thus earns a higher return abroad than does foreign type-1 capital, fig. 16.2's factor-price frontier for the advanced technology used in producing the first commodity shows that if the real wage is lower abroad, the real return to capital

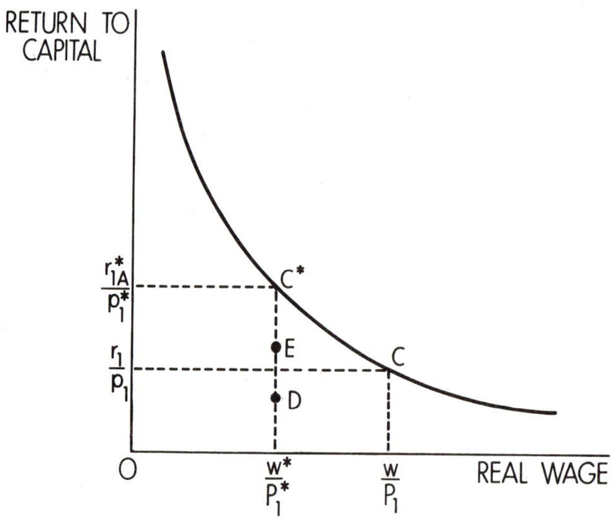

Figure 16.2

[7] Findlay [5] assumes that foreign investors pay a higher wage than do local firms. We abstract from this possibility.

[8] I have also illustrated the advanced sector adopting more capital-intensive techniques (at G) than does the backward sector (at H), but this is not a necessary requirement.

earned in the advanced sector abroad (r^*_{1A}/p^*_1) can exceed that earned by this same type of capital at home (r_1/p_1). Indeed, this discrepancy motivated the export of technology. The high wage home country is at C and the combination of factor returns in the advanced sector abroad is at C^*, two points on the common frontier determined by the home country's technology for producing commodity 1. Not drawn is the factor-price frontier derived from the foreign technology used in producing the first commodity in the backward region abroad. It would lie below the advanced technology frontier. At the foreign real wage, w^*/p^*_1, it could cut at D (showing a lower return to foreign capital than to home capital at home) or at E. Foreign capital is at a technological disadvantage in producing the first commodity compared with home capital located abroad (D and E lie below C^*), but works with lower-paid labor than does home capital at home, and thus may end up earning more than r_1/p_1 (as at E).[9]

Real wages are lower abroad. If sector 1-type capital embodies the superior technology and can be shipped abroad, why should any of this capital remain at home if r^*_{1A} exceeds r_1? Taxes provide one possible answer: perhaps a tax imposed by the home country on earnings of home capital located abroad, at rate t, brings *net* private returns, $r^*_{1A}(1 - t)$, into equality with r_1. This suggests the notion of a 'scientific tax', designed precisely to offset the attraction to home capital of cheap labor abroad. I reject the possibility that tax structures are so carefully tailored and, instead, assume that home owners of capital demand a risk premium in order to invest abroad. Furthermore, the extent of the premium rises as the amount of home capital invested abroad, K^*_A, increases. This behavior is captured by the rising *RR* curve in fig. 16.3. The vertical axis shows the ratio of after-tax returns on foreign investment to returns at home and the horizontal axis the extent of foreign investment. The positive slope of *RR* could reflect the increased fear of expropriation the greater the size of alien capital abroad (which becomes increasingly irritating to foreign nationals). The *RR* curve could start at unity on the vertical axis (as drawn) or from a higher point if some positive premium is required in order that *any* foreign investment takes place.

Of course the advantage offered by the relative cheapness of foreign labor could outweigh the risk premium so that *all* productive activity for commodity 1 is located abroad. (This need not wipe out foreign production in the backward region.) I assume this is not the case in order to examine the intermediate possi-

[9] I assume commodity 2 is always freely traded so that p_2 and p^*_2 (the foreign price) are always the same. However, trade taxes could cause p_1 and p^*_1 to diverge. Nonetheless, I assume that the return earned by home capital invested abroad, r^*_{1A}, exceeds the home return, r_1, as well as r^*_{1A}/p^*_1 exceeding r_1/p_1 as shown in fig. 16.2.

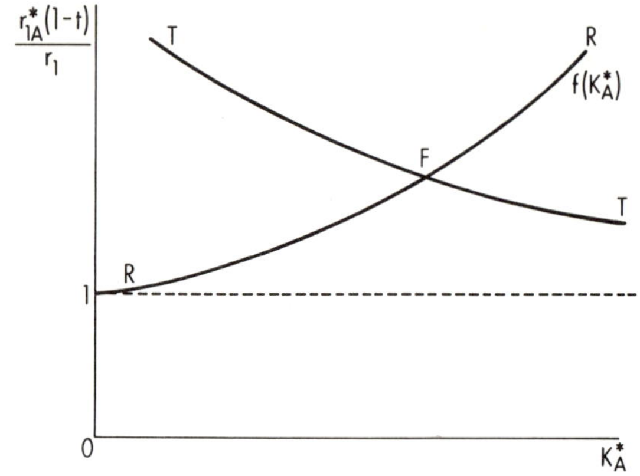

Figure 16.3

bility of commodity 1 being produced in both countries, with the export of technology causing two different techniques to be used abroad.

In a competitive world the equilibrium volume of exported technology must equate the after-tax foreign return, $r^*_{1A}(1-t)$ to $f(K^*_A)r_1$, where $f(K^*_A)$ shows one plus the risk premium (fig. 16.3). But for given tax rates and commodity prices, the ratio of returns to capital in the two countries depends on the technologies and the quantity of exported capital. This relationship is shown by the downward-sloping *TT* schedule. At given terms of trade an increase in technology exports drives down the return to capital invested abroad, r^*_{1A}, and raises r_1 at home. Thus, in fig. 16.3 point *F* shows the equilibrium export of technology.

A change in commodity prices or the tax rate would shift the *TT* schedule and thus affect rates of return and the quantity of technology exports. So, also, a lowering of the risk premium would shift the *RR* schedule clockwise and encourage technology exports. To probe more deeply, suppose risks do diminish so that K^*_A expands. What effect does this increase in exports of advanced technology have on incomes in the two countries and on world outputs?

An outflow of capital from sector 1 at home to the advanced sector abroad will drive up wages abroad at the expense of the return to all kinds of capital. At home the reverse takes place – labor loses at the expense of all capitalists. (Recall that commodity prices are being held constant.) With less type-1 capital at home, production of x_1 falls. Production of x_2 rises since some labor is driven from the first sector to the second sector. Abroad the situation is more complicated since there are two different sectors producing commodity 1, as well as a sector producing commodity 2.

In more detail, the influx of capital with its embodied technology in the advanced sector abroad causes output there to expand. Labor will be released from sector 2 and from the backward sector producing commodity 1. The net effect on output of commodity 1 must be positive. The analysis is somewhat simplified by noting (i) the influx of K_A^* would, if there were *no* labor movements, raise output in the advanced sector by precisely the marginal product of capital times the increase in K_A^*. (ii) Any transfer of labor from the backward sector producing the first commodity to the advanced sector has *no* net effect on output of commodity 1. This follows since the real wage (reflecting labor's marginal product) is equated between sectors. (iii) Output in the advanced sector is expanded even further to the extent that the rise in wages causes labor to be released from sector 2. The extent of this release depends upon the size of sector 2, and the general flexibility of 2-technology compared with the rest of the economy.

If an increase in technology exports causes net output of the first commodity to rise abroad and fall at home, what can be said about net *world* output of commodity 1? There is a presumption, but no certainty, that it will rise. The presumption stems from the asymmetry in the returns to type-1 capital in the two countries; r_{1A}^* exceeds r_1 (assuming zero tax) by the amount of the risk premium demanded by foreign investors. The difference between the real returns to capital in the two countries indicates the increase in net world outputs of the first commodity that would be caused by this further export of technology *if* labor allocations in each country did not change. But at home labor is absorbed into 2's production, with a reverse movement abroad. Thus, a further comparison of productive structures in the two economies would be required. Much of this comparison involves the characteristics of the *advanced* technology used to produce commodity 1. Both countries share this technology, although actual techniques differ because real wages differ. Therefore distributive factor shares will generally be different from country to country, and these shares are an important part of the comparison.[10]

Although the *TT* schedule in fig. 16.3 is drawn as of constant commodity prices, I have argued that an increase in K_A^* might presumably be expected to raise world output of commodity 1 and thus lower the price of 1. The consequences of this possibility are developed below. But first ask the reverse question: How would an exogenously-given increase in commodity 1's relative price affect the export of technology? With reference to fig. 16.3 the question is whether an increase in p_1 serves to shift *TT* upwards or downwards.

The answer must once again be 'it depends'. It is clear that an increase in p_1 encourages production of the first commodity everywhere. And both r_1 at home and

[10] The reader is again referred to the appendix in Berglas and Jones, *op. cit.*

r^*_{1A} in the advanced sector abroad are driven up (even relative to p_1). There is a presumption that the absolute gap $(r^*_{1A} - r_1)$, widens. Indeed, this presumption is based exactly on the same considerations as previously stated for the effect of an increment in technology exports on net world output of the first commodity.[11] But such a presumption disappears for the *ratio*, r^*_{1A}/r_1, which, by assumption in fig. 16.3 is the crucial variable linking risk and the volume of technology exports.

For policy purposes we can ask about the possibility of government interference in commodity markets via trade taxes and/or interference directly in the export of technology. It proves convenient to analyze government actions in the special case in which there is no interference in commodity markets. The only instrument by which the government can affect the equilibrium export of technology is the tax on earnings of foreign investors. By raising this tax, the government can restrict K^*_A. Should it do so? To the extent that a restriction on capital outflows raises the return to capital invested abroad, there is a clear gain to aggregate real income at home. This is a 'terms-of-trade' effect applied to the export of technology.[12] But commodity prices may have to adjust to clear the market. I have argued above that there is a presumption that a restriction of technology exports for the first commodity would lower 1's world output. I now extend this presumption by arguing that such restriction would tend to raise the world price of commodity 1. Does this represent a gain or loss to the home country?

Any restriction on technology exports that serves to raise commodity 1's price must *in part* be favorable to the home country because such a price rise directly raises the return to technology and capital invested abroad. But more is involved – the price change directly affects home real incomes if commodity 1 is traded. Of crucial importance is the *direction* of trade.

It may seem plausible to assume that the home country, with an assumed superiority in the technology whereby the first commodity is produced, emerges as the exporter of this commodity. However, there are several qualifications that must be made. First, differences in factor endowments between countries also affect trade patterns. Secondly, the home country may also have superior technology in producing the second commodity. Finally, and most importantly for this discussion, the technology is itself being exported, and foreign investment directly competes with home production. The trade pattern could run either way.

If the home country exports the first commodity as well as the technology to

[11] This is an application of Samuelson's *reciprocity* relationship.

[12] The analysis of this kind of problem for capital flows not involving technology transfers is found in Kemp [11], and in Chapter 12, for the two-country, two-commodity, Heckscher–Ohlin model.

produce the first commodity abroad, it has an interest in raising that commodity's price. Having ruled out export taxes, which would bring this about directly, the home country could instead restrict technology exports with a tax on repatriated earnings from abroad. The presumption is that this would serve indirectly to raise p_1 by restricting world output of the first commodity.

The case involving a potential conflict between attempting to obtain better commodity terms of trade and a higher return to technology exports has the home country importing the first commodity. Clearly, much depends on the significance of commodity imports versus technology exports. The less important are technology exports, the more likely is the home government to subsidize these exports in order to benefit by lower import prices for the first commodity.

Although this analysis introduces an element of 'monopolistic' behavior in examining the optimal level of taxation in order to have the government maximize the home country's real income, there is an alternative element of 'monopoly' behavior perhaps more typically associated with this problem. Suppose that owners of type-1 capital can band together into what might be called a multinational corporation interested in maximizing their own real income. Furthermore, suppose they are incapable of *discriminating* by establishing different commodity prices in the two countries. (After all, foreigners also produce commodity 1 with their own – albeit backwards – technology and capital.) That is, domestic p_1 and foreign p_1^* are the same, precisely as in the case of free trade just analyzed. Assume no government tax interference. Nonetheless, home owners of type-1 capital could cut back on the exports of technology below the competitive level suggested by point F in fig. 16.3. If they do so, a relative spread between r_{1A}^* and $f(K_A^*)\,r_1$ is created, and this could be contrasted with the government's optimal tax wedge in order to see if a multinational would restrict technology outflow by more or less than would an aggregate-real-income maximizing government.

Such a comparison is most simple to make if the repercussions on commodity markets can be ignored. In that event the model throws up a strong conclusion: a multinational corporation would restrict technology exports by *less* than would a government intent upon maximizing society's real income. Indeed, a multinational could go as far as promoting technology exports beyond the competitive level. The rationale is clear. Starting from a competitive position the government would wish to restrict technology exports in order to drive up the return abroad to capital already invested there – a pure 'technology' terms-of-trade consideration. But such a restriction drives *down* the rate of return to type-1 capital at home. This latter effect is balanced by other changes in the distribution of income internally (primarily a gain by workers) and such pure redistribution of income would be ignored by a government whose objective function is real *national* income. However, it would not be ignored by a multinational with direct control over the allocation of its capital and embodied technology.

These remarks reveal the importance of the assumption that technology is embodied. An export of technology involves an export of capital, leaving *less* in the home country. Opposed to this is the case of a company that could just sell off its technological secrets for a positive price abroad. That would always be profitable *if* the changes in commodity prices could be ignored.

When the effect of restriction of technology on the commodity terms of trade is considered, the analysis obviously gets more complicated. But an essential difference between multinational control on the one hand and government control (in the national interest) on the other gets revealed. Recall that if the nation *imports* the first commodity, the government has an impetus to lower the price of the first commodity (ignoring the repercussion on the rate of return). But the multinational would never share such behavior. Its interest as a 'producer' of the first commodity always outweighs its interest as a 'consumer'.[13] The situation in which the multinational might adopt a *more* restrictive policy on technology exports than would be optimal for the economy as a whole is precisely the situation in which the home country depends heavily on imports of the commodity in question.

4. Labor skills and technology transfer

'Learning by doing' is the catch phrase used by economists since the basic paper by Arrow [1] to suggest that skills and knowledge about technology can be acquired by experience in production. This concept is important for this discussion of technology exports in two fundamental ways: (i) technological knowledge may be embodied in labor so that some form of migration may be required in order to export the technology, and (ii) if 'doing' encourages 'learning', this tends to be focused on the *kinds* of techniques actually used. Or, to use the phrase adopted by Atkinson and Stiglitz [2], technological change tends to be 'localized' around a region of the isoquant representing actual factor proportions being utilized. To these two themes we suggest a third: there may be 'forgetting by not doing'. Even 'advanced' countries may have an absolute technological disadvantage in producing commodities by highly labor-intensive techniques compared to backward countries if the latter have recent experience with such techniques and the former do not.

[13]The multinational's interest is actually 'magnified', as r_1 and r^*_{1A} rise in greater proportion than does p_1

Fig. 16.4 shows three unit isoquants for producing the same commodity.[14] Consider just isoquants (*1*) and (*2*). Each of these summarizes the technology available to a particular country – (*2*) to an advanced high-wage country and (*1*) to a relatively backward low-wage country. Neither isoquant dominates. The advanced country has concentrated on improving relatively capital-intensive techniques compared with the backward country, and a combination of 'learning by doing' and 'forgetting by not doing' explains their relative shapes. Points *A* and *B* showing actual techniques adopted reflect the relatively high wages paid in the advanced country. As drawn, the technology developed by the advanced country is *not* relevant to the backward country. But it would become profitable to transmit the advanced technology when and if real wages rise over time. The existence of different factor prices in the two countries has had two effects – it has induced different technologies over time, and it makes one country's technology at any point in time less relevant (or irrelevant) for the other country.

Now consider the case of two countries, each developing over time, accumulating capital, and experiencing steady increases in real wages. Suppose there is a steady lag – the advanced country's level of real wages remains, say, ten years ahead of that of the relatively backward country. At an early stage the advanced country has developed technology (*2*) and produces at *A* in fig. 16.4, whereas the lower-wage country is at *B* using technology (*1*). Technology (*2*) becomes useful to the backward country only when its real wages rise beyond the position in-

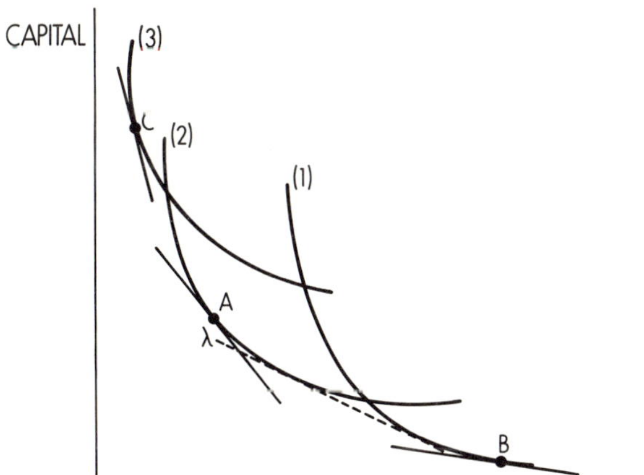

Figure 16.4

[14] This diagram and much of this discussion is based on Jones [10]. See also Chapter 15.

dicated by the slope of the λ-line. But by this time the advanced country has developed technology (*3*), which is more relevant to it, as its real wages have risen as shown by point *C*. Technology (*3*) is not useful at this stage to the backward country.

To this tale of 'vintage' technologies continuously being developed and then discarded by one country, subsequently to be adopted by another, add the notion of 'vintage' labor. Each technology in the advanced country is developed by, and experience in production acquired by, a certain generation of labor. As time progresses, the skills acquired by this generation would prove less useful as compared to new skills developed by a younger generation in connection with developing and experiencing more advanced technologies. However, the embodied skills of the older generation become more useful to countries further behind in their development efforts. The generation in the advanced country trained in techniques at *A* may find a ready market for their skills once the backward country's real wages rise beyond the λ-line.

If the possibility of international labor mobility helps support the demand and returns to older workers in the advanced country, it may help suppress the demand for the relatively skilled workers abroad. These foreign workers have no experience in (*2*) type technologies, and thus are at a disadvantage compared to mobile older home workers. This is an ironic story in which international labor mobility encourages a more equal distribution of wage incomes for each country's nationals, but enhances the gap between lower-paid workers in the advanced country and relatively better paid labor in the backward country. Labor mobility provides the advanced country an opportunity to export labor and skills no longer in local demand and the backward country to import labor and skills not found in their own labor force.

Of course a different form of labor migration may take place. The relatively backward country may send its younger workers to the home country for education and on-the-job training, learning techniques which later can prove useful if these workers return to the foreign country.

5. Conclusion: other issues in the export of technology

Is the export of technology more likely to develop from an advanced economy to a relatively underdeveloped economy, or between countries at relatively similar stages of development and factor prices? In a recent article, Findlay [5] cites Veblen and Gerschenkron as supporting the former view that the rate at which a backward country's technology can improve is positively related to the extent of the technology gap.[15] This is a view which may be easiest to defend if advances in technology take the form of relatively uniform shifts of isoquants in towards the origin. In such a case the potential saving in costs is greater the larger the technology gap, regardless of differences in economic structure (factor endowments, factor prices) between countries. However, in the preceding section we argued that if human labor skills are an important ingredient in explaining technical progress and if such progress tends to be 'localized', through a combination of 'learning by doing' and 'forgetting by not doing' progress in one country may not prove relevant for countries with markedly dissimilar factor prices.

These remarks apply strictly to a comparison of technologies available to produce a particular commodity. But there is a broader and deeper question concerning the degree of similarity in technologies for producing different commodities. A bold hypothesis would maintain that commodities that require roughly similar factor proportions also have more technological processes in common than do commodities with more disparate factor proportions. If so, it may be expected that new processes developed for producing commodities in one country can be exported, with suitable modifications, to countries producing other commodities close to those in input proportions. Indeed, two-way trade in technology can easily be envisaged for countries at roughly comparable stages of development.

The development literature frequently asks why multinational corporations seem to pay scant attention to production techniques that require relatively intensive use of unskilled labor found in abundance in less developed regions. That is, multinationals are frequently charged with exporting technologies that are inappropriate given factor prices and availabilities in the host country.[16] One set of explanations for such behavior points to the illusory nature of cheap labor in such countries. (Labor costs per unit of productivity may be high; minimum wages may distort the labor market, etc.) But even if factor prices correctly represent factor availabilities, Magee [13] provides an interesting explanation why the actual technologies exported might be biased towards the complex capital intensive and skilled-labor-intensive direction. These techniques are harder to imitate. The extra variable is that the ability of the firm to appropriate to itself the returns from its technology exports depends upon the factor mix embodied by the technology.

Finally, how does the export of technology differ in principle from the export of commodities? They are often viewed as competing alternatives. Country A may produce locally and export its produce to country B, or it may choose to invest

[15] This view has also been expressed more formally by Nelson and Phelps [14] and by Kmenta [12].

[16] For a good summary of this issue see Helleiner [6].

abroad and exports its capital, labor skills, and technology instead.[17] The choice between the two depends not only upon a comparison of factor prices and risks in the two countries (as was emphasized in section 3) but also upon the tax policies in the host country. In this respect commodity trade taxes (tariffs) have a different role to play than do other forms of taxation. Tariffs can distort the pattern of commodity trade and protect local industries. Tariffs can also be used to attract foreign investment that produces for the local market. But taxation of factor incomes can significantly affect the location of production for *export*.

Country *B* may have a limited local demand for a commodity produced by country *A* and exported to a number of regions. An appropriate production subsidy could encourage an export of capital and technology and result in *B* becoming the new major supply source for this commodity, exporting to third countries (and perhaps back to *A*). Why should *B* be willing to subsidize production? Because it could more than recoup through the income tax on the firm's earnings. International tax agreements, whereby host countries get first crack at earned income, provide an incentive for countries to attract foreign investment and foreign technology. And unlike straightforward trade in commodities, where protection can result in a proliferation of production to service local protected markets, the possibility of trade in factors and technology offers countries the opportunity to create new *export* industries, whose limits are not set by local demand. Tax arrangements provide the incentive for such behavior.

References

[1] Arrow, K.J., 'The Economic Implication of Learning by Doing', *Review of Economic Studies* (June 1962).

[2] Atkinson, A. and H. Stiglitz, 'A New View of Technological Change', *Economic Journal* (September 1969).

[3] Caves, R.E., 'International Corporations: The Industrial Economics of Foreign Investment', *Economica* (February 1971).

[4] Findlay, R. and H. Grubert, 'Factor Intensities, Technological Progress, and the Terms of Trade', *Oxford Economic Papers* (February 1959).

[5] Findlay, R., 'Relative Backwardness, Direct Foreign Investment and the Transfer of Technology: A Simple Dynamic Model', unpublished.

[6] Helleiner, G.K., 'The Role of Multinational Corporations in the Less Developed Countries' Trade in Technology', *World Development* (April 1975).

[7] Horst, T., 'The Theory of the Multinational Firm: Optimal Behavior under Different Tariff and Tax Rates', *Journal of Political Economy* (September/October 1971).

[8] Horst, T., 'The Industrial Composition of U.S. Exports and Subsidiary Sales to the Canadian Market', *American Economic Review* (March 1972).

[17] Several papers by Horst [7, 8] focus on this issue. See also the discussion in Swedenborg [17].

[9] Johnson, H.G., 'Economic Development and International Trade', in: Caves and Johnson, eds., *Readings in International Economics* (Irwin, 1968).

[10] Jones, R.W., 'Comments on Technology, Technical Progress and the International Allocation of Economic Activity', unpublished.

[11] Kemp, M., 'The Gain from International Trade and Investment: A Neo-Heckscher–Ohlin Approach', *American Economic Review* (September 1966).

[12] Kmenta, J., 'Economic Theory and Transfer of Technology', in: Spencer and Woroniak, eds., *The Transfer of Technology to Developing Countries* (Praeger, 1967).

[13] Magee, S., 'Information and the Multinational Corporation: An Appropriability Theory of Direct Foreign Investment', unpublished.

[14] Nelson, R. and E. Phelps, 'Investment in Humans, Technological Diffusion and Economic Growth', *American Economic Review* (May 1966).

[15] Solow, R., 'Technical Change and the Aggregate Production Function', *Review of Economics and Statistics* (August 1957).

[16] Solow, R., 'Investment and Technical Progress', in: Arrow, Karlin and Suppes, eds., *Mathematical Methods in the Social Sciences*, 1959 (Stanford, 1960).

[17] Swedenborg, B., 'Towards a Theory of International Direct Investment', unpublished.

Chapter 17

TECHNICAL PROGRESS AND REAL INCOMES IN A RICARDIAN TRADE MODEL

Countries that are linked together by international trade cannot expect to find their real incomes unaffected by changes in economic structure taking place in other countries. The outcome typically expected is that growth in one country will have favorable spill-over effects for its trading partners. But the trade literature has for a long time considered the possibility of one of two exceptions: (i) in the case of immiserizing growth, an outward shift in the home country's production possibilities curve so damages that country's terms of trade that real income at home actually falls; or (ii) at the other extreme, home expansion of outputs may serve to worsen the terms of trade for other countries and thus cause negative spill-overs for foreign real income. The most obvious example has the home country's growth concentrated in import-competing sectors.

This chapter considers one particular source of growth, technical progress. It is supposed that progress takes place in one country (the home country) in just one type of production. Thus, at the outset growth imposes an alteration in some relative prices. If this were the only change, a lowering of one commodity's price relative to all others, the distribution of the gains from growth would be easy to identify. But in models with more than two commodities there may be other price changes required to clear commodity markets. As I shall argue, the Ricardian labor-theory-of-value model is well suited to the analysis of the impact of technical change in a world of many commodities since it isolates (i) the change in the price of the commodity in which technical progress takes place relative to all other prices of commodities produced at home, and (ii) the price level of commodities produced at home relative to commodities produced abroad. Other price movements that might complicate the analysis are precluded in the Ricardian model.

I begin the analysis with the more simple case in which cost structures between the home and foreign country are connected by virtue of a commodity produced in common by both countries. Call this commodity 2, and let it serve as numeraire in a free trade world. The home country also produces commodity 1, in which it possesses a technological comparative advantage. Analogously, the foreign country is the sole producer of commodity 3. The case in which the home country experiences technical progress in intramarginal commodity 1 differs from that in which its costs are reduced in commodity 2, produced in both countries, so I consider first the case in which home labor costs per unit of x_1 produced, a_{L1}, are lowered.

Since commodity 2 serves as numeraire and since home a_{L2} and foreign a^*_{L2} are both fixed, home and foreign wages are undisturbed. Therefore the price of commodity 3, p_3, also produced abroad, is constant. As for commodity 1, technical progress insures that at a constant wage rate,

$$\hat{p}_1 = \hat{a}_{L1} < 0. \tag{1}$$

The foreign country obviously gains from such a change. The only price change involves a reduction in price for a commodity being imported. Let $\mathrm{d}y^*$ represent the change in foreign real income, defined as $p_1\mathrm{d}D^*_1 + \mathrm{d}D^*_2 + p_3\mathrm{d}D^*_3$, where D^*_i is foreign consumption of commodity i. Foreign production is located on a two-dimensional transformation line for goods 2 and 3. With the slope of this line given by the p_2/p_3 price ratio, any required output changes abroad (in either direction, depending upon world demand behavior) leave the value of produced income unaltered. That is, $\mathrm{d}x^*_2 + p_3\mathrm{d}x^*_3$ is zero so that by the budget constraint,

$$\mathrm{d}y^* = -D^*_1\mathrm{d}p_1. \tag{2}$$

At home the calculation of the real income change, $\mathrm{d}y$, is more complicated since technical progress has shifted the transformation line outwards, and this is an ingredient in $\mathrm{d}y$. More specifically,

$$\mathrm{d}y = (x_1 - D_1)\mathrm{d}p_1 + \{p_1\mathrm{d}x_1 + \mathrm{d}x_2\}. \tag{3}$$

The first term suggests a loss as home terms of trade deteriorate. But the second expression is positive. By the assumption that all labor is fully employed,

$$a_{L1}x_1 + a_{L2}x_2 = L. \tag{4}$$

Differentiate, and note that progress reduces a_{L1}:

$$a_{L1}\mathrm{d}x_1 + a_{L2}\mathrm{d}x_2 = -x_1\mathrm{d}a_{L1}. \tag{5}$$

Multiply by the wage rate, w, and recall that unit costs, wa_{Li}, equal p_i. Thus

$$\{p_1\mathrm{d}x_1 + \mathrm{d}x_2\} = -p_1x_1\hat{a}_{L1} = -x_1\mathrm{d}p_1. \tag{6}$$

Technical progress in x_1 has increased the value of output at constant prices by an amount proportional to total output of commodity 1, whereas the terms of trade deterioration is proportional to exports, $x_1 - D_1$. Netting these out in (3) leads to

$$dy = -D_1 dp_1. \tag{7}$$

These results, of course, generalize in a Ricardian model with any number of commodities as long as cost structures between countries are linked by a commonly-produced commodity. Technical progress in any intramarginal commodity produced solely in one country has positive spill-over effects on both countries' real income. The division of real income gains depends *only* upon the share of that commodity *consumed* in each country. The home country might devote 90% of its resources to producing this commodity, but if it consumes little of it the lion's share of the gains from technical progress will accrue to foreigners.

Consider, now, the borderline case in which home technology improves in that commodity which both countries produce, commodity 2. If this commodity is still being treated as numeraire, the reduction in a_{L2} causes a proportional rise in home wages, and this, in turn, drives up the costs of producing the first commodity at home. That is,

$$\hat{w} = -\hat{a}_{L2} > 0, \tag{8}$$

and

$$\hat{p}_1 = \hat{w}. \tag{9}$$

Foreign a^*_{L2} is assumed unaffected, and therefore the foreign wage rate and the price of commodity 3 are also unchanged. The foreign country thus unambiguously suffers a worsening in its terms of trade and real income: dy^* is, as before, given by (2), but dp_1 is now positive. Home real income is favorably affected both by the terms of trade improvement (the $(x_1 - D_1)dp_1$ term in (3), or $D^*_1 dp_1$) and by the increase in the value of aggregate produced income at initial prices. This term is now shown by

$$\{p_1 dx_1 + dx_2\} = p_2 x_2 \hat{p}_1. \tag{10}$$

It is proportional to the extent of technical improvement in the second sector (captured by the wage rise, or $\hat{p}_1$) and the size of the second sector.

Note that nothing has been assumed about the initial trading patterns. In particular, the foreign country might have been an importer of the second commodity. Nonetheless, it suffers a decline in real income if technical progress takes place at home. If production is originally finite, a small improvement in home technology will not serve to wipe out foreign production. Instead, the foreign wage rate drops in relation to home wages, thus preserving foreign competitiveness in the second commodity. In a many-commodity world the interpretation is that all intramarginal commodities produced at home experience price rises proportional to the increased labor productivity at home in the marginal, commonly-produced commodity whose price is being held constant.

If no commodity is produced in common by both countries, a wider variety of spill-over effects is made possible since more than one relative price can change. Suppose the home country has a technological comparative advantage in commodities 1 and 2 and the foreign country in commodity 3 in the sense that at initial equilibrium wage rates the foreign country can only compete in commodity 3 and the home country concentrates on commodities 1 and 2. What are the effects of a technological improvement at home in producing one of its export commodities? Suppose a_{L1} is reduced, with commodity 2 again serving as numeraire. Since a_{L2} is constant, home wage rates are unaltered and the price of commodity 1 must decline in proportion to the technical change. But the cost and price of commodity 3 are no longer linked to numeraire good 2 since the foreign country produces none of the second commodity. Instead, p_3 will rise or fall as required by the condition that markets be cleared.

With the foreign country completely specialized in x_3^*, the entire burden of clearing the market falls on world demand, $D_3 + D_3^*$. If λ_3 and λ_3^* represent, respectively, the fraction of the world supply of the third commodity consumed by the home and foreign countries, p_3 must adjust so that

$$\lambda_3 \hat{D}_3 + \lambda_3^* \hat{D}_3^* = 0. \tag{11}$$

At home D_3 depends upon prices and real income

$$D_3 = D_3(p_1, p_3, y). \tag{12}$$

Let E_3^j denote the substitution elasticity, $\{(p_j/D_3)\cdot(\partial D_3/\partial p_j)\}$ and m_3 the marginal propensity to consume the third commodity at home. Then total differentiation of (12) leads to

$$\hat{D}_3 = E_3^1 \hat{p}_1 + E_3^3 \hat{p}_3 + \frac{m_3}{p_3 D_3} \mathrm{d}y. \tag{13}$$

The expression for $\hat{D}_3^*$ is precisely analogous.

The breakdown of the change in home real income shown by (3) must be amended in this case to allow for the adverse impact on y of any rise in p_3 (or benefit to home residents of a fall in p_3). Thus (3) is modified to

$$\mathrm{d}y = (x_1 - D_1)\mathrm{d}p_1 - D_3 \mathrm{d}p_3 + \{p_1 \mathrm{d}x_1 + \mathrm{d}x_2\}. \tag{14}$$

The change in the value of national output at initial prices is once again shown by (6) so that the expression for dy becomes

$$\mathrm{d}y = -p_1 D_1 \hat{p}_1 - p_3 D_3 \hat{p}_3. \tag{15}$$

This can be substituted into (13) to yield

$$\hat{D}_3 = \left[E_3^1 - \frac{p_1 D_1}{p_3 D_3} m_3\right] \hat{p}_1 + [E_3^3 - m_3]\hat{p}_3. \tag{16}$$

The coefficient of $\hat{p}_3$ must be negative (assuming no commodities are inferior), whereas the sign of the coefficient of $\hat{p}_1$ is positive if commodities 1 and 3 are gross substitutes for each other.

Foreign real income is disturbed only by changes in the terms of trade; it benefits to the extent that p_1 falls, but would suffer if its export commodity 3 were to fall in price. Thus, since foreign exports $(x_3^* - D_3^*)$ provide all of home consumption, D_3,

$$\mathrm{d}y^* = -p_1 D_1^* \hat{p}_1 + p_3 D_3 \hat{p}_3. \tag{17}$$

Substituting (17) into the foreign version of (13) yields

$$\hat{D}_3^* = \left[E_3^{1*} - \frac{p_1 D_1^*}{p_3 D_3^*} m_3^*\right] \hat{p}_1 + \left[E_3^{3*} + \frac{D_3}{D_3^*} m_3^*\right] \hat{p}_3. \tag{18}$$

The (negative) value of $\hat{p}_1$ is given by the extent of home technical progress in the first commodity. The amount by which p_3 must adjust to clear markets is found by substituting (16) and (18) into (11). This yields

$$\hat{p}_3 = \frac{1}{\Delta}\left\{\lambda_3 \left[E_3^1 - \frac{p_1 D_1}{p_3 D_3} m_3\right] + \lambda_3^* \left[E_3^{1*} - \frac{p_1 D_1^*}{p_3 D_3^*} m_3^*\right]\right\} \hat{p}_1, \tag{19}$$

where

$$\Delta \equiv -\left\{\lambda_3 E_3^3 + \lambda_3^* E^{3*} + \frac{D_3}{D_3 + D_3^*}(m_3^* - m_3)\right\}.$$

Stability in commodity markets leads to a positive value for denominator Δ.[1] The numerator shows that in each country at initial p_3 a drop in p_1 encourages substitution away from the third commodity (assuming 1 and 3 are net substitutes), but that if commodity 3 is a normal good the increased real income in each country (again, at initial p_3) spills over into increased demand for the third

[1]See the appendix to chapter 10 for this version of the stability criterion.

commodity. Income and substitution effects conflict, with substitution effects the more powerful if commodities 1 and 3 are gross substitutes.

Suppose these two commodites are gross substitutes. In a stable world market the price of commodity 3 must fall since demand is drained away towards commodity 1 at initial p_3. This, of course, benefits the home country. But foreigners are adversely affected. Expression (17) shows how the drop in p_1 favors foreigners, but a fall in p_3 would by itself harm real incomes. Could this latter effect dominate? If so a somewhat curious result emerges: a technical improvement in producing a commodity for which a country depends completely on imports may end up hurting that country.

With commodities 1 and 3 assumed now to be gross substitutes, is there any presumption from (19) as to the extent to which p_3 can fall relative to the technologically determined drop in p_1? I would argue that if all goods are net substitutes and if substitution effects are generally high, the fall in p_3 will not be relatively as great as the fall in p_1. The rationale lies in the observation that in each country the 'own' substitution term, $-E_3^3$, is the sum of the cross substitution terms, E_3^1 and E_3^2, and thus exceeds either of them if both are positive. Thus the numerator of $\hat{p}_3$ in (19) would tend to be smaller than the denominator.[2] Of course this reasoning collapses if commodities 2 and 3 are net complements, in which case the cross effects, E_3^1 and E_3^{1*} would exceed, respectively, the own effects, $-E_3^3$ and $-E_3^{3*}$.

Suppose that the fall in p_3, which hurts foreigners, does not exceed, in relative terms, the fall in p_1, which improves foreign real incomes. Does this preclude a fall in foreign real incomes? The key observation about eq. (17) is that the weight attached to the fall in p_3, (p_3D_3), must exceed the weight attached to the change in $p_1(p_1D_1^*)$. The foreign country is in a position of balanced trade. It exports only commodity 3, and the total value of these exports is given by home consumption, p_3D_3. Its imports are spread over commodities 1 and 2 so that $p_1D_1^*$ is a fraction of p_3D_3. This suggests the kind of situation in which technical progress at home in a commodity not produced abroad may nonetheless worsen foreign real incomes. Suppose commodities 1 and 3 are gross substitutes but commodity 1 represents a small fraction of the foreign import bill. (After all, commodity 2 represents an amalgam of all those commodities produced in the home country for which no technical progress has occurred.) Then the lowering of 1's price has relatively little favorable effect on foreign real incomes, but may have a significant impact on world commodity markets and thus on p_3.

If substitution effects are generally weak, the familiar possibility of immiserizing

[2]The adjustments required for the income terms in (19) would tend to be negligible if substitution elasticities are high.

growth in the home country must be considered. As eq. (15) shows, a drop in p_1 that causes initial excess demand for foreign commodity 3 (as positive income effects spill over to that market) may cause a rise in p_3 sufficient to reduce home real incomes. From (19) there is no limit to the possible rise in p_3 if Δ is small (but still positive). And, in (15), there is no necessary connection between the weights attached to each price change. Note the variation to the familiar explanation of immiserization required in the Ricardian model: commodity 1 falls in price, but only by the extent of the change in technology relative to all other commodities produced at home. It is not low elasticities for commodity 1 *per se* that are crucial. Instead, immiserization at home depends upon low elasticities (throughout the world) for the entire range of commodities produced abroad.

Earlier I showed that if technical advance at home in means of producing the first commodity occurs in a state of trade in which both countries produce a common commodity (2), the prices of all other goods produced abroad (3) remain constant relative to all goods produced at home not subject to technical change (2). The same kind of result is achieved in the absence of the connecting link provided by joint production of commodity 2 if taste patterns in the two countries satisfy the requirement that the fraction of income spent on each commodity is constant. This is the case dividing gross substitutes from gross complements. It corresponds to underlying Cobb–Douglas utility functions or, in the language of trade theory, to Graham demand functions. It is the special assumption employed recently by Dornbusch, Fischer and Samuelson [1], to allow simple aggregation of world demand in a Ricardian model with a continuum of commodities. It ensures that when technical progress lowers p_1 relative to other commodities produced at home, third markets are not disturbed, so that only one relative price change takes place. It is when demand functions either display much less substitutability than this norm that the home country might suffer a loss in real income, or much more substitutability than this norm that foreigners might lose out despite the fact that the disturbance initially lowers the price of a commodity they import.

Finally, observe the simplifications for a problem of this type that a Ricardian multicommodity model possesses over, say, a pure-exchange model with many commodities. In the latter case suppose the home country possesses only commodities 1 through 12 and the foreign country fixed supplies of 13 through 28.[3] An increase in the home country's endowment of the first commodity would, in general, lower its price relative to other commodities. But, except in special cases, twenty-six other relative prices can be expected to change, greatly com-

[3] It matters little if both countries have endowments of some commodities in common.

plicating the search for real income divisions. In the Ricardian model at most two relative prices would be altered with a change in the technology of producing a single commodity, and this suffices to reveal how both countries can gain, or how either might gain at the expense of the other.

Reference

[1] Dornbusch, R., S. Fischer and P.A. Samuelson, 'Comparative Advantage, Trade, and Payments in a Ricardian Model with a Continuum of Goods', *American Economic Review* (Dec. 1977).

PART VI

DIMENSIONALITY IN TRADE THEORY

INTRODUCTION TO PART VI

This concluding section of the book contains the piece I prepared for the Graham lecture at Princton University in 1976. Frank Graham was an economist with many interests, but is best known in trade theory for his insightful criticisms of the assumption typically made that classical trade theory could rely on small-scale models: two countries trading in two commodities. This assumption about dimensionality also characterizes most of Heckscher–Ohlin theory. I took my invitation to prepare a lecture in honor of Frank Graham as an opportunity to discuss the issue of dimensionality in trade theory not only in Ricardo–Graham and Heckscher–Ohlin models but in wider areas of the literature on trade theory.

Not mentioned explicitly in this lecture is the phenomenon discussed in Chapter 17. In a two-commodity Ricardian model in which two countries produce no commodity in common, technical progress at home must have favorable spill-over effects on real incomes abroad. In a many-commodity model, however, such technical progress may so draw demand away from foreign exportables that foreign real incomes fall. A necessary ingredient in this scenario is the existence of more than one market. Analogous problems are discussed in section 4 of chapter 18.

Chapter 18

'TWO-NESS' IN TRADE THEORY: COSTS AND BENEFITS*

1. Introduction

The number 'two' is undoubtedly encountered more frequently in the theory of international trade than in any other field of economics. It is a large number: two countries provide a more complex setting for analysis than just one. The analysis of two countries trading two commodities, each produced with one or possibly two factors of production, eschews the partial-equilibrium one-thing-at-a-time approach standard in so many areas of economics in favor of general equilibrium. But two is also a small number. It is the smallest number that can be used to describe international trade when countries have genuinely different commodities to exchange with each other.

The basic defense offered in casting so much of trade theory in 'twos' is ease of exposition and lack of ambiguity in conclusions. Two dimensions are ideally suited to blackboard diagrams. Koopmans [25, p. 175] has suggested that 'Only unnecessary and self-imposed tool limitations can explain why almost the entire literature on the theory of international trade has been confined to models of two countries trading in two commodities.' I suggest there are other reasons. Fundamentally, there exists a belief that most of the useful and valid points in trade theory can be made in the context of two countries, two commodities, and one or two productive factors. If so, there is surely some advantage to using such a streamlined vehicle of communication. Combined with this is the fear that general-

* Delivered as the Frank Graham Memorial Lecture at Princeton University in April, 1976, and appearing as no. 12 in the Special Papers in International Economics, Princeton University.

equilibrium analysis of higher-dimensional cases cannot be coaxed into yielding definite and unambiguous comparative-statics results.

But can the simple two-by-two models in trade theory be relied upon to provide answers to basic questions that have hopes of generalizing fairly accurately to a world with many commodities, countries, and factors? Listen to some of the critics: Pearce [37, p. 320], in discussing trade and production models, states: '... many textbooks of international trade theory (even the most advanced) lay a great deal too much emphasis upon *propositions which are true only for models with two commodities and two factors of production*' (italics supplied). Hahn [13, p. 297], in a review of a recent book by Negishi, remarks: '... it is well known that an economy with only two goods has a number of important properties which do not carry over to the general case.'

Perhaps the clearest note of criticism was that sounded by Frank Graham [11] whose volume, *The Theory of International Values*, culminated several decades of pioneering work aimed at setting the pure theory of trade on a much firmer foundation than had been provided by Ricardo, Mill, and Marshall. Graham [11, p. 284] states explicitly, '... one of the very strongest reasons for rejection of the classical doctrines is that the classicists themselves made their analysis in such simple terms (two-country, two-commodity trade) and then erroneously projected their results into complex trading situations'. In reviewing Graham's book, Elliott [8, p. 16] summarizes Graham's attitude toward received doctrine in trade theory by remarking. 'In the theory of international trade, classical and neoclassical writers were led astray ... by generalizing from the case of two countries and two commodities.'

The issue I wish to address in this chapter concerns the appropriateness of 'two-ness' as an assumption in the theory of international trade. I shall start where Graham left off, with a brief analysis of the issue of dimensionality in the classical, or neo-Ricardian, world characterized by constant returns in production to composite units (labor). From there I shall branch more widely into several diverse areas of international trade theory in which standard work has been characterized by the 'two-ness' assumption but in which it is also possible to consider the consequences of moving beyond two. To conclude, I shall appraise the post-classical (or modern) approach known as the Heckscher–Ohlin theory in the light of our quest for higher-dimensional truths. In particular, I shall argue that the sharp distinction often drawn between Ricardian 'climatic' models and the Heckscher–Ohlin theory can disappear when one heeds Graham's insistence on basing the analysis of trade upon a model with many countries and many commodities.

In my discussion, I shall in large measure (but not exclusively) pick examples from my own work. For the past twenty years I have taken seriously the kind of question concerning dimensionality that was posed so forcefully by Graham. But perhaps I have been more conservative – trying to reveal how the 'two-ness' assumption can often be salvaged to play a useful role in expressing basic economic truths. As I shall argue, this defense of the simple models is frequently made possible only after basic concepts are reformulated to take account of economic relations more clearly viewed in higher dimensions.

2. The classical trade model and Graham's criticism

The basic Ricardo–Mill–Marshall model that attracted so much criticism from Graham can be sketched as follows. In each of two countries, fixed labor costs (man-hours) per unit of output would be required to produce one unit each of two commodities (wine and cloth). In the absence of international exchange, each country would supply its own residents' consumption demands and wine and cloth would exchange for each other according to their relative (labor) costs of production. For countries not sharing the same technology (or climate), these costs ratios would differ between countries. Once free trade is made possible, some ratio of commodity exchange is struck between the limits set by the cost ratios in the two countries. Although Ricardo was mute concerning precisely how such terms of trade were established, both Mill and Marshall asserted that the forces of reciprocal demand – in each country for the product in which the other country possessed a comparative advantage – would determine an equilibrium trading ratio.

Perhaps the feature of this solution that most disturbed Graham was the assertion that the terms of trade would lie *between* the cost ratios in either country. With occasional remarks to the contrary, most classical writers illustrated, in their numerical examples, a trading ratio lying *strictly* between the cost ratios in each country. This is what Graham called a 'limbo' ratio, one not anchored by costs of production, since each country specializes in a different commodity. The striking feature of such a limbo solution is that changes in tastes cause prices to change but there is absolutely no response in supply.

The alternative, which Graham viewed as 'normal', involves terms of trade equilibrated to the cost ratio in one of the countries, with at least one commodity produced in common by more than one country. He provided numerical examples with either more than two countries or more than two commodities, or both, in which an 'intermediate' commodity or country served as a link between the two countries' cost structures. Thus, in a three-commodity, two-country case, each country could produce the commodity in which it possessed the greatest comparative advantage as well as the intermediate commodity. Labor costs in each country would then serve to bind the price of the intermediate commodity to each of the other two commodities. In such a world, according to Graham, changes in the structure of world demand could be accommodated by reallocations of labor in each country between the two goods that country produces without any change in the terms of trade.

The role of intermediate commodity thus described could alternatively be played by a third country. To the two-country, two-commodity case now add a third country whose cost ratio is intermediate between the two other countries. Fig. 18.1 illustrates this cost ratio by the slope of intermediate line (3). If the world terms of trade coincide with the cost ratio in the third country, a shift in tastes could serve just to alter production patterns in the intermediate country instead of changing the terms of trade.

Since Graham's work, there has apparently emerged an agreement among writers in this area that an eclectic view is appropriate. In a world of many countries and many commodities, a disturbance to trade may be met primarily by price changes, on the one hand, or production changes, on the other. Limbo price ratios may occur and are not as 'unstable' as Graham would have led us to believe. The analytical concept that supports this view is of a world production-possibilities surface which, in the Ricardian world of constant returns to single primary inputs in each country, consists of 'flats', 'ridges', and 'corners' of various

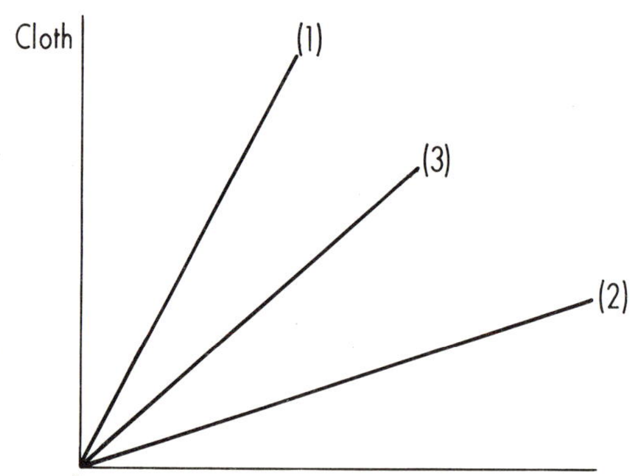

Figure 18.1

dimensions, depending upon the number of commodities and countries.[1] A simple two-commodity, three-country version is illustrated in fig. 18.2. The slope of each segment corresponds to the cost ratio in the designated country (as shown also in fig. 18.1).

Imagine now being able to describe world taste patterns by a set of smoothly bowed-in indifference curves. A point of 'tangency' between one such curve and the transformation locus could take place anywhere along the surface. If it takes place at *C* (as illustrated), intermediate country (3) indeed fulfills its Graham role of producing both wine and cloth, leaving country (1) to produce just cloth and (2) to concentrate on wine. But a different taste pattern (not drawn) could easily result in a corner (or limbo) solution such as *A*, with prices strictly between the slopes of (2) and (3).

It is certainly the case that Graham forces us to consider the possibility that the terms of trade will be reflected in the cost ratio of some country that is incompletely specialized. But is it necessary to abandon the simple two-by-two world to illustrate this point? Not at all. Indeed, Graham argued strongly that, even in a world composed of two countries and two commodities, the terms of trade would be unlikely to lie strictly between the cost ratios in each country. More likely, in his view, would be a disparity either in country size or in the relative importance of commodities that would drive one of the countries to produce both commodities.

The appropriate criticism of the two-by-two model, then, is not that it excludes the possibility that the terms of trade may correspond to some country's cost

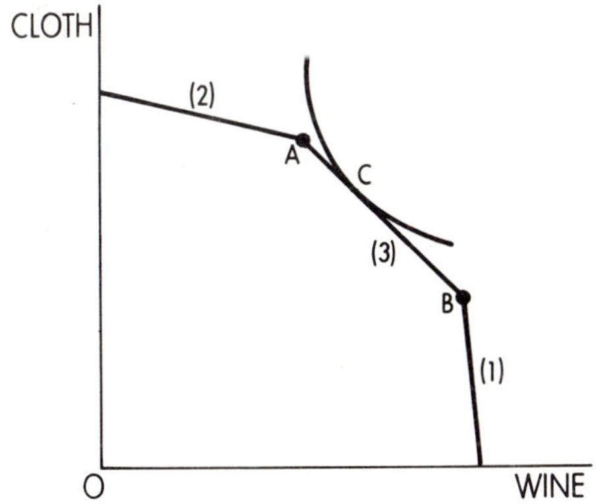

Figure 18.2

[1] This concept was used by Whitin [47] and McKenzie [30].

ratio but that it suggests such a possibility is *extreme*. In such a model, there is a whole range of possible equilibrium terms of trade. All the ones 'in the middle' are limbo ratios. The solution that Graham terms normal can be found only at one extreme ratio or the other, for example, the slopes of rays (1) or (2) in fig. 18.1 when country 3 is absent. I refer to this more generally as the phenomenon of the *excluded middle*, a trait of 'two-ness' that will show up in other contexts. In general, I submit that, if a wide variety of solutions is possible, some midway solution suggests itself more naturally than an extreme solution. Certainly, Ricardo, Mill, and Marshall found this case seductive in most of their arithmetic examples. The difficulty with the structure of the two-country, two-commodity model is that there is no middle solution that is capable of expressing what to Graham was normal – terms of trade that are a reflection of opportunity costs.

Graham points out as well that the higher-dimensional cases admit a richer variety of possible outcomes than does the two-by-two model. Can a fall in world demand for a nation's export commodity improve that country's welfare? Certainly not in the two-country, two-commodity case. In suggesting the alternative possibility, Graham is stressing that today's exports may become tomorrow's imports. With sufficient commodities and countries explicitly considered, the entire trading (and production) pattern in a country can change when tastes are altered. By contrast, in the two-by-two case each country has only one commodity it can ever export (excluding technical progress).

The criterion for comparative advantage in the two-by-two case involves a double bilateral-ratio comparison: the ratio of labor costs in wine and cloth in one country compared with a similar ratio in the other country. Now enlarge the scope of the model: three countries (America, Britain, and Continental Europe – *A* *B*, and *C*) each capable of producing three commodities, say corn, linen, and cloth. Some years ago, I analyzed this kind of model and provided a numerical solution in which America was assigned production of linen, Britain production of corn, and Continental Europe production of cloth. With the labor-cost figures chosen,[2] it turned out that each country had a bilateral comparative advantage in the commodity assigned to it relative to either of the other countries compared

[2] See Chapter 3. This example was suggested by a diagrammatic illustration in McKenzie [30]. For ease of reference I reproduce the numerical example here. Each number represents man-hours per unit of output:

	America	Britain	Continental Europe
Corn	10	10	10
Linen	5	7	3
Cloth	4	3	2

with the commodity assigned to each of them. That is, if a_j^i represents the labor cost (man-hours) in country i per unit output of commodity j,

$$a^A_{\text{linen}}/a^A_{\text{corn}} < a^B_{\text{linen}}/a^B_{\text{corn}}; \quad a^A_{\text{linen}}/a^A_{\text{cloth}} < a^C_{\text{linen}}/a^C_{\text{cloth}},$$

and

$$a^B_{\text{corn}}/a^B_{\text{cloth}} < a^C_{\text{corn}}/a^C_{\text{cloth}}.$$

These are the comparisons suggested by the two-by-two model. However, with the numbers chosen, it turns out that this set of production assignments could never be tolerated in a free-trade competitive world. The criterion that was used in the two-by-two model turned out not to be incorrect, but rather to be *insufficient* in a genuine multilateral world. An alternative assignment (America in corn, Britain in cloth, and Continental Europe in linen) turned out also to satisfy the appropriate bilateral rankings. No comparison between the efficient specialization (America in corn, etc.) and the inefficient one (America in linen, etc.) was possible using just a pair of countries and commodities at a time.

Lest these remarks serve to cast doubt on the generalization of the concept of comparative advantage, I hasten to add that the appropriate general criterion for choosing among production assignments in a Ricardo–Graham model does, of course, reduce to the standard bilateral comparison in the two-by-two case. It just appears in slightly different guise. Both specializations cited above for the three-by-three model involved the specialization of each country in a different commodity (and thus all three commodities were produced – each by a different country). How many patterns of production should be considered? There are six candidates for this 'class' of assignments.[3] (There are three choices for corn. Each leaves two for linen, with the remaining country in cloth.) The optimal (or efficient) assignment in this class is the one that *minimizes* the product of labor coefficients. Thus, the second of the two specializations I cited had

$$a^A_{\text{corn}}\, a^B_{\text{cloth}}\, a^C_{\text{linen}} < a^A_{\text{linen}}\, a^B_{\text{corn}}\, c^C_{\text{cloth}} \quad (90 < 100).$$

This minimum-product rule can be translated into the bilateral-ratio rule in the two-by-two case. For example, the first bilateral-ratio comparison previously can be written as

$$a^A_{\text{linen}}\, a^B_{\text{corn}} < a^A_{\text{corn}}\, a^B_{\text{linen}}.$$

The criterion in the two-by-two case thus rewritten serves as the appropriate guide for the multilateral case.

[3] As I have defined the term, a 'class' of assignments specifies how many countries are to be completely specialized in each commodity. Here there is one country in each commodity (see Chapter 3).

This phenomenon will occur again in comparing a model characterized by 'two-ness' with a higher-dimensional version: alternative and equivalent criteria in two-by-two cases may not prove equivalent in more general settings. But knowledge of the general case can aid in recasting criteria in the simple model so that it can generalize.

Let me make one final remark about this Ricardo–Graham model before turning to other issues. In general, we can specify two categories of production assignments of countries to commodities. Some assignments are efficient, and, if world prices (or world demands) are appropriate, these production patterns could be observed in a free-trade world. Other assignments are inefficient, so that no conceivable pattern of demand (or prices) could coax them into existence given the competitive pressures of free trade. Indeed, the doctrine of comparative costs should, I think, be viewed as telling us not what *will* be produced (for that depends on demand as well) but what patterns *cannot* be produced in a worldwide competitive framework. Suppose we restrict ourselves to patterns of production in which each country is completely specialized in some one commodity. If there are n commodities and r countries, there are n^r possible assignments of this type. In a two-by-two model there are four.[4]

How many of these assignments are inefficient? In a two-by-two world, only one (each country assigned the commodity in which it has a comparative disadvantage). That is, in the basic two-by-two world the doctrine of comparative advantage can be used to knock out only 25% of the possible production patterns based on complete specializations. In this sense, the two-by-two model does insufficient justice to the power of the doctrine. In a three-by-three world, a full 17 out of 27 (or 63%) of the assignments are ruled out; in a four-by-four world, the percentage of inefficient production assignments rises to 86. Multilateral models of comparative advantage – of the kind considered by Graham – reveal more forcefully than the classical two-country, two-commodity model the ruthlessness with which a regime of free trade requires countries to abstain from inefficient production assignments.

3. New possibilities in a multicommodity, multifactor setting

A natural formal objection to models characterized by 'two-ness' is that they are automatically precluded from displaying compositional features that can emerge in higher-dimensional cases.

[4]One assignment has both countries producing wine, one has both producing cloth, and two have one country in wine and the other in cloth.

To illustrate, consider the relationship between commodity outputs and prices along a smoothy bowed-out production-possibility schedule. Suppose the price of commodity 1 rises, all other commodity prices remaining constant. Output in the first sector must rise. This is a common property of general-equilibrium models that holds regardless of the number of sectors. In a two-sector economy, such output expansion in the first sector must draw resources away from the second. But in a multisector model this condition does not usually generalize to *every* other sector. Some sectors may expand when p_1 rises – those that are complementary to the first sector. Formally, if p_1 rises in an n-sector model (other prices remaining constant). $\Sigma_{j \neq 1} p_j \mathrm{d}x_j$ must be negative. But *some* other outputs may expand.

A similar observation can be addressed to demand behavior along smoothly bowed-in indifference surfaces. With real income held constant, a rise in p_1 would induce a fall in demand for commodity 1 (D_1) and a substitution toward *some* other commodities. Indeed, $\Sigma_{i \neq i} p_i \mathrm{d}D_i$ would have to be positive. But not *all* other D_i's need rise. Some may be complements of good 1 in consumption, a feature precluded in the two-by-two models.

This possibility of complementarity lies at the root of a phenomenon discussed recently by Gruen and Corden [12]. In the standard two-commodity model, a country might improve its terms of trade by levying a tariff. A duty on imports, so the argument goes, could serve to depress the world price of imports by artificially creating a reduction in home demand. Symmetry compels the same conclusion to emerge in the case of an export tax: the world price of the country's exports could be bid up. The exception to this result follows in the case in which the home country is too small to be able to exercise any influence over world prices. In this event, a tariff (or export tax) would leave the terms of trade unaffected.

By adding one more commodity (and one more factor), Gruen and Corden provide an example in which a tariff serves to *worsen* the terms of trade. In addition, their example usefully points out how in a multicommodity world a country may be 'small' in some markets but not in others. Their example is intended to capture some of the features of the Australian economy. Only one commodity is imported (textiles), and it utilizes capital and labor. Two commodities are exported – wool and grain and each requires land and labor (but not capital). Of these two export items, wool employs a higher proportion of land to labor than does grain.

This description ensures that wool and textiles are complements in production. Suppose the domestic price of textiles rises because a tariff is levied on textiles and the country is too small in the world textile market to influence world prices. If the prices of grain and wool are (temporarily) held fixed, what resource shifts are induced? Clearly, textiles draw labor away from the export sectors. Wool and grain production together form a subset of the economy in which total land availability is constant (land is not used in textiles), and in which labor supply has been depleted (the departure of workers to the protected textile industry). At constant prices (for wool and grain), the standard Rybczynski [40, pp. 336–341] result for a two-sector economy asserts that labor-intensive grain output falls but land-intensive wool output actually rises.

Gruen and Corden use the complementarity between textiles and wool in this example to establish their 'paradox' by assuming further that, although the country cannot influence grain prices, it can affect the world price of wool. The tariff on textiles has caused local output of wool to rise. If this exceeds any rise in local demand, the world price of wool will be depressed. Thus, the only influence on world prices exerted by the initial tariff on textiles is a lowering of the wool price. A tariff has worsened a country's terms of trade. Complementarity, either in production or consumption (or both), is thus a new feature introduced by moving beyond the world of twos.

There are also *problems* that cannot effectively be posed without introducing more than two commodities, factors, or countries. For example, the theory of customs unions requires at least three countries in order to capture the phenomenon of two or more nations banding together to create a tariff structure that discriminates against other countries in favor of the nations in the union.[5]

At a more basic level, the presence of more than two commodities is required in order to raise the question of optimal tariff *structures*. A simple illustration involves a country too small to affect world prices that imports two commodities (2 and 3) in exchange for exports of another commodity (1). Suppose that the country has imposed a tariff at rate t_2 on its imports of commodity 2, and that this rate cannot be changed. (For example, strong trade-union pressure has forced protection in the second industry.) Also, suppose there is required free trade in the market for its exportables. Should this small country levy a duty on its imports of commodity 3? If so, at what level?

The analysis of this case is straightforward. Since the country is small, there are no terms-of-trade effects. Real income is affected only if the volume of trade is altered in any market in which world price (p_j^*) differs from domestic price (p_j). By assumption, no such discrepancy exists in the nation's export market, but it does in the market for the second commodity. A small initial duty on imports of commodity 3 would, if commodities 2 and 3 were substitutes, tend to shift demand toward 2 and production away from 2. On both counts, imports of 2 would rise; this would raise real income, since the local value of the second commodity to

[5] For recent treatments of the customs-union issue, see Kemp [22] and Berglas [1].

home residents is reflected in the domestic price, p_2, which exceeds the cost of obtaining commodity 2 on world markets (p_2^*) by the amount of the fixed tariff rate, t_2. But this reasoning also suggests that further increases in the duty on commodity 3 will introduce some harmful effects on real income as a tariff wedge in the market for good 3 is established and imports of good 3 are reduced.

Formal analysis in this case reveals that, if all goods are substitutes, the small country should impose a duty on the third commodity, but *at a lower rate* than the fixed duty on the other importable. If M_j denotes excess demand for good j, the change in home real income (measured in units of the first commodity) as tariff rate t_3 is increased is given by

$$\frac{\mathrm{d}y}{\mathrm{d}t_3} = \sum_j (p_j - p_j^*) \frac{\mathrm{d}M_j}{\mathrm{d}t_3}.$$

Real income reaches a maximum when this expression is zero, or when tariff rate t_3 is given by

$$\frac{t_3}{1 + t_3} = \left[\frac{p_2(\mathrm{d}M_2/\mathrm{d}t_3)}{-p_3(\mathrm{d}M_3/\mathrm{d}t_3)}\right]\frac{t_2}{1 + t_2}.$$

With p_3 the only variable price, and since in the neighborhood of the point of maximum utility the real-income effects of a tariff rise vanish,

$$\frac{\mathrm{d}M_j}{\mathrm{d}t_3} = \left(\frac{\partial D_j}{\partial p_3} - \frac{\partial x_j}{\partial p_3}\right)p_3^*,$$

where the consumption effect, $\partial D_j/\partial p_3$, reflects only a substitution term. For substitution effects in consumption, $\sum p_j(\partial D_j/\partial p_3)$ equals zero. For movements along the transformation frontier, $\sum p_j(\partial x_j/\partial p_3)$ is also zero. Therefore,

$$\frac{t_3}{1 + t_3} = \left[\frac{p_2\left(\dfrac{\partial D_2}{\partial p_3} - \dfrac{\partial x_2}{\partial p_3}\right)}{p_1\left(\dfrac{\partial D_1}{\partial p_3} - \dfrac{\partial x_1}{\partial p_3}\right) + p_2\left(\dfrac{\partial D_2}{\partial p_3} - \dfrac{\partial x_2}{\partial p_3}\right)}\right]\frac{t_2}{1 + t_2}.$$

If all commodities are substitutes in consumption and production, each term in parentheses is positive, and optimal t_3 is a positive fraction of predetermined t_2. Thus the introduction of a second import commodity suggests, for the small country, a *nonuniform tariff structure*. Note that if the two imports become highly substitutable for each other, the optimal value of t_3 approaches tariff rate t_2, while if exportables and commodity 3 are highly substitutable instead, good 3 should be (almost) freely traded. These are the limits suggested by the two-commodity model.

The 'second-best' flavor of this example should be stressed. Since the country is assumed not to be able to affect the world terms of trade, the optimal tariff on good 2 would be zero. If t_2 cannot be reduced, an alternative route is to impose an export tax on commodity 1 and a tariff on commodity 3, both at the same rate as t_2. It is only when a fixed *relative* tariff wedge is prescribed – between export commodity 1 and import commodity 2 – that a second-best nonuniform tariff structure is revealed as more commodities are added to the model.[6]

4. The role of nontraded commodities

In traditional two-sector models, both commodities are traded. No room is left for commodities which, by virtue of high costs of transport, are neither imported nor exported. It would seem that a basic case against 'two-ness' in trade theory can be launched with the assertion that the introduction of nontraded commodities can significantly alter traditional findings in models with only importables and exportables. I shall argue later that the role of nontradeables can frequently be analyzed without sacrificing the essential 'two-ness' of the model. But first let me sidestep this issue in order to suggest the nature of the new phenomena which the incorporation of nontradeables allows the model to reveal.

The distinguishing characteristic of nontradeables is that their market is national instead of international. Any local excess supply of nontradeables cannot be disposed of on world markets. Instead, the local price must fall. The 'small country' case, in which the home country has no control over the prices of traded goods, points up in extreme fashion this distinction between tradeables and nontradeables. An immediate consequence of this distinction is that to determine the impact of any change abroad on local consumption and production it is necessary to incorporate the effect of this change on the market for nontradeables *and* the subsequent feedback to the markets for tradeables. It would be fallacious to argue that if models of international trade are ultimately concerned only with

[6] A more complicated problem in tariff structure is provided in the literature on optimal taxes on foreign investment when an optimal tariff policy is simultaneously being pursued. The details of the relationship between capital and outputs in the production process (both at home and abroad) are involved in the question of the optimal pair of tax distortions (see Chapter 12 and Kemp [21]). A point to emphasize about this literature, however, is that it involves only two countries, two commodities, and two productive factors. The problem of tariff *structure* is introduced by allowing trade in capital services as well as in the two commodities.

markets for exportables and importables, they can usefully ignore the background adjustments in the nontraded-goods markets.

This potentially crucial role for nontraded goods can be illustrated by examining the following question. Suppose the price of a small country's exportable (say commodity 1) rises on world markets, the prices of all other *traded* goods remaining constant. Must this price encourage the production of exportables? We argued in the preceding section that moving to a model with many commodities did not disturb the conclusion that a rise in p_j *alone* would cause output, x_j, to rise. At issue here is the potential for overturning such results when account is taken of required changes in prices of nontradeables.

Although this example can be handled in a general three-commodity model, new results can more easily be obtained by assuming that the community consumes none of export commodity 1 and produces none of import commodity 2, although of course it must both produce and consume a nontradeable commodity (N).[7]

Start by assuming that the price of export commodity 1 is driven up in world markets. The repercussion on the market for nontradeables is discussed with reference to fig. 18.3. The supply curve shows the influence of a rise in p_N/p_1 in attracting resources to the nontradeable sector. With only nontradeables and exportables produced (by assumption), this supply curve is invariant as world p_1 rises. Not so the demand curve. Since the community consumes commodities 2

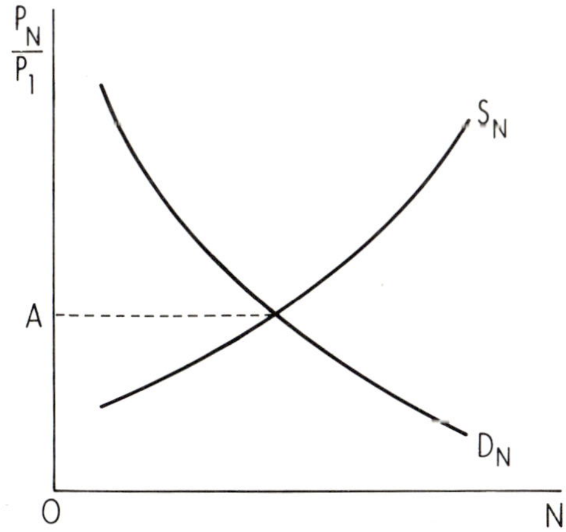

Figure 18.3

[7]These assumptions were exploited in Jones [15].

and N, the demand curve in fig. 18.3 is drawn as of given terms of trade (p_2/p_1). The price of importables, p_2, is held fixed, but when p_1 rises, initial *relative* price OA (fig. 18.3) indicates a higher price for nontradeables as well. That is, at initial OA there has been a rise in p_N/p_2. The substitution effect in consumption would serve to shift the D_N curve leftward.[8] But the terms of trade have improved with the rise in p_1, and the consequent real income gain serves to shift the D_N curve rightward. If the income effect dominates, the relative price and output of nontradeables rise. That is, output of exportables falls as a consequence of an increase in their price.

The criterion sufficient to ensure this paradoxical-sounding result can be put in more recognizable form. An equivalent percentage rise in export and nontraded-goods prices (keeping the ratio at OA in fig. 18.3) at a constant p_2 has the same impact on real quantities as a fall in p_2 at constant p_1 and p_N. In the latter event, the absolute value of income produced is also constant. The quantity of importables demanded would rise, but the aggregate value of spending on importables would fall if the ordinary elasticity of demand for importables was less than unity. Suppose it is. Then the value of spending on home goods (the only other outlet for spending) rises and, to clear the market, p_N/p_1 would have to rise. That is, a rise in the price of exportables serves actually to *reduce* the quantity of exportables produced if the demand for importables is inelastic, since in this case the price of home goods is driven up by more than the price of exportables.[9]

In a two-commodity model, the sensitivity of a nation's demand for imports to a change in the terms of trade is linked directly and unambiguously to the extent of producer and consumer response to prices. Indeed, the elasticity of import demand can be expressed as the straightforward sum of an elasticity of consumer demand for importables and an elasticity of production response for exportables (or importables) (for explicit statements, see Caves and Jones [2, ch. 6]). When nontradeables are added, this view must be modified. For example, in the

[8] Alternatively, the D_N curve shifts downward (for the substitution effect) by the same relative amount as p_1 has increased. With real income and p_2 constant, the absolute price of p_N would have to remain constant in order to ensure that the same quantity is demanded.

[9] Brief mention can be made of another paradoxical-sounding case in the literature that is closely related. In Kemp and Jones [23] the following question is raised: If the price of one traded good rises relative to another, can output of the first good actually fall? Yes, if the labor–leisure choice is made explicit. Suppose as the price of exportables rises, the demand for leisure also rises. If exportables are labor intensive and labor supply is backward bending, production of exportables might actually fall. Much depends also on the possibility of complementarity between leisure and the produced commodities. The point to emphasize here is that leisure is a nontraded commodity. However, in this case the price of leisure (the wage rate) is determined *not* by local demand but rather by world prices for traded goods.

simplified version of the model just considered – with no local consumption of exportables or production of importables – ask whether the elasticity of demand for imports (with respect to the terms of trade) is increased if the elasticity of supply of exportables (along the transformation curve) is increased. A straightforward affirmative answer cannot be given: it depends upon demand behavior.

The logic of this position is illustrated by the offer curve (reciprocal demand curve) for imports drawn in fig. 18.4. Import demand is elastic in the neighborhood of *A* and inelastic near *B*. Following the preceding analysis, suppose the price of exports rises and import prices are constant. If the terms of trade are initially given by ray *OA*, such an improvement in the terms of trade raises exports, since import demand is elastic. As already shown, behind the scenes the home-goods market is cleared with a rise in the price of nontradeables that is less than the rise in export prices. The production of exportables (and therefore the volume of exports) rises because the relevant price ratio, p_1/p_N, rises. The higher the elasticity of export production along the transformation curve, the more elastic will be the offer curve. Contrast this with the situation if the terms of trade are initially shown by ray *OB*. An increase in p_1 causes production of exportables to fall. This paradoxical-sounding case reflects a behind-the-scenes rise in the price of nontradeables that exceeds the rise in export prices. This, in turn, was caused by the inelasticity in demand for importables, which channeled so much of the increase in real income provided by the terms-of-trade improvement into the nontradeables market. With p_1/p_N falling, the greater the value of the elasticity of export supply, the more *inelastic* will be the offer curve in region *B*.

Discussions during the 1940s and 1950s of stability conditions in trade or condi-

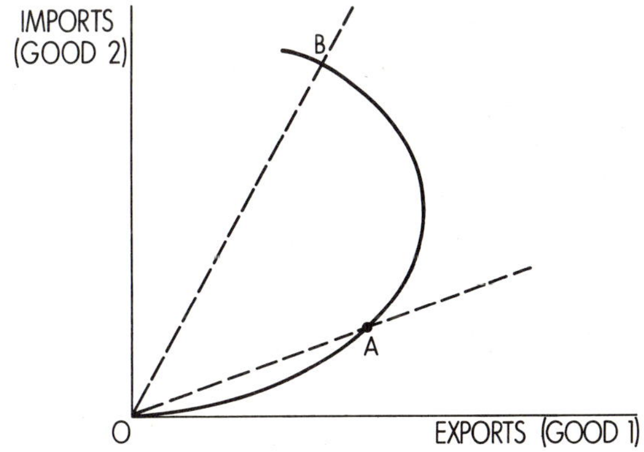

Figure 18.4

tions required for successful devaluation [10] noted this peculiar relation between supply elasticities for exportables and demand elasticities for imports. Even if 'stability' was threatened by low values of demand elasticities, low (rather than high) values for supply elasticities might save the day(see Metzler's [34, p. 227] discussion). This is a peculiarity of the model totally absent in the two-sector version and reflects the background adjustments in the home-goods market.

Not surprisingly, almost all results in two-sector trade theory are modified to some extent if a nontraded sector is added. For example, the criterion in a two-sector model stating in which direction the terms of trade will move when one country makes a transfer to another is extremely simple: it involves only a comparison of marginal propensities to import. More generally, it becomes necessary to ask how a transfer affects markets for traded goods at initial terms of trade when the markets for home goods have cleared. The criterion for a terms-of-trade deterioration for the transferor thus becomes complicated by demand and supply elasticities that capture responses to the required adjustment in the price of nontradeables even at the initial terms of trade. [11]

It is interesting to note that the importance of nontraded goods for the transfer issue was clearly discussed at an early stage by Frank Graham. This is perhaps not surprising, given Graham's insistence that trade theory be made more realistic by incorporating many commodities – even those not entering international trade (see Graham [11, pp. 184–200 and 277]).

5. Functional 'two-ness'

I have thus far taken a view of 'two-ness' that is, I would argue, too narrow. The number 'two' has been used to count the number of commodities, countries, and factors of production. For example, in the last chapter I showed how introducing

[10] I do not mean to imply that the issue of market stability is equivalent to the effect of currency devaluation on the trade balance. But these issues were confused with each other during this period (see, for example, Ellsworth [9] or Metzler [34]).

[11] Full discussions of the transfer problem when nontraded goods are present can be found in Chapter 10 and in Chipman [6]. The tariff literature can also be reassessed when nontraded goods are present. As I show in Jones [16], a country may expand its demand for imports when the terms of trade deteriorate if its exportables use the import as an intermediate good and if it also produces a nontradeable. The concept of effective protection is relevant here. In this discussion I have avoided mention of the theory of effective protection and its collection of paradoxes. For example, see the Ramaswami – Srinivasan [38] result: output in a sector granted effective protection may fall. See also my analysis of this problem in Jones [14]. These 'paradoxes' are as much a consequence of the concept of a 'value-added product' as of moving beyond the two-commodity or two-factor case. For a general discussion, see Corden [7].

a third, nontraded commodity could alter some of the conclusions derived in a two-commodity world. And yet, in a sense, a model with *three* commodities – exportables, importables, and nontradeables – is a model characterized by 'two-ness' if you focus on the number of *markets*. What makes life so simple (and restricted) in a two-commodity general-equilibrium trading model is that there is only *one* market – in which exportables exchange for importables.

Even this argument still restricts the number 'two' to identifying the quantity of similar items: commodities, countries, factors of production, or (with the above extension) markets. I would stress the possibility of a more functional view. Simple models can be constructed that stress two *types* of commodities, factors, or countries.

The analysis of trade models with nontraded commodities provides a key illustration. Suppose a small country produces many commodities that are exchanged at constant world prices as well as some commodity that is not traded. The Hicksian composite commodity theorem allows all the traded commodities to be lumped together, since their prices are fixed relative to one another. The model then usefully reduces to a two-commodity model: tradeables and nontradeables. Indeed, it was the belief that in some circumstances the relative price ratio of nontradeables to tradeables was more important than the terms of trade that motivated extensions of the standard two-commodity model (see, for example, Pearce [36]). When a small country devalues its currency, how can resources be reallocated if it cannot change world prices? If the price of nontradeables can be suppressed relative to higher prices for both exportables and importables, a resource transfer toward tradeable goods can signal a successful devaluation. As Salter [41] and others have shown, the techniques of analysis long familiar in standard two-commodity trade theory – transformation curves, indifference curves, and the like – are directly applicable to the tradeables – nontradeables distinction in small-country models (see also the discussion in Caves and Jones [2, ch. 19]).

The procedure of lumping all traded goods together would break down if the terms of trade changed. In the preceding section, I analyzed a problem of this type: the price of importables was fixed, the price of exportables rose, and the price of nontradeables had to adjust to clear markets. However, the simplifications chosen in that discussion allowed many of the features of 'two-ness' to be preserved: the country only consumed a pair of commodities (nontradeables and importables) and only produced a pair of commodities (a different pair – nontradeables and exportables).

More generally, I would argue that the two-sided nature of the distinction between tradeables and nontradeables can be exploited even in 'large'-country cases in which the terms of trade are endogenous. The transfer-problem literature bears this out. To ask about the impact of transfer on the terms of trade, it is useful first to ask about the realignment of world demands and supplies at *given* terms of trade. This permits one to examine in each country the flow of resources into or out of tradeables as a group. With the price of nontradeables in each country adjusting to clear home-goods markets, the state of excess demands for the *two* tradeables can then be examined for the ultimate direction of change in the terms of trade – much as in the easier two-good model.[12]

Implicit in these remarks is another useful type of two-sided distinction between sizes of countries. There is no doubt that the concept of a 'small' country has been extremely productive in trade theory. For many issues, it is unimportant to examine the compositional pattern of changes in the 'rest of the world' if the disturbance introduced by a small country cannot materially affect world prices.

Just as the degree of 'tradedness' can characterize two classes of commodities, so can the degree of intersectoral mobility characterize two classes of productive factors. One of the oldest production models portrays each of two sectors producing a unique output with the use of two productive factors. One of these is specific to that sector while the other is used in both industries and is sufficiently mobile to earn the same return in each. Although this is a three-factor model, the sense of 'two-ness' is maintained in that only two inputs are required for each output. More important, there are only two *types* of productive factors: specific and mobile. Indeed, most features of this three-by-two model faithfully project themselves to the n-sector, $(n + 1)$-factor extension. One factor (say labor) is freely mobile between sectors, while in each sector some other specific factor is used only in that sector.[13]

Two-sector models naturally invite bilateral comparisons. These comparisons can still be made in a multisector model, but the number of possible pairings rapidly multiplies. Often a sense of 'two-ness' can be preserved in a multisector setting by contrasting any sector in which one is particularly interested with the *average* over all sectors. These averages, in turn, often possess properties quite

[12] All this assumes the markets are stable. For details, see Chapter 10.

[13] The three-factor version of the specific-factors model is analyzed in Chapter 6 and Samuelson [43]. Applications to the distinction between short-run and long-run models are found in Mayer [33] and Mussa [35]. The $(n + 1)$-factor, n-commodity version is presented in Jones [17]. An analogous distinction can be made between factors tied to a particular country and factors internationally mobile. Indeed, some factors (say capital) may be relatively mobile between countries but not between occupations, while others (labor) may be immobile internationally but competitive as between sectors internally. An exposition of the case of internationally mobile capital is provided in Chapter 13.

stable relative to the structural detail in each individual sector. Examples are provided in section 8 below.

6. The identification problem

In criticizing classical doctrine, Graham [11, ch. 9] devoted an entire chapter to spelling out the difficulties in the concept of 'reciprocal national demand'. The problem, according to Graham, involved the incorrect identification of demand *for* commodities with demand *by* countries:

> When, instead of discussing the *total* reciprocal demand (supply) for the various products in an integrated trading system, the classicists split demand (supply) into irrelevant national parts, with assumed reciprocal national demands for fixed sets of commodities of mutually exclusive composition (supposed, qualitatively, to represent the unalterable output of each of the several trading countries), they were indulging in pure fantasy [pp. 158–159].

This is a pitfall made all the easier to step into if the dimensionality of the analysis is limited to two countries and two commodities. With each country committed to a particular export commodity, its demand for the other commodity is easier to identify with its demand for imports. In a general multilateral setting, by contrast, it would seem more natural to focus in turn upon all nations' demands and supplies of particular commodities.

The point Graham is making can be illustrated by considering the classic market-stability condition in the two-country, two-commodity case that is associated with the names of Marshall and Lerner.[14] Suppose ϵ_i denotes the (positive) elasticity of demand for imports in country i – defined as (minus) the relative change in quantity of imports demanded along that country's reciprocal demand curve divided by the relative change in that import price. The market is stable if

$$\sum_{i=1}^{2} \epsilon_i > 1.$$

Suppose a third country is added to this two-commodity world. Is stability more likely? Does the stability criterion, the sum of import demand elasticities exceeding unity, generalize by adding more countries?

To ask the question this way is to betray the negative answer. But suppose the two-commodity, two-country stability criterion had been rewritten to emphasize

[14] The references are to Marshall [32 Appendix J] and Lerner [29].

the behavior of *world* excess demand for one of the two commodities, say commodity 2. Let me simplify in an inessential way by posing the problem in an exchange model in which each country's production of the second commodity is invariant to prices. If p denotes the relative price of commodity 2, and D_2^i country i's demand for 2, stability requires that

$$\sum_{i=1}^{2} \frac{\mathrm{d}D_2^i}{\mathrm{d}p} < 0.$$

To put this into elasticity notation, let

$$\omega_2^i \equiv -\frac{p}{D_2^i}\frac{\mathrm{d}D_2^i}{\mathrm{d}p}.$$

Then the condition can be written as

$$\sum_{i=1}^{2} \frac{D_2^i}{D_2}\omega_2^i > 0,$$

where D_2 is total world demand for commodity 2, $\sum D_2^i$. This statement, equivalent to the Marshall–Lerner condition, more readily generalizes to many countries because it states that a weighted average of the various countries' elasticities of demand for commodity 2 is positive.[15] Adding a third country reduces the weight that any individual country receives.

Along this same theme, consider a model characterized throughout by 'twoness': two countries, two commodities, and two currencies.[16] The fact that the same number of countries (or currencies) as commodities is specified makes it more tempting to identify the commodity-price ratio (the terms of trade) with the currency-price ratio (the exchange rate). As Graham [11, p. 280] observed. 'There is even some tendency to confuse rates of exchange of currencies with the ratio of exchange of goods.' As Graham went on to state, this confusion would be more supportable if each country were specialized in a different commodity and the price in each country for the single commodity produced by that country were pegged in terms of the domestic currency. The terms of trade do, indeed, then change in proportion to the exchange rate. However, a difficulty with this story is that it suggests that exchange authorities charged with setting exchange rates must really be in the buffer-stock business of supporting commodity prices in each country in terms of that country's currency.

[15] More insight into the nature of the condition could be obtained by decomposing each ω_2^i into a substitution term and an income term. The latter would normally be negative for exporters and positive for importers. For details, see Caves and Jones [2, pp. 56–57].

[16] The number of productive factors behind the scenes could exceed two.

In any case, the point I wish to stress is that an identification of the exchange rate with a commodity-price ratio would be much less likely if the number of commodities greatly exceeded two.

As a final remark on this theme, return to the case discussed by Gruen and Corden [12] in which a country produces one import-competing commodity (textiles), and two exportables (grain and wool). It levies an import duty on textiles, and this opens the possibility that its terms of trade may deteriorate. In a two-commodity model, the Lerner [28] symmetry theorem establishes that an import duty is equivalent to an export tax in its real effect on the terms of trade. In the Gruen–Corden three-commodity case, suppose the country had levied an export tax on wool instead of an import duty on textiles. The possibility of the paradoxical worsening of the terms of trade would disappear: the world price of wool would be driven upward. The symmetry theorem in this case states that an import duty on textiles is equivalent to an export tax on *both* exportables. It would be incorrect to equate a tariff on textile imports with a tax just on wool exports.

7. The aggregation problem

Two-sector models are often defended on the grounds that each sector represents an aggregate of a number of individual commodities. Thus a nation might import 53 different types of commodities and yet speak of the effect of a rise in the import price level on the aggregate quantity of imports demanded. If these 53 commodities differ from each other significantly in the extent to which the demand for (or production of) each is sensitive to price, it would be unreasonable to expect any individual elasticity of import demand to be accurately mirrored by the aggregate elasticity of import demand. But suppose symmetry is the order of the day: a 10% increase in the price of any individual import item always reduces the quantity demanded of that import by the same relative amount (say 15%). Will this figure be reflected in the aggregate elasticity of demand for imports?

This type of question could also be asked of an aggregate export sector. Any aggregate elasticity of export supply would of course tend to mask radical differences in the response of any individual export commodity to price changes. But suppose a rise in p_j of 10% – other prices remaining constant – serves to raise exports in the jth sector by 5%, regardless of which export commodity j is chosen. In such a case, if the price of each and every exportable rises by 10% – all other prices (importables) remaining constant – will there be a 5% increase in the *aggregate* volume of exports? No. In fact, the quantity of each and every export supplied may *fall!* Quite aside from the possible diversity among individual commodities, the mere act of aggregation serves systematically to reduce the aggregate elasticity of export supply below the mean of the individual values.[17]

The key to understanding this aggregation problem is that the effect on demands and production of a rise in the price of a single commodity is different from that of an equi-proportionate rise in the prices of all commodities belonging to that aggregate sector (either importables or exportables). The latter change invokes cross-substitution effects in production and consumption that are absent in the case of a single price change, as well as an income effect of a different order of magnitude.

Consider how this works out for a single importable, say the twelfth commodity in the class of imports. If only p_{12} rises, the quantity of imports, M_{12}, falls both because of an 'own' substitution effect in demand and an increase in production and because real income is reduced proportionally to the volume of imports of commodity 12. What further effects on M_{12} can be expected if the prices of all other importables rise by the same relative amount as p_{12}? Suppose, on balance, that commodity 12 is a substitute both in consumption and production for other importables. As their prices rise, demand is deflected back toward commodity 12 (substitution effect) and production drawn away from commodity 12. These cross effects work partially to counter the initial effect of the rise in p_{12}:M_{12} will not be reduced by as much.[18] But an income effect must also be taken into account. The rise in all the other import prices serves to lower real income by a much greater extent than would be the case if just p_{12} rose. This greater income effect serves to cause M_{12} to be reduced even more. When all import prices rise (instead of just p_{12}), two kinds of corrections are required in estimating the further impact on M_{12}: the cross effects of price changes would tend to lower the value of the elasticity of import demand, but the heightened income effects would tend to raise it. There is no reason to suppose these effects precisely cancel.

On the export side, two types of corrections are also involved in considering how the exports of, say, the twenty-first export item is affected when the prices of *all* exportables rise by 10% as opposed just to a rise in p_{21}. But, instead of tending to counteract each other, they reinforce one another. Suppose a 10% rise in p_{21} by itself raises exports in the twenty-first sector, X_{21}, by 5%. When all other export prices rise as well, the cross-subsitution effects cause an increase in local demand for the twenty-first commodity and a fall in production (as resources are lost to the other export sectors). On this account, X_{21} is reduced. But the favorable

[17] This phenomenon is explored more carefully in Jones and Berglas [18].

[18] Note that p_{12} has still risen relative to all exportables, so that M_{12} can be expected to fall on this account.

extra income effect of a rise in the prices of all other exportables tends to raise local demand for the twenty-first commodity and thus *further* to reduce X_{21}. Indeed, the net effect may be a fall in exports of this commodity as all export prices rise.

In two-sector models of international trade, it is not at all unusual to find diagrams illustrating a decline in exports as the relative price of exports rises. All that is required is inelasticity in the demand for imports. Fig. 18.4 above shows import demand inelastic at a point such as *B* where the reciprocal demand curve bends backward. And yet, how easy is it to find a real-world example in which a nation will supply less of some item for export in response to a rise in export price? This can, of course, be the response in a two-commodity world – the labor–leisure choice with a possible backward-bending supply curve of labor provides the classic textbook example. But the real world is not a two-sector world, and it seems much harder to find examples of single commodities exhibiting such a backward-bending response to a rise in own price.

The importance of the preceding aggregation result lies in its demonstration that exports in the aggregate can respond precisely as shown in text-book diagrams of the fig. 18.4 type even if no single commodity would mirror this behavior. If the world is made up of many sectors, the two-commodity illustrations in trade theory are appropriate indicators of aggregate behavior but should not be identified with the 'representative export'.

8. Generalizations in Heckscher–Ohlin theory

In the literature on the theory of international trade in the past quarter century, the Ricardian trade model has yielded pride of place to the Heckscher–Ohlin model, particularly the two-factor version. Indeed, much of the criticism levied against the use of 'two-ness' in trade theory is aimed most specifically at the two-factor, two-commodity production model that has served as the basis for such propositions as the Stolper–Samuelson tariff theorem, the Rybczynski theorem, the factor-price equalization theorem, and the Heckscher–Ohlin theorem itself.

Attempts to break down the dimensionality limitations of the simple two-by-two model have generally followed two paths. On the one hand, economists have endeavored to discover conditions sufficient to have an n-factor, n-commodity model replicate in detail the results of a two-sector model. For example, the Stolper–Samuelson result posits that in the two-sector model a price increase will unambiguously raise the return to the factor used intensively in that sector and reduce the return to the other factor. In the n-by-n case, can each factor of production be associated with a particular industry so that, if the price of that industry rises, the designated factor's *real* return rises and *all other* factors lose? Only in highly special cases could such a strong version of the Stolper–Samuelson result be expected.[19] The other path of inquiry asks what generalizations can be established without making highly restrictive assumptions – even if these results do not conform precisely to the two-by-two parable.[20] Since I have recently written on this topic in detail, I limit myself here to a few summary remarks.

The concept of relative factor intensity used in the two-sector, two-factor trade model is typically not stated in a way that usefully generalizes. The second output is said to be relatively capital intensive if and only if it employs a higher capital/labor input ratio than the first. Of course, regardless of the number of factors and commodities, it is always possible to make a bilateral comparison of capital to labor ratios between any pair of commodities. But consider the usefulness of this ranking in the following example:

Let both industries 1 and 2 employ three factors of production: labor (L), capital (K), and land (T). Suppose that the first sector employs a higher labor/capital ratio than the second and that the wage rate (w_L) rises by 10%, the return to capital (w_K) falls by 10%, and the rental on land (w_T) remains constant. Does this change in factor prices raise or lower the relative cost of producing the first commodity? If labor and capital were the only factors used, the relative cost of producing commodity 1 would have to rise. But suppose the distributive shares of factor i in industry j in this three-factor model are shown by θ_{ij}:

$$\theta_{L1} = 0.2; \quad \theta_{L2} = 0.5,$$

$$\theta_{K1} = 0.1; \quad \theta_{K2} = 0.3,$$

$$\theta_{T1} = 0.7; \quad \theta_{T2} = 0.2.$$

Since θ_{L1}/θ_{K1} exceeds θ_{L2}/θ_{K2}, the first industry does indeed employ a higher labor/capital ratio than the second. What happens to unit costs? The presumed rise in wage rate and fall in return to capital serve to raise costs (or price, p_1) in the first industry by 1%. (Let a '$\hat{\ }$' over a variable denote relative changes):

$$\hat{p}_1 = \theta_{L1}\hat{w}_L + \theta_{K1}\hat{w}_K + \theta_{T1}\hat{w}_T$$
$$= 0.2(10\%) + 0.1(-10\%) = 1\%.$$

[19] See Chipman [5] and Uekawa [45]. Many other sources are cited in the bibliographies of the articles mentioned in the next footnote.

[20] Two recent papers pursuing this route are Ethier [10] and Jones and Scheinkman [20], summarized in Chapter 8.

In the second industry, costs (or price) have risen by 2%:

$$\hat{p}_2 = \theta_{L2}\hat{w}_L + \theta_{K2}\hat{w}_K + \theta_{T2}\hat{w}_T$$
$$= 0.5(10\%) + 0.3(-10\%) = 2\%.$$

This increase in the wage/rent ratio has lowered relative cost in the industry employing the higher labor/capital ratio.[21]

This example is cited not to establish a paradox but rather to point out that a particular form of expressing factor-intensity rankings that succeeds in indicating relative cost changes in a two-by-two world need not continue to do so in a model with many productive factors. There is, however, an alternative specification of factor intensities that is equivalent to the physical ratio comparison in the two-by-two model but accurately captures the link between intensities and costs in the multi-factor case. Industry k is said to be labor intensive compared with industry j if labor's distributive share in the kth industry, θ_{Lk}, exceeds labor's share in the jth sector, θ_{Lj}. By this criterion, industry 2 was labor intensive in the preceding example ($\theta_{L2} - \theta_{L1} = 0.3$). It was also the case that industry 2 was capital intensive ($\theta_{K2} - \theta_{K1} = 0.2$), but the degree of capital intensity fell short of the degree of labor intensity, and this is crucial for a cost comparison when wages rise 10% and the return to capital falls 10%.[22]

The basic relationship linking factor and commodity prices is the competitive profit relationship already cited in this example. If factors are combined in each industry to produce a unique output, and if production levels are positive in a competitive equilibrium.

$$\hat{p}_j = \sum_i \theta_{ij}\hat{w}_i.$$

That is, each commodity-price change is a positive weighted average of all the factor-price changes.[23] From this it follows that if all price changes are ranked,

[21] Notice that the return to land was kept constant throughout. If a two-factor (capital and labor) ranking is relied upon to provide comparisons when other factors are available in differing amounts (and prices), obvious errors can be made. For example, it proved inappropriate to examine American trade patterns solely on the basis of capital and labor endowments and requirements when other factors, such as natural resources, were present but unaccounted for. See the statement of the Leontief paradox in Leontief [27] and criticisms by Vanek [46] and Kenen [24].

[22] Of course, the first industry is land intensive ($\theta_{T1} - \theta_{T2} = 0.5$). The use of distributive shares to indicate factor-intensity rankings in the two-by-two case was made in Chapter 4.

[23] If a_{ij} denotes the input of factor i per unit output of j, then p_j equals unit costs, $\Sigma_i w_i a_{ij}$. Cost minimization requires $\Sigma w_i \mathrm{d}a_{ij}$ to equal zero, from which the relationship $\hat{p}_j = \Sigma_i \theta_{ij}\hat{w}_i$ follows. For further details, see Caves and Jones [2, ch. 8 and 9], or Chapter 4.

so that

$$\hat{p}_1 > \hat{p}_2 > \cdots > \hat{p}_n,$$

there must exist some factors i and h such that

$$\hat{w}_i > \hat{p}_1 > \cdots > \hat{p}_n > \hat{w}_h.$$

The magnification effect of commodity-price changes on the factoral distribution of income is the basis for the appropriate generalization of the Stolper–Samuelson theorem, and it rests not upon the dimensionality of the model but upon the assumption of no joint production.

Closely related to the Stolper–Samuelson theorem is the Rybczynski [40] theorem, whereby the increase in just one factor endowment, all other factor endowments and commodity prices remaining constant, must cause a reduction in at least one commodity output. In the n-by-n model this is especially easy to establish, since the factor-price equalization theorem asserts that factor prices remain constant if commodity prices are assumed constant. Therefore, techniques of production are also given and full employment of each factor requires that if that factor supply, V_i, changes, either all outputs rise at the same relative rate or some rise relatively more than the endowment and others relatively less. Formally stated, if λ_{ij} indicates the fraction of factor i employed in the jth industry, and $\hat{x}_j$ the relative change in output in the jth sector, full employment and constant prices require that

$$\sum_{j=1}^{n} \lambda_{ij}\hat{x}_j = \hat{V}_i, \quad \text{for all } i = 1, \ldots, n.$$

Therefore, if some factors grow but some others do not, at least one output must fall. The key assumption once again is the lack of joint production rather than the size of n (equal to the number of factors and goods).

If the number of factors exceeds the number of commodities, the Rybczynski result does not generalize as well as the Stolper–Samuelson result, because keeping commodity prices constant (a condition of the Rybczynski theorem) does not suffice to keep factor prices and techniques constant. Nonetheless, some results can be obtained by using what Samuelson [42] has called the 'reciprocity theorem'. This remarkable result states that in any general-equilibrium model, regardless of the number of factors or commodities, and even including the possibility of joint production,

$$\frac{\partial x_j}{\partial V_i} = \frac{\partial w_i}{\partial p_j}.$$

In words, the increase of the ith factor endowment on the jth output (with all other endowments and commodity prices held constant) equals the impact that a rise in the jth commodity price would have on the ith factor return (if no other commodity prices change and endowments are kept constant).

This result, combined with the earlier statement of the competitive profit conditions and the full-employment equations of change, can be used to establish the following generalizations of the two-by-two model if the number of factors equals the number of commodities.[24]

(1) A rise in any single commodity price, p_j, will cause at least one factor to gain in real terms ($\hat{w}_i > \hat{p}_j$) and at least one other factor to lose.

(2) A rise in any single factor endowment, V_i, will cause at least one commodity output to rise by a greater proportional amount and at least one other output to fall, assuming commodity prices are kept constant.

(3) Every factor, i, has at least one 'natural enemy' in the sense that there is at least one industry, j, such that if p_j alone rises, w_i must fall.

(4) Every factor, i, need not have at least one 'natural friend'. That is, for factor i it may be impossible to find any single industry j (and therefore any group of industries) such that if p_j rises (other prices kept constant) w_i will rise by a greater relative amount. This has an important implication for tariff theory: Is it possible to impose a tariff structure that would unambiguously raise the real return to a preselected factor, i? Yes, in a two-by-two world; not necessarily, in an n-by-n world.[25]

(5) For each industry, j, it is possible to find some factor, i, such that if endowment growth is concentrated solely in factor i, the output of j must fall at constant commodity prices.

(6) It may not be possible to find any factor, i, such that, if the endowment of i alone rises, a preselected jth industry would rise by a greater relative amount at constant prices.

If the number of factors of production exceeds the number of outputs, proposition 1 remains valid, as does the general Rybczynski result (5). But propositions 2 and 3 do not generalize to this 'uneven' case.

One particular feature of the two-by-two model deserves special emphasis, because it singles out the peculiar quality of the restriction to two factors in a world with no joint production. Suppose relative commodity prices change. Then each factor of production either unambiguously gains or unambiguously loses. I term this the phenomenon of the 'excluded middle'. With no joint production,

[24] Proofs are supplied in Jones and Scheinkman [20] and Chapter 8.

[25] As demonstrated in Chapter 8, factor i must indeed have at least one natural friend if i is 'unimportant enough' in the sense that $\Sigma_j \theta_{ij}$ is less than unity.

every commodity-price change must be bounded by factor-price changes. If there are only two factors in the model, a change in relative commodity prices must serve to raise one w_i by more than any commodity price and to lower the other relative to any commodity price. This feature makes the two-factor model somewhat inappropriate in tariff analysis, for it leaves out of account any factor that genuinely 'doesn't care'. That is, there is no factor 'in the middle' such that a change in tariff structure has ambiguous effects on real returns. The two-factor model would thus not capture the general apathy that characterizes perhaps a large section of the population when tariff changes are considered.[26]

Any model with more than two factors opens up the possibility that some factor return may not be 'extreme' compared with commodity-price changes. In particular, let me consider briefly the 'specific factors' model mentioned earlier. In the small-scale (three-by-two) version, let land be used only in one sector (food) and capital in the other (machines), with labor used in both and earning the same return because it is mobile between sectors. If relative commodity prices change, labor is always a middle factor in the sense that the wage will fall in terms of the commodity that has risen in price and rise in terms of the other commodity.[27] This is also the case in the large-scale $[(n+1) \times n]$ version in which each industry uses a single factor specifically tied to that industry as well as sharing in a common labor force. If commodity prices change, the change in the wage rate is a positive weighted average of the commodity-price changes:

$$\hat{w}_L = \sum_j \beta_{Lj} \hat{p}_j,$$

where $\beta_{Lj} > 0$ *and* $\sum \beta_{Lj} = 1$.

This expression can help to illustrate a remark I made earlier about the usefulness of a bilateral comparison of one sector with an average trait for the economy as a whole, even in multisector models. Suppose only the *j*th commodity price rises. By how much will this increase the wage rate? More particularly, would the wage rate rise (relatively) by more or less than the average change for

[26] This is discussed in more detail in Ruffin and Jones [39].

[27] This model was used in Chapter 6 in discussing the problem in economic history posed in Temin [44]. Suppose that the real wage (deflated by the price of food) *and* the interest rate (the return to capital deflated by the price of machines) in mid-nineteenth-century America can be shown to be higher than in the United Kingdom. Is it possible to conclude that America possessed a superior technology? In a two-factor model, the factor-price frontier must be negatively sloped for a given technology. But not so in a three-factor world. If food is relatively cheap in America, the same technology as is available in Britain could support a higher real wage and interest rate.

all factor prices? The average of all the relative factor-price changes is simple to find. Letting α_j denote the output share of industry j in the national income and α^i be factor i's distributive share throughout the economy,

$$\sum \alpha^i \hat{w}_i = \sum \alpha_h \hat{p}_h .$$

The average over all factor-price changes, shown on the left, would equal industry j's output share, α_j, times $\hat{p}_j$ if the price of j is the only commodity price that rises. The change in the wage rate, $\hat{w}_L$, is given by $\beta_{Lj}\hat{p}_j$, and it is easy to show (see Ruffin and Jones [39]) that

$$\beta_{Lj} = \lambda_{Lj} \frac{\gamma_{Lj}}{\sum_i \lambda_{Li}\gamma_{Li}},$$

where the new term, γ_{Lj}, represents the elasticity of labor's marginal-physical-product schedule in the jth sector.

The point I wish to stress is that in asking how labor fares (compared with the average of all factors) as a result of the rise in the price in sector j, it is necessary to know something about sector j and about the average over all sectors, but *not* the detailed composition in each and every other sector. More precisely, the larger is γ_{Lj} compared with the economywide average, $\sum_i \lambda_{Li}\gamma_{Li}$, the greater will be labor's gain. Suppose the elasticity of labor's marginal-physical-product schedule in sector j is given precisely by the average elasticity for the economy as a whole. Then the comparison of the wage-rate change with the average over all factors depends on the intensity with which the jth sector employs labor, λ_{Lj}, relative to the importance in the economy of the jth sector, α_j. Indeed, the ratio λ_{Lj}/α_j provides a bilateral ranking of industry j's labor intensity *not* with some other particular sector but with the economy as a whole. If λ_{Lj}/α_j exceeds unity, call the jth sector labor intensive and conclude that the wage rate would rise by more than the average over all factors.[28]

9. Ricardo and Heckscher–Ohlin: reconciliation in a multicommodity world

Two striking differences distinguish the Ricardian model from the standard Heckscher–Ohlin model, regardless of the number of commodities and countries

[28] It is easy to show that λ_{ij}/α_j equals θ_{ij}/α^i. Note the double bilateral comparison of one factor use relative to another in one industry compared with another for the two-by-two model is replaced generally by the assertion that 'industry j is i intensive if θ_{ij}/α^i exceeds unity'.

we wish to consider. The Ricardian model completely ignores differences in factor intensity and mobility between sectors. Homogeneous productive resources are converted into outputs at constant costs, so that it is just as useful to say that in the Ricardian model only one factor of production (labor) is employed. The Heckscher–Ohlin model assumes there are two inputs freely mobile between sectors but used in different proportions in each.[29] Also, the Ricardian model assumes that countries differ in 'climate' or in the productivity of labor in the same occupation. By contrast, the Heckscher–Ohlin model is based on an assumption that knowledge of the best productive techniques is available to all countries.

In each model, there is a standard or typical solution in the two-country, two-commodity case. For the Ricardian model, it is a solution with each country completely specialized and limbo terms of trade established between the cost ratios in each country. Commodity prices are equalized by trade but factor prices (wage rates) are not. For the Heckscher–Ohlin model, the typical solution shows each country *in*completely specialized, producing both goods with the same techniques as are used in the other country, and with factor prices equalized between countries. Of course, if factor endowments are sufficiently dissimilar, one (or both) countries may be driven to specialize completely, but this case is often made to appear extreme. The country's factor endowments would have to lie on one side or the other of the 'cone of diversification'.[30]

The question of what appears 'standard' and what does not is significantly affected by the dimensionality of the model. For this reason, I turn to the many-commodity, two-factor Heckscher–Ohlin case. In particular, I concentrate on the role of factor endowments in determining production and trade patterns by considering two small countries sharing access to the same technology but differing in their endowments of capital and labor. Some trade may take place between these countries, but they each rely mainly on an outside world market in which commodity prices are determined. World prices reflect technology and climate in various parts of the world, and I assume these bear no necessary resemblance to the technology shared by the two small countries.

For each of these small countries, technology plus world prices combine to yield a locus showing minimal combinations of capital and labor that can produce those quantities of one or more commodities worth exactly $1 at world prices. This locus is constructed from the separate unit-value isoquants shown in fig.

[29] In this section, I restrict the discussion to the two-factor version of the Heckscher–Ohlin model.
[30] This phrase is used by Chipman [4].

18.5.[31] Five commodities are illustrated. For each is shown a bowed-in locus of the minimal combinations of capital and labor which would produce a dollar's worth of that commodity. A doubling of that commodity's price would radially shift the unit-value isoquant halfway toward the origin. Some commodities, like commodity 5, could not be competitively produced in either of the small countries at prevailing world prices. The dashed tangent chords, *AB*, *CD*, and *EF*, form part of the inner frontier, since it is possible to employ capital and labor to produce a pair of commodities instead of just one. For example, point *G* is halfway between *F* and *E* on chord *FE*. The input bundle shown by *G* can be split into two parts. One part would consist of half the labor and capital combination shown by *E* and could be used to produce 50 cents' worth of the third commodity. The other part would be the bundle halfway between *F* and the origin. It can produce 50 cents' worth of commodity 4. Thus bundle *G* can produce a dollar's worth of output.

The individual country's capital-labor endowment ratio would dictate the location of production along this composite unit-value isoquant and the country's wage/rent ratio. For example, suppose the endowment ray from the origin cuts the composite unit-value isoquant at point *H*. The country would specialize in

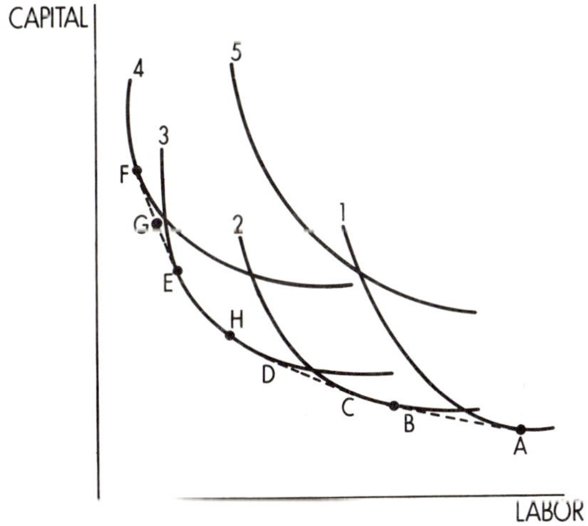

Figure 18.5

[31] This construction, and much of the succeeding argument, is based on Chapter 2 of this book and on Caves and Jones [3, ch. 7].

producing commodity 3 and the wage/rent ratio would be reflected by the slope at *H*. The resulting connection between factor endowments and factor prices is illustrated in fig. 18.6. The upward-sloping portions correspond to complete specialization in one of the commodities forming part of the composite unit-value isoquant. The flat portions illustrate the factor-price equalization result for a two-by-two world. For example, if the country's factor endowments are in the ratio shown by *G* in fig. 18.5, it can produce commodities 3 and 4 along the highest horizontal section shown in fig. 18.6. In that range, any small rise in the capital/labor ratio would not increase relative wages. Instead, it would change the composition of production – increasing production of capital-intensive commodity 4 at the expense of more labor-intensive commodity 3.

Fig. 18.6 is particularly useful in illustrating how a many-commodity model can suggest 'natural' results which would appear 'extreme' in a two-sector model. For example, does trade lead to incomplete specialization? This depends on the endowment proportions. As the capital/labor endowment ratio rises from low to high values, the country becomes alternatively completely specialized and incompletely specialized. It would be incorrect to characterize incomplete specialization as associated only with middle values of the endowment proportions and complete specialization only with extreme values.

In the standard two-by-two model, factor-price equalization between countries is associated with incomplete specialization. But the degree of specialization does not provide the key to this issue. As fig. 18.6 makes clear, two countries sharing the same technology could each be incompletely specialized in two commodities without having factor prices brought to equality – one country could be producing commodities 2 and 3 and the other commodities 3 and 4. Countries that are quite similar in their endowment proportions are more likely to have their factor

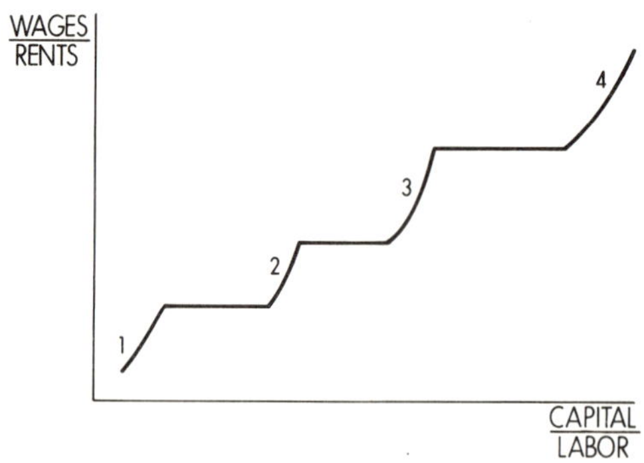

Figure 18.6

prices equalized by free trade. But this tendency toward factor-price equalization would be incomplete if one (or both) of the countries were completely specialized.

I emphasized earlier that the Ricardian and Heckscher–Ohlin models are distinguished from each other by the assumption concerning a commonly shared technology. Moving to a multicommodity setting allows this strict distinction to be blunted. Suppose one of the two countries produces commodities 2 and 3 and the other country produces 3 and 4. Although production functions are identical, the techniques actually adopted to produce commodity 3 will differ between countries *because* the wage/rent ratio is higher in the more capital-abundant country. The difference between countries in labor productivities that is asserted by assumption in the Ricardian model can be deduced from differences in factor endowments in a Heckscher–Ohlin model.

International trade allows countries to concentrate their resources on one or a few commodities in which they possess a comparative advantage. Multicommodity models are better suited than two-commodity models to bring home this point precisely because multidimensional models have more scope for distinguishing between the *number* of commodities that will be produced with trade and the number that will be consumed. In the typical version of the two-by-two Heckscher–Ohlin model, a country produces and consumes the same number of goods. Graham [11, ch. 6] provided two numerical examples of multicountry, multicommodity trade with ten countries and ten commodities. On average, with trade, each country consumed ten commodities and produced only two.[32] In the five-commodity Heckscher–Ohlin example discussed here, a small country would produce one or two commodities while consuming all five.[33] Of course, the objection to the two-commodity version is not that it is incapable of showing this asymmetry between numbers of goods produced and consumed. It is that the restricted dimensions of the model make it more difficult to highlight the extent to which trade weeds out inefficient production.

Just as in Graham's strictures on the two-by-two classical model, the many-commodity Heckscher–Ohlin model exhibits a richer variety of trade patterns than does the two-sector version. Changes in world tastes that rearrange world prices can cause a country to shift completely out of commodities it previously produced into others it previously imported. Furthermore, multicommodity

[32] With trade, two countries each produced four goods, one country produced three, another produced two, and the remaining six were completely specialized. A recent discussion of Graham's techniques in finding numerical solutions is contained in McKenzie [31].

[33] The tendency of trade to force concentration in the number of commodities produced is also emphasized by Krueger [26].

models allow a *pattern* of trade that a two-sector model is too limited to display. A country can import commodities which, if produced at home, would require a higher capital/labor ratio than that embodied in its exports and simultaneously import commodities that are more labor intensive than are exportables.[34] A truly multicommodity model can show how a country's factor-endowment proportions determine which commodity or commodities it can appropriately produce in the spectrum of all commodities. The country will rely on trade with other countries to provide commodities that are both more labor intensive and more capital intensive than its own production choice.

10. Conclusion

The design of theoretical models frequently reflects a conflict between generality and simplicity. Most questions in the pure theory of international trade involve issues of composition – distinguishing between gainers and losers among countries, expanding and contracting sectors in the economy, or factors of production intensively used in one sector of an economy but not the other. The number 'two' provides the lower bound in dimensionality for most of these issues. There is no doubt that trade models characterized by two countries, two commodities, and one or two productive factors have borne most of the burden in developing the present corpus of trade theory.

What have been the costs of this heavy reliance on such simple models? Frank Graham argued that these costs were considerable in the classical trade model. The primary thrust of his argument was to discredit the notion propagated in the classical literature that the network of comparative costs had so little to do with determining the precise values of equilibrium world prices. His concern for the supply side of the model provided a healthy antidote to the typical classical illustrations. I would argue, and he would have agreed, that the classical models were capable of exhibiting some of the characteristics he wished to see in the solution – prices reflecting actual cost ratios in some country. But it remains the case that trade models with more than two countries and more than two commodities offer a richer variety of solutions, in many of which the existence of countries producing commodities in common would seem less extreme than in the two-by-two setting.

[34] With reference to figs. 18.5 and 18.6, the country might produce goods 2 and 3 while importing commodities 1 (more labor intensive), 4 (more capital intensive), 5 (whose factor endowments are somewhat similar to 2 or 3, but for which home technology is inferior to that of other countries), and (perhaps) some of 2 or 3, which it also produces. It exports either 2 or 3 or both.

Moving beyond Ricardian-type models, I have argued that the addition of more commodities, countries, and factors often requires that conclusions based on simple models be qualified to allow for feedback effects from other markets. Even so, these qualifications often remain just that – a catalogue of possible exceptions to, or modifications of, a result from models characterized by 'two-ness' that retains its general validity in higher-dimensional cases.

One exception to this remark is provided by what I called the 'aggregation problem'. Even when all the sectors being aggregated are fairly similar, cross effects of price changes and the scale of income effects argue in favor of distinguishing between 'aggregate' response to price changes and 'typical' response to price changes in any one sector. The real world consists of many sectors, and it may be difficult to find individual ones that seem actually to portray the characteristics imputed by small-scale models even though real-world aggregates may do so.

The two-sector Heckscher–Ohlin model presents a series of propositions which, although challenged because of the two-dimensionality assumption upon which they seem to rest, in large part reflect the widely held assumption that productive techniques involve an array of inputs combined to produce a unique output in each sector. That is, the assumption of no joint production injects an asymmetry into the input–output constellation, and this asymmetry gets reflected in magnified relationships between output prices and factor prices, on the one hand, and factor endowments and industry output (at constant prices) on the other. This is an area of theory where, I would argue, the two-by-two results are fairly robust. Nonetheless, it is clear that assuming a greater number of productive factors creates new possibilities, perhaps the most important of which is that relative price changes leave certain factor returns fairly constant in real terms. The excluded middle can be filled in when there are more than two productive factors.

The force of Graham's contribution is most keenly felt when considering trade in many commodities between many countries. The sharp distinction between Ricardian and Heckscher–Ohlin trade models is blurred because an assumption of commonly shared technologies need not be translated into identically used techniques and equality of factor prices. Furthermore, in both models the extension to many commodities allows more adequate expression of the impact of free trade in forcing a concentration in production but not in consumption. The question of concentration is ultimately a 'numbers' game, and it should come as no surprise that a limit to the number of commodities the model can encompass serves to inhibit this point's being forcefully made.

I should conclude by pointing out that I have no special plea to make for the number 'two' *per se*. Instead, I would argue the advantages of stripping any theoretical argument down to its essential core, and if an excess number of commodities, countries, or factors is present, this core may prove unnecessarily stubborn in revealing itself. However, arguments based on higher dimensions may be required both to explore problems that essentially involve a move beyond 'twoness' and to examine how criteria applicable in the general case should be formulated in more simple models. Two-dimensional building blocks not only provide the firm foundations upon which trade theory is constructed but present a standard of comparison against which truly multidimensional results can be appreciated.

References

[1] Berglas, E., 'On the Theory and Measurement of Gains from Preferential Trading', unpublished.

[2] Caves, R.E. and R.W. Jones, *World Trade and Payments: An Introduction* (Little, Brown, Boston, 1973).

[3] Caves, R.E. and R.W. Jones, *World Trade and Payments: An Introduction*, rev, edn. (Little, Brown, Boston, 1977).

[4] Chipman, J., 'Survey of the Theory of International Trade: Part 3, The Modern Theory', *Econometrica*, 34 (January 1966) 18–76.

[5] Chipman, J., 'Factor Price Equalization and the Stolper–Samuelson Theorem', *International Economic Review*, 10 (October 1969) 399–406.

[6] Chipman, J., 'The Transfer Problem Once Again', in: G. Horwich and P.A. Samuelson, eds., *Trade, Stability, and Macroeconomics* (Academic Press, New York, 1974).

[7] Corden, M., *The Theory of Protection* (Oxford University Press, London, 1971).

[8] Elliott, G.A., 'The Theory of International Values', *Journal of Political Economy*, 58 (February 1950) 16–29.

[9] Ellsworth, P.T., 'Exchange Rates and Exchange Stability', *Review of Economics and Statistics*, 32 (February 1950) 1–12.

[10] Ethier, W., 'Some of the Theorems of International Trade with Many Goods and Factors', *Journal of International Economics*, 4 (May 1974) 199–206.

[11] Graham, F., *The Theory of International Values* (Princeton University Press, 1948).

[12] Gruen, F.H. and W.M. Corden, 'A Tariff that Worsens the Terms of Trade', in: I.A. McDougall and R.H. Snape, eds., *Studies in International Economics* (North-Holland, Amsterdam, 1970).

[13] Hahn, F., 'Review of Takashi Negishi's General Equilibrium Theory and International Trade', *Journal of International Economics*, 3 (August 1973) 297–298.

[14] Jones, R.W., 'Effective Protection and Substitution', *Journal of International Economics*, 1 (February 1971) 59–81.

[15] Jones, R.W., 'Trade with Non-Traded Goods: The Anatomy of Interconnected Markets', *Economica*, 41 (May 1974) 121–138.

[16] Jones, R.W., 'The Metzler Tariff Paradox: Extensions to Non-Traded and Intermediate Commodities', in: G. Horwich and P.A. Samuelson, eds., *Trade, Stability, and Macroeconomics* (Academic Press, New York, 1974).

[17] Jones, R.W., 'Income Distribution and Effective Protection in a Multi-Commodity Trade Model', *Journal of Economic Theory*, 12 (August 1975) 1–15.

[18] Jones, R.W., and E. Berglas, 'Import Demand and Export Supply: An Aggregation Theorem', *American Economic Review*, 67 (March 1977).

[19] Jones, R.W. and R.J. Ruffin, 'Trade Patterns with Capital Mobility', in: M. Parkin and A.R. Nobay, eds., *Current Economic Problems* (Cambridge University Press, New York, 1975).

[20] Jones, R.W. and J. Scheinkman, 'The Relevance of the Two-Sector Production Model in Trade Theory', *Journal of Political Economy* (October 1977).

[21] Kemp, M.C., 'The Gain from International Trade and Investment: A Neo-Heckscher–Ohlin Approach', *American Economic Review*, 56 (September 1966) 788–809.

[22] Kemp, M.C., *A Contribution to the General Equilibrium Theory of Preferential Trading* (North-Holland, Amsterdam, 1969).

[23] Kemp, M.C. and R.W. Jones, 'Variable Labor Supply and the Theory of International Trade', *Journal of Political Economy*, 70 (February 1962) 30–36.

[24] Kenen, P.B., 'Nature, Capital, and Trade', *Journal of Political Economy*, 73 (October 1965) 437–460.

[25] Koopmans, T.C., *Three Essays on the State of Economic Science* (McGraw-Hill, New York, 1957).

[26] Krueger, *Growth, Distortions, and Patterns of Trade Among Many Countries*, Princeton Studies in International Finance, no. 40 (Princeton, N.J., 1977).

[27] Leontief, W.W., 'Domestic Production and Foreign Trade: The American Capital Position Re-examined', *Proceedings of the American Philosophical Society* (September 1953).

[28] Lerner, A.P., 'The Symmetry Between Import and Export Taxes', *Economica*, 3 (August 1936) 306–313.

[29] Lerner, A.P., *The Economics of Control: Principles of Welfare Economics* (Macmillan, New York, 1944).

[30] McKenzie, L.W., 'Specialization and Efficiency in World Production', *Review of Economic Studies*, 21 (June 1954) 165–180.

[31] McKenzie, L.W., 'Why Compute Equilibria?' in: J. and M. Loś, *Computing Equilibria: How and Why* (North-Holland, Amsterdam, 1976).

[32] Marshall, A., *Money, Credit and Commerce* (Macmillan, London, 1923).

[33] Mayer, W., 'Short-Run Equilibrium for a Small Open Economy', *Journal of Political Economy*, 82 (September/October 1974) 955–968.

[34] Metzler, L.A., 'The Theory of International Trade', in: H.S. Ellis, ed., *A Survey of Contemporary Economics* (Blackiston, Philadelphia, 1949).

[35] Mussa, M., 'Tariffs, and the Distribution of Income: The Importance of Factor Specificity, Substitutability, and Intensity in the Short and Long Run', *Journal of Political Economy*, 82 November/December 1974) 1191–1204.

[36] Pearce, I., 'The Problem of the Balance of Payments', *International Economic Review*, 2 (January 1961) 1–28.

[37] Pearce, I., *International Trade* (Norton, New York, 1970).

[38] Ramaswami, V.S. and T.N. Srinivasan, 'Tariff Structure and Resource Allocation in the Presence of Factor Substitution', in: Bhagwati *et al.*, *Trade, Balance of Payments, and Growth* (North-Holland, Amsterdam, 1971).

[39] Ruffin, R.J. and R.W. Jones, 'Protection and Real Wages. The Neo-Classical Ambiguity', *Journal of Economic Theory* (April 1977) 337–348.

[40] Rybczynski, T.M., 'Factor Endowment and Relative Commodity Prices', *Economica*, 22 (November 1955) 336–341.

[41] Salter, W.E.G., 'Internal and External Balance: The Role of Price and Expenditure Effects', *The Economic Record*, 35 (August 1959) 226–238.

[42] Samuelson, P.A., 'Prices of Factors and Goods in General Equilibrium', *Review of Economic Studies*, (February 1953) 1–20.

[43] Samuelson, P.A., 'Ohlin Was Right', *Swedish Journal of Economics*, 73 (1971) 365–384.
[44] Temin, P., 'Labor Scarcity and the Problem of American Industrial Efficiency in the 1850s', *Journal of Economic History*, 26 (September 1966) 277–298.
[45] Uekawa, Y., 'Generalization of the Stolper–Samuelson Theorem', *Econometrica*, 39 (March 1971) 197–217.
[46] Vanek, J., 'The Natural Resource Content of Foreign Trade, 1870–1955, and the Relative Abundance of Natural Resources in the United States', *Review of Economics and Statistics*, 41 (May 1959) 146–153.
[47] Whitin, T.H., 'Classical Theory, Graham's Theory, and Linear Programming in International Trade', *Quarterly Journal of Economics*, 67 (November 1953) 520–544.

INDEX